CHRISTIAN ETHICS

CHRISTIAN ETHICS

A Case Method Approach

FIFTH EDITION

Laura A. Stivers
James B. Martin-Schramm

ORBIS BOOKS
Maryknoll, New York 10545

Founded in 1970, Orbis Books endeavors to publish works that enlighten the mind, nourish the spirit, and challenge the conscience. The publishing arm of the Maryknoll Fathers and Brothers, Orbis seeks to explore the global dimensions of the Christian faith and mission, to invite dialogue with diverse cultures and religious traditions, and to serve the cause of reconciliation and peace. The books published reflect the views of their authors and do not represent the official position of the Maryknoll Society. To learn more about Orbis Books, please visit our website at www.orbisbooks.com.

This is a substantially revised edition of Christian Ethics: A Case Method Approach, Fourth Edition, edited by Laura A. Stivers, Christine E. Gudorf, and James B. Martin-Schramm, Maryknoll: NY: Orbis Books, 2012.

Published by Orbis Books, Box 302, Maryknoll, NY 10545-0302.

Manufactured in the United States of America
Manuscript editing and typesetting by Joan Weber Laflamme

Library of Congress Cataloging-in-Publication Data

Names: Stivers, Laura A., author. | Martin-Schramm, James B., author.
Title: Christian ethics : a case method approach / Laura A. Stivers, James B. Martin-Schramm.
Description: Fifth edition. | Maryknoll, NY : Orbis Books, 2020. | Includes bibliographical references. | Summary: The fifth edition of this classic introduction to Christian ethics via the case method approach, utilizing case studies of contemporary ethical issues.
Identifiers: LCCN 2020006710 (print) | LCCN 2020006711 (ebook) | ISBN 9781626983977 (trade paperback) | ISBN 9781608338610 (ebook)
Subjects: LCSH: Christian ethics—Case studies.
Classification: LCC BJ1251 .C49 2020 (print) | LCC BJ1251 (ebook) | DDC 241—dc23
LC record available at https://lccn.loc.gov/2020006710
LC ebook record available at https://lccn.loc.gov/2020006711

For Laura's children, Marijke and Annelies,
and
Jim's children, Joel and Josh, and granddaughters,
Anna Rose and Caroline Gannon

Contents

PART VIII
LIFE AND DEATH

Introduction

Christian Ethics
and the Case Method

The student pensively approached the case teacher after class and finally mustered some words: "That case really hit home. The characters were different, but they could just as well have been my family. Not long ago we went through exactly the same thing." Another student, waiting for the first to finish, finally edged up and joined in, "And the question that woman in the front row asked about euthanasia, that's the precise question I wanted to ask but couldn't find the right words."

These two statements, often encountered in one form or another by case teachers, reflect something enduring in human behavior: while every individual is unique, ethical problems and questions about what is right or good are persistent if not universal. These recurrences and the dilemmas they represent can be recorded and revisited to help others learn to make better ethical choices. Case studies are one way to capture past occurrences, and case teaching is a method to enable individuals and groups to make better choices.

This book is about making ethical choices and forming Christian character. It contains sixteen cases. Accompanying each case study is a commentary that is intended to aid understanding of the case from a Christian ethical perspective. The purpose of the book is to offer an approach to contemporary social issues and to underscore the importance of the Christian ethical dimension in the issues and in character formation. The authors are enthusiastic about the case approach as one way to prepare individuals and communities to make ethical decisions and form character. Since the method was first developed at the Harvard Law and Business Schools, it has moved far beyond these origins, receiving wide acceptance nationally in business and law schools. During the past four decades it has also been successfully applied to religious studies. This proven track record and personal experience with the case approach are the bases of the authors' enthusiasm for this teaching and learning approach.

MAKING ETHICAL DECISIONS

Ethical decisions are made on a number of levels. On one level decision-making seems to flow easily. Individuals follow their gut-level intuitions and muddle through situations reactively. This approach may be effective if the individual is caring and the situation is uncomplicated and more or less personal. It is less effective in complex social situations and can be disastrous when the individual is uncaring, ethically immature, or locked into a narrow social world.

On another level, making ethical choices is both difficult and complex. Logical and abstract reasoning comes hard to some. In certain situations the decision-maker is bombarded by a bewildering array of conflicting and complex facts. Finding relevant ethical norms or guidelines from Christian traditions to apply to particular situations is difficult at best and can easily be short-circuited or sidetracked with simplistic appeals to authority.

Once relevant norms are discovered, their application is often tricky. The norms frequently offer conflicting counsel. Indeed, this is the primary reason that ethical decisions are problematic. There is seldom a straight path from a single norm to an easy decision. If there were, no problem would exist. The decision-maker is most often caught between equally attractive or unattractive alternatives. Worse, the path is usually made treacherous by intersecting problems and relationships that complicate situations and suggest exceptions to the rules. Finally, and hardly necessary to point out, relationships themselves present complicating factors. The moral decision-maker possesses limited freedom and is quite capable of being arbitrary in its use.

The case method of instruction recounts real ethical dilemmas in order to assist individuals and groups through complexity to good or at least well-reasoned choices. Cases may help sort out the choices and give the person with the dilemma an opportunity to move down the path from the identification of norms through the maze of intersecting facts, relationships, and exceptions to the selection of the best alternatives.

There are many types of case studies. They range from imagined scenarios, to in-depth histories of organizations, to one-page "verbatims" that report a single incident. The cases in this volume are descriptions of actual situations as seen by a writer, usually through the eyes of a participant involved in the problem. The situations normally entail a decision to be made that is left sufficiently open to allow students to enter the process of ethical reflection and decision-making.

Such a method is well suited to the study of Christian ethics, for it drives the student to take the insights of tradition and theory, apply them to an actual situation, and then reconsider the adequacy of theory and tradition. Involved in this movement from theory to practice and back to theory are all the elements that go into an ethical decision.

THE ELEMENTS OF AN ETHICAL DECISION

Element I: The Relationship of Faith

A pervasive historical problem for most Christian traditions has been human sin. Sin results from deep-seated anxieties and separation from God, self, others, and nature. It issues forth in specific acts that break relationships. Sin is magnified in groups and hardens in institutions. From another angle, sin is the refusal to accept God's gracious power of love, a refusal that leads to a sense of alienation and judgment.

While sin runs deep and is universal, it does not necessarily paralyze the moral life. In his person and work Jesus Christ reveals resources for living with integrity in the midst of sin. Jesus identifies God, the source of these resources, as a power who creates inner wholeness and the possibility of right relationships.

Primary to most Christian traditions is the affirmation of God's power as love. Love redeems humans from sin and reunites them with others without violating human freedom. Love is a free gift, never a possession, and cannot be obtained by an effort of the will alone. The continuing presence of love in all situations is called the work of the Holy Spirit.

The starting point for Christian ethics is being in love. This is not something the self can do alone, however. It is something that God does in cooperation with the self, although the self is constantly tempted to think otherwise and take control, thus furthering sin and alienation. Being in love is first a matter of receiving love and letting it work in the self to produce inner wholeness and transformation. Action follows being in love. This is more or less the central message of most Christian traditions, although there is considerable variation in particulars. Thus, Christian ethics has its foundation in being or life in the Spirit. Faith is a matter of relationship, of being in love first with God and then responsively with self, others, and nature.

The word *spirituality* is often used to identify the core relationship to God. God's power is experienced in quite different ways, the common element being the integrated and transformed self that emerges. Most Christians readily recognize the customary religious ways of experiencing God: worship, prayer, singing, participation in the sacraments, and the preached word. God is not limited to these religious ways, but rather, according to most traditions, God is free to be present in a variety of ways consistent with love.

Spirituality, alternatively being in love or being in the Spirit, inspires acts of justice in society and nature and also leads the loving self intuitively to specific acts in particular situations. In coming to decisions, however, other things are needed, because inspiration and intuition by themselves are not always accurate guides for doing what is right or good. This is especially true in complex social situations. The doing of good acts requires thought as well as heart, knowledge as well as inspiration and intuition. The Christian doer, while inspired and empowered, is also sensitive to relationships in specific situations and deeply interested in the facts and theories that give order to situations as well as the traditions that provide ethical norms for human actions.

Sensitivity to relationships involves a strong element of good intentions. It also involves a sense of the Spirit already at work in a situation, of the character of the human actors, and of the needs of plants and animals. Sensitivity to relationships is constantly in tune with feelings and the subtle changes that make certain situations exceptional. It is aware of the self, its state of being, and its tendencies to sin, both in one's own self and in the selves of others.

Interest in the facts and norms that guide decisions are more a matter of knowledge than heart. They require the thoughtful analysis and assessment of a situation, the next two elements in making an ethical decision.

Element II: Analysis

Good ethical decisions and actions depend on good information, and getting good information depends on hard work and a certain amount of savvy. There are several components to consider in analyzing a situation or case study, not all of which apply in any given situation or case. First is to consider how *personal experience* shapes the way the self perceives a situation. One way to do this is for students to ask themselves what they personally have at stake, what personal history—for example, race, class, gender, habits, and attitudes—they bring to the situation.

The second component is *power dynamics*. Who are the key players, and how is power distributed among them? Whose voices are heard? Whose are ignored?

A third component is *factual information*. Are there historical roots to the problem? What are the key facts? Are there facts in dispute? Are the theories that give coherence to the facts in conflict?

Fourth is the larger *context* of the situation. Most cases are seen through the eyes of a single person and involve personal relationships. The decision-maker must go beyond the close confines of his or her own personal life to see how society and nature affect and in turn are affected by the actions of the people in the case. As the old adage goes: Don't lose the forest for the trees.

Fifth is attention to the *complicating factors* in a situation. Is this an exceptional case? Is crucial information missing? Are there things that are hard to grasp?

Sixth is a careful delineation of *relationships*. Sometimes relational factors produce a situation that is not normal and to which traditional ethical guidelines do not apply. Decision-makers must ask if there are relational or character issues that complicate choices.

Seventh is to identify the primary and secondary *ethical issues* in the situation. Case studies almost always involve multiple issues, and students must select among them in order to focus.

Finally, the eighth component is the identification of *alternative courses of action* to address the issues and the consequences of each. What seems to be appropriate action may on second glance reveal consequences that make it inappropriate or even harmful.

Element III: Assessment

The main task in assessment is locating norms or ethical guidelines in the traditions of the church that are relevant to a given situation. In ethics, norms refer to broad directives that provide guidance for moral life. Norms help to determine what usually should be done in a particular situation. They reflect the wisdom and experience of past decision-makers as they faced similar situations and generalized about what is good. Their insights are passed down in traditions and usually offer wise counsel as current decision-makers face the same kinds of situations or even new situations.

Norms

Norms come in many forms. A few illustrations will suffice to demonstrate this variety and to identify the most important norms. Three very important norms are love, justice, and peacemaking. The experience of God's love leads to an intention to love one's neighbor. In Christian ethics justice is a *general principle* and means fairness or equity with a special concern for the poor and those on the margins of society. In the ethic of ecological justice this norm is given further expression in the principles of sustainability, sufficiency, participation, and solidarity (see the case "Sustaining Dover"). Peacemaking as a norm includes understandings of nonviolence and reconciliation and gives foundation to three normative *perspectives*: pacifism, the justifiable war, and the crusade (see the case "American Idol").

Virtues are norms insofar as they represent patterns of behavior worthy of emulation. The best, but not the only, example in Christian ethics is the person and work of Jesus. The popular but well-worn question "What would Jesus do?" points to how his example is a moral guide for many.

Theological interpretations also guide. Different interpretations of how God is at work in a given situation, for example, are important in cases of life and death. Theological understandings of sin, death, and the work of the Holy Spirit and the church are important to decisions in other cases.

Finally, the most familiar norms are stated as *rules, laws*, and *commands*. The Ten Commandments are the most obvious. In using laws as guides, care must be taken, however, to avoid legalism, the tendency to follow rules slavishly even if the consequences are unloving. In Christianity, all laws and rules are grounded in and tested by love, the most basic guideline of all.

Sources of Norms

Christians look to a number of sources for ethical guidance. The *Bible* has traditionally been the first and most important source. Gleaning ethical guidance from the Bible is not as easy as it might seem, however. The many books of the Bible were written in different periods and reflect quite a variety of contexts and situations. The biblical writers wrote from their own locations in diverse societies and culture. They saw and understood things differently from one another and certainly from persons of the modern age, who live in a thoroughly changed world. Biblical writers sometimes disagreed with one another, and what they thought was ethically acceptable in their own time—for example, slavery—has changed as culture has evolved. Compounding these differences, and complicating matters immensely, present-day decision-makers must interpret what biblical writers meant and then apply these meanings. The Bible does not interpret itself or make decisions. And while biblical scholars have developed a wide range of tools to do the task of interpretation and ethicists offer their best wisdom on interpretation, their disagreements are commonplace. Indeed, ethical conflicts are sometimes matters of interpretation and use of biblical texts.

In spite of these complications, themes do run through the Bible, and these themes can be identified with a degree of accuracy. The biblical writers experienced the same loving God as modern people and faced many of the same problems. The Bible remains a good source of guidance.

Theology is the second source of norms. Understandings of God's power and human sin have already been identified. The nature of God's power as love inspires and leads decision-makers to love their neighbors and to be sensitive to the work of the Spirit in situations. Different understandings of sin lead to conflicting views, such as on matters of sexuality. Seeing sin as deep and universal leads decision-makers to realistic actions that factor in the human tendency to misuse freedom.

The third source of norms is the *historical traditions* of the church. Christians through the centuries have devoted considerable thought to issues of, for example, violence, sexuality, the poor, and nature. The traditions change and sometimes yield a multiplicity of guidelines, but they also show continuity and reflect a certain amount of practical wisdom. Traditions on justice are critical to this volume.

The fourth source of norms is the *church* in its many forms. The three previous sources all grew in church ground. The church ranges from the church catholic or universal, to specific church organizations such as the Roman Catholic Church and specific Protestant denominations, to associations of churches, to the local brick and mortar church, to what in the Bible is referred to as "where two or three are gathered together." Likewise, the ethical guidelines range from traditional historical perspectives, to comprehensive church studies and pronouncements, to rules of church organizations, and to the wisdom and guidance of a good friend.

The final source is the broad category of *secular ethical traditions and other religions*. Christian and secular philosophical traditions in the West have had a close and mutually edifying relationship for centuries. Native American traditions are rich in their sensitivity to nature. Taoism is likewise rich in its search for balance. Buddhism holds to the interrelation of all beings and talks about attachment or desire as the chief problem. Christians are free to appropriate the insights of other traditions, to enter into dialogue with adherents of these traditions, and to join in common actions.

Using these five sources to establish norms that relate to a given case is complex and requires practice. The situation or case itself offers an obvious starting point. So, for example, if the situation involves violent conflict, norms dealing with violence and nonviolence apply.

Many aids are available to help in locating relevant norms. Concordances help to locate specific words in the Bible and texts containing these words. The critical commentaries that follow each case in this volume identify norms and help with interpretation. Dictionaries of Christian ethics are widely available and provide short summaries for those whose time is limited. Scholars have studied most ethical issues, and their publications usually develop norms. Most major denominations have well-established positions on major ethical issues. If cases are discussed in a classroom setting, teachers may provide background in lectures. Also, decision-makers may turn to the local church, where communities of believers frequently work through ethical issues, often guided by competent leaders.

Conflicting Norms

Once decision-makers have identified the relevant norms and reflected on their meaning for a specific situation, they must jump at least one more hurdle. Ethical problems are frequently encountered because two or more norms conflict. For example, in matters related to the use of violence, nonviolence is an obvious norm. So is justice. The conflict between the two in certain cases has led some Christians to elect the normative perspective of the justifiable war as their guide. So, if a large measure of justice can be won for a small measure of violence, violence may be justifiable if certain conditions are met. Another frequent conflict is between human economic benefit and care for other species and ecosystems.

What should the decision-maker do when conflicting norms make for a close call? There is no one right answer to this question. Prayer helps, but finally choices must be made. Martin Luther's famous dictum, "sin bravely," applies in some cases.

Method

Method is the process of pulling intuitions and norms together and applying them to analysis. No single method of relating norms, facts, theories, contexts, and relationships to one another and to specific situations can be called distinctively Christian. There are a number of methods, each with advantages and disadvantages. The authors have not tried to impose a particular method in their approach either to the cases or to the commentaries that follow them. They are convinced that method is important, however, and that an adequate method seeks to touch base with the elements relevant to making a particular ethical decision.

The case approach is conducive to the teaching of method. A specific case can even be used to focus on method. Over the course of a semester or study series the teacher can use and ask participants to use a single method so that they will acquire skill in employing that particular methodology. Alternatively, the teacher can employ several methods and request that students experiment with and evaluate each. Or finally, consciousness of method may be left to emerge from the process of doing ethical reflection.

The commentaries that follow each case are organized around the elements of making an ethical decision. The commentaries do not spell out how these elements are to be put together to reach a decision. The authors would be remiss, however, if they did not indicate a few typical approaches.

The approach that starts with and stresses norms is called the *deontological* or *normative approach*. The word *deontological* comes from the Greek word *deon*, which means "binding," and refers to the study of duty and moral obligation.

The tendency in this approach is to let norms, rules, principles, standards, and ideals be decisive or binding in making choices. The degree of decisiveness that should be afforded to norms has been a matter of contention in Christian ethics. To call an approach normative means that norms have a fairly high degree of decisiveness. Most of those who take a normative approach, however, are willing to admit some exceptions to norms occasioned by contextual or relational factors and conflicting norms. Used in a flexible way, the normative approach is appropriate. Indeed, the authors are of a common mind that considerable attention should be given to norms in all situations.

The extreme of the normative approach, legalism, presents difficulties, however. Following rules to the exclusion of contextual and relational factors is a problem for Christians because of its rigidity, frequent heartlessness, and the obvious polemic against it in the sayings of Jesus and the epistles of Paul.

The second approach is called *teleological* from the Greek *telos*, which means "end" or "goal." Those who take a teleological approach are interested in achieving an end or maximizing a goal as much as possible. Another way to put this is to say they seek good consequences or results. Hence this approach is also called the *consequentialist approach*, a common example of which is utilitarianism, generally defended by secular ethicists like Peter Singer. People differ, however, about the goals they seek and the ends they pursue. Some may wish simply to amass wealth and power in life, while others may seek to maximize the welfare of others, including other species. Not all ends or goals are morally desirable, however. For Christians, norms derived from the five sources and especially fundamental norms like love and justice guide evaluation of these ends or goals. Teleologists weigh the costs and benefits of various alternatives as they figure out how to maximize the good they seek to achieve. For teleologists, the ends sometimes justify the means, even morally questionable means in some cases. A weakness here is that teleological thinking can run roughshod over others as it makes ethical concessions in order to maximize the good. So, ends do not justify all means. A strength of this approach is that it takes consequences seriously.

The third approach is called the *areteological approach* or sometimes *virtue ethics* or the *ethics of conscience*. The word comes from the Greek *arete* and refers to excellence of moral character. Those who take this approach think that good ethical decisions will be made by good people. The first task, therefore, is to cultivate excellence of character through education, training, and spiritual formation, that is to say, through the internalization of norms so that they become intuitive. One of the products of this moral formation is the conscience that exists within an individual or community. Those who employ this approach often appeal to their consciences as the basis of their perception of an ethical problem or as a justification for the particular solution they prefer. Ends and means are evaluated in terms of how consistent they are with one's moral character and conscience.

An advantage of this approach is that life is complicated and often requires ethical decisions that have to be made quickly. In situations where norms are not clear or there is insufficient time to calculate costs and benefits, recourse to one's conscience and moral intuition can be a very effective way to exercise ethical judgment. One of the problems, however, is that a sound conscience depends on a well-formed moral character. Many who perpetrate great evils sleep all too well at night. In addition, intuitive appeals to conscience can be very subjective. Ultimately, good ethics requires that reasons be given to justify decisions. Vague appeals to conscience can be a way to dodge this responsibility.

Few teachers have consciously used the case approach to form character. Case discussions are a good resource for character formation, however, and in the process of repeatedly making moral judgments, moral maturity may be expected to increase, or at least that has been the experience of case teachers. Character development may therefore be an unintended positive side effect of the case method. Many teachers may prefer leaving it that way, but there is no reason why character development cannot be made more explicit.

So which of these approaches is the best? All three are good and may be used effectively alone or in combination. The authors suggest a combination, although combinations will not be effective in all cases. Decision-makers should be self-conscious, however, about which approach they are using.

Ethical Assessment

The last step of assessment is actually to do it. Having done the analysis, identified relevant norms, and selected one or more of the methods, decision-makers should evaluate alternative courses of action, strategies, and tactics as well as their viability and consequences. No magic formula or foolproof way exists. The process is dialogical. Norms, methods, and the factors of analysis should be massaged together to find what is appropriate or fitting.

The decision follows. It is sometimes difficult to make because alternative courses of action are equally satisfactory or equally unsatisfactory, but the relationship of faith calls the decision-maker to decide. Cases do, of course, allow the luxury of "fence sitting," but the ethical dilemmas of life do not. Also, not to decide may be a wise course of action in some cases, but it is a decision nonetheless.

Once a decision has been made and a course of action chosen, these conclusions need to be justified to others. Ethics should normally be a community enterprise. Reasons supporting the decision should be consistent with analysis, appeal to relevant moral norms, use an appropriate method, and carry a sense of proportionality. A well-justified ethical decision will also explain why this is the best choice given the circumstances of the case. In addition, a well-crafted decision will also anticipate and respond to the most significant counterarguments others may raise.

Element IV: Action

Cases in this volume end with decisions to be made. They are open-ended. Discussions of cases usually end at the point of decision, but in life situations this will not be the case. In this final stage decision-makers are called not only to decide but also to act on their decisions.

Reflection should then follow action so that decision-makers will learn from successes and failures. Finally, there is even a tiny bit of reward. When decisions and actions are done well, decision-makers may bask in the glow and enjoy the inner peace that follows. And even when things do not turn out all right and mistakes are made, and wrong choices selected, with repentance there are resources of forgiveness. Guilt may be a mark of sin, but it is never the last word in Christian ethics. The Good News is the last word. You are forgiven.

FLEXIBILITY

Cases can be used to form character, to analyze problems, to teach method, to understand human relationships, and to employ a method. The case approach is flexible, and this flexibility makes the goals of the teacher in using the method of great importance. Cases lend themselves to one purpose or a multiplicity of purposes, and teachers need to be clear about what they are trying to accomplish. Purpose should govern the selection of cases, how they are taught, and the outcome. This cannot be emphasized enough. Purpose governs use.

What the authors have not done, and in fact cannot do, is set the purpose for participants and facilitators. We suggest a range of options, for example, introducing students to complex social issues, using cases as an entry into the tradition, the teaching of method, and the development of character, but application must remain with the user. This also means that cases can be misused for the purpose of indoctrination and manipulation. Teachers and students should be aware of this, although misuse of method is not peculiar to the use of cases.

Flexibility has still another dimension. The case method is appropriate to a variety of learning situations such as the classroom, church groups, and the informal discussions found in coffee shops, dorms, and living rooms. Those who use the method regularly find that it stimulates discussion, breaks up the one-way flow of lectures, and eliminates the silence that often permeates abstract discussions. The method is dialogical and thus meets the needs of instructors and learners who prefer more engaged pedagogy. But discussion is only the most frequent way cases are used, and discussion can be more or less structured by teachers depending on their goals.

The method also has internal flexibility. Role plays, small groups, voting, and mini-lectures, a fuller description of which can be found in the Appendix, are only a few of the ways cases can be engaged. Cases are not particularly good for presenting normative material and scientific theories. Experienced case teachers have found that lectures and outside reading are more appropriate for introducing this kind of material. Thus, where significant background information is required for intelligent choices, the authors recommend using cases for the purposes of opening discussions of complex problems, of applying theory and the insights of traditions, of bringing closure and decision, and of encouraging the development of a critical consciousness.

ISSUES AND COMMENTARIES

The issues that the cases raise were given careful thought. A characteristic of a good case, however, is that it raises more than one issue. Some cases raise numerous issues, and beyond these are what might be called connecting components. There is no case, for example, that is explicitly about women or men, yet several address changing relationships of contemporary women and men, including nonbinary relationships. Racism is a central issue in at least two cases and a related one in several others. Teachers may want to use these connecting components to structure their courses so that themes are addressed consistently.

Each case is followed by a commentary that is provided because past experience shows that interpretive reflections help decision-makers by providing leads into avenues of analysis and assessment. These commentaries are not definitive interpretations. They are the observations of individuals trained in Christian theology, ethics, and the case method. They are not out of the same mold, although they do attempt to use the elements that go into an ethical decision as their starting point. There are stylistic differences and variations in emphasis resulting from their multiple authorship. They are intended as aids and not as substitutes for creative thinking, analysis, and decision-making.

As mentioned before, the content of the interpretive reflections is not arbitrary. It is organized around the elements that go into making an ethical decision; however, for the sake of variety and flexibility the authors decided that each commentary did not necessarily have to discuss all of the elements or to do so in the same order. The commentaries are designed to touch base with these elements, although for a given case each element may not be covered with the same thoroughness. Brevity has also governed design. In some of the cases, analysis of one or more of the components does not add significant insight. No doubt in these commentaries there are things omitted that teachers will want to add and points made that facilitators will disagree with and want to comment upon critically.

ADDITIONAL RESOURCES

Ahearn, David Oki, and Peter R. Gathje, eds. *Doing Right and Being Good: Catholic and Protestant Readings in Christian Ethics*. Collegeville, MN: Liturgical Press, 2005.

Birch, Bruce C., Jacqueline E. Lapsley, Cynthia D. Moe-Lobeda, and Larry L. Rasmussen. *Bible and Ethics in the Christian Life: A New Conversation*. Minneapolis: Fortress Press, 2018.

Crook, Roger H. *An Introduction to Christian Ethics*. 6th ed. Upper Saddle River, NJ: Prentice Hall, 2013.

De La Torre, Miguel. *Doing Christian Ethics from the Margins*. 2nd edition. Maryknoll, NY: Orbis Books, 2014.

———, Miguel, ed. *Ethics: A Liberative Approach*. Minneapolis: Fortress Press, 2013.

Jung, Patricia Beattie, and Shannon Jung. *Moral Issues and Christian Responses*. Minneapolis: Fortress Press, 2012.

Lovin, Robin W. *An Introduction to Christian Ethics: Goals, Duties, and Virtues.* Nashville: Abingdon Press, 2011.

Martin-Schramm, James B., Daniel T. Spencer, and Laura A. Stivers. *Earth Ethics: A Case Method Approach.* Maryknoll, NY: Orbis Books, 2015.

McCracken, Vic, ed. *Christian Faith and Social Justice: Five Views.* New York: Bloomsbury Academic, 2014.

Ott Marshall, Ellen. *Introduction to Christian Ethics: Conflict, Faith, and Human Life.* Louisville: Westminster John Knox Press, 2018.

Wells, Samuel, ed. *Christian Ethics: An Introductory Reader.* Hoboken, NJ: Wiley-Blackwell, 2010.

Wilkens, Steve, ed. *Christian Ethics: Four Views.* Westmont: Spectrum Multiview/Intervarsity Press, 2017.

PART I

FAMILY

Case

Rigor and Responsibility

David Trapp hung up the phone and paused to reflect. He had just spoken with his good friend Al Messer. Al had offered to build the cabin. For several months David and his wife, Nancy, had considered building on the two acres of Clark Lake property left to them the year before by David's uncle. The nagging question returned to David. Now that the means were there, was it right to build?

David lived with his wife and two children on a quiet residential street on the outskirts of Toledo, Ohio. David was a lawyer with a downtown law firm that encouraged him to spend up to 15 percent of his time with clients who could not afford to pay. David always used the full allotment, considering it one way he could respond in faith to a pressing human need. David was also active in community affairs. He was vice-president of a statewide citizens' action lobby for more progressive taxation. Locally, he was on the board of directors of an environmental organization whose goal was the cleanup, restoration, and preservation of Lake Erie, and he led adult education classes at his church. What troubled David the most was relating his sense of outrage at injustice to his enjoyment of good food, travel, and water sports.

Nancy Trapp was a buyer for an office-furniture supplier. Her work involved increasing responsibility, and she found it difficult to leave unfinished business in the office. Recently she had been elected to a two-year term as president of the P.T.A. at the children's school. She had not foreseen the constant interruptions such a position would bring. The telephone never seemed to stop ringing, especially on the weekends when people knew they could find her at home.

Decision-making was more or less a family affair with the Trapps. David and Nancy seldom disagreed on family matters and to David's recollection

---

This case and its commentary were prepared originally by Robert L. Stivers and have been updated by Laura A. Stivers and James B. Martin-Schramm. The names of persons and institutions have been disguised, where appropriate, to protect the privacy of those involved.

never on a major one. The children, Darcy and Ben, ages ten and eight, were consulted on major decisions and their voices taken into account.

Nathan Ferguson was the pastor of the local congregation in which the Trapps were active participants. Nathan had recently sold a piece of property he had once intended for recreational purposes. The proceeds from the sale had been donated to a church-sponsored halfway house for drug addicts in downtown Toledo. Shortly after Nathan had sold the property, he had begun to preach and teach in a low-key way on the subjects of possessions, overconsumption, and the materialism of American society. His eventual aim was to have some of his parishioners understand and consider forming a community based on the one in Jerusalem described in the opening chapters of the Book of Acts. He envisioned this community as one that would be environmentally sensitive, hold possessions in common, limit consumption to basic necessities, and give liberally to programs among the poor that were based on a principle of self-reliance.

Clea Parks was David's colleague and an active participant in the church's adult education classes. What amazed David was how she could combine a concern for the poor with a way of living that allowed for occasional extravagances. Like David, Clea made full use of the firm's 15 percent allotment to work with poor clients. She was also on the board of the halfway house for drug addicts. In contrast, she and her husband regularly traveled to Bermuda for tennis and golf and to Sun Valley for skiing. Last year they had flown to the Amazon for an eco-tour. This fall they were headed to the Holy Land for three weeks.

Shortly after the settlement of his uncle's will, which in addition to the two acres included enough cash to construct a modest cabin, David and Nancy had discussed the matter of building. David expressed his ambivalence. He wondered about limits to self-indulgence. His desire for the cabin seemed to be locked in a struggle with his conscience. "How can we build a second place," he asked, "when so many people are living in shelters without roofs or simply do not have a home at all? Can we in good conscience consume as heavily as we do while others are crying out for the very things we take for granted and consume almost at will? And what about the animals? Our consumption contributes to the degradation of their habitat."

He also considered the matter of energy consumption. Again directing his reflections to Nancy, he said: "Think about the energy used in construction and all the driving back and forth that will follow. Is this good stewardship of resources? Does it reflect our responsibility as Americans to conserve fuel? What sort of legacy are we leaving to our grandchildren, not to mention the lessons we are teaching our own children?"

He then rehearsed once again a pet theme: the excessive materialism of American society. "The Bible is quite explicit about possessions," he insisted. "Possessions can easily plug our ears to the hearing of God's word. A person cannot have two masters. The rich young ruler went away empty because he was unwilling to give up his possessions. The tax collector, Zacchaeus, is commended by Jesus for his willingness to give one-half of his possessions to the poor. And Jesus himself lived without possessions, commanding his disciples to do likewise."

He paused to think about this further. "Is it possible," he asked, "to avoid the spirit-numbing nature of possessions short of self-denial? And if I'm not going to opt for self-denial, then I at least have to ask in what way my consumption helps to perpetuate a system that is getting further and further away from the simplicity of Jesus." He paused, then added: "I guess it all boils down to the ethics of the Sermon on the Mount that Pastor Ferguson keeps talking about. Does the rigor of the sermon's ethic represent the only valid Christian option? Is it possible to live in excess of basic needs if this ethic is taken seriously? And if we conclude that the sermon is not a new set of laws, what is its relevance anyway?"

Nancy's response was slow in coming both because she was sensitive to David's imaginative conscience and because she wanted a place to separate herself from work and to teach the children the water sports she and David both enjoyed. "I can understand your commitment," she told him. "It's not a matter of guilt for you. But I just don't feel quite as strongly about those things as you do. The pressure has been getting worse lately, and I feel the need to share time with you and the children in a more relaxed setting. The kids are getting older fast, and in a few years they'll be beyond the age where they'll be around to learn water sports.

"The materialism you are so concerned about," she went on to say, "has also made for creative new possibilities. It's not possessions themselves, but how we use them that makes a difference. It's the willingness to give, and we give enough what with the 15 percent of your time and the giving of more than 10 percent of our incomes to church and charity. And think about what giving up our possessions will do. Without programs to transfer our abundance to the poor, giving things up will go for naught or perhaps contribute to the loss of someone's job. That is just the way things are. Think about Al Messer."

David was not quite sure what to make of Nancy's comments. The old nagging questions kept coming back. His conscience would not let him off easily.

Then Nathan Ferguson had begun his sermons and more recently had conducted a series of six sessions in the adult education class that David led. Nathan returned time and again to the teachings of Jesus: to the Sermon on the Mount, to the rich young ruler, to Zacchaeus, to the sharing in early Christian communities, to the call of the prophets to justice and care for the poor, and to Jesus's love for the birds of the air and fish of the sea. Nathan had not talked in a demanding or accusatory fashion, but neither had he let his parishioners off the hook. To David it seemed that Nathan's every thought had been directed straight at him.

At the office Clea hit him from the other side. At first she had merely commented on Nathan's sermons and classes. She thought Nathan was too much of a perfectionist. She appreciated his concern for the poor and the environment and how possessions can close one's ears to the word of God. She did not, however, see how individual sacrifices produced the social change they all wanted.

She also had a contrasting view of the Sermon on the Mount. "We cannot live the sermon," she explained. "It's impossible, and anyway, it wasn't intended for everyone. Ethical rigor is right for folks like Nathan, but what most of us are called to is responsibility: to the right use of possessions, to a willingness to give, and to advocacy of justice in word and deed. The choice is not between self-indulgence and self-denial. There is a third option: living responsibly with concern for all those issues Nathan talks about and still appreciating the finer things in life."

When David told her about the lake property and Nancy's needs, Clea had begun to push him a bit harder. "Come on, David," she said, half joking, "it's all right with Jesus if you build. Jesus enjoyed life and participated in it fully. The church tradition is quite ambiguous on possessions, wealth, and nature." Another time she put it bluntly, "What right have you to force your values and views on Nancy and the children?" Lately she had been teasing him. Just the other day with a big grin on her face she called him "the monk."

Al Messer's call had jolted David and increased his sense that something had to give. Al had told David that he could build the cabin out of used lumber and had found a place where he could get insulation and double-pane window glass at reduced prices. Al had also indicated he needed the work because business had been a bit slow lately.

Nancy entered the room and guessed what was troubling David. "I know what's bothering you," she said. "If we build, those old questions about the poor, materialism, and limits to consumption will nag at you. You might not even stick to a decision to build. If we don't build, you'll feel you have let the kids and me down and miss your favorite water sports. How should we decide this?"

Commentary

Taken at face value this case is about David and Nancy Trapp struggling to decide whether to build a vacation cabin. But at a deeper and more comprehensive level the case is addressed to all non-poor Christians; the issue is how to live as a Christian in a materialistic world where ostentatious luxury, grinding poverty, and environmental degradation exist side by side.

This question of how to live can be given greater specificity by considering the title of the case. Should an affluent family give up what it has and follow the rigorous "holy poverty" of Jesus, or is there an alternative called "responsible consumption" that stresses right use and good stewardship of material resources? Realizing that a continuum of options is possible between the "either" of rigor and the "or" of responsibility, these two options may be contrasted for the purpose of analyzing the decisions the Trapps must make.

Before addressing these two contrasting perspectives, however, there are several related issues that should at least be mentioned. The two most important are poverty and environmental degradation. David and Nancy's decision is not hidden in a vacuum. It stands out in a context where, according to the World Health Organization, 821 million people are undernourished (one in nine) and live in miserable poverty. It stands out in a global economy in which the gap between rich and poor is wide and expanding. It stands out in an economic system that needs high levels of consumption to stimulate growth and jobs. It stands out in a planetary system where unprecedented numbers of species are going extinct largely due to human actions and where there is serious concern about the sustainability of natural resources and the capacity of ecosystems to absorb pollution. These issues raised by the context of the case are the very issues raised to prominence by this volume.

There are six other issues important for this case but peripheral to the main concerns. The first is family decision-making. How is this family to decide? The second stems from the Trapps' need to "get away." Would the addition of a cabin really solve the more pressing problems of overwork and over-involvement in the community? The third is the matter of educating children. What messages do David and Nancy send Darcy and Ben by overwork and by building a second home? What sort of character are they trying to instill?

The fourth issue is raised by the inheritance. Are David and Nancy really free to give their inheritance to the poor? Although the case does not say, they probably live within the context of a larger family grouping, some of whose members might be a little upset with such unilateral action. The fifth issue is guilt. Should Christians and Americans feel a sense of guilt for their high levels of consumption? And what is the function of guilt in the Christian life? Sixth is the issue of individual action in a world fast approaching eight billion people that is dominated by large social organizations. How do people like David and Nancy influence others to do justice and exercise Christianity's call for solidarity? Will individual acts of self-sacrifice make a difference?

Beyond these six issues, there are a number of issues raised by Christian traditions. How should the Bible and theology, for example, guide the Trapps' choice? What in fact do the traditions say about the issues in the case?

THE MAIN QUESTION

So how are Christians to live in a world of continuing poverty and environmental degradation? Most students react to David's dilemma with at least mild astonishment. They seem to assume that consuming goods and services in quantity is the natural thing to do and have difficulty comprehending why building is a dilemma at all. This is not surprising given the daily barrage of commercial advertising whose main purpose is to sell a way of life that encourages heavy consumption. Indeed, heavy consumption has become a way of life to many Americans.

The norm of justice makes the gap between rich and poor and the grinding poverty of so many people that goes side by side with this consumption difficult to justify. The emphasis on material things underlying this consumption is difficult to reconcile with biblical norms on wealth and consumption. The environmental degradation that this level of consumption causes is a serious problem for sustainability of the earth's ecological systems. On these grounds David and many Americans have good reason to be troubled by their consciences.

Consider first the norm of *justice*. Justice is rooted in the very being of God. It is an essential part of God's community of love and calls followers of Jesus Christ to make fairness the core of their social response to other persons and the rest of creation. Included in this biblical concern for justice is solidarity with the poor and also with nature.

The biblical basis of justice and solidarity with the poor starts with God's liberation of the oppressed Hebrew slaves in Egypt and the establishment of a covenant with them (Exodus). This theme continues in the prophetic reinterpretation of the covenant. Micah summarized the law:

> to do justice, and to love kindness,
> and to walk humbly with your God. (Mic 6:8)

Amos was adamant that God's wrath would befall Israel for its injustice and failure to care for the poor (Amos 5:21–24). Isaiah and Jeremiah were equally adamant (Is 1:12–17; 3:13–15; 58:6–9; Jer 22:13–17).

In the Christian scriptures the emphasis on justice is somewhat muted in comparison to the prophets, but the concern for the poor may be even stronger. Jesus himself was a poor man from a poor part of Israel. His mission was among the poor, and his message was directed to them. He blessed the poor and spoke God's judgment on the rich. On the cross he made himself one of the dispossessed. In the early Jerusalem community, as recorded in Acts 1—5, the basic economic needs of all members were taken care of as the wealthier shared their possessions so none would be deprived.

Second are biblical and theological understandings of wealth and consumption. Two traditions have dominated, offering two not very compatible understandings of what it means to live sufficiently. One stresses a rigorous response to Jesus's teachings, including self-denial, the giving of what one has to the poor, and a radical freedom from possessions. The other accents the right use of possessions and emphasizes responsibility and willingness to share. The first tradition may be called *rigorous discipleship* and the second *responsible consumption.* These are not meant to be polemical titles. Responsible consumption has its element of rigor, and rigorous discipleship is certainly responsible. While the differences between them are significant, it is possible to accept both as valid Christian ways of living.

Parenthetically, these two traditions also give a foundation for solidarity with the poor. Historically, many Christians have identified completely with the poor, even to the point of considerable self-sacrifice. Widely known modern examples, such as Mother Teresa and Dorothy Day, have continued this tradition. At the same time and not so spectacularly, Christians work responsibly in everyday vocations serving Christ with varying degrees of intensity and frugality.

The choice between these traditions is David's dilemma and is worthy of further exploration. The dilemma is the age-old one of the ideal and the real. On the one hand, Jesus offers glimpses of the ideal in his teachings on the community of God and in his person. The community of God, he says, is already present with power, and Jesus asks his disciples to live in this power and to drop what they are doing and follow him. On the other hand, paradoxically, the community of God is still to come in its fullness.

Reality is a mixture of powers: human power rightly and wrongly used and God's power of love. God's community of love stands alongside and often in contradiction to human power, and Christians must live in a world where perfect choices are seldom presented.

These two normative traditions both have biblical bases. The Hebrew scriptures take the responsible consumption side. They praise the rich people and place a high value on riches gained through honest work (Gen 13:2; 26:13; 30:43; 41:40). Alongside this praise is the obligation to care for weaker members of society (Amos 8:48; Is 5:8–10; 10:1–3). Nowhere do the Hebrew scriptures praise self-imposed poverty or beggars.

The two sides are found in the teachings of Jesus. His announcement of the coming community of God carries with it a call for unparalleled freedom from possessions and complete trust in God. The service of God and service of riches are incompatible (Mt 6:24; Mk 8:36; 9:43–48; 10:17–25; Lk 12:15; 8:14, 18–23; 19:1–10). Jesus tells the rich young ruler who has kept all the laws to go sell what he has and give it to the poor (Lk 18:18–24). Jesus himself had no possessions (Mt 8:20; Mk 1:16; 6:8–9; Lk 9:3; 10:4) and prodded his disciples to go out on their missionary journeys taking nothing with them (Lk 9:3; 10:4).

Nevertheless, Jesus took for granted the owning of property (Lk 6:30; 10:30–37; Mt 25:31–40). He was apparently supported by women of means (Lk 8:2) and urged that possessions be used to help those in need (Lk 6:30). Jesus did not ask Zacchaeus to give up all his possessions (Lk 19). He dined with hated tax collectors and was fond of celebrations, especially meals of fellowship. The examples echo the Hebrew scriptures' stress on the right use of wealth and possessions.

This mixed mind continued in the early church. On the one side was the Jerusalem community, where goods were shared in common (Acts 1—5). This seems to follow Jesus's teachings about radical freedom from possessions. The letter of James offers little solace to the wealthy (Jas 1:11; 2:1–7; 5:1–6). On the other side is Paul, who did not address the problem of wealth, although he himself seems to have had few possessions and was self-supporting as a tentmaker (Phil 4:11–13). He did, however, stress right use, made clear his center in Christ, and called on the congregations he served to support the poor in Jerusalem. The letter to Timothy, while hard on the wealthy, leaves the door open to right use of possessions (1 Tim 6:6–10, 17–19).

From these two traditions a dual ethic emerged. For monks and nuns, who surrendered their possessions and elected a life of chastity, holy poverty, and nonviolence, the rigor of Jesus was binding. For the great majority the rigor of Jesus became "counsels of perfection." It was deemed impossible of fulfillment and therefore binding only on those who would be perfect.

These two ways of living existed side by side with the authority of the church sanctioning both and holding them together. Implicit in this resolution of the dilemma was a troublesome hierarchy of perfection and the unbiblical notion of special merits that practicing rigor was claimed to confer. Thus, while the church held things together, it did so at the price of grading perfection and discouraging the rigor of ordinary Christians.

Protestants, following Martin Luther's dictum of the priesthood of all believers, eliminated special merit, but at the price of restoring the dilemma. Monasteries and convents were closed, and all believers were, according to Luther, to serve God in whatever vocation they found themselves. Where there had been two ways of life in one church, now there was one way of life with two tendencies in many churches. Still, rigorous discipleship has continued to the present in the monastic movement within the Roman Catholic Church and in many sects that have flourished in Protestantism.

One statement by Martin Luther during a "table talk" in the winter of 1542–43 catches the mind that is suspicious of wealth:

> Riches are the most insignificant things on earth, the smallest gift that God can give a man. What are they in comparison with the Word of God? In fact, what are they in comparison even with physical endowments and beauty? What are they in comparison to gifts of the mind? And yet we act as if this were not so! The matter, form, effect, and goal of riches are worthless. That's why our Lord God generally gives riches to crude asses to whom he doesn't give anything else.[1]

The biblical witness on consumption follows much the same twofold pattern. The basic issue is frugality versus contentment with a moderate level of consumption.

Theologically the two traditions take their cues from the paradoxical "here, but yet to come" teaching of the early church. This paradox appears in the earliest pages of the Bible. Human beings are created in the image of God (Gen 1) but with Adam and Eve fall away from God into sin (Gen 3). It reappears again and again in the history of Israel as the Israelites wrestle with the responsibilities of the covenant and their own unrighteousness.

Jesus advises his disciples to be sheep among the wolves and to have the wisdom of the serpent and the innocence of the dove (Mt 10:16). For

---

[1] Henry F. French, ed., *Martin Luther's Table Talk: Abridged from Luther's Works*, vol. 54 (Minneapolis: Fortress Press, 2017), 26.

Christians, this paradox is preeminent in the cross and resurrection. The cross is reality at its worst and points to the depth of human sin. Sin is not some minor defect to be overcome by new techniques. Ordering force and occasionally even coercion are needed to keep it in check.

Yet the cross is not the last word in Christianity. It is followed closely by the ever-new word of the resurrection. The resurrection points to God at work overcoming sin and death. It points as well to the possibility of the "new creation" in the lives of individuals and groups and to the creative potential of love and justice. It teaches Christians that while they still live in the age of sin and death, God's love has broken in, there is hope, and their efforts in response to God's love are not in vain. Christians are invited, as a result, to deal with a partly open future in which even small responses can make a difference.

Finally, the paradox is highlighted by Paul's sense that Christians live between the ages. They live in the old age of sin, death, injustice, and limits. Yet they are called to live according to the new age inaugurated by Jesus Christ and made present by the Holy Spirit. Insofar as they live in the old age, Christians give limited support to such things as prison systems, to less than perfect but still functioning economic and political systems, and even to wars of liberation and defense. Living in the old age involves compromises, many of which appear to be "cop-outs" to those who take the rigorous path.

Nevertheless, Christians are not to be serpents or to live according to the old age. They are to live in the resurrection according to the love and justice of the new age. This means pushing beyond what merely is and seeking just and sustainable societies. Living in the new age means witnessing to the ideal and may seem utopian to those who enjoy luxury and even some who follow the path of responsible consumption.

In summary, the rigorous tradition builds on Jesus's call to radical discipleship, his living without possessions frugally and simply, and his freedom from materialism. This tradition calls the disciple to a life of simplicity and sharing. It is a life of commitment to the community of God. And even if all the details are not lived perfectly, at least the disciple should aim in that direction and pray that the grace of God will provide the resources to reconcile aim and action.

As for living between the ages, the path of rigorous discipleship emphasizes the new age almost to the exclusion of the old. This exclusion comes not from failure to see the sin of the old age, but rather from the assumption that Christians are free from the old age through the power of God. Hence radical changes in ways of living come naturally, and followers make these changes with enthusiasm.

The path of rigorous discipleship is attractive. It does not bog down in the inevitable relativities and compromises of the old age. It is simple, direct, and often accompanied by communities that seem full of the Spirit. It is a valid Christian option.

Unlike the path of rigorous discipleship, the path of responsible consumption does not take its main cues from the teachings of Jesus. This does not mean it is less biblical, but that it rests more heavily on the main themes of the Bible, in particular on the theological tension between the old and the new ages. Like those on the path of rigorous discipleship, Christians on this path are concerned for the poor and aware of being tied to possessions. They do not, however, take the frugality and simplicity of Jesus literally or urge the surrender of all possessions.

Reduced to basics, those who follow this tradition wrestle with what it means to live between the ages, taking both ages seriously. In contrast to the heavy stress on the new age, they point to the realities of the old age or to the ambiguity of life between the ages. The problem for them is not rigorous discipleship but how to act responsibly and to begin a process of change that will lead to greater justice and more sustainable communities. Their mood is sober, their programs moderate and reformist in nature. They also have a greater appreciation of material consumption.

This path is attractive to less ascetic Christians and to those who are deeply involved in existing structures. It is a valid Christian tradition and avoids the excesses that sometimes accompany the rigorous tradition. Most important, it accounts for the complexities of living in the world as it is.

While Christianity has been of two minds, it has been clear on one guiding norm, *sufficiency.* Sufficiency for humans is the timely supply of basic material necessities, defined as the minimum amount of food, clothing, shelter, transportation, health care, and education needed to live at some margin above mere subsistence. Sufficiency is, of course, more than a given batch of goods and services. Philosopher Martha Nussbaum has established something she calls the "flourishing life" as the goal of her development scheme. She has advanced two lists of what constitute "the human form of life" and "good human functioning."[2] She insists it is the responsibility

---

[2] Martha Nussbaum and Jonathan Glover, *Women, Culture, and Development: A Study of Human Capabilities* (Oxford: Clarendon Press, 1995), 76–85. Nussbaum and Glover argue that the "human form of life" consists of (1) mortality; (2) the human body including the needs for food, drink, and shelter, and sexual desire; (3) the capacity for pleasure and pain; (4) cognitive capability including perceiving, imagining, and thinking; (5) early infant development; (6) practical reason; (7) affiliation with other human beings; (8) relatedness to other species and nature; (9) humor and play; (10) separateness; and (11) space to move around in. "Basic human functional capabilities"

of political and economic institutions to ensure that everyone is capable of functioning at a human level. While her lists are exhaustive and beyond the capacity of most governments, they are a good starting place for understanding what sufficiency means.

Sufficiency for other species revolves first around the preservation and restoration of habitat for wild species. Humans do not have the capacity to oversee the survival of many species, but they can cease degrading critical habitats. Habitat loss is a major cause of species extinction. As for domestic animals, more is required. Sufficiency for them means the provision of basic material needs and proper care. This opens up a wide range of options including alternative farming techniques and even vegetarian diets.

Sufficiency must also include future generations. Sufficiency must be sustainable over long periods of time. Another norm influencing the Trapps' decision is therefore *sustainability.* The issue that sustainability raises for the Trapps is whether the forms of consumption they are contemplating degrade the environment. One small cabin on an already developed lake front will hardly do much damage, but if their behavior were to be generalized, it certainly would. Earth can ill afford eight billion people who consume as if they were affluent North Americans.

What then are David and Nancy to do? How are they to live? If they will to live responsively to the power of God and to be guided by Christian norms, they will avoid heavy consumption, materialism, and selfish individualism. They will live sufficiently free to pursue rigorous discipleship or responsible consumption as they feel called. They will put trust where trust belongs, that is to say, in God's community, not in material possessions. What this means in practice is something that finally is a matter of conscience. Blueprints and prescriptions are not available.

GUILT

Is David driven by guilt over his own privileged place in the world—white, American, male, intelligent, and wealthy—or is *guilt* an inappropriate

---

include (1) being able to live to the end of a human life of normal length; (2) being able to have good health; (3) being able to avoid unnecessary and non-beneficial pain; (4) being able to use the senses; (5) being able to have attachments to things and persons outside ourselves; (6) being able to form a conception of the good and to engage in critical reflection about the planning of one's life; (7) being able to live for others; (8) being able to live with concern for and in relations to animals, plants, and the world of nature; (9) being able to laugh, play, and enjoy recreational activities; and (10) being able to live one's own life in one's own surroundings and context.

word to describe his struggle with rigor and responsibility? The case does not reveal the answer. Giving David the benefit of doubt, however, it is better to see his struggle as a conscientious effort to deal with an ambiguous tradition and a changing environmental context. Christians like David may be genuinely perplexed as they try to figure out the right course, because valid norms sometimes suggest quite different courses of action.

Even if David did not feel guilty, it is important to recognize that guilt is an all too common human experience and should be taken seriously. Guilt may be a warning sign of serious inner alienation. It may be telling David that he really is living a sinful way of life and needs to change (repent).

More important for those who would categorize David as "guilt-ridden" is the possibility that they are projecting their own guilt in order to be free for a life of affluence. To dismiss David's dilemma as guilt is to miss the main point of the case.

Finally, guilt is not something that needs to paralyze action. Guilt may be genuinely experienced and may legitimately point to sin, but it is not the place to rest. Just as the resurrection follows the cross, so do forgiveness and the possibility of new life follow sin and guilt.

INDIVIDUAL ACTION

Does it really make a difference what David and Nancy decide? Does David's struggle over options available to only a select few trivialize the more important problems of world poverty and environmental degradation?

Discussions of individual action are permeated with optimistic and pessimistic extremes. The optimists insist that successful social movements are usually started and led by individuals who are deeply concerned and motivated. They urge their listeners to take the challenge and change the world. The pessimists, in turn, dismiss individual action as not having a chance in a world of large organizations. They urge their listeners to join movements or counsel withdrawal.

Christians are neither optimists nor pessimists. They are hopeful and realistic; hopeful because God is at work in even the darkest times, realistic because of sin. Christians act first in response to the love of God they experience spiritually and only second to achieve results. If good results follow from faithful discipleship, they should be embraced. If they do not, action is still forthcoming because of its spiritual foundation.

This simple truth does away with the debate between optimists and pessimists over individual action. The debate is misplaced. It misses the essential inspiration of Christian ethical action and substitutes reliance on human action alone.

Is David's dilemma trivial? By no means! His struggle with his conscience over appropriate levels of consumption is essential in a poverty-stricken, environmentally degraded world. It is essential for everyone, especially for those who consume heavily or could potentially consume more. Whether it is a cabin, a television set, a new computer, or a trip to the Amazon, personal consumption makes an ethical statement. It says a lot about character. While David's specific decision will not be recorded in history books, what this generation does to relieve poverty and preserve the environment will.

ADDITIONAL RESOURCES

Brueggemann, Walter. *Money and Possessions*. Louisville: Westminster John Knox Press, 2016.

———. *Sabbath as Resistance: Saying No to the Culture of Now*. Louisville: Westminster John Knox Press, 2017.

———. *The Prophetic Imagination*. 40th anniversary edition. Minneapolis: Fortress Press, 2018.

Cloutier, David M. *The Vice of Luxury: Economic Excess in a Consumer Age*. Washington, DC: Georgetown University Press, 2015.

Cobb, John B., Jr. *Sustainability: Economics, Ecology, and Justice*. Eugene, OR: Wipf and Stock Publishers, 2007.

Dauvergne, Peter. *The Shadows of Consumption: Consequences for the Global Environment*. Cambridge, MA: MIT Press, 2010.

Fadling, Alan. *An Unhurried Life: Following Jesus' Rhythms of Work and Rest*. Westmont, IL: InterVarsity Press, 2013.

Foster, Richard J. *Freedom of Simplicity: Finding Harmony in a Complex World*. New York: HarperOne, 2005.

Francis. *Praise Be to You: Laudato Si': On Care for Our Common Home*. San Francisco: Ignatius Press, 2015.

Hartman, Laura M. *The Christian Consumer: Living Faithfully in a Fragile World*. New York: Oxford University Press, 2011.

Hinson-Hasty, Elizabeth L. *The Problem of Wealth: A Christian Response to a Culture of Affluence*. Maryknoll, NY: Orbis Books, 2017.

Horsley, Richard A. *Covenant Economics: A Biblical Vision of Justice for All*. Louisville: Westminster John Knox Press, 2009.

Johnson, Jan. *Abundant Simplicity: Discovering the Unhurried Rhythms of Grace*. Westmont, IL: InterVarsity Press, 2011.

Kavanaugh, John K. *Following Christ in a Consumer Society: The Spirituality of Cultural Resistance*. Maryknoll, NY: Orbis Books, 2006.

McFague, Sallie. *Blessed Are the Consumers: Climate Change and the Practice of Restraint.* Minneapolis: Fortress Press, 2013.

Nash, James A. "Toward the Revival and Reform of the Subversive Virtue: Frugality." In *Consumption, Population, and Sustainability: Perspectives from Science and Religion,* edited by Audrey R. Chapman, Rodney L. Petersen, and Barbara Smith-Moran. Washington, DC: Island Press, 2002.

Pahl, Jon. *Shopping Malls and Other Sacred Spaces: Putting God in Place.* Grand Rapids, MI: Brazos Press, 2003.

Poole, Eve. *Buying God: Consumerism and Theology.* London: SCM Press, 2018.

Rasmussen, Larry L. *Earth-Honoring Faith: Religious Ethics in a New Key.* New York: Oxford University Press, 2013.

Ritterhouse, Bruce P. *Shopping for Meaningful Lives: The Religious Motives of Consumerism.* Eugene, OR: Cascade Books, 2013.

Rohr, Richard. *Simplicity: The Freedom of Letting Go.* Updated edition. New York: Crossroad Publishing Company, 2005.

Shi, David. *The Simple Life: Plain Living and High Thinking in American Culture.* Athens: University of Georgia Press, 2007.

Sider, Ronald. *Rich Christians in an Age of Hunger: Moving from Affluence to Generosity.* Reprint edition. Nashville: Thomas Nelson Publishers, 2015.

Slaughter, Michael. *The Christian Wallet: Spending, Giving, and Living with a Conscience.* Louisville: Westminster John Knox Press, 2016.

Stevenson, Tyler Wigg. *Brand Jesus: Christianity in a Consumerist Age.* New York: Seabury Books, 2007.

Related Websites

The Story of Stuff Project
https://storyofstuff.org/

Case

What God Has Joined

Linda glanced through the large glass window of the restaurant and saw Beth and Jennifer already seated in a corner booth. She hesitated a moment at the door, then moved toward them, hugging and greeting each in turn. They had been good friends in college, but after graduation they had drifted apart. When the fourth member of their college quartet, Joanne, had died of breast cancer eight years after graduation, the remaining three had come together again to support her in her last months and to share the pain of her passing. Over the next two years they had remained close. The lunch today was a kind of a celebration for Jennifer, who had concentrated on her career as an accountant after college rather than marrying and having children like the other three. Now, as the three survivors of the quartet approached thirty-five, Jennifer was engaged to be married to another partner in her accounting firm. Next Saturday there was to be a big party, but this lunch was just for the three of them.

Twenty minutes later, having admired Jen's ring and listened to the couple's wedding plans, Linda was shifting uncomfortably in her seat. She realized both Beth and Jennifer were staring, waiting for her to volunteer information. Finally, Jennifer, not the most patient or tactful of the trio, blurted out, "Tell us what's the matter, Lin. We both know that things haven't been great for a while at home, but you seem desperately unhappy. We love you. What's going on?"

It was more than Linda could do to control the gulping sobs that rolled out of her. "I don't know what to do. It's all come back, and I can't go on. David's drinking, and he's hit me. I can't take it anymore."

When Linda had calmed down, Beth pulled the story from her a piece at a time. Beth and Jen knew that Linda's husband, David, had rarely used alcohol before he lost his job as manager of a bank branch, but both had

This case and commentary were prepared originally by Christine E. Gudorf and have been updated by Laura A. Stivers and James B. Martin-Schramm. The names of persons and institutions have been disguised, where appropriate, to protect the privacy of those involved.

seen him inebriated at least twice in the last six months. They knew David had not found another job. But both were shocked to hear that he had hit Linda. They immediately asked for details, for neither would have thought David capable of violence. Both remembered the extraordinary gentleness he had displayed in the hospital nursery holding and feeding Megan, the couple's tiny premature firstborn.

Linda began by defending David, citing the pressures of unemployment on him, the stress of seeing their unemployment insurance run out, and the prospect of their savings running out as well. With only the part-time secretarial work that Linda had found with the school board, they would not be able to keep up house payments. "He's drinking, but he's not really drinking that much. He has hit me two or three times but always stops after the one slap. The real problem is me. It's all coming back. I love him, but I can't stand for him to get near me. And he thinks I'm rejecting him, that I don't love him anymore because he doesn't have a job."

Both Beth and Jennifer understood that Linda was referring to her memories of years of sexual abuse by her grandfather. From the time she was eight until his death when Linda was fourteen, her grandfather had used his position as her after-school babysitter to sexually molest her. Her family had more or less dismissed both attempts she made to tell about the abuse. She later suspected that her mother had been abused before her. When she arrived at college, Linda never dated. When the topic of child incest came up in a sociology class, Linda spoke to the professor, who referred her to individual therapy and to a support group for child victims of incest. After six months of therapy Linda had met David, declared herself cured, and quit the therapy. But both Beth and Jennifer remembered Linda's screaming nightmares and her fear and distrust of men. And they knew that though she kept in touch with her family, she never went back home after college and never left her children with any of her family.

"Are you and David talking, Linda?" Jennifer asked.

"What can I say? He doesn't believe me when I say that he's not the reason I don't want sex. He keeps telling me I was over the abuse years ago, that I have loved sex for all these years, that the only thing that could be turning me off is him. Maybe he's right, and the memories are just an excuse. Maybe I have invented them. That's what mother and Aunt Lucy told me when I was little. That I made them up. I don't really know how I feel, or whether I love him, or what I want to do. But I can't go on. Sometimes I just go and hide in a closet for hours at a time. I can't face anyone. I don't know how I got here—I haven't been outside the house in weeks."

Linda was calmer by the end of the lunch. Both Jennifer and Beth were disturbed by Linda's depression and her expressions of self-doubt and self-blame. They urged her to seek therapeutic help. Beth volunteered to make appointments for both David and Linda separately to see her neighbors, the Spencers, a husband-and-wife therapy team. Beth assured Linda that they worked on a sliding-scale fee schedule.

LONG-TERM RECOVERY ISSUES

Six weeks later, when the friends met after Jen's wedding, Linda reported that some things were better and some things were worse. David had liked Dr. Dan Spencer from the start. By the second session he had stopped drinking, and though there were no more incidents of either verbal or physical violence, David continued to work with Dan Spencer on issues around alcohol and violence. Linda reported that Alice Spencer was pushing her to face the violent episodes, to look at the effect they had had on her and on the marital relationship, and to think about how she might react to violence or the threat of violence from David in the future. David was continuing to look for work in surrounding communities. But he still had trouble accepting that Linda was not rejecting him when she declined sex.

Sitting in Beth's kitchen while Linda's and Beth's children played outside the backyard window, Linda confided, "Sometimes I really do want him to hold me, to give me affection. But the minute it turns sexual, I want to scream. For him, if I don't want sex, I don't love him. He tries sometimes to just be affectionate, but it really hurts him when I panic and push him away from me. Sometimes I can't even stand him being close; other times I want to be held but then push him away later. He complains that he never knows what I want. And I don't know what I want. I don't know why it all came back. There was no clue for all those years. We were really happy until he lost his job. But it's been almost a year since we made love, and three months since I was last willing to try."

"What does Alice Spencer think of your situation?" asked Jennifer.

"She says that I need to concentrate not on David or the relationship but on my own feelings. She thinks that's why it all came back—I didn't stay in therapy long enough to heal from the abuse. I'm not good at explaining it, but what the years of abuse did was to teach me to respond to other people's needs and desires and to lose sight of my own. She says now I need to respond to my own feelings, but first I have to learn what they are. And in some areas of my life I don't have a clue as to which feelings are mine and which are David's, or my grandfather's, or even other people's—like yours. So many 'shoulds' in my life have come from outside me, without any conscious consideration or adoption on my part. She insists I can heal, that I can find my authentic self. But I don't know. In some things, yes, but I can't imagine ever having sex again and enjoying it without remembering the pain and hatred and ultimate emptiness inside. What does that mean for our marriage? Do I love David? Can I make him wait for what may never happen? Shouldn't I be working on accepting sex so I can stop hurting him? My rejection is hurting him much worse than his slaps ever hurt me. Can there be a marriage without sex? A real one with love and warmth, the kind we vowed to have?"

Jennifer responded, "That's a tough one. I remember that Christian churches used to forbid totally impotent men to marry, because sex was important to marriage, but I think so long as they had sex once, it didn't matter if they never did again. I don't know. I'm the newly married one here. Can there be a real marriage without sex? Won't that depend on what David wants and needs, too? Do you want to be married? Why don't you talk to somebody with some expertise? You like Pastor Link, and we've all known him for years. Why don't you and David talk to him?"

At that very moment David sat in Dan Spencer's office. "All right, all right. I am coming to see that she really is going back through all that past abuse. I don't understand why. I thought she was through it before we got married. She was never tense or nervous about sex, never afraid of being forced or hurt. She knew I would never hurt her. I just don't understand why it came back now, if not in response to me. But I can't do this much longer. I know that when I feel really threatened by her withdrawal that I want to drink too much, and I know that if I drink, the hurt and threat will come out in anger. I don't know how I'd live with myself if I ever forced her to have sex. But not drinking is only a little part of the answer."

David continued thoughtfully, "I know I haven't slept the whole night through in over six months. Some nights I have to get up and get away from her, so I won't start making love to her while she's asleep. I have to go lie down on the couch. I love Linda. When I hold her or hug her or just sit in the car with her driving the kids to Sunday school, I want to make love to her. And I want her to love me. It's not just selfish or lust. I want to give her pleasure, to make her feel better, to show her that she can trust me with her body and her heart. Sometimes I think it would be easier to just stay away from her. But to avoid her, to get separate beds, or even separate rooms when we could afford them, would be like divorce. When will this be over? How long does it take? Will she ever get better? Is divorce the only option?"

When Linda picked up David at Dr. Spencer's, she asked if he was interested in seeing Pastor Link. David agreed and offered to make the appointment. When David called the church, he was told that Pastor Link was out of town for three weeks but that the associate pastor, Reverend Deerick, was available. David made an appointment with Reverend Deerick, explained the general situation to him, and mentioned that he and

Linda were in therapy with the Spencers. Reverend Deerick asked for their authorization to speak with the Spencers. When David and Linda appeared the following week for their appointment, Reverend Deerick had briefly discussed the case with the Spencers. Linda and David began by describing their feelings about each other and their marriage, and ended with a flurry of questions about the nature of marriage. Was their marriage over? Could the wounded child in Linda ever really heal after all these years? If not, would remaining together be merely a hypothetical front, or would it be a heroic fidelity to the vows they had taken? Could there be a real Christian marriage without sharing either genital pleasure or touch and affection? What did the church teach?

When they had finished, Reverend Deerick was still for a few moments and then said: "I'm not sure that anyone can answer all your questions. I have never been married myself. And you probably know that our church, like most Christian churches, is in the midst of rethinking various aspects of our teachings regarding sexuality and marriage. I could tell you what Augustine or Luther would say to you, but I don't think that would do much good. From what you have told me, you didn't marry either to have children or to prevent fornication. You married because you loved each other in a deeply interpersonal way and because you found that the whole of the other person—body and soul—helped put you in touch with ultimate reality, with God. This contemporary understanding of the purpose and goal of marriage is radically different from Augustine's, or Luther's, or any of the other classical Christian thinkers. So their likely advice in this situation—that you purify and consecrate your marriage by giving up sexual intimacy, living as brother and sister as you rear your children—would probably strike you as effectively ending the marriage.

"Our theological tradition simply doesn't give us a lot of useful contemporary guidance about sexuality in marriage. But I do have some suggestions. The first one is personal prayer. I don't mean that you should pray that all this will mysteriously disappear. Prayer is communication with God. Sometimes it is spoken; more often it is silent. Sometimes we write our prayers. Think of prayer as a way of making a friend of God.

"David, I am very moved by your pain and your love for Linda. But you express a great deal of need for her, and that need clearly puts emotional pressure on her. Most men in our society are socialized to fulfill virtually all their intimacy needs in one sexual relationship. Developing an intimate relationship with God could not only take away some of your pain and need, but it could also let you focus on Linda's needs more clearly. Linda, prayer for you could be a source of hope and strength for healing. Some victims of sexual abuse by males have a difficult time with prayer and with God because of the traditional images of God as masculine. You may need to focus on the femininity of God, on God as Mother, to be able to pray. But regardless of what gender you attribute to God, the object is that you let yourself feel God's love for you and God's support for your healing. Feeling God's support for healing could help you feel more legitimate investing so much time and energy in the healing process. A prayerful relationship with God could help you reclaim feelings of trust, self-worth, and responsibility for your own life.

"You both have many questions about marriage and your future that I think only prayer can answer. Prayer can be a process of uncovering, one piece at a time, all our questions about who we are and what we should do. If you like, I would be glad to meet with you periodically to discuss developments in your individual prayer life. Or I have some books or articles you could read, if you prefer."

As David and Linda drove home from the meeting, they wondered how valuable Reverend Deerick's advice had been. In some ways it evoked simplistic notions of passive religion in which prayer is the answer to everything. But Reverend Deerick had supported their therapeutic process with the Spencers as helpful and seemed to want to coordinate this spiritual direction with that process. Perhaps prayer could help David find more patience with Linda's withdrawal and could help Linda feel stronger and more worthwhile. Halfway home Linda asked, "David, do you want to consider divorce as an option? I would understand if you did. I don't think it's right for me to ask you to continue with our marriage if that's not what you want, but for myself I prefer to work on our marriage. I'm just not sure how we work on rebuilding it, or what we can legitimately ask of each other. What do you want to do, David?"

Commentary

Some of the social and moral issues requiring analysis in this case include alcoholism, domestic violence, and child sexual abuse (child incest). But as David's and Linda's questions indicate, the central question for them is whether they should remain together. This question raises the theological issues undergirding the nature of marriage. Let us begin with the more specific problems.

ALCOHOLISM

Linda and David both seem to treat David's drinking as a minor problem; Beth and Jennifer also seem to accept that judgment. However, Dan Spencer continues to ask about and treat alcohol as a possible ongoing problem, for he is not sure that alcohol is only temporarily a problem due to David's loss of work or Linda's withdrawal. While the use of alcohol has not been regarded as a moral problem within most of Christianity—certainly not within scripture—the abuse of alcohol has been consistently condemned from scriptural times to the present. It is not clear from the case that David's alcohol abuse is part of a larger pattern of alcoholism, but David's misuse of alcohol under the pressure of unemployment and his wife's withdrawal might well signal a pattern of relying on alcohol to cope with pressure.

Research has not determined whether persons who have had trouble with alcohol dependency in response to stress are permanently at risk. Alcoholics Anonymous says yes and insists on lifelong abstinence. There are some people who seem to be able to return to moderate, even abstemious, use of alcohol after an episode of alcohol abuse and to maintain that lower level of use for years. But there are not reliable methods for separating those with such potential from those unable to use alcohol responsibly. If David does not decide to give up alcohol altogether, he needs careful monitoring and oversight of his consumption and response for some time.

DOMESTIC VIOLENCE

Linda's friends are perceptive to question her facile dismissal of David's violence against her. The Spencers need to elicit from both Linda and

David their accounts of violence in the relationship. All too often domestic violence follows a pattern: psychological violence leads to verbal violence, which leads to physical violence (including sexual violence), which may even lead to homicide. It is important to discover whether there has been a pattern of escalation in the violence within the relationship.

According to the National Coalition Against Domestic Violence, one in every four US women and one in every nine US men will be involved at some time during their lives in a relationship of domestic violence. One in every three female murder victims is killed by an intimate partner. While more women than men are victims of domestic violence, women can also be perpetrators, especially in the case of verbal or psychological abuse. Furthermore, domestic abuse is not confined to heterosexual partnerships but occurs in same-sex relationships as well. In addition, one in fifteen children are exposed to intimate partner violence each year, and 90 percent witness it firsthand. On a typical day, domestic violence hotlines nationwide receive over twenty thousand calls.

Christianity also bears some responsibility for high rates of domestic violence. Violence against women has been tolerated and sometimes actively supported in the churches. In Christianity before mandatory clerical celibacy was imposed at the end of the first millennium, and among Protestants after the Reformation, clergy were encouraged to be especially severe in beating their wives, since their wives were to be examples of wifely submission for other women. Scriptural verses that embody the household code of the Roman Empire, such as Ephesians 5 and Colossians 3, enjoin wives to obey their husbands and husbands to love their wives. These texts were interpreted to require beating as a form of loving discipline, ignoring the fact that the Colossians text reads: "Husbands, love your wives and never treat them harshly" (Col 3:19).

The staggering level of domestic violence in modern society is supported by an attitude of social silence. Neighbors close the windows when they hear slaps, crashes, and shouting next door rather than intervene or call the police. Family members ignore bruises and black eyes in silence or whisper to one another that John and Mary "aren't getting along." Police sometimes treat domestic abuse as if it were another barroom brawl in which both parties are equally at fault and merely need a short separation to "cool down." Too often the churches are totally silent about domestic violence and sexual abuse, assuming that such things do not occur in the homes of church members but only among the unchurched. Such an attitude discourages victims from turning to the church as a resource and fails to call abusers to accountability.

Domestic violence is not accidental and is not typically about blowing off steam. Nor is the victim accidentally chosen. Domestic violence maintains control over the spouse. The batterers feel that they are losing control over their spouse and so "accidentally" lose control of themselves in violence. Afterward, abusers frequently argue that they should be forgiven because they were not themselves; they were under the influence of alcohol, or temper, or fear, and did not mean the abuse. In fact, batterers' recourse to alcohol is itself usually deliberate, as is the attempt to find issues over which to explode (the quality of dinner, the size of a bill, the behavior of the children, the length of a phone call, and so on). These are pretexts for recourse to violent acts that then terrorize the spouse into capitulating to the control of the abuser. When the violence is done and the abuser's control restored, typical abusers apologize for the damage, pledge their love, and woo the victim into both remaining in the relationship and forgiving them. Even during this expression of repentance, however, abusers typically refuse to accept responsibility. They insist that the victim was responsible for triggering violence brought on by alcohol, stress, or other factors not under their control.

Given this common pattern in domestic abuse, the Spencers need to ask both Linda and David questions about control in the marriage. Is there any evidence that David's use of violence in response to Linda's sexual withdrawal is part of a pattern of David's controlling Linda through violence or threat of violence? It is important to probe the issue of violent abuse because of Linda's past victimization. Her earlier sexual abuse has obscured her own feelings and interests so that she seems better able to focus on David's suffering and pain than on her own. Does Linda's tendency to brush off the violent episodes mask a low self-esteem that makes her see herself as an appropriate object for violence? Or is her easy dismissal of violence the result of over ten years of knowing David as a gentle, non-controlling partner demonstrating abiding love for her and the children?

Questions need to be asked about violence in either Linda's or David's interaction with their children as well, and about how the children have been affected by David's violence and alcohol abuse and by Linda's emotional condition. We have no indications that either parent has directed violence at the children, and we do not know the ages of these children. The children should be told as much about what is going on with their parents as is appropriate for their ages. Linda and David should explain in simple terms why they are upset, that they are working on their problems, that the children have no responsibility for their parents' problems, and that no matter how they work out their particular problems, the parents will both continue to love the children. Having some idea of what is occurring may help the children feel secure enough to ask for additional reassurance when they need it.

CHILD SEXUAL ABUSE

The real prevalence of child sexual abuse is not known because so many victims do not disclose or report their abuse. According to the US Centers for Disease Control and Prevention, adult retrospective studies show that one in four women (25 percent) and one in six men (16.7 percent) were sexually abused before the age of eighteen. One of every twenty young girls is the victim of stepfather-daughter incest or father-daughter incest, which is generally considered the most traumatic type of incest, though specific incidents of other types of incest can cause as much or more trauma. In this case we have no mention of Linda's father; her grandfather may or may not have functioned as a father substitute.

The extent of the trauma in child sexual abuse depends upon four factors: the intrusiveness of the abuse; the length of time the abuse continued; the degree of prior trust the victim had invested in the abuser; and the degree of pain, coercion, or threat used to obtain compliance from the victim. We have no information here about the intrusiveness of the abuse or the degree of coercion, pain, or threats in Linda's incestuous abuse as a child. But the abuse continued for several years, and it involved betrayal of trust. In Linda's case the abuser was not only a family member acting in a caretaker role, but the abuse was supported by her primary caretaker's refusal to believe her. Linda's experience is not unusual. Nor is she unusual in experiencing trauma from the incest many years after she thought she had put it behind her. It is often not clear what triggers such memories, but greater social awareness of incestuous abuse of children has supported many unhealed adult victims in getting help rather than remaining trapped in nightmarish fear, distrust, and self-loathing.

The United States is generally considered to have among the lowest child sexual abuse rates in the world. But data is not readily available for most parts of the world, and even US data is incomplete. In general, researchers are coming to believe that large numbers of the world's children are at risk for sexual abuse. Both religious and secular cultures here and elsewhere include strong supports for child sexual abuse, including socialization of children to universal respect and unquestioning obedience to parents and other adults; failing to recognize children's rights over their own bodies; and a silence about sex that prevents both information flow and ease of communication around sex, even between intimates. Both church and society, which hold up the family as a protector of children, have been largely blind to familial abuse of children.

Healing from sexual victimization is almost always a long and painful process. When victimization is endured as a child and is unaddressed for decades, the internalization of the abuse, which usually does the most damage, is often unobstructed, even reinforced. In Linda's case, however, it is extremely positive that she did not suppress all memories of the abuse and that she seems to have a history of both sexual satisfaction and intimacy with David. Whatever deficiencies existed within that intimacy (there are always greater depths of intimacy to achieve), the fact that both partners experienced the relationship as intimate for over a decade testifies to the advantage Linda has over incest victims in general. Many victims find themselves unable to trust others enough for intimacy and unable to feel that they have an authentic self worthy of being disclosed to another. While Linda may always carry some degree of damage from her childhood experience, she may well develop moral strengths from her battle that help her resist and heal from her family's sinful abuse.

It is important for Christians to insist that Linda can heal, both because there is objective evidence of the healing of other victims and because Christians believe in the resurrection, the ground of Christian hope. What Christians mean when they speak of Jesus Christ's resurrection as victory over sin is not that sin ceases to exist. Victims of child sexual abuse are victims of sin. Rather, Christians mean that sin is not final and decisive; because of Jesus Christ's resurrection, others can overcome and recover from the effects of sin. It is through healing from sin that Christians participate in the resurrection of Jesus. In this case there is a very real possibility that dealing with the present problems in the relationship—the memories that plague Linda, and David's recourse to alcohol and violence—may allow them to reestablish and strengthen their earlier intimacy.

In order for that to happen, David needs to move beyond his present step of acknowledging that Linda is not yet healed from the earlier abuse. He needs to become truly supportive of that healing. Perhaps, as Reverend Deerick suggested, prayerful intimacy with God could alleviate some of David's intimacy needs so that he could become more supportive of Linda's healing. Only support from David himself can remove the sense of demand Linda now feels about David's desire for sexual intimacy. Her feelings of guilt about not being able to give him what he wants echo lessons learned in the abuse and interfere with her ability to concentrate on her own healing process. If David could learn to rely less on sexual intimacy as symbolic of the overall intimacy of the relationship and be more open to emotional intimacy and non-genital physical intimacy with Linda, he could assist Linda's healing and satisfy physically some of his own need to be reassured of Linda's love for him.

At the same time, it would be wrong to demand that David immediately accept a marriage without genital relations or even physical touch. Human beings are integrated persons, and their relationships and growth and development should be integrated. While David seems to be extremely focused on physical and even genital activity for expressing his feelings for Linda and meeting his own intimacy needs, other avenues of interpersonal interactions should be developed in addition to, and not in place of, sexual activity. Genital activity in marriage is an important foundation for other forms of intimacy because of its symbolic power. Both nakedness and the letting go of consciousness and control in orgasm are powerful images of trust and self-giving, of vulnerability. Shared pleasure in sex both rewards lovers for their willingness to offer themselves to the other and bonds lovers together.

Linda should be encouraged to assume that she can heal and that the healing process will include her ability to reclaim her sexual feelings and activity. Healing will mean ending the power of the abuse to dictate her feelings, her actions, and her life. To assume from the beginning that she will never be able to resume a full marital relationship is "victimism," accepting that the effects of victimization are permanent.

SPIRITUAL COUNSELING

Reverend Deerick's offer of support for guiding Linda's and David's prayer life seems to include spiritual counseling around the specifics of their situations. Spiritual counseling when coordinated with psychological counseling frequently complements it and is often the most effective therapy for dealing with lingering feelings of guilt and sinfulness in victims of sexual abuse. Spiritual counseling for Linda might also include encouragement to approach her family as a mature adult who needs to have her suffering and the family's responsibility acknowledged in ways that allow her to get on with her life. We do not know whether she faced her mother (or her aunt) with the fact of her abuse after it ended, whether they feel estranged from her, or, if so, if they know the reason for the estrangement. Even though her grandfather is dead and Linda is not close to her family, she may need, for her own sake, to confront them with her abuse. Spiritual counseling could also help protect Linda from family pressure for premature forgiveness and reconciliation.

MARRIAGE AND DIVORCE

There is little doubt that both David and Linda are experiencing great pain and suffering and asking serious questions about the permanency of marriage. Even though some denominations recognize divorce, Christian understandings of marriage have always taught that marriage should be undertaken as a permanent commitment. Some variety of the "for richer or poorer, in sickness and health, until death do us part" vow has been a part of the Christian wedding service for centuries. The degree of suffering involved is not, in itself, an indication of the appropriateness of divorce. A physician would not help a patient with appendicitis to die merely because the immediate pain is severe. Far more important is the prognosis for restoring health and alleviating the suffering.

For many readers the question of whether David and Linda should remain married is moot, because they are both clear that they love each other. Until the twentieth century there would have been no theological support for the understanding that marriage endures only when love endures, even though it was increasingly common after the sixteenth century to understand that love was a motive for marriage. Because women were not economically franchised, and because of the association of marriage with the bearing and rearing of children, it was assumed that women and children required the presence of the husband/father for their well-being.

Today Christian churches are divided in their understanding of marriage and divorce. The Roman Catholic Church does not recognize divorce and therefore forbids remarriage. However, if Linda were a Catholic, she might be able to obtain an annulment—a declaration that no true marriage ever existed with David—on the grounds that she was not fully free to consent to marriage because of the unresolved trauma of child sexual abuse. Most other Christian churches do not exclude the divorced and remarried, though their preference for permanency is clear. Across denominational lines the criteria that divide marriages in crisis into viable and nonviable categories are disputed among pastors and pastoral counselors. The most common question is whether contractual obligations in marriage endure after feelings of love have been lost. A related question is whether fidelity to the contractual obligations can, over time, rekindle lost feelings of love. Is love more than a feeling? There are no clear answers to these questions, which is one probable reason for Reverend Deerick's focus on personal prayer in response to David's and Linda's questions about the future of their marriage.

A second reason for Reverend Deerick's shift of focus from church teaching on marriage to prayer is that the positive and useful insights on marriage in scripture are embedded within and often distorted by patriarchal depictions of women as men's property. Women achieve virtue through fruitful wombs, sexual fidelity, and homemaking skills. The Mosaic Law and scriptural authors allow little scope for the personhood of women; while a few women are singled out, only an exceptional handful of women are recognized for their own initiatives rather than for their submission or for the fruit of their wombs. For this reason, it is difficult to apply any of the scriptural stories or teachings to the crisis in David's and Linda's marriage. From the perspective of many of the communities from which scripture emerged, Linda would have no right to deny David the sexual use of her body, and David would be expected to exercise his rights regardless of her wishes. Linda might not even feel sexual aversion from her childhood memories, for she would have been raised to understand women's bodies as the property of men and might well regard her abuse by her grandfather as a universal hazard of being female. At the same time, the expectations of David and Linda of their marriage would have been significantly different had they lived in scriptural communities. They would have understood the marital bond as characterized much less by interpersonal intimacy and more by contract, especially contract between clans or families.

Theological treatment of marriage as a covenant modeled on the covenant between Yahweh and Israel is a contemporary reversal of the biblical attempt to personalize the covenant relationship. Ancient Israelites came to see their relationship with Yahweh as more personal and intimate than the feudal covenant between lords and vassals that gave the covenant its form and name. The Israelites came to image the covenant as a marriage, the most personal and intimate relationship they knew. In a society in which women were chattel that husbands bought from fathers, the inequalities of power, status, and worth in the divine/human relationship were not barriers to the effectiveness of the analogy. Saint Paul later extended the marital analogy to Christ and the church. But when the contemporary church uses the relationships of Christ/church and Yahweh/Israel relationships to understand and explain marriage, it imports into the marital relationship assumptions about inequalities of power, worth, and initiative between the partners that are alienating, making the analogies less than effective.

Until the modern age, theological treatment of marriage focused almost exclusively on procreation as the purpose and chief blessing of marriage, rather than on the quality of the relationship, which has become the central theological concern over the last few centuries. Few helpful historical resources on the role of sexuality in Christian marriage exist. Between the early medieval era and the Reformation, Christianity taught total impotence as an absolute bar to marriage and sexual consummation of marital vows as necessary to finalize marriage. Before the Reformation, and in Roman Catholicism even afterward, couples were often encouraged to consider Josephite (celibate) marriages, and clergy regularly cautioned couples to abstain from sex on Sundays, holy days, and during Lent, as sex was understood as an obstacle to prayer and contemplation. Procreation was regarded as a sufficient good to justify sexual activity and consequent pleasure. But sexual pleasure was morally suspect and forbidden as a motive for marital sex. The difficulty of resisting sexual pleasure in marriage caused pre-Reformation Christianity and post-Reformation Roman Catholicism to understand celibate religious life as a holier vocation than marriage.

The Reformers raised the status of marriage compared with vowed celibacy and gradually abandoned some of the more negative traditional attitudes toward sex. For the most part, however, the churches of the Reformation continued to understand procreation as the primary purpose of marriage and sex. For limited numbers of Protestant Christians, sexual activity came to be seen as an important way to cherish the spouse and as a source for generating warmth and intimacy that could influence children and the wider community. Among the Puritans and Quakers, for example, new understandings of marriage as primarily a personal bond, within which children were an additional but not the central blessing, gave rise to an appreciation of sex in marriage.

Within American Christianity a positive understanding of sex in marriage has been in tension with a more traditional and more widespread understanding of sex as morally dangerous and sexual desire as something to be resisted by the virtuous. Contemporary Christian theologians are attempting to recover and develop the few examples of positive treatment of body, sexuality, and sex found in Christian theological traditions. Since Christian faith is grounded in the incarnation—the doctrine that the Second Person in the Godhead became fully embodied in flesh—there should be no room for hatred or suspicion of the human body, its appetite or actions per se.

Some Catholics point out that though the traditions of Catholic moral theology were decidedly anti-sexual, the sacramental tradition regarding marriage incorporated a number of positive elements, including the understanding that sexual intercourse (especially orgasm itself) operates as a primary sacramental sign. Marital sex does not merely represent the spousal love that it signifies but actually contributes to the creation and development of that love. It has even been suggested by a Catholic clergy/lay team in a document commissioned and funded by the United States Conference of Catholic Bishops, in its 1986 document Embodied in Love, that mutually pleasurable marital sex is perhaps the most accessible human experience of the love that characterizes the Persons of the Trinity.

CONCLUSION

What should David and Linda do about their marriage? Under what circumstances should they divorce? Despite all their problems and pain, they both state their concern for each other and act as if they care very much about the other. For that reason they may not want to abandon the marriage now but may prefer to continue work with the Spencers and perhaps to begin seeing Reverend Deerick to work on personal prayer as a means of clarifying what they should do. The teachings of Christian churches on the issues of permanency in marriage and sex in marriage have begun to shift away from fear and suspicion of sex in marriage and from insistence on marital permanence regardless of the costs to those involved. Christian churches have come to see that marital sex can be an integral part of both interpersonal intimacy and communion with the Divine, and that the costs of preserving marriage in some circumstances can include physical and emotional violence and the erosion of selfhood. Ultimately, only Linda and David can decide what level of cost is acceptable to them and to their children in the attempt to rebuild their marriage.

ADDITIONAL RESOURCES

Bass, Ellen, and Laura Davis. *The Courage to Heal: A Guide for Women Survivors of Child Sexual Abuse.* 4th edition. New York: Harper Paperbacks, 2008.

Bolz-Weber, Nadia. *Shameless: A Sexual Reformation.* New York: Convergent Books, 2019.

Bromley, Nicole Braddock. *Breathe: Finding Freedom to Thrive in Relationships after Childhood Sexual Abuse.* Chicago: Moody Publishers, 2009.

Brown, Joanne C., and Carole R. Bohn, eds. *Christianity, Patriarchy, and Abuse: A Feminist Critique.* New York: Pilgrim Press, 1989.

Clark, Ron. *Setting the Captives Free: A Christian Theology for Domestic Violence.* Eugene, OR: Wipf and Stock, 2005.

Ellison, Marvin, and Kelly Brown Douglas, eds. *Sexuality and the Sacred: Sources for Theological Reflection.* 2nd edition. Louisville: Westminster John Knox Press, 2010.

Farley, Margaret. *Just Love: A Framework for Christian Sexual Ethics.* New York: Continuum, 2006.

Gudorf, Christine E. *Body, Sex, and Pleasure: Reconstructing Christian Sexual Ethics.* Cleveland: Pilgrim Press, 1994.

Hammond, Adam. *Alcohol in the Home: An Analytical Guide to Understanding and Ministering to Families Affected by Alcohol Abuse.* Bloomington, IN: CrossBooks Publishing, 2011.

Jung, Patricia, Mary E. Hunt, and Radhika Balakrishnan, eds. *Good Sex: Feminist Perspectives from the World's Religions.* New Brunswick, NJ: Rutgers University Press, 2001.

Miles, Al. *Domestic Violence: What Every Pastor Needs to Know,* 2nd edition. Minneapolis: Fortress Press, 2011.

Nason-Clark, Nancy, Barbara Fisher-Townsend, Catherine Holtmann, and Stephen McMullin. *Religion and Intimate Partner Violence: Understanding the Challenges and Proposing Solutions.* New York: Oxford University Press, 2017.

Ruether, Rosemary Radford. *Christianity and the Making of the Modern Family: Ruling Ideologies, Diverse Realities.* Boston: Beacon Press, 2000.

Vieth, Victor. *On This Rock: A Call to Center the Christian Response to Child Abuse on the Life and Words of Jesus.* Eugene, OR: Wipf and Stock, 2018.

Related Websites

National Coalition against Domestic Violence
   http://www.ncadv.org/
National Sexual Violence Resource Center
   http://www.nsvrc.org/publications/child-sexual-abuse-prevention-overview

PART II

VIOLENCE/
NONVIOLENCE

Case

A Life for a Life?

There were only two days left in the Florida legislative session. Manny sighed in relief just thinking about it. He was tired of Tallahassee and tired of commuting home to Sarasota on weekends for the last two months. Florida, unlike many other states, was limited by its constitution to a two-month annual legislative session. The big work—getting agreement on the budget—had just been finished. No one was satisfied with the bill, but that was the nature of compromise.

As Manny picked up his briefcase and headed out the door of his office he spotted Alice Browner speaking with one of the House members from the Florida Keys. Manny ducked back within his office, shutting the door softly. He liked Alice, but he knew what she wanted and that she might latch onto him if she saw him now. Alice was an unpaid lobbyist for religious groups trying to get the death-penalty statute off the books in Florida. It was an interesting time in Florida. Like the rest of the United States, over 56 percent supported capital punishment for those convicted of murder, but when Floridians were asked in a recent poll to choose between the death penalty and a lifetime sentence without the possibility of parole, nearly 58 percent supported the latter. Buoyed by these new poll numbers, Alice's group was full of enthusiasm for full elimination of the death penalty. In 2005, they had won their struggle to restrict the death penalty to adults, those over eighteen years of age, when the Supreme Court declared capital punishment for minors unconstitutional.

The issue of the death penalty for minors had arisen in Florida following a few trials that had become media affairs. Three Miami area boys, between twelve and fourteen years of age, had been arrested for murder: one for shooting a teacher, another for beating to death a six-year-old girl, and one for slicing the throat of a classmate in the boys' restroom at a

---

This case and its commentary were prepared originally by Christine E. Gudorf and have been updated by Laura A. Stivers and James B. Martin-Schramm. The names of persons and institutions have been disguised, where appropriate, to protect the privacy of those involved.

public school. The first two had been tried as adults, and in the first case the prosecutors had asked for the death penalty. In the end both boys had gotten sentences of life in prison without parole. The case of the one who had killed the six-year-old while wrestling with her in his home had been a real mess, Manny recalled. The boy's mother had refused to let him take the plea to a lesser charge offered by the prosecutor because she was sure her son would be acquitted. But when he was found guilty of first-degree murder, the mandatory sentencing statute kicked in, and he was saddled with life in prison without parole. He had just been released, however, after serving three years, because a court determined that the state should have done competency testing on him before going to trial since there was strong evidence that he was mentally impaired. Now the third of these child-killers was about to be tried, and it looked like he also would be tried as an adult and could face the death penalty. Due to the publicity over the possibility of these very young minors getting death penalties, many Floridians, including Manny, had come to agree with the Supreme Court that the death penalty was inappropriate for minors.

But now Alice's group and a number of other civic and religious groups were lobbying to end the death penalty in Florida altogether; they had introduced a bill to that effect. With the state budget out of the way, they hoped the legislature would use some of its remaining days to deal with this bill.

Manny had talked to two other House members about the bill just days ago: John Benvenuti from Winter Garden, and Saul Weiss from Jacksonville. Saul had initiated the discussion over dinner one night as they finished revision of an amendment to an insurance bill they wanted passed.

"Do you know how you'll vote if Alice Browner and her group get the death-penalty bill on the agenda?" Saul had asked.

John had responded, "I don't see how I could live with myself if I didn't vote for it, but I don't see how I can get the voters to support such a vote. My district is strong on law-and-order issues, and when it sees death penalty, it thinks 'urban crime,' 'blacks and Hispanics.' My constituents don't see convicted criminals as belonging to the same species as their families and friends."

"Do you really see this as an issue of conscience, John? I didn't know you opposed the death penalty," asked Manny, surprised.

"My church did a program on the death penalty last year, and it really had an impact on me," said John. "You know, since the death penalty was reintroduced in 1973, over 165 people have been released from death row with evidence of their innocence. From 1973 to 1999 there was an average of 3.1 exonerations a year. From 2000 to 2013 there has been an average of 4.29 exonerations a year. Of the death-penalty convictions vacated in the United States, twenty-nine have been in Florida—we have had the largest number in the country. Illinois is next with twenty-one, then it drops down to thirteen in Texas. The program at church brought in the sister of a guy who had been on death row for fifteen years when another man confessed, and DNA testing—not available when he was tried—proved he had not done the rape and murder for which he was convicted. But it came too late for him; he died of cancer in prison weeks before he would have been released. That's the piece of it that gets me—that some of them really are innocent. That's why in 2000 the governor of Illinois, George Ryan, put a moratorium on executions and commuted so many sentences, and his successor, Pat Quinn, signed a bill abolishing the death penalty in Illinois in March 2011. It became hard to have faith in the system's ability to deliver justice. I don't see how I could ever vote for the death penalty. It may cost me my seat. I'm glad we are only part-timers here." He added wryly, "Conscience would be a lot tougher to follow if this were my entire bread and butter." John referred to the fact that he, like almost all House members, had a normal career; they were lawyers, insurance agents, corporate officers, and a variety of other professions, but they earned just under $30,000 in addition to a per diem of $152 for expenses in state compensation for a little more than sixty days of service every year.

"I hear you," said Saul, "but that's not where I am. I'm not pandering to my constituents here. I agree with them. There are monsters out there, and they deserve the death penalty. I'm all for improving the justice system—I admit all these people being released from death row doesn't inspire confidence in the system—but I think the answer is to fix the system, not junk it. And don't think for a minute that all these people released from death row are innocent—a lot of the reversals were for police or prosecutor misconduct in the first trials, but by the time those verdicts were reversed evidence had been lost or witnesses had died, so prosecutors simply didn't file for retrials. That doesn't mean those people were innocent. Our job is to write the rules that protect the innocent, and I think the death penalty helps do that."

Manny shook his head. "I just don't know. My district, like John's, thinks killers only come out of urban pits like Miami, that the death penalty is necessary for black and Hispanic criminals and a handful of white 'trailer-trash.' I'm not sure many of them would even care if they knew some of these vacated convictions were clear results of southern racism in the fifties and sixties."

John put in, "The role of race in death-penalty sentences is scary, all right. Much higher percentages of blacks than whites get death sentences, but the real surprise is that regardless of the race of the killer those who kill whites are three times more likely to get sentenced to death than those who kill blacks, and four times more likely than those who kill Latinos. That just shouldn't be."

"I agree that's wrong," responded Saul. "But just because there have been racists voting for the death penalty doesn't mean all death-penalty verdicts are racist. I think those prosecutors who decided to try twelve-year-olds and fourteen-year-olds as adults were wrong and that they were racially motivated. But they aroused what I think is an overreaction against the death penalty in the Supreme Court and among citizens. I don't have any problem with executing monsters of sixteen or seventeen, maybe even some fifteen-year-olds. We keep hearing that what we need to do to reform the system is to give judges more discretion in sentencing, instead of tying their hands with mandatory sentences. I say let the judges decide, but give them the option to grant the death penalty if that's what the state asks for and it's appropriate to the circumstances."

"Saul, do you really think that the criminal justice system is ever color blind?" asked John.

"Are you calling me racist?" asked Saul indignantly.

"No, I'm talking about the racism in our constituents, who so clearly intend the death penalty for minority groups. Or even the system itself—remember that *Miami Herald* series that showed the huge differences in how the juvenile justice system treats whites and blacks? When convicted of the same crime and with the same juvenile record, most white youth got probation or community service, and most black youth were sent to reformatories. People who work in the adult system say the same thing happens—whites have more money to hire private lawyers, and so they either get off altogether, or, when they are convicted, get lesser sentences."

"Wait a minute, John," protested Saul. "I do remember that series, and it explained that the reason for the different sentences involved the kids' support networks—family and community. Black kids less often had intact homes with effective parents who could monitor their behavior and also had fewer contacts with community organizations willing to supervise community service. Those sentences were based on the individual situation of the kids, not racism in the system."

"Kind of a vicious circle, isn't it?" asked John. "Because one kid has a father in prison, or who skipped town, and a mother who works three jobs to support her kids, the kid gets into trouble. And the very reasons he got into trouble in the first place are the same reasons he goes to reformatory, while a white kid in the same trouble goes free."

"I can't fix every broken home," responded Saul. "That's not my job. All I'm saying is that not everything that differentiates the races is due to racism. Some differences just occur, and individuals bear some responsibility for what happens to them. Not all kids with absent fathers and overworked mothers get into trouble. These kids had a choice."

Manny asked, "You know that Alice's latest argument is that we should eliminate the death penalty as a budget reduction measure? Some think tank figured out that Florida could save $51 million a year by commuting all its death-penalty cases to life without possibility of parole. In fact, the governor of California recently declared a moratorium on executions, which he says will save the state $170 million a year. California has spent over $5 billion enforcing the death penalty since the state reintroduced it in 1978. What do you think, Saul? Would you and your voters be persuaded by the cost-savings argument?"

"Maybe," Saul replied, "as a temporary budgeting solution. But I think that only death fits some of these crimes, and I know some of my constituents agree."

As the three of them left the restaurant to return to the session, John and Saul shifted the topic to procedural moves on the insurance bill, but Manny remained quiet. This was a really tough issue for him.

Manny had grown up thinking that unjust executions only happened in other countries, like Cuba, where one of his mother's brothers had been executed as a young man for opposing Castro. He had always seen the justice system in the United States as a model for the world. But his years in the legislature had taken some of the shine off that model. He saw how large a role politics, personalities, the press of time, and sometimes even corruption had in the creation of laws and state budgets, and it made him wonder if the implementation of laws was necessarily any more careful than the creation of those laws. The best evidence of that, he thought, was the March rape and murder of a nine-year-old girl abducted from her home not too far from Manny's district. It had taken many days to discover the body and catch the killer—an ex-con sexual predator who later confessed—because the state database that was supposed to track the registered locations of sexual predators was so out of date that it did not know that the rapist had moved into the girl's neighborhood months before. He tended to agree with his wife, Pina, that these sexual predators seemed to be impossible to reform and that the death penalty was the only way to safeguard society, especially the children.

Now Manny was torn. While he thought he could support capital punishment for sexual predators, he knew that there could be cases in which people were wrongly convicted as sexual predators. He agreed with Saul that the level of death-row acquittals proved the system was not well run and should be improved, but he wasn't sure it could be fixed well enough to justify capital punishment.

Manny also knew that Pina would be appalled if he voted for Alice's bill to eliminate the death penalty. The little girl recently killed had been a student at the school where Pina taught kindergarten, and that had made Pina and most other parents see the perpetrator as a threat to all the children there, including Pina's and Manny's two little girls. But it was also true that Manny was a second-term legislator with a strong likelihood of reelection, and he and Pina had counted on the income from one more term to finance the master's degree in education she planned to finally begin in the fall. Their oldest son would graduate from a state university in December, and it was supposed to be Pina's turn now, while the younger kids were still in elementary and junior high school. Pina was a kindergarten teacher who had to earn a master's degree soon or lose her job, which she loved. If he lost the November election over this issue, his regular salary would only go up about $6,000 before taxes, because he already took one month of the legislative session as paid vacation from his job and only one month as unpaid leave. From $30,000 to $6,000 in salary for that month was a big drop. Could Pina understand if he not only defended the right to life of sexual predators who preyed on children, but if also, because of his taking that position, they weren't able to fund her return to the university? More than that, how would they manage to send the other kids to college if Pina lost her job?

Manny lifted his head and ended his reverie. Surely he had waited long enough for Alice to leave. He walked down the hall, hearing nothing. But just as he turned the corner to the elevator, Manny saw Alice. She saw him, waved, and made a beeline toward him. It was crunch time.

Commentary

Christian tradition has not been historically unanimous on the issue of killing. While the first three centuries of Christianity saw a strong pressure for pacifism at all levels, in the fourth century earlier refusals to grant Christian burials to those who had taken life—whether in self-defense, military service, or wantonly—were relaxed, and Christian theologians such as Augustine began to argue that Christians could serve in the army, since the army protected the Roman Empire and, thus, Christianity. From that time on, the dominant Christian position has been that Christians are allowed to kill on behalf of the state in certain situations, and even in some very limited personal situations, notably self-defense.

This teaching has not been by any means unanimous. There have been, especially since the Protestant Reformation, a number of pacifist denominations who oppose killing in all forms. These denominations include the Mennonites, the Amish, the Quakers, the Brethren, and a number of other smaller denominations. Jehovah's Witnesses are often counted with this group, as they oppose all obedience to the state and deny the right of the state to demand military service or any other type of service, including oaths. Many theologians have agreed with the American courts, however, that Jehovah's Witnesses are not pacifist in the same sense as these other groups because they insist they will take up arms in the last days to fight in the army of the Lord to punish sinners.

Christian ethical analysis of this case must examine at least three questions: (1) the justice of capital punishment in general; (2) the way widespread DNA testing is overturning wrongful convictions; and (3) whether for Christians there are other values (for example, forgiveness or mercy) that can or should trump justice in capital cases.

CAPITAL PUNISHMENT, JUST WAR, AND RACE

The dominant Christian position regarding violence has been called the just-war position. Capital punishment has been subsumed under the just-war position, as it, too, argues that at some times the state must take human life in order to defend the common good against serious attacks—war from outside and capital crimes inside. The basic limitation was that the life taken must be guilty. While it could be permitted to kill, it was never permissible to kill innocent life.

The development of the just-war position occurred over many centuries; many theologians and churchmen contributed to it, including Augustine, Bonaventure, and Aquinas. In their arguments defending the possibility of a just war, they often used examples of capital punishment, which was generally accepted. At the same time that Christians generally accepted the need for the state to execute criminals (not always for what we might consider serious crimes), the question of whether Christians should be allowed to be executioners was raised again and again. Many jurisdictions ruled that executioners must be hooded, so that they might avoid some of the moral disapproval that generally accompanied the job.

While there has been a great deal of debate about just war—conditions for just war in particular—within the dominant tradition, there has been little debate about capital punishment until fairly recently. Historically, the self-understanding of the church as an institution parallel to, and similar to, the state, caused the church to assume that the legal system of the state was generally just and efficient. That assumption has been radically called into question in the last century in a new way.

In the past there were occasionally periods in which it was apparent to the church and to the wider society that the law and the legal system itself were being manipulated by the powerful, often by the monarchs themselves, to produce injustice: innocents wrongfully accused and executed, their property coveted and appropriated. Such things even occurred sometimes within the church itself. But when law and order were restored, the interval that had just ended was considered an exception to the normal prevalence of justice.

This worldview is still prevalent in many American Christians. The National Assembly of Evangelicals, the Christian Coalition, Christian Reconstructionists, Southern Baptist churches, Latter-Day Saints (Mormons), Missouri Synod Lutherans, and many Pentecostal churches support the death penalty for serious crimes. Important for many of these churches is the biblical evidence that the Hebrew scriptures support capital punishment, even "requiring" the death penalty for over a dozen crimes in addition to murder. That said, these churches no longer see most of these Old Testament "crimes" as deserving capital punishment today (for example, working on the Sabbath, being disrespectful toward parents, teaching another religion, being an unbeliever, and entering the Temple). Furthermore, supporters of the death penalty quote Matthew 5:17–19 to the effect that Jesus intended the Mosaic Law to remain unchanged: "Do not think that I have come to abolish the law or the prophets; I have come not to abolish but to fulfill it. For truly I tell you, until heaven and earth pass away, not one letter, not one stroke of a letter will pass from the law until all is accomplished."

But by the twentieth century there were many people who questioned not only the specific workings of one legal system or another but the very assumption that human systems of legal justice could be more or less just. There were a number of reasons underlying such suspicions. One was the gradual acceptance by the majority of the idea, spread initially by Marxism, that modern societies are class societies in which power tends to be wielded by the wealthy in their own interests. In this conception the legal system functions to support social control by the wealthy elite.

Even many who do not accept that modern capitalist societies inevitably have legal systems in which the interests of those with less power and wealth carry less weight recognize that this is often the case. In the United States, for example, extensive analysis of convictions and sentencing has shown that the best predictor of the severity of punishments for murder, rape, and assault is the race of the victim. If the victim is white, conviction rates are higher and sentences are stiffer than if the victim is black or Hispanic. The second-best predictor is the race of the accused: blacks accused of crimes were convicted more often, and when sentenced for the same crime as whites, got higher sentences than whites when the victims were white, but not necessarily when the victims were black. Race-based economics undoubtedly plays a part in discrepancies in convictions and sentencing in general, in that higher percentages of blacks are poor and thus forced to utilize overworked and underpaid public defenders, who are not as successful in defending their clients as are the private attorneys more often hired by whites.

The following statistics on death-row exonerations and clemency come from the Death Penalty Information Center; its website includes state-by-state data on executions and exonerations throughout the United States. Since Florida first reintroduced the death penalty in 1976, there have been twenty-nine exonerations for those on death row and six instances of clemency. The language used for the reversals of capital convictions is telling. Supporters of capital punishment point out that the vacation of these sentences does not mean that the person is innocent of the crime; sometimes it merely means that there is insufficient evidence to convict, or the process in the trial was faulty. Inevitably, some guilty persons are released, too.

Details on the twenty-nine Florida cases in which death-row prisoners were set free illustrate that sometimes the reversals do indicate proof of police or judicial misconduct rather than full innocence. The cases fall into the following categories:

- Two were pardoned by the governor of Florida after another man confessed;
- Ten were set free because appeals found insufficient evidence for them to be charged with the crime;
- Four were released after new DNA evidence revealed the convict was not the perpetrator;
- Two were released when other suspects were found and charged with the crime;
- One was exonerated when new evidence was uncovered during a follow-up investigation;
- Five were exonerated due to prosecutorial misconduct in the original trial, including knowingly allowing false testimony to be introduced at trial, improper use of evidence, misuse of expert testimony, and the withholding of critical evidence;
- Five were set free after it was proven that key witnesses had committed perjury, retracted their statements, or were incompetent.

The suspicion of unequal justice, supported by many different analytic reports of how the legal system actually works, has influenced American churches, even those with long histories of acceptance of capital punishment. Since 1974 the US Conference of Catholic Bishops (USCCB) has opposed the death penalty, which was reinstated after a long legal hiatus in 1976, despite over a millennium and a half of ecclesial support for capital punishment. In 2005, the USCCB declared in *A Culture of Life and the Death Penalty*:

We reaffirm our common judgment that the use of the death penalty is unnecessary and unjustified in our time and circumstances. Our nation should forgo the use of the death penalty because:

- The sanction of death, when it is not necessary to protect society, violates respect for human life and dignity.
- State-sanctioned killing in our names diminishes all of us. Its application is deeply flawed and can be irreversibly wrong, is prone to errors, and is biased by factors such as race, the quality of legal representation, and where the crime was committed.
- We have other ways to punish criminals and protect society.

The Vatican has become a strong supporter of abolishing the death penalty, frequently appealing on behalf of individual convicts awaiting execution. In 2018, Pope Francis approved a new revision of paragraph number 2267 of the *Catechism of the Catholic Church*, which declares that "the death penalty is inadmissible" because "a new understanding has emerged of the significance of penal sanctions imposed by the state."

The USCCB and Pope Francis point to significant problems impeding justice within the system of capital punishment, including the possibilities of mistakes, long delays, unfairness in sentencing due to poverty and racism, as well as the extinction of all possibility for reform and rehabilitation of the convict. The bishops have also pointed to racial and economic inequalities in the system of justice—that the poor and persons of color are disproportionately more likely to receive the death penalty than middle-class or white persons convicted of the same crimes.

Regardless of the continued criticism of the death penalty by the Catholic bishops of the United States, a majority of the Catholic population in the United States supports the death penalty. This is also true for many members of denominations that officially oppose the death penalty, which include the Eastern Orthodox Christian Churches, the Methodist Church, the Evangelical Lutheran Church of America, the Episcopal Church, the Presbyterian Churches, the United Church of Christ, the Reformed Church in America, the Unitarian Universalists, and the National Council of the Churches of Christ. One notable exception is black Christians. They have been especially prominent in their opposition to the death penalty, influenced by the history of lynching in the United States, in which there was often collusion between officials of the justice system and the lynch mobs, and also by clear evidence of racial bias in the application of the judicial death penalty.

It is also important to understand the premises upon which a majority of Catholics or other American Christians approve the death penalty. When the question is asked in a vacuum (Do you support the death penalty or not?), many respond yes because they understand the alternative to be less than life sentences, which release on parole dangerous people, such as sexual predators who prey on children. When the question is stated a different way, "Do you favor a sentence of life without parole instead of the death penalty?" there is a significant shift in the numbers, and a slight majority favors eliminating the death penalty. Elimination of the death penalty in the present situation of overcrowded prisons, which exerts pressure on prosecutors, judges, and parole boards to make prison space available by shortening sentences and granting parole, simply has not been acceptable to many. A number of legislatures are debating whether their state should join the twenty states that have abolished the death penalty, but the grounds for debate are not moral so much as economic. Death-penalty trials cost much more than trials over life sentences, and the execution process, with all its appeals, costs many millions of dollars more. The stakes are high: As of October 1, 2018, there were 2,721 people on death row in the United States, of whom 354 were in Florida.

DNA TESTING DEEPENS OPPOSITION
BY EXPOSING ERRORS IN CONVICTIONS

DNA evidence was first introduced into trials in 1989. According to the Innocence Project, it has resulted in 365 exonerations in thirty-seven states to date. This number includes 130 people who were wrongfully convicted for murder and 20 who spent time on death row. On average, each one of these 365 exonerees served fourteen years in prison. Demographically, 62 percent were African Americans, 30 percent were Caucasian, and 27 percent were Hispanic.

The number of vacated sentences has increased due to DNA testing, and as the role of race in prosecution and sentencing has also become more apparent, an increasing number of states have reversed their stance on the death penalty. According to the Death Penalty Information Center, as of 2020 twenty-one states have abolished or overturned the death penalty and in four other states it has been suspended or eliminated via executive action by the governor. The trend is not uniform, however. For example, while the Nebraska legislature voted to repeal the death penalty in 2015, the governor vetoed the bill. When the legislature overrode the governor's veto, the governor helped to fund a successful statewide referendum to reinstate the death penalty. As a result, Nebraska is preparing for its first state execution since 1997.

To return to the central ethical questions in the case, we must ask to what extent the errors in the administration of capital punishment in the United States since 1977 are an inevitable part of a death-penalty system and whether they can be eliminated by reform. About this, people differ. Some point out that the justice system not only includes the original trial and sentencing, but also the very appeal process through which many have been exonerated. They insist that the high number of sentences vacated is proof that the appeals process works. Those who oppose the death sentence point to the fact that two-thirds of the vacated sentences have come about through some kind of initiative from outside the justice system itself, usually from volunteer legal organizations such as a law-school class in Illinois that began the process of appealing for DNA testing in old death-penalty cases in that state. In the vast majority of capital cases, however, the convict does not have such advocates.

In 2009 a coalition pulled together by the Constitution Project published a report, "Smart on Crime," with recommendations for the Administration and Congress. That report listed the chief needs in the criminal justice system as, among others, adequately trained counsel in all capital cases; protections for the mentally ill or disabled from execution; safeguards in habeas corpus (which anti-terrorism legislation since 1996 has undermined); and safeguards against racially biased capital prosecution.

JUSTICE, MERCY, AND CONSCIENCE

Beyond these questions of justice is yet another, often invoked by leaders of Christian churches, about the primary values of the gospel. When we stand before the throne of God, how do we want to be treated? With justice, or with mercy? What makes God worthy of worship is not power (in the sense of the ability to impose one's will on another), but the power of goodness, of compassion and mercy, even for sinners. This is the center of the incarnation and redemption: God's compassion and mercy for us as sinners. What God asks of us, say many authorities in the Christian tradition, is that we treat others as we are treated by God.

So strong is this argument from within Christian theology that it completely rules out arguments by Christians for retribution in the criminal justice system. Christians may make arguments for sentencing based on the need to protect the innocent in society from future victimization or on the need for action to reform and rehabilitate criminals (in order that they not be a danger to others), but Christians cannot make arguments that invoke the gospel for the necessity of making criminals suffer for their sins. That is not only exclusively God's prerogative, but it is one that God has been shown to forgo in the interests of mercy. Thus, the question becomes one of whether or not we live in a situation in which the only way to protect the innocent requires us to give up any hope of rehabilitation in the criminal and end his or her life. Clearly, in the past many societies felt that there was no alternative to capital punishment if society was to be truly protected. But today, the United States is one of only a handful of developed nations that have not abolished the death penalty.

Some have argued that it is opponents of the death penalty who have imposed the heaviest burdens on those sentenced to death, in that they are responsible for the long delays before execution. These delays are not simply years—over fifteen years on average, but sometimes twenty or more—spent in prison. Death-row prisoners are kept in isolation. They spend about twenty-three hours a day in their single-person cells, separated from the rest of the prison population, allowed out of the cell only for a shower every other day and a daily half-hour alone in the exercise yard. Two hundred years of prison studies have shown that because human nature is relational, solitary confinement is inhumane treatment that can and often does undermine sanity. Some feel that death-row conditions are so inhumane that it would be better to risk taking the lives of a few innocents by shortening the time between sentencing and execution in order to spare prisoners decades on death row. Opponents of the death penalty, however, insist that the proposals to limit appeals and speed up executions do not simply raise the risk of executing a "few" innocent people. The *average* death-row exoneration occurs slightly more than eleven years after receiving the death sentence; cutting appeal time to any less time means the majority of those now released would be executed. Radically curtailing the time from conviction to execution to one or two years, as proposed by some, would condemn almost all those who presently are exonerated.

Manny's decision in this case seems to hinge a great deal on his concern for his family. He is worried that his wife may not understand if he votes to end capital punishment, especially if it means that he then loses his seat and she is unable to start her master's degree. But if Manny's conscience speaks, it should be obeyed, regardless of the political or the personal consequences.

At another level, however, it is possible that his concern that Pina might not accept whatever stance he takes is rooted in a longstanding process of developing shared moral feelings, which is appropriate to marriage. One purpose of marriage is the "perfection of the spouse," as some vows used to say. Spouses often help each other recognize their moral blind spots and address them, and they learn to lean on each other for this. If Manny has been accustomed to take many of his moral signals from Pina, he may be uneasy at taking a differing position on this issue. But conscience is personal. Part of the process of moral development is being able to stand alone, even against our own community and our own family, when God speaks to us in conscience. Manny needs to listen to the voice of conscience and not let his anxieties about whether he will lose his seat, or whether Pina will understand, or how much clout Alice and her organization have, obscure that voice. Perhaps his problem is that conscience is not speaking at all, in which case he needs to continue to gather evidence, listen to both sides, pray, and listen for that voice. If conscience does not speak in a clear voice, then he will need to do the best job he can of weighing the risks and benefits of both options, and choose what seems to be the better option.

Manny's decision comes at an interesting time. Public support for the death penalty, which has been steadily declining since the late 1990s and reached a four-decade low in 2016, has lately been increasing. According to a May 2018 poll conducted by the Pew Research Center, 54 percent of Americans favored the death penalty for people convicted of murder, while 39 percent opposed it. As an elected official, to what extent should public opinion affect the positions Manny takes on issues? To what extent should his personal religious and ethical views shape Manny's decision whether or not to abolish the death penalty in Florida?

ADDITIONAL RESOURCES

Alexander, Michelle. *The New Jim Crow: Mass Incarceration in the Age of Colorblindness.* New York: The New Press, 2010.

Brugger, E. Christian. *Capital Punishment and Roman Catholic Moral Tradition,* 2nd edition. Notre Dame, IN: University of Notre Dame Press, 2014.

Claiborne, Shane. *Executing Grace: How the Death Penalty Killed Jesus and Why It's Killing Us.* San Francisco: HarperOne, 2016.

Evangelical Lutheran Church in America. *The Death Penalty: A Social Statement.* Chicago: Division for Church in Society, 1991.

Gross, Samuel R., et al. "Exonerations in the United States: 1989 through 2003." University of Michigan Law School. April 19, 2004.

Gudorf, Christine E. "Christianity and Opposition to the Death Penalty: Late Modern Shifts." *Dialog* 52, no. 2 (2013): 99–109.

Kay, Judith W. *Murdering Myths: The Story behind the Death Penalty.* Lanham, MD: Rowman and Littlefield Publishers, 2005.

Prejean, Helen. *Dead Man Walking: An Eyewitness Account of the Death Penalty in the US.* New York: Random House, 1993.

Santoro, Anthony R. *Exile and Embrace: Contemporary Religious Discourse on the Death Penalty.* Boston: Northeastern University Press, 2013.

Steffen, Lloyd. *Executing Justice: The Moral Meaning of the Death Penalty.* Cleveland: Pilgrim Press, 1998.

Stevenson, Bryan. *Just Mercy: A Story of Justice and Redemption.* New York: Spiegel and Grau, 2014.

United States Conference of Catholic Bishops. *A Culture of Life and the Penalty of Death: A Statement of the United States Conference of Catholic Bishops Calling for an End to the Use of the Death Penalty.* Washington, DC: USCCB, 2005.

Wallis, Jim. *America's Original Sin: Racism, White Privilege, and the Bridge to a New America.* Grand Rapids: Brazos Press, 2016.

Related Websites

Death Penalty Information Center
http://www.deathpenaltyinfo.org

Innocence Project
   https://www.innocenceproject.org/
Pew Research Center, "Religious Groups' Official Positions on Capital Punishment"
   https://www. Pewforum.org/2009/11/04/religious-groups-official-positions-on-capital-punishment/
Pro-Death Penalty.com
   http://www.prodeathpenalty.com/.

Case

An American Idol?

It was April 27, 2019. Pastor Eric was shaken. Again. After yet another shooting in a house of worship—the Chabad of Poway Synagogue in California—he was sad and angry and determined to do something, finally. Some congregation members had approached him in 2015 after the attack on Emanuel African Methodist Episcopal Church in Charleston, South Carolina. A young white supremacist had killed nine African American parishioners at "Mother Emanuel" and wounded three others during a bible study. The shooter was a baptized Lutheran and had been attending a Lutheran church in Columbia, South Carolina.

Pastor Eric's parish, St. Peter's Lutheran Church, was a predominantly white congregation in Iowa that had become a thriving and well-known LGBTQ-friendly community. Before marriage equality was legal, Pastor Eric had presided at same-sex weddings with the full blessing of the church council. When the Evangelical Lutheran Church in America (ELCA) changed the rules in 2009 to welcome LGBTQ pastors and embrace their families, the congregation threw a party. In the process, some conservative members left the congregation. The folks who remained, however, were clear about their commitments. They welcomed queer leadership and formed new friendships. And the whole city knew it.

Those commitments were tested after the 2016 Pulse nightclub shooting in Orlando, Florida, when an American man with Islamic State sympathies murdered forty-nine and wounded another fifty-three people. The vast majority had been gay Hispanic men. The members of St. Peter's mourned deeply and held a vigil that packed the house with people who hadn't seen the inside of a church in years. Then they got anxious, aware of their vulnerability to some bigot with an AR-15. Would they be targeted too? In worship on Sunday mornings they felt like sitting ducks. The congregation

This case was prepared by Jean Larson and the commentary by James B. Martin-Schramm. The names of persons and institutions have been disguised, where appropriate, to protect the privacy of those involved.

was only fifteen minutes from the police station, but anybody armed with a semi-automatic gun could murder and injure many in just a few seconds. What could they do to protect themselves?

The congregation started to answer this question after an attack on the Tree of Life Synagogue in Pittsburgh, Pennsylvania, killed eleven people in 2018. Pastor Eric had asked the church council to form a safety committee to research the issue and recommend the best response. It had been a terrible year for gun violence—beginning with the mass shooting at Marjory Stoneman Douglas High School in Parkland, Florida, only eight months before. Although desire for effective action gripped much of the nation, no national gun-safety legislation had been signed into law since 1994. At the state level, Iowa did not bar weapons from houses of worship. It was clear to the safety committee that it had to act. It had to find ways to protect the congregation. The question was how best to do so.

The first meeting of the five-member safety committee was chaotic.

Morrie knew his way around guns. He collected them, was an avid hunter, and had a concealed carry (CCW) permit. He volunteered to carry his gun in worship on Sunday mornings to be able to respond on the spot to an active shooter. He offered to recruit a buddy to help him out.

Ed, a retired cop, chaired the committee. He knew how much training was required to respond to critical incidents, and he was pretty certain he was the only member of the congregation who had that training. But he was retired. He'd also been in the midst of a shooting and knew how fast and chaotic those situations were. He was dead set against arming parishioners, even those who were proficient with guns. Armed "good guys" had been mistaken for "bad guys" in previous incidents. Law enforcement couldn't tell one from the other. Innocents had been killed and wounded.

Kathy, a single woman in her late twenties was appalled at the thought of guns anywhere in church, even for protection. Jesus went to the cross without violence. He taught his disciples to turn the other cheek. Could anyone really countenance the idea of using deadly force in the sanctuary, even against a "bad guy"? Wasn't this an assault on Christian faith itself? She was willing to suffer the consequences of unarmed defense, but she was losing sleep over the possible outcome for other members of the congregation who did not share her pacifist views.

Patrick, a newer member, had known a person who was wounded in the Pulse shooting. It had taken him a long time even to come to worship because of the spiritual abuse he had suffered as a gay teen in his previous church. After months of hiding in the back pews, Patrick began to trust that the peace at St. Peter's was genuine. He could be safe there. He was determined to work hard to keep the church safe and return worship to a sense of peace in the presence of God. He had no idea how.

Pastor Eric also sat on the committee. The congregation had started receiving anonymous threats after the vigil held following the Pulse shooting. He had informed the police and the executive committee of the church council, but they had decided not to tell others in order to keep panic at bay. Pastor Eric was determined to keep guns out of worship. He saw the threat of deadly force as a contradiction to Christian faith. He believed it would make true worship impossible. Nevertheless, he wanted St. Peter's to be a safe space for everybody.

The safety committee decided it needed to meet with the church's insurance agent, Ruth, whose company insured many churches. What were the implications for the church's liability with any of the choices they might make? The insurance company suggested a six-video class on training for active-shooter scenarios. In addition, Ruth advocated holding active-shooter drills in church. The committee was overwhelmed.

The committee did view a six-minute video on YouTube, "Run, Hide, Fight." Kathy and Patrick had a hard time dealing with the violence involved in preparing to prevent violence. Nevertheless, Ruth did help narrow their options. Her company advocated against Morrie's desire to arm himself and another parishioner because the liability to the congregation was too great if things went awry. Pastor Eric was relieved. Ruth advised them that, if the congregation decided to hire an armed security team, hiring professionals was highly recommended. But what would that cost? What would it do to worship to have armed security agents on church property on Sunday mornings?

Ruth had one more suggestion—to train people to use a nonlethal, gel-based pepper spray. Sold under the brand name Reflex Protect, the product disables a shooter from fifteen to twenty feet away. The gel sticks to the target and does not cross-contaminate the area, as gas sprays do. In addition, another chemical quickly reverses the effects of the spray. The gel does no permanent harm to either the shooter or an innocent person sprayed by accident. Ruth noted that some schools, hospitals, and churches are using it. Congregation members who volunteer would have to be trained in its use and be prepared to carry it on Sunday mornings. However, the protector would have to get within twenty feet of the shooter to make the spray effective and thus risk getting shot in the process. Could the congregation ask anyone to accept that much risk?

The safety committee had much to consider. Kathy went to work researching different approaches and discovered the ELCA had passed a social policy resolution in 2016 titled "Gun Violence Prevention." It focused on advocacy and encouraged bishops, pastors, and lay leaders to communicate with state and national legislators. Two issues were highlighted: (1) universal background checks on all gun purchases, and (2) renewing the federal assault weapon ban, which had expired in 2004. Kathy was also encouraged by a 2018 statement from the ELCA Conference of Bishops after the Marjory Stoneman Douglas shooting. In their "Statement in Solidarity with our Children and Youth," the bishops cited a 1994 ELCA social message, "Community Violence":

> Christians, as salt of the earth (Mt 5:13) and light of the world (Mt 5:14), are called to respond to violent crime in the restorative ways taught by Jesus (Mt 5:38–39) and shown by his actions (Jn 8:3–11). We are empowered to take up the challenge to prevent violence and to attack the complex causes that make violence so pervasive.

In addition, Kathy consulted with the social ministry committee at St. Peter's. Two members of that committee were active in the local chapter of Moms Demand Action for Gun Sense in America. Kathy got a quick introduction to the work they had been doing with the state legislature— testifying before committees, phone calling or texting when an important bill came up, and educating themselves on effective gun safety measures. Moms Demand Action also had a program for gun safety in the home, Be SMART, which the social ministry committee was going to introduce to Sunday School parents.

Kathy thought it would be great to have an adult forum at St. Peter's on the work of Moms Demand Action and to encourage church members to join and support the organization. When she mentioned this to her friends on the social ministry committee, she was cautioned. Another church in town had invited a Moms Demand Action member to a gun-safety forum, and she'd been ambushed by two vocal National Rifle Association (NRA) members who took over the conversation, accused the presenter of lying, and made the whole event something of a fiasco. Kathy had no idea who might be an NRA member at St. Peter's. Maybe Morrie? Could she talk with him? She had no desire to cause dissension in the congregation. She just wanted to protect its sacred, peaceful space for the people who had found refuge there.

At the next meeting of the safety committee Kathy urged the members to work upstream of the problem by advocating for gun laws proven to reduce violence, such as universal background checks. She wanted congregation members to get involved with the gun violence prevention movement. She believed that this approach was consistent with church teaching and what it means to follow Jesus. It would be a positive response to members' anguish. And it would harm no one.

Morrie was firmly opposed. He believed in the right to bear arms enshrined in the Second Amendment to the US Constitution. Though he understood that stricter gun laws may keep guns out of the hands of the wrong people, he thought it was unfair to ask people who were already abiding by the laws to jump through even more hoops to acquire a gun legally. He emphasized that it's the bad people in society that St. Peter's needs to address, not guns. In addition, he emphasized that self-defense is a legal right and that protection of the innocent is a moral obligation.

Patrick agreed with Kathy about advocating for gun control, but he also wanted to try the gel spray, so that there would be some reasonable defense in case the congregation was attacked. He didn't want to see any more people murdered when there was a way to stop it.

Ed was dubious about the spray, but the option recommended by the insurance agent of using an armed security team seemed to be more than the congregation could handle, financially and spiritually. He thought it would be good to show the whole congregation the "Run, Hide, Fight" video and to practice it in the church. He also wanted St. Peter's to consider hiring a consultant to teach the staff and volunteers how to make the church's facilities more secure.

Pastor Eric was grateful for the hard work of the committee. That said, he wanted a safety protocol in place sooner rather than later. Within the human and financial resources of the congregation, what was the best approach to deal with the danger of gun violence in worship? What was the congregation's responsibility in advocating for gun safety legislation? Which strategy was most compatible with the church's teaching? What was faithful to the way of Christ? What should St. Peter's Lutheran Church do about gun violence?

Commentary

This case addresses a very painful topic in contemporary American life—the scourge of gun violence that has shattered the lives of so many individuals, families, and communities. It is truly an exceptional situation. No other industrialized country suffers from the scale of gun violence that plagues the United States. This commentary explores the broader context for the case, identifies various Christian perspectives on the problem, and closes by exploring policy options to reduce the number of deaths associated with widespread ownership of deadly firearms.

CONTEXT OF US GUN VIOLENCE

Death. According to the most recent data available from the Centers for Disease Control and Prevention (CDC), 39,773 people died from gun-related injuries in the United States in 2017. In other words, that year 109 people lost their lives each day to gun violence. Sadly, this is not the exception but rather the rule. Since 1979, the nation's gun deaths have not dropped below 32,000 per year. More Americans have been killed by guns over the past two decades than have been killed in all of the nation's foreign wars. More poignantly, the number of children killed by guns since the infamous killing spree at Sandy Hook Elementary School on December 14, 2012, is larger than the number of US soldiers who have been killed in overseas combat since the terrorist attacks on September 11, 2001. According to the CDC, the number of deaths per 100,000 people was greater in 2017 for those killed by firearms (12.2) than by motor vehicle accidents (11.9).

This case focuses on gun violence in houses of worship. The shooting at Chabad of Poway Synagogue in California was the last straw for Pastor Eric. Even though only one person was killed and three persons were injured, the prospect for more widespread bloodshed was very real since the shooter used a semi-automatic rifle that can fire up to ten rounds per second. The case also refers to the 2015 murder of nine people at Emanuel African Methodist Episcopal Church in Charleston, South Carolina, and the 2016 Pulse nightclub shooting that resulted in forty-nine deaths.[1]

---

[1] At the time, this was the deadliest mass shooting in US history. Sadly, it was eclipsed by the deaths of fifty-nine people when a shooter used twenty-three military-

Other examples include a 2018 assault on the Tree of Life Synagogue in Pittsburgh that killed eleven congregants, a 2017 massacre of twenty-six people worshiping at First Baptist Church in Sutherland Springs, Texas, and the murder of six people in 2012 at a Sikh temple in Wisconsin. A 2018 article published by the Associated Press reports a dozen more mass shootings at houses of worship since 2012. According to an article published in *Politico,* all but two of the mass shootings in the United States since 1982 have been committed by men, and most were white men.

While the public is rightly alarmed by what, on average, are daily mass shootings—events that result in the deaths of four or more people—including those in houses of worship, the associated fatalities represent only about 2 percent of all gun-related deaths in the United States. Suicides have long accounted for the majority of gun-related deaths. In 2017, approximately 60 percent of gun-related deaths were suicides (23,854), while 37 percent were murders (14,542). The remainder were law-enforcement related (553), unintentional (486), or had undetermined circumstances (338).

Suicide has been on the rise in the United States in recent years and is currently the tenth leading cause of death. Gun suicides rose 41 percent between 2006 and 2017. Every thirty minutes someone in the United States takes his or her life with a gun. While guns are not the most common way people attempt suicide, they are by all means the most lethal. Eighty-five percent of suicide attempts with a gun end in death, whereas drug overdoses (the most frequent means) are fatal less than 3 percent of the time. Having a gun in the home triples the risk of suicide. Of children who commit suicide, 80 percent use a family member's gun. Veterans are especially at risk. Their suicide rate is 22 percent higher than that of the general public, and two-thirds of them use a gun.

According to the CDC, there were 12.2 gun deaths per 100,000 people in 2017, which is the highest rate in more than two decades (but below the 16.3 gun deaths per 100,000 people in 1974, the highest rate in the CDC's online database). If the focus is just on homicide, per capita murder rates are much higher in some developing countries like El Salvador (39.2), Venezuela (38.7), Guatemala (32.3), Colombia (25.9), and Honduras (22.5). As noted in one of the other cases in this volume, "Detain and Deport," this is one of the main reasons so many are fleeing their homes in these countries and migrating to the United States.

Nevertheless, homicide rates in the United States are much higher than those in other industrialized countries. According to data published by the

---

style weapons, some modified with bump stocks, to fire more than eleven hundred bullets into a crowd at an outdoor music festival from a hotel room in the Mandalay Bay Hotel in Las Vegas on October 1, 2017.

United Nations Office on Drugs and Crime, the United States has 29.7 homicides per million people. Switzerland is second with 7.7, Germany has only 1.9, and Australia has 1.4. Gun murder rates in the United States are seventeen times higher than Australia, thirty-five times higher than Germany, thirty-seven times higher than Spain, and 355 times higher than Japan. According to an article published in *Bloomberg Business*, gun-related murders are the leading cause of death for black men between the ages of fifteen and thirty-four in the United States. They are four times more likely to die from gun violence than in a motor-vehicle accident. According to the *American Journal of Public Health*, guns are also the leading cause of death for law enforcement officers; 90 percent of those killings are committed with a gun.

Guns. These statistics are alarming. Some might draw the conclusion that Americans are extraordinarily violent people. This would be erroneous. The problem isn't the people but the number of guns. The Federal Bureau of Investigation (FBI) estimates there are 350 million guns in the United States. According to an analysis by the Small Arms Survey, Americans make up less than 5 percent of the world's population, but they own about 45 percent of all the world's privately held firearms.

The results of a 2019 Gallup Poll revealed that 30 percent of US adults say they personally own a gun, and 43 percent report having a gun in the household. Remarkably, 50 percent of non-Hispanic white households report having a gun in the house, and a 2017 Pew Research Center survey showed that 41 percent of white Christian evangelicals report owning a gun. Republicans (45%), men (43%), and self-identified conservatives (40%) are most likely to personally own a gun. Women (17%), Democrats (16%), and Hispanics (15%) are the least likely to report personal gun ownership. Some households and individuals have many guns. According to a 2016 article published in *USA Today*, 3 percent of the US population owns half of the country's privately held guns—on average, seventeen guns per person.

Regulation. These large and disconcerting numbers regarding gun ownership are directly related to the ease with which a person can acquire a gun in the United States. According to *Business Insider*, there were 14,146 McDonald's restaurants and 25,400 grocery stores in the United States at the end of 2016, but there were 60,417 legal firearm dealers. In other words, there are four times as many gun dealers as there are McDonald's and more than twice as many gun dealers as grocery stores. According to the Brady Campaign to End Gun Violence, roughly 5 percent of these gun dealers are unscrupulous. As a result, about 90 percent of guns recovered in crimes are traced back to these dealers. More troubling is the estimate that 40 percent of all firearms sold in the United States are acquired from unlicensed sellers who sell weapons over the Internet or at an estimated five thousand gun-and-knife shows that take place in all fifty states each year. Private sellers are not required to conduct background checks on buyers and typically conduct their transactions in cash.

The wide access to and ability to purchase an unlimited number of guns is due to relatively lax regulation in the United States, at least when compared to other industrialized nations. Federal law requires background checks for sales by licensed gun dealers and for any interstate sales of firearms. The acquisition of guns is also regulated by various state laws that vary significantly in their form and degree of stringency. In general, Southern states have the weakest gun laws, the most guns per capita, and (not surprisingly) the most gun deaths per capita.

Presbyterian theologian James Atwood identifies a host of ludicrous aspects regarding the current federal regulation of firearms in *Gundamentalism and Where It Is Taking America.* For example, he notes that the Gun Control Act of 1968 gives the Bureau of Alcohol, Tobacco, Firearms, and Explosives (ATF) the authority to check gun dealers for illegal sales, but they can only do so once every twelve months. As a result, only about 7 percent of gun dealers are checked annually. It does not help that the ATF has the same size staff it had when it was established in 1972—twenty-five-hundred agents. While licensed gun dealers must keep specific records regarding each firearm sale, the ATF is prevented by law from compiling an electronic database of all gun owners. In addition, when firearm dealers go out of business, they are required to send all of their records to the ATF's National Tracing Center in Martinsburg, West Virginia. These paper records have to be filed by hand because, in 1986, Congress enacted the Firearms Protection Act, which bans the ATF from creating a computerized registry of guns, gun owners, or gun sales. Atwood also points out that The Consumer Protection Act of 1972 prohibits the Consumer Protection Agency or any other agency from examining the quality or safety of any gun or piece of ammunition. No other sector in the American economy enjoys such legal protection.

One option in the case is for Morrie and his friends who have concealed carry permit to bring their guns to St. Peter's Lutheran Church on Sunday with the assumption that "good guys" with guns will be able to stop any "bad guys" with guns. Every state now has some sort of concealed carry permit. In thirty-three states law enforcement is required to supply a CCW permit if a citizen passes a background check and applies for one. In Iowa, the state is even willing to issue such a permit to persons who are legally blind.

The Second Amendment. This key passage in the US Constitution is central to national debates about gun control: "A well regulated Militia, being necessary to the security of a free State, the right of the people to keep and bear Arms, shall not be infringed." At least two things should be kept in mind about the Second Amendment. The first is that the authors would have had in mind flintlock muzzle-loader rifles and pistols used by the Continental Army during the American Revolutionary War. It took the average militiaman about a minute to reload the weapon by ramming gunpowder and the new shot down the barrel. Today, we are talking about guns that can fire ten rounds a second versus one round a minute. The second thing to consider is that the well-regulated militias were state militias constituted for the protection of each state.

In 2008, however, the US Supreme Court's decision in *District of Columbia v. Heller* overturned two hundred years of prior judicial rulings when it interpreted the Second Amendment as an *individual right* to bear arms as opposed to a *collective right* to defend the state. The court said "it is an individual right with reasonable restrictions and it does not infringe upon gun rights." Justice Antonin Scalia wrote the majority opinion:

> This individual right is not an unlimited or unrestricted right. It does not cast doubt on long-standing prohibitions on the possession of firearms by felons and the mentally ill, or laws forbidding the carrying of firearms in sensitive places such as schools and government buildings, or laws imposing conditions and qualifications on the commercial sale of arms. . . . Like most rights, the Second Amendment right is not unlimited. It is not a right to keep and carry any weapon whatsoever in any manner whatsoever and for whatever purpose.

James Atwood describes uncompromising supporters of the Second Amendment as "gundamentalists." He points out that they only focus on the second half of the Second Amendment, not the first; that is, they refuse to acknowledge the part that refers to a well-regulated militia. Atwood says gundamentalists peddle fear to Americans that one day there is going to be a gunfight with tyrannical "Big Government," which will come to seize their guns and control their way of life. He offers Timothy McVeigh as a prime example. Angry about the federal siege of the Branch Davidian compound in Waco, Texas, McVeigh blew up the Federal Building in Oklahoma City in 1995, killing 168 people and injuring 600. Atwood also singles out former Governor of Alaska, Sarah Palin, who advised her followers, "Don't retreat, reload." On her website Palin placed crosshairs on Gabby Giffords's congressional district. Giffords was later shot along with six other people outside a grocery store in her congressional district. Atwood offers these examples of gundamentalist extremism to illustrate his claim that "words matter." Indeed. Extreme rhetoric can lead to violent results.

The National Rifle Association (NRA). No discussion about the Second Amendment, and extremist views about it, would be complete without discussing the key role of the NRA, which was founded in 1871 to promote "skill, accuracy, and marksmanship" in the use of firearms, especially in hunting and sport. Today the NRA has approximately five million members, which is less than 2 percent of the US population of 329.4 million people in March 2020. Nevertheless, the organization has considerable political muscle.

In 2004, the NRA successfully lobbied Congress to let the Federal Assault Weapons Ban expire. In 2005, the NRA backed the Protection of Lawful Commerce in Arms Act, which prevents firearms manufacturers and dealers from being held liable for any negligence if any crimes are committed with their products. In 2016, the NRA's Political Victory Fund contributed $30 million to support Donald Trump's campaign for the White House. In 2019, the NRA offered to pay President Trump's legal expenses associated with impeachment proceedings in Congress.

A former executive officer of the NRA, Warren Cassidy, once said: "You would get a far better understanding of the NRA if you approached us as if you were approaching one of the great religions of the world." Charlton Heston offered similar remarks couched in religious overtones when he addressed the group during his term as president of the NRA. Holding aloft an old flintlock rifle, Heston said: "Sacred stuff resides in that wooden stock and blue steel when ordinary hands can possess such an extraordinary instrument that gives the most common man the most uncommon of freedoms that symbolize the full measure of human dignity and liberty."

THEOLOGICAL AND ETHICAL PERSPECTIVES

Biblical scholar Walter Wink writes: "Violence is the ethos of our times. It is the spirituality of the modern world. It has been accorded the status of a religion, demanding from its devotees an absolute obedience to death. . . . It, and not Christianity, is the real religion of America."[2] There is much evidence to support his claim. In fiscal year 2019, the US Department of Defense's budget authority was nearly $700 billion. The United States has 662 military bases located in the United States and thirty-eight other countries around the world. According to the deficit hawk, Peter G. Peterson Foundation, the United States spends more on defense than the next seven nations combined—China, Saudi Arabia, India, France, Russia, Germany,

---

[2] Walter Wink, *Engaging the Powers: Discernment and Resistance in a World of Domination,* 25th anniversary edition (Minneapolis: Fortress Press, 2017), 13.

and the United Kingdom. The Poor People's Campaign claims the United States spends over $20,000 per second on defense and notes that fifty-three cents of every discretionary federal dollar goes to the military (compared to only fifteen cents to alleviate poverty). Estimates are that gun violence in America is costing the nation at least $100 billion a year in rising insurance premiums, emergency medical bills, legal costs, and lost productivity. Some estimates place the figure at $229 billion a year, or almost $700 per American citizen.

On the basis of statistics like these, two prominent Christian theologians, Shane Claiborne and Michael Martin, articulate the following conviction: "We have a problem. We have a pathological, spiritual illness. . . . Saying more guns will solve our problem is sort of like a drunk saying he just needs more whiskey, or like thinking that the solution to a flood is more water."[3]

Idolatry

James Atwood explores the toxic combination of American views about divine blessing and manifest destiny, which he thinks "have led millions of Americans to believe that God has given Americans both the right and the responsibility to own guns so that they can protect their families, private property, and their neighbors."[4] He associates this view with gundamentalists who, like the NRA, argue that "the only thing that will stop a bad guy with a gun is a good guy with a gun." This seems to be Morrie's view in the case. Atwood argues that "redemptive violence is the theology of gundamentalists."[5] They think violence caused by guns can save the innocent and that those who wield these guns are doing the work of God. Atwood goes further: "The weapons of gun extremists become absolutes, i.e., *another* god or idol. These are good folks who have been seduced by an idol masquerading as an Ultimate Good."[6]

Claiborne and Martin agree with Atwood. They note that idols and false gods should not only be associated with primitive societies in the past but are very real and powerful in the present. To paraphrase Martin Luther's counsel in his Large Catechism, "Your god is that within which you place your ultimate security." Claiborne and Martin write: "Think of all the promises a gun pledges to its owner—power, control, safety, protection,

---

[3] Shane Claiborne and Michael Martin, *Beating Guns: Hope for People Who Are Weary of Violence* (Grand Rapids, MI: Brazos Press, 2019), 178–79.

[4] James A. Atwood, *Gundamentalism and Where It Is Taking America* (Eugene, OR: Cascade Books, 2017), 11.

[5] Ibid., 15.

[6] Ibid.

deliverance, self-confidence, self-determination, ridding the world of evil. If the gun were actually able to keep all its promises, then we would be like God."[7] They argue that idolatry warps true Christian worship as well as the moral character of Christians:

> True worship is when we let God change us and make us more like God. Idolatry is when we try to change God and make God more like us. . . . What's just as important as whether or not we worship God is the character of the God we worship and what our worship of God does to us. Does it make us more loving, more concerned about life, or compassionate for the marginalized? Or does it make us more ag-gressive and angry and self-righteous and violent?[8]

Pastor Eric and Kathy share these concerns in the case. They are worried about the message it would send to have armed guards in church. After all, Christians worship a God of life, not of death. They are also worried about what a reliance on guns for security might do to the character of the Christian community worshiping at St. Peter's Lutheran Church. How does a willingness to kill affect one's ability to love?

Self-Defense

The views above probably resonate with many readers, but they may also cause cognitive dissonance for some. After all, the legal right to self-defense is assumed by most and appears self-evident to many. Morrie certainly feels this way in the case. David French, an Iraq War veteran and senior writer for *National Review,* has developed a full-blown defense of the biblical and natural right of self-defense. He begins by noting God's words to Noah after the Flood: "Whoever sheds the blood of man, by man shall his blood be shed, for God made man in his own image" (Gen 9:6). He goes on to note that Mosaic Law does not condemn killing when it occurs in defense of one's home: "If a thief is found breaking in and is struck so that he dies, there shall be no bloodguilt for him" (Ex 22:2). French also refers to passages in Nehemiah and the Book of Esther where "the morality of self-defense is not only presumed, the act of self-defense is permitted and even mandated by key Biblical figures."[9] Finally, French notes that Jesus's disciples carried swords for self-defense and that Jesus

---

[7] Claiborne and Martin, *Beating Guns,* 172.

[8] Ibid., 175.

[9] David French, "The Biblical and Natural Right of Self-Defense," *National Review,* January 25, 2013.

even instructs his disciples, "If you don't have a sword, sell your cloak and buy one" (Lk 22:37).

Pacifism

There is no question, however, that Jesus chose not to defend himself when faced with crowds who shouted, "Crucify him, crucify him" (Lk 23:21). He urged his followers to "love your enemies and pray for those who persecute you" (Mt 5:44). Early Christian leaders embraced this stance. For example, Tertullian (160–220 CE) writes, "In our way of life it is more permissible to suffer death than to inflict it." And Origen (185–254 CE) states: "God did not . . . allow the killing of any man whatsoever." Twelve hundred years later Martin Luther urged fellow Christians not to engage in self-defense:

> Christ says that we should not resist evil or injustice but always yield, suffer, and let things be taken from us. If you will not bear this law, then lay aside the name of Christian and claim another name that accords with your actions, or else Christ himself will tear his name away from you, and that will be too hard for you.[10]

Kathy feels called to this classical understanding of pacifism. Here, in the words of Mennonite theologian John Howard Yoder, "forgiveness absorbs hostility."

Creative, Nonviolent Resistance

That said, Kathy also worries about the welfare of other members of the congregation who do not share her pacifist views. Patrick is similarly concerned. What can they do to defend others without resorting to lethal violence? How can they engage in creative, nonviolent resistance against those who would harm their neighbors? When Jesus enjoined his disciples to "turn the other cheek" and "go the extra mile" (Mt 5:38–40), these were examples of creative, nonviolent resistance against evil. The goal was to ignite the conscience of the oppressor and thus to create the possibility for repentance and change. This is easier to contemplate when one is face to face with someone seeking to do you harm; it is another thing when that person has several semi-automatic weapons and is firing from a distance

---

[10] Martin Luther, "Admonition to Peace: A Reply to the Twelve Articles of the Peasants in Swabia," in *Luther's Works*, ed. Helmut T. Lehmann and Robert C. Schultz (Minneapolis: Fortress Press, 1967), 28–29.

into a crowd. Nevertheless, in some instances the gel-spray option would fit under this approach to creative, nonviolent peacemaking. While it does harm the assailant, the harm is temporary and reversible. That said, while these approaches may be *faithful* to the life and witness of Jesus, they may not be *effective*, which brings us to the final and most commonly used approach to violence by Christians.

Just-War Criteria

Christians have wrestled with the justifiable use of violence for centuries—especially after Constantine made Christianity the official religion of the Roman Empire in the fourth century. While Luther urged Christians to forsake self-defense, he emphasized that they had a duty to wield the sword and come to the aid of their defenseless neighbors if called upon to do so by legitimate authorities. Over time, seven criteria emerged. Five were to be applied *ad bellum* (before violence was used) and two were to be applied *in bello* (as violence was being used).

Before War (Jus ad Bellum)

1. last resort
2. just cause
3. right intention
4. declared by a legitimate authority
5. reasonable hope of success

During War (Jus in Bello)

6. discrimination—between combatants and noncombatants
7. proportionality—the means must be proportional to the ends

Marvin Lim, a Roman Catholic attorney for the Campaign to Keep Guns Off Campus, has very creatively applied some of these criteria to the moral challenges posed by the scourge of gun violence in the United States.[11]

- *Last resort:* Lim thinks the church should argue that guns, by their very nature, "encourage people to think that they have exhausted all nonviolent options in a particular scenario, and that violence is the last resort. . . . Guns encourage people to think that violence is justified even in scenarios where they are not physically threatened."

---

[11] All the quotations following in this section are from Marvin Lim, "The Church Has a Stance on War, But Needs a Stance on Guns," *National Catholic Reporter,* December 1, 2016.

- *Just cause:* Lim argues that, under this just-war criterion, force may be used only to correct a grave evil, like aggression or the mass violation of human rights. He expresses concern that "stand your ground" laws "encourage people to think they have just cause to defend their honor or property even if there is no imminent bodily threat." Lim thinks these laws "encourage the escalation of precarious situations that, even if self-defense in one instant might be legitimate, could have been avoided entirely."
- *Proportionality:* Lim points out that "for many ardent gun rights advocates, the principle of proportionality is irrelevant: To them, the liberty to own and use a gun is absolute, regardless of the cost to life." Lim thinks that even though guns can be used legitimately in self-defense, "the proliferation of guns in society, legal and illegal, causes disproportionate harm in the way of accidents and suicides as well." Just as proportionality should stop the military from taking otherwise advantageous action if it might cost too many innocent lives, so too should it constrain civilians in the case of self-defense.
- *Discrimination:* Lim argues that "guns, by their very nature, encourage viewing all people as potential threats and thus, in effect, as 'combatants.'" He argues that much of the rhetoric around self-defense "encourages 'otherization,' which, in this context, results in people— and inevitably those of certain minority groups—being seen not for their value, but for their risks." This criterion is directly relevant to the case. The members of St. Peter's Lutheran are worried they will become targets of a homophobic murderer outraged about their open, loving, and welcoming embrace of those in the LGBTQ community.

Lim concludes by arguing that the Roman Catholic Church "can, and must do more to build a comprehensive theory on the evils of gun violence." He encourages all Christians to draw on the church's historical affirmation of human dignity to protect human life, but to resist doing so by quickly turning to violence.

POLICY OPTIONS

There are two important issues raised by the case. The first is what St. Peter's Lutheran Church can do to ensure greater measures of safety for its members during worship and during other hours of the day when the church is used for various purposes. The second is how St. Peter's should engage in legislative advocacy around the national issue of gun violence. Both are very important.

Congregational Options. The case outlines various possibilities. One that all seem to agree on is active-shooter training. The "Run, Hide, Fight" training program has been used widely in public schools, at colleges and universities, and in other large institutional settings. Another option, which some are uneasy about, and that the insurance company discourages, is the use of congregational members with concealed carry permits.[12] An FBI study recently concluded that only 3.2 percent of active-shooter events have been stopped by people with concealed carry permits. As a retired police officer, Ed knows how chaotic shootings can be and how easy it is for law-enforcement officials to confuse those using their concealed guns in defense with the actual assailant. The hiring of professional, trained security officers would be likely to alleviate much of this concern, but the cost of doing so would be quite prohibitive for most congregations. Pastor Eric also seems troubled by the message it would send to have armed officers at the doors of a church that ostensibly worships the Prince of Peace.

An option that seems to get some traction in the case is the use of a gel-form pepper spray to incapacitate the shooter. A study in *Field & Stream* found that hunters would have a better chance of stopping a charging grizzly bear if they used pepper spray rather than their guns. Once the spray gets into the eyes, it causes significant pain and disorientation, which leads assailants to stop what they are doing as they rub their eyes, try to restore their vision, and attempt to reduce the associated pain. Studies indicate that pepper spray will incapacitate shooters for thirty to forty-five minutes and that the spray does not have irreversible effects. While the spray can also cause the same reactions among others who accidentally get caught in the stream, there is a chemical that can be applied to counteract the effect. As noted earlier, however, the problem is that the person using the spray needs to get within fifteen to twenty feet of the shooter, which is obviously close enough to become a target. Use of the spray would require substantial training and also great courage.

Public Witness. Claiborne and Martin offer some examples of public witness that are rooted in the worship life of the congregation rather than in the world of legislative advocacy. They lift up the possibility of congregations collaborating with local police departments to host no-questions-asked weapons-collection events that could be accompanied by a worship service

---

[12] Claiborne and Martin offer a poignant remark on this topic: "After the gruesome massacre at Emanuel AME Church in Charleston—where nine members of a Bible class lost their lives, including South Carolina State Senator Reverend Clementa C. Pinckney—NRA board member Charles Cotton declared, 'Pinckney voted against concealed carry. Eight of his church members might be alive today if he had expressly allowed members to carry handguns in church. Innocent people died because of his position on a political issue'" (*Beating Guns,* 152).

that emphasizes repentance and forgiveness. They also describe workshops that involve literally "beating swords into plowshares" (Is 2:4; Joel 3:12; Mic 4:3). Their book contains several color photos of ways guns have been transformed into gardening implements and other useful products. Finally, they discuss how they have organized prayer vigils outside gun dealers who have been accused of selling guns to criminals in crime-ridden neighborhoods. James Atwood frames this sort of public witness by means of a powerful quotation from Rabbi Abraham Heschel: "Prayer is meaningless unless it is subversive, unless it seeks to overthrow and to ruin the pyramids of callousness, hatred, opportunism, and falsehood."[13]

Legislative Advocacy. In the case, Kathy is very interested in what St. Peter's can do to reduce the number of guns and to better regulate them in the first place. It appears that Kathy is in a growing majority in the United States. Public opinion polls by Gallup and other pollsters show that support for gun control measures is rising—especially after mass shooting events. In a Quinnipiac poll, a solid majority (61 percent) of Americans said they favor stricter gun laws in the United States, but the breakdown by party is striking. Whereas 91 percent of Democrats think gun laws should be stricter, as do 59 percent of Independents, only 32 percent of Republicans agree.

Universal background checks receive widespread support. In a 2019 poll, 89 percent said they supported background checks for gun purchases at licensed dealers as well as at unlicensed gun shows or other private sales. According to Atwood, this includes 85 percent of all gun owners as well as many members of the NRA. Atwood claims background checks have stopped over two million gun purchases by dangerous people since 1993, when federal legislation mandated them for purchases from licensed gun dealers.

Others argue that licensing and registering guns is an even more effective step because it is more comprehensive and virtually eliminates impulsive gun purchases motivated by crime or the intention to cause self-harm. Atwood supports this measure as well and includes the use of fingerprinting: "The United States registers births, deaths, marriages, divorces, cars, trucks, boats, trailers, bicycles, houses, lands, livestock, dogs, and cats. Everything except guns."[14]

Another option that also enjoys widespread support is the reinstatement of the Federal Weapons Ban on Assault Weapons. This measure has support within several Christian denominations, including the ELCA and the Presbyterian Church USA. "Red Flag" laws, which enable family members and/or law enforcement to go to court to request that guns be temporarily

---

[13] Abraham Joshua Heschel, "On Prayer," in *Moral Grandeur and Spiritual Audacity: Essays*, ed. Susannah Heschel (New York: Farrar, Straus, and Giroux, 1996), 263, cited in Atwood, *Gundamentalism,* 82.

[14] Atwood, *Gundamentalism,* 135.

removed from a person who is a danger to self and/or others, are another option.

Kathy and the other members of St. Peter's Lutheran Church should take the time to learn more about what their denomination's legislative-advocacy office supports both at the state and federal level. They would also do well to get involved in national organizations with local chapters like Moms Demand Action. They might also consider engaging in acts of creative, nonviolent resistance like some of the students who were traumatized by the violence at Marjory Stoneman Douglas High School in Parkland, Florida. Many of these students, and others, have engaged in strikes and have conducted sit-ins in the offices of Congressional representatives to disrupt the status quo and demand action on gun violence.

CONCLUSION

We are witnessing a *kairos* moment. . . . People across the country have started talking about guns. . . . When preachers use their moral authority and preach on the topic, and Sunday school classes debate the rights and risks of having a gun in the home, when lay leaders discuss the latest gun tragedy, or the latest headline about a mass shooting, and folks at potluck suppers talk about the dangers their young people face because so many guns are out there . . . a grassroots movement is gaining steam.[15]

James Atwood believes this with all his heart. While guns speak the language of power and fear, Christians live in the confidence that "perfect love casts out fear" (1 Jn 4:18). As Martin Luther King Jr. said: "Darkness cannot drive out darkness; only light can do that. Hate cannot drive out hate; only love can do that."[16] It appears that an increasing number of people are realizing that the mass violence that plagues American life doesn't happen in other industrialized nations to the degree and with the frequency that it happens in the United States. Americans are starting to realize that it is in their power to do something about it. While it is not possible to eradicate violence, it is possible to make it less lethal and more rare. What it requires is political courage and a willingness to stick together against forces the Bible calls "principalities and powers" that benefit from the status quo and will do all they can to preserve it.

---

[15] Ibid., 190.

[16] Martin Luther King Jr., *Strength to Love* (Minneapolis: Fortress Press, 2010), 47.

ADDITIONAL RESOURCES

Atwood, James E. *Gundamentalism and Where It Is Taking America.* Eugene, OR: Cascade Books, 2017.

Atwood, James E., and Walter Brueggemann. *America and Its Guns: A Theological Exposè.* Eugene, OR: Cascade Books, 2012.

Belew, Kathleen. *Bring the War Home: The White Power Movement and Paramilitary America.* Cambridge: Harvard University Press, 2019.

Claiborne, Shane, and Michael Martin. *Beating Guns: Hope for People Who Are Weary of Violence.* Ada, MI: Brazos Press, 2019.

Douglas, Kelly Brown. *Stand Your Ground: Black Bodies and the Justice of God.* Maryknoll, NY: Orbis Books, 2015.

Gabor, Thomas. *Enough! Solving America's Gun Violence Crisis.* Lake Worth, FL: Center for the Study of Gun Violence, 2019.

Gaffney, Donald V. *Common Ground: Talking About Gun Violence in America.* Louisville: Westminster John Knox Press, 2019.

Hawes, Jennifer Berry. *Grace Will Lead Us Home: The Charleston Church Massacre and the Hard, Inspiring Journey to Forgiveness.* New York: St. Martin's Press, 2019.

Pearson, Sharon Ely, ed. *Reclaiming the Gospel of Peace: Challenging the Epidemic of Gun Violence.* New York: Morehouse Publishing, 2015.

Wallis, Jim. *On God's Side: What Religion Forgets and Politics Hasn't Learned about Serving the Common Good.* Ada, MI: Brazos Press, 2013.

Wink, Walter. *Engaging the Powers: Discernment and Resistance in a World of Domination.* Minneapolis: Fortress Press, 1992.

———. *Jesus and Nonviolence: A Third Way.* Minneapolis: Fortress Press, 2003.

Related Videos

HBO, *Requiem for the Dead: American Spring.* 66 minutes. 2015.

PBS, *Gun Violence and Second Amendment Rights.* 27 minutes. 2018.

Related Websites

Brady Campaign
   https://www.bradyunited.org/
Coalition to Stop Gun Violence
   https://www.csgv.org/

Evangelical Lutheran Church in America, A 60–Day Journey toward Justice in a Culture of Gun Violence
https://www.elca.org/60days
Everytown for Gun Safety
everytown.org
Moms Demand Action
momsdemandaction.org
Gun Violence Archive
https://www.gunviolencearchive.org/
Presbyterian Peace Fellowship
https://www.presbypeacefellowship.org/gun-violence/
Vox, Gun Violence
https://www.vox.com/gun-violence-shootings

PART III

POVERTY

Case

Homelessness:
The How and Why of Caring

Walking to where she works as a counselor and case manager, Tracy drops a dollar bill into the paper cup in Gerald's extended hand. Gerald is fifty-five, nearly toothless, and debilitated due to a car accident years ago. As she walks on, Tracy wonders what Gerald will do if the new panhandling legislation is passed by the City Council next week.

While there is currently a law on the books against aggressive panhandling, citations are only issued when someone files a formal complaint. In such cases 80 percent of those arrested are convicted. The new legislation gives police the added power to offer citations for any intimidating conduct toward another person if the conduct is accompanied by an act of solicitation. If a "reasonable person" feels "fearful or compelled to give money" due to behavior such as intentional blocking or interference, use of threatening physical gestures or profane language, repeated solicitation, provision of unrequested services without consent, or solicitation at ATMs or parking pay stations, the conduct is considered intimidating. Under the new law Gerald could be fined $50 and receive a civil infraction if a police officer thinks he has crossed the line and intimidated someone. Failure to pay the fine or show up in court could mean criminal prosecution and jail.

Gerald recently managed to secure a subsidized downtown studio apartment after being homeless off and on for a number of years, but he panhandles to supplement the meager $1,050 a month he gets from the state disability program. Tracy has worked with Gerald and many other people

This case and commentary were prepared and updated by Laura A. Stivers. The names of persons and institutions have been disguised, where appropriate, to protect the privacy of those involved. Some of the material from the commentary was previously published in Laura A. Stivers, *Disrupting Homelessness: Alternative Christian Approaches* (Minneapolis: Fortress Press, 2011).

who have ended up homeless, especially women with children, helping them negotiate the complex array of services available and the paperwork needed to secure them. Gerald had been lucky (after waiting for several years) to be placed in a "Housing First" subsidized apartment provided for individuals who have been chronically homeless. Gerald needs to pay only 30 percent of his income toward rent, but that leaves little to cover food, clothing, and other essentials.

Originally part of a fivefold program designed by the City Council to address homelessness, so far the anti-panhandling legislation has been the only piece of the program that council members have tried to put in place. Also part of the program is increased police presence and services for the homeless. The former includes more police foot patrols in downtown areas and hiring new police officers to enable the neighborhood policing plan. The latter includes street outreach offering support services to the homeless and increased housing capacity combined with support services for homeless individuals struggling with mental health and/or chemical dependency challenges.

Like most other urban areas nationwide, the county commissioned a ten-year plan to end homelessness several years back. Yet in this year alone, due to tight city and county budgets, human-services funding was reduced by half, youth shelters eliminated, and food-bank funding slashed. At the state level, funding for general assistance, the State Housing Trust Fund, drug treatment, and basic health care were also drastically cut or ended. Legislation against panhandling seems to Tracy to be a relatively cheap way for the City Council to appear to be addressing homelessness. She notes, however, that many panhandlers like Gerald are not even homeless.

While Tracy opposes the impending panhandling legislation, her employer, Fairmont Christian Housing Alliance, and several other service providers are publicly supporting the new law. In fact, she was hurrying this morning to the meeting the executive director had called to discuss the issue.

"As you all know, I've called this meeting to explain our organization's perspective on the pending panhandling legislation up for vote in the City Council next week and to answer any questions you might have," declared Bob Knowles, executive director of Fairmont Christian Housing Alliance. "Our mission is to help low-income and/or homeless individuals and families who are seeking to improve their lives and secure housing. As we all know, there are some homeless people on the streets of our city who have addiction disorders and who do not seek to better their lives but instead harass people to fund their drug or alcohol consumption."

While Tracy agreed with Bob's statement, she wasn't sure making criminals of these people was going to solve their addiction problems or stop their panhandling. Bob went on to state, "We believe that a combination of new laws, more officers on foot patrol, and increased services and housing will both address homelessness and improve the safety and quality of life for everyone in the downtown area."

One of the drug and alcohol counselors, Kurt Trimmer, spoke to Tracy's unease. "You seem to be saying that the people we serve are 'deserving' because they want help, but the people with addictions who are living on the street are no less deserving. They will never get off the streets if we simply recycle them through jails instead of helping them address the underlying roots of their addictions."

Fairmont Alliance chaplain David Smith added, "Until they surrender their lives to Jesus Christ, there isn't anything that is going to save them. We can offer all the support services in the world but unless people come to the realization that they cannot kick an addiction by themselves, they will continue to mess up their lives and end up in jail. All of God's children are deserving, but to help them we need to embody God's tough love and not be enablers. With God's grace homeless addicts can learn discipline and recover, but they have to want to do so. Sometimes it takes hitting bottom before such a conversion happens."

Bob replied, "The panhandling legislation is only a part of the fivefold plan the City Council intends to pursue. Our organization also supports more low-income addiction-recovery programs and housing." Housing coordinator Lynn Fields spoke up from the back, "Unfortunately, the City Council is only focusing on the anti-panhandling part of the plan. Coming out publicly in support of it pits us against many of the other organizations in the city that work with the homeless. The editors of the *Street Beat* homeless newspaper, the Interfaith Alliance Against Homelessness, the Star County Coalition on Homelessness, and even the American Civil Liberties Union all oppose the legislation. The ACLU claims that panhandling is a civil right and that this law targets the poor, especially people of color. That's racial profiling."

Jasmine Gould, a long-term volunteer peer mentor who was homeless at one point in her life, chimed in, "The city's Human Rights Commission is unanimously opposed to this law. In its fifteen-page report it shows that the majority of people cited under a similar anti-panhandling law in San Francisco were people of color. The report points out that 80 percent of the cases were dismissed, resulting in large administrative and court costs."

Another staff member noted, "The city that this upcoming legislation is patterned after never actually had to enforce the ordinance, but proponents said it acted as a deterrent nevertheless." Jasmine replied, "But our city already has a law against aggressive panhandlers that works fine when there is a complaint, so why do we have to give undue power to police officers to cite anyone they deem aggressive? I know from experience that many police officers, despite excellent training, are not immune from stereotypes about who is deviant."

Wanting to get on with the day's work, Bob cut short further comments and said, "I realize not all of you support our institutional stance on this legislation, but in the big picture we will be able to do our work more effectively if we publicly support this bill. While our stance might cause some difficulty with organizations we collaborate with on the issue of homelessness, we have to keep in mind our financial viability to further our mission." Tracy noticed that except for Lynn and Jasmine, the room emptied quickly. She thought that Bob had not adequately responded to the points they made and wondered what he had meant about keeping in mind the organization's financial viability.

Tracy overheard Jasmine say to Lynn, "I simply cannot in conscience support this legislation, even though I really like my position as peer mentor here at Fairmont. My community-organizer friends at *Street Beat* have invited me to a protest at City Hall tomorrow. Would you like to come with me? We're meeting at 11:00 on the front steps."

Lynn looked uncomfortable as she replied, "I agree with your position, but as a single mom of two children I can't risk losing my job over conscience. I also understand why Bob is supporting this legislation. He is on the board of the Downtown Association, a group of highly influential business leaders whose mission is to promote a healthy downtown core. This legislation is one of its three policy priorities this year. Fairmont Christian Housing Alliance relies heavily on city contracts and the beneficence of city business leaders, so it would not be prudent for Bob to oppose this legislation. There are at least five other service organizations in the same boat. Funding sources sometime limit organizational autonomy."

"I get the funding issue," Jasmine noted, "but what a waste of our time and energy to support a law that doesn't even address homelessness. The Downtown Association released a list of the thirty most prominent panhandlers to support its position, yet only three of them were labeled aggressive. I bet those three are not even homeless. This law will not address the public's discomfort and fear of the homeless. It will simply target the poor and people of color." Lynn agreed, "Yeah, the Downtown Association keeps trying to connect homelessness with deteriorating public safety, but as you and I both know, the homeless have more to fear from crime than anyone else. I think the association members are mostly interested in hiding poverty and homelessness so that their businesses can rake in the tourist dollars."

"I hope you will go to the protest and relay my tacit support to colleagues in service organizations opposing the legislation," said Lynn. "I know Jack Fields from the Interfaith Alliance will be there. He'll understand that while some of us are not there in body, we are there in spirit. I'm just sorry that his energy is being diverted to oppose this bill. His organization is doing such good outreach ministry to the homeless, and advocacy from the churches in his alliance got the new mayor to offer a permanent site for the homeless residents of the tent city."

Tracy joined the conversation, "The churches that have set up shelters and/or food pantries cannot keep up with the need. Poverty and inequality are negatively affecting more and more people." Jasmine retorted, "Instead of addressing the structural issues of low wages, an inadequate number of jobs, and insufficient affordable housing in our city, the council is focusing on individual deviance by intensifying surveillance and policing. In effect, it is blaming the poor for societal failure. In the neighborhood I grew up in, jobs were few and far between, drug sales were rampant, and housing was decrepit and dangerous." Exasperated, Jasmine passionately proclaimed, "I'm going to City Hall tomorrow with a sign that says 'Target poverty, not the poor!'"

At dinner that evening with John, her husband of twenty years, Tracy mentioned the City Hall protest the next day. "Despite my employer's stance for the anti-panhandling legislation and Reverend David's point about individual responsibility, I would like to join Jasmine in protesting a policy that seems to blame the poor." She continued, "I really respect the work the *Street Beat* organizers are doing to publicize structural causes of homelessness, most notably the lack of affordable housing and living wages, but also non-housing issues that affect family flourishing, such as safe neighborhoods and good schools, affordable quality child care, health care, and meaningful ways of citizen participation in setting public policies."

John replied, "The stories you've shared with me of the individuals and families you work with point to some of the structural issues that cause chronic poverty, yet you relate some pretty dysfunctional behavior and complain that many of your clients need to make better choices."

"I agree that people sometimes cause their own problems," Tracy replied, "but our own extended middle-class family and plenty of our friends have enough dysfunction to go around. The difference is that most of us have a safety net to fall back on in times of crisis."

She continued, "Perhaps there is a role for multiple approaches to homelessness. The structural causes of poverty must be addressed, but as Jack of the Interfaith Alliance said at the Forum on Homelessness the other day, many people cannot even access the resources that are already out there. He pictured the resources to help people who are homeless as a large apple tree with many branches, but argued that thousands of people cannot reach the fruit. For example, a single mother with two small children might want to take advantage of scholarships for education and job training, but if she doesn't have a place to live or cannot find affordable quality child care, how is she going to attend school?" John replied, "But that example only confirms that addressing the problem of homelessness requires structural changes to make basic needs accessible in many areas, not just housing."

"Jasmine clearly wants to move to the structural level first," Tracy noted. "Jack, in his outreach ministry, emphasizes how to help homeless people even get to the table. My work has a similar focus, but I think we need to come at it from both ends." Tracy thought about all the times she had heard Jack speak and shared some of his insights: "Jack says that most congregants come to the issue of homelessness as problem-solvers rather than listeners. Furthermore, when they come in contact with people who are homeless, they treat the relationship as a transaction, providing what they think people need. He argues that a relationship of trust needs to be built first. Presence and treating people with dignity, he says, is the most powerful response because of the isolation, separation, and shame that homeless people experience."

John thought about their recent adult Sunday School class on hospitality and the ministry of Jesus. "While we are called to open up God's banquet table to all (that is, address the structural issues so that all have access to the 'apples on the tree'), we are also called to see the divine in each person we meet and treat them accordingly. Through his presence Jesus continually brought healing and acceptance to marginalized people." Tracy nodded, "I try to remember that every time I pass a homeless person on the street and whenever I get frustrated with the behavior of my clients."

Tracy reflected: "I sometimes have trouble with the notion of hospitality, however. I think a lot of people in our Sunday school class have a patron- izing form of hospitality. They talk about hospitality as a responsibility for those who have been blessed by God with abundance. It never occurs to them that hospitality is not practiced only by those with power and privilege. After all, God's blessings are not only about material abundance. They also seem to confine hospitality to charitable exchange rather than reciprocal relationship."

"One thing I have always admired about you is your ability to develop relationships with the people you serve," John replied. "You sure received hospitality the other day when four-year-old Evan gave you a drawing of the playground at the transitional housing unit where he is living, and his mom brought you hand-picked flowers. That relationship has taken time to form, but it has become one of mutual care, concern, and trust. Are we still going to have them over for dinner next week?"

Tracy was too deep in thought to respond to the dinner question. "I just worry that my power as counselor and case manager could lead to a form of patronizing compassion if I'm not organizing *with* the homeless for broader structural change to prevent poverty and homelessness. I often wonder, what is the best way to offer care and hospitality to those in need? Can I be in solidarity with people on the margins when I control distribution of goods and services they are seeking? Is joining Jasmine tomorrow to protest the proposed anti-panhandling legislation the best use of my energy? Can I look Gerald and other homeless people in the eyes each day if I do not act on my conscience?" John smiled, "You've got a lot to think about, honey, but I know that whatever you decide, your heart is in the right place."

Commentary

Tracy is struggling with how best to put compassion and hospitality into practice in relation to the problem of homelessness. She takes seriously the Christian call to love our neighbor no matter who that is, as illustrated by her chosen profession and the deep relationships she has developed with people she serves. She is aware, however, that sometimes our most well-meaning efforts to help people are not what is most liberating for them and that we often settle for responses of charity without seeking to remedy the injustices that caused the need for charity in the first place.

Practical realities sink in, however. She has a secure job, and she does make a difference in the lives of people who become homeless. Can she be in solidarity with the people she works with, however, if she simply focuses on charity? How should she be involved in ending homelessness from a structural perspective? While protesting the anti-panhandling law would be a way to stand in solidarity with the homeless, what constructive change needs to happen to keep people from becoming homeless? Are compassion and hospitality on an individual level without attention to structural realities adequate? It appears Tracy tries to walk in the footsteps of Jesus and treat everyone as a child of God, but she seems to be questioning whether Christian discipleship requires more of her.

Tracy is also troubled by the fact that funding considerations have muted the prophetic voices that her workplace and other organizations could have. Does the potential loss of funding sources to help the homeless justify not standing up against policy that might result in unjust criminalization of some homeless people? And what about her organization's working relationships with other groups that are in solidarity with and advocating for the homeless? Working in coalitions is the only way that larger social change to end homelessness will occur. There is power in numbers. This power can be thwarted, however, by funding sources that use their donations to divide and conquer groups who are advocating for substantial policy changes to promote social and economic justice. How does Tracy follow Jesus as a role model when it comes to politics and social policy?

DEMOGRAPHICS AND CAUSES OF HOMELESSNESS IN THE UNITED STATES

The common denominator among people who are homeless is extreme poverty. Some people are transitionally homeless due to unemployment, divorce, or eviction. Others are episodically homeless; that is, they cycle in and out of homelessness for differing amounts of time. While the majority of people who are homeless are in these two groups, traditionally we associate the face of the homeless with chronic homelessness—people like Gerald who have lived on the streets or in shelters for prolonged periods of time. However, the fastest-growing segment of the homeless population today is children, like four-year-old Evan.

Estimates on the number of people who are homeless depend on how homelessness is being defined. For example, the Department of Housing and Urban Development (HUD) counts only those who are literally homeless (on the street or in homeless shelters), while the Department of Education includes people who are sharing the housing of others due to loss of housing or economic hardship as well as people who are living in such places as hotels, camp grounds, or parking lots. In 2018, the HUD homeless count estimated 553,000 people are homeless in one night, but homeless organizations believe the number is much higher. The problem is most acute in California, where one in five homeless Americans live; New York follows with 15 percent of the nation's homeless population.

The US Conference of Mayors' Hunger and Homelessness Survey estimates that, of the single homeless population, 60 percent are male, but of the homeless families with children, a majority are households headed by a female. The largest increase in homelessness was among unaccompanied children and youth who now make up 6.5 percent of the homeless population. Based on 2018 HUD estimates, the national racial makeup of the homeless population is roughly 40 percent African American, 49 percent European American, 3 percent Native American, and 1 percent Asian American. By ethnicity, 22 percent of the homeless are Hispanic Americans. Clearly, homelessness and racism are linked. A larger percentage of people of color experience poverty, and while overt segregation was ruled illegal with civil rights legislation, neighborhoods and schools continue to be segregated by both race and class, perpetuating inequality and unequal opportunity. Further, studies on racial discrimination have consistently shown unequal treatment in areas such as job hiring, housing, and banking.

According to the Urban Institute, up to one-fourth of the urban homeless are employed. The National Coalition for Homeless Veterans says that veterans make up 11 percent of people who are homeless, down from

20 percent ten years ago. HUD estimates that the number of veterans experiencing homelessness was cut in half between 2010 and 2017, in part due to a supportive housing program that combined HUD rental assistance and Veteran Affairs (VA) case management and clinical services. A study by the National Institute of Mental Health found that 20–25 percent of people experiencing homelessness suffer from mental health issues (compared to 6 percent of all Americans). In addition, studies indicate that at least one-third and perhaps as many as two-thirds of all homeless persons suffer from addiction disorders.

While race, marital status, and health matters play important roles in homelessness, poverty and a severe lack of affordable housing are the central causes. Poverty has increased in the last forty years due to eroding wages and benefits for work as well as declining public assistance, while affordable housing, especially rental housing, has decreased. After World War II there was plenty of affordable rental housing and inexpensive single room occupancy (SRO) housing, but rents increased in the 1970s and 1980s and SROs were demolished in urban-renewal efforts. According to the National Low-Income Housing Coalition, there are now 7.2 million more extremely low-income households than there are affordable housing units. Today, many families are paying considerably more than the 30 percent of their income that is typically considered affordable for housing.

While poverty and lack of affordable housing are the predominant causes of homelessness, the personal factors determine *who* is homeless. Addiction, disability, mental illness, and experiences with foster care, jail/prison, and domestic violence can be contributing causes of homelessness, and oppression based on race, gender, class, sexual preference, or disability plays a factor in who is the most vulnerable in a competitive economy. The presence of a sufficient safety net in society determines whether structural or individual factors will cause homelessness.

A race and gender analysis of both declining wages and weakening public assistance helps explain some of the disparities of homelessness. For example, single mothers with children under the age of six cannot afford child care on low-wage jobs, yet according to the National Alliance to End Homelessness, only one of ten children who is eligible for child-care assistance under federal law gets any help. Studies from the Economic Policy Institute indicate that around 60 percent of minimum-wage workers are female and 40 percent are people of color.

Since the 1980s the *number* of people who are homeless has steadily increased, although the *percentage* of people in the overall population who are homeless has decreased. Although funding for homelessness has been one of the few areas of social-safety-net spending that has increased in recent years (mainly to address chronic homelessness through shelters and housing with services, like the Housing First apartment Gerald received), there has been little funding for low-income rental assistance. According to the Center for Budget and Policy Priorities (CBPP), spending on public housing is minimal and rental assistance to offset the cost of market rate housing is available for only one in four households that qualify for it. Serious economic downturns also increase the ranks of the homeless. During the 2008–10 recession, 2.8 million US properties received foreclosure notices. Twenty percent of the foreclosed properties were rentals. During the Covid-19 global pandemic, millions of Americans suddenly found themselves out of work and unable to pay their rent or mortgages. Low-income families and minority communities are hit the hardest during recessions, and many find themselves homeless as a result.

APPROACHES TO HOMELESSNESS

If poverty and lack of affordable housing are the predominant causes of homelessness, it would make sense for public policy and institutions to focus on addressing the causes of poverty and providing more low-income rental housing. However, approaches to homelessness have generally been punitive for those who are considered the "undeserving homeless" and charity-based for those who are seen as the "deserving homeless." Like many cities nationwide, the City Council in this case has focused its efforts on anti-panhandling laws that give police more authority to "clean up" the city—especially the downtown—by removing "undesirables." While many people like Jasmine and Tracy, who work in Christian organizations, might see the need for approaches focused more on justice than charity, long-term organizing to address poverty takes time and energy and often has no quick tangible gains to show for the work. Further, constructing low-income housing takes substantial capital. The efforts by nonprofits to build low-income housing are laudable but remain small compared to the substantial need.

Punitive approaches are based on prevailing social myths including the claim that all homeless people are unreliable, incompetent, and/or mentally unstable and the belief that they are homeless primarily because of a personal fault or characteristic (laziness, addiction, lack of education, disability). Many even believe that people are homeless because they choose to be. These views lead some to think that the only way to stop people from being lazy and overly dependent on charity is to punish such behavior. Many cities have adopted anti-panhandling laws. Other cities have enacted "quality-of-life" ordinances under which police can arrest people for sleeping or sitting on sidewalks. Some argue that such criminalization of the homeless has led to an increasing number of attacks on the homeless, primarily by young men. Many believe, as drug and alcohol counselor Kurt Trimmer points out, that recycling people through jails will not remedy the issue of homelessness but rather exacerbate it because it does not address the root cause of addiction.

Charitable approaches might or might not blame the homeless for their plight. Some people who offer direct charity realize that structural conditions in our economy are a major cause of homelessness. Others offer charity along with self-help assistance based on the assumption that homeless people need to be reformed in some way. That is, they believe the homeless need to gain a work ethic, a more virtuous character, middle-class values, or more job and life skills. Often the homeless who agree to the procedures of reform and assimilation are deemed "deserving" and offered charitable aid (housing assistance, welfare, shelter), but they remain subject to a whole array of social workers, rules, and regulations in their lives.

Some Christian programs of reform claim that the primary problem the homeless face is spiritual, not economic. Thus, their solution is for the homeless to accept Jesus into their lives. Chaplain David Smith voices this perspective when he claims the homeless cannot "kick an addiction by themselves" but can only do so through God's grace and through better discipline. His assumption is that most homeless people have addictions and that the solution to homelessness lies in changing the individual (the spiritual self), not in economic policies and structures.

Since the 1930s there has been an emphasis in the United States on promoting home ownership. Home owners are envisioned as everything the homeless are not—secure, autonomous, industrious, and virtuous (that is, they have middle-class values). Through tax deductions and credits (such as home mortgage deduction, deduction for property taxes, capital gains exclusion for home sales, and exclusion of net imputed rental income), state and federal tax systems have financially supported home ownership over rental assistance. While not technically budget expenditures and thus not considered part of the housing budget allotted to HUD, the amount of money not collected from home and rental property owners far exceeds any amount of money spent on low-income housing assistance. According to the CBPP, 60 percent of federal housing spending goes to households with incomes over $100,000. While many renters do not get needed assistance, those with the means can use the home mortgage-interest deduction to reduce the cost of owning two homes.

Ending poverty and homelessness is a goal shared by Christians from different theological backgrounds and denominations. Some congregations have worked to find ways to make their communities open and welcoming to people of all stations in life. Others have organized to respond to the needs of people who are marginalized in their local communities and cities through creation of programs and through advocacy for particular city and county policies. Still others are actively advocating for anti-poverty policies at state and national levels.

COMPASSION, HOSPITALITY, AND JUSTICE

While there is no perfect response to poverty and homelessness, any adequate response should include both compassion and justice. While structural changes are necessary to address the root causes of homelessness, advocacy efforts ought to be grounded in a deep level of compassion for *all* our neighbors. Church communities can and should offer a strong moral voice and commitment to the movement for a just and compassionate world; just as important, individual Christians and Christian communities must *practice* hospitality, compassion, and justice.

We often stop short of fulfilling these values out of fear. For example, we cite liability concerns to avoid letting homeless people sleep on church grounds or issues of safety and security to ban low-income housing in our neighborhoods. In the case, fear of losing funding becomes the obstacle for the Fairmont Alliance. Often the real obstacle, however, is a stereotype that turns our neighbors into "others" who are dangerous. Many Christians volunteer at soup kitchens and shelters, or help build homes, or assist people they know who are struggling financially, but often we continue to hold stereotypes of the homeless unless we get to know them.

Tracy appears to do a good job of relating to the homeless without stereotyping them. Working shoulder to shoulder with people who are homeless might have aided her in doing so. Many parishioners in churches have contact with people who are homeless only at a distance or for short periods, and often their main experience is of street people who are chronically homeless. They might have known people who are episodically homeless without even realizing it. A handful of churches have challenged the turning of our neighbors into "others" by becoming radically inclusive. These churches have oriented their mission toward supporting the homeless and have developed outreach and worship that appeal to people in all walks of life. They believe compassion requires solidarity, that is, a "walking with" others, not simply "doing for" others.

Getting to know the homeless and making their lives central to ethical analysis of social policy gives insight into what obstacles prevent flourishing lives. How would Christian approaches change if we quit seeing the homeless as having the problems? How would such approaches look if we saw the gospel as less about an individual relationship with Jesus Christ and more about the physical, spiritual, and mental health of people within God's community? Assuming that the spiritual crisis only pertains to individuals without addressing the ways our society is spiritually impoverished blames the victims of such a society.

Christian communities must ask what it means to take seriously a call to be disciples of Jesus Christ in the world. Compassionate responses of hospitality and charity, resistance to injustice and exploitation, and advocacy for systems and institutions that support justice and well-being are equally important. The way of Jesus suggests a bottom-up approach that moves from caring for each person in our life to making a flourishing home for all in God's community.

Thus, hospitality must be connected to justice. Hospitality as justice was a foundation of all morality in biblical times. Having been freed by God from slavery, the people of Israel understood that a covenant with God included caring for all within their midst by sharing their bread with the hungry and bringing the homeless poor into their houses (Is 58:7). Jesus also modeled hospitality as justice. At the Last Supper, and throughout his ministry, Jesus opened the banquet for all to be seated at the table in relationship with God and one another. Jesus envisioned abundant life for all, a life in which humans are not only physically housed but are truly at home within caring, inclusive, and sustainable communities. Paul sought to make such a vision of *koinonia* community a reality in the early church. Translations for *koinonia* include "fellowship," "contribution," "sharing," and "participation." The early church aimed to embody these values by caring for all its members, distributing goods according to need, and worshiping and praying together (Acts 2:42–47). Each member of the community participated fully in the fellowship and worship of the community because hospitality as justice was practiced with God's gifts shared sustainably by all.

The problem of homelessness is not about people who find themselves without a place to sleep; it is a reflection of our collective identity as a people and a society. Do we want to be a society that puts people in jail because they do not have a home, or do we want to be a society that claims homelessness simply is not an option? Our high value in the United States on individualism and each person being responsible for himself or herself can hinder our ability to envision alternatives to what seems inevitable. Many Americans have been socialized to accept a dominant cultural worldview that promotes individual initiative, enterprise, and achieving the "American Dream," but a society founded on such a competitive worldview privileges the winners and marginalizes the losers. The early church did not assume there must be losers, nor did it believe homelessness is inevitable.

Jesus challenged those who tried to limit the seats at the banquet table and who were only willing to share crumbs rather than abundant loaves.

Hospitality as charity does not afford recipients full human dignity in ways that enable them to participate fully in community and fellowship. The bountiful goods at the banquet table are not earned but are gifts from God, meant to be sustainably shared by all (Lev 25:18–19, 23–24). God's creation is interdependent, with each one an intricate part contributing to the whole. Love of neighbor entails both being a neighbor to others and allowing others to be neighbors to us. As the story of the starving widow who serves Elijah (1 Kgs 17—18) attests, those who are poor and outcast can be just as hospitable as those who are rich and powerful.

While there is no single blueprint, there are basic levels of human and environmental flourishing for which we should aim. For one, all people in a society ought to have decent housing, access to adequate health care and a good education, and, if they are able, work that allows them to live healthy lives and contribute to a healthy society. For people who are not able to contribute through work, we ought to find other ways that they can contribute to society and have services and safety nets so they can live well. Basic goods are not all that is necessary for people to flourish, however. Meaningful avenues for participation for all individuals in communities and the broader society are also important. If we are all to participate in society and relate to one another as neighbors, then there also needs to be a rearrangement of wealth and power. While protesting anti-panhandling legislation is important, more deep-seated change is necessary. Substantial inequality as we have in our society today blocks solidarity among people and thwarts just and compassionate communities. Charitable paternalism that sustains the status quo supplants solidarity and justice.

Practicing hospitality as justice entails building a social movement to end homelessness and poverty. Such an agenda is not simply a liberal enterprise; conservative and evangelical Christians are also concerned about ending homelessness and poverty. Top priority in such a movement would be advocacy for more affordable rental housing (not simply home ownership) and jobs with livable wages and benefits. Relying on nonprofits and churches to build and maintain affordable housing will not be enough. Being in solidarity with the homeless and working poor means advocating both local and federal government to ensure the number of decent low-income rental housing units meets the need. Government intervention is needed to promote zoning for rental housing, require developers to include a certain percentage of low-income rental housing in their developments, and hold landlords accountable to fair rental practices and safety standards. The ways to eradicate homelessness are well documented, but the political will waxes and wanes (usually the latter) without a sustained movement to promote change.

Both Tracy and Jasmine are beginning to see that Christian disciple-ship requires more than charitable hospitality. They are clear that being disciples of Jesus Christ includes care and compassion for those who are marginalized in society, but they are still figuring out how to practice and organize for hospitality as justice so that all may have a home not only in God's community but in our all-too-human communities as well. While organizing against poverty and for more affordable rental housing is clearly an important long-term goal, Tracy must decide how to respond in the short term to legislation that serves to punish rather than empower the homeless. She has to keep in mind, however, her institutional role and how she can continue to work directly with people who experience homelessness. Such work requires funding. Thus, pragmatic as well as prophetic concerns are on Tracy's mind.

ADDITIONAL RESOURCES

Abramsky, Sasha. *The American Way of Poverty: How the Other Half Still Lives*. Brooklyn: Nation Books, 2014.

Bouma-Prediger, Steven, and Brian J. Walsh. *Beyond Homelessness: Christian Faith in a Culture of Displacement*. Grand Rapids, MI: Eerdmans, 2008.

Corbett, Steve, and Brian Fikkert, John Perkins, and David Platt. *When Helping Hurts: How to Alleviate Poverty Without Hurting the Poor and Yourself*. Chicago: Moody Publishers, 2014.

Desmond, Matthew. *Evicted: Poverty and Profit in the American City*. New York: Broadway Books, 2017.

Greenfield, Susan Celia, ed. *Sacred Shelter: 13 Journeys of Homelessness and Healing*. New York: Empire State Editions, 2018.

Keenan, James F., and Mark McGreevy, eds. *Street Homelessness and Catholic Theological Ethics*. Maryknoll, NY: Orbis Books, 2019.

Kusmer, Kenneth L. *Down and Out, On the Road: The Homeless in American History*. New York: Oxford University Press, 2002.

Parsell, Cameron. *The Homeless Person in Contemporary Society*. New York: Routledge, 2018.

Rennebohm, Craig, and David Paul. *Souls in the Hands of a Tender God: Stories of the Search for Home and Healing on the Streets*. Boston: Beacon Press, 2008.

Russell, Letty M. *Just Hospitality: God's Welcome in a World of Difference*. Edited by Shannon J. Clarkson and Kate M. Ott. Louisville: Westminster John Knox, 2009.

Ruthruff, Ron. *The Least of These: Lessons Learned from Kids on the Street.* Birmingham: New Hope Publishers, 2010.

Stivers, Laura. *Disrupting Homelessness: Alternative Christian Approaches.* Minneapolis: Fortress Press, 2011.

Related Videos

Homeless: The Motel Kids of Orange County. By Alexandra Pelosi. 60 minutes. TV Movie. 2010.

The Hidden Face of Homelessness. 60 minutes. Cozzi Video Productions. 2009.

Under the Bridge: The Criminalization of Homelessness. 74 minutes. By Don Sawyer. 2017

Without a Home. By Rachel Fleischer. 74 minutes. Breaking Glass Pictures. 2011.

Related Websites

National Alliance to End Homelessness
    http://www.endhomelessness.org
National Coalition for the Homeless
    http://www.nationalhomeless.org
National Law Center on Homelessness and Poverty
    https://www.nlchp.org/
Shelter Force: The Journal of Affordable Housing and Community
    http://www.shelterforce.org/

Case

Detain and Deport

Alamosa County Sheriff Frank Styles was feeling very uncomfortable after his phone conversation with an agent at the US Immigration and Customs Enforcement (ICE) field office in Denver. The ICE agent wanted to detain Javier García Lopez, an undocumented eighteen-year-old who had been living in Alamosa for the past eight years. Lopez had recently been arrested and booked into the county jail. The ICE agent had requested that Sheriff Styles detain Lopez for forty-eight hours beyond when he was supposed to be released so that one of the Denver field agents could drive to Alamosa to take Lopez into custody for deportation proceedings. His last words to Styles were, "Let us know when you're going to release him."

While the call had not really surprised Frank, he had hoped to avoid having to make a decision like this. He knew it was really only a matter of time before he would get such a call from ICE since half of Alamosa's fifteen thousand residents are Hispanic, and some are undocumented. Perhaps if Javier were a hardened criminal Sheriff Styles wouldn't feel so conflicted, but he was simply a troubled teenager who got suspended for getting into a fight at school. He was arrested when he tried to pick more fights and enter his high school before his suspension was over. After thirty-four years as a law enforcement officer in a rural community with few resources, Frank didn't think one of his priorities was to help ICE deport a teenager who had done something stupid. Based on conversations with his wife, Frank was well aware of the obstacles youth like Javier face when they come to the United States.

Unlike most of his rural law-enforcement counterparts, Sheriff Styles was a Democrat with Libertarian views on issues like recreational marijuana and same-sex marriage. His progressive views didn't extend to immigration and border security, however. Frank had seen the ravages of heroin in his community and therefore supported building a wall along the United States–

This case and commentary were prepared by Laura A. Stivers. The names of persons and institutions have been disguised, where appropriate, to protect the privacy of those involved.

Mexico border to stop drugs and criminals, especially Mara Salvatrucha (MS-13) gang members, from entering the United States. Nevertheless, Frank was bothered by ICE's request. Police officers fingerprint people who are booked into the local jail, and they usually send the fingerprint records to the FBI to check criminal history and arrest warrants. It had never really concerned Frank that ICE can access this information in both FBI and US Department of Homeland Security (DHS) databases to check immigration status and enforce immigration laws. However, fulfilling an ICE request to detain undocumented immigrants for up to two extra days, regardless of whether they had been convicted of a crime, felt like a much bigger deal to Frank.

The majority of police officers Frank managed also leaned to the Right when it came to immigration issues. His good friend and former partner, John Kearny, had just said to Frank that morning: "I can't believe the Mayor of Oakland alerted undocumented immigrants that there was going to be an ICE raid in her city. How can local law enforcement in those California cities protect illegal immigrants from deportation? The sanctuary city movement is bullshit! It is against the law to enter the United States illegally. These people should immigrate through legal channels; if not, they should be prosecuted and deported."

Frank had replied, "I agree with you that people shouldn't come into the US illegally, but I worry that it is unconstitutional to honor ICE requests for detention without a warrant. Recently the legal counsel for the County Sheriffs of Colorado advised sheriffs to avoid legal trouble by not honoring ICE detainers.[1] The Fourth Amendment prohibits holding people behind bars without a warrant signed by a judge."

"The ICE detainers might be unconstitutional," John noted, "but at least ICE is trying to protect American jobs and our national identity."

Two nights prior, Frank had been talking with his wife, Sheri, about the difficulties they each face at work. He shared his concern that he would get caught in the crosshairs of ICE's priority to deport undocumented immigrants and the White House's pressure on local law enforcement to cooperate with ICE. Sheri talked about her struggles to meet the needs of young children of poor families in her role as family advocate for the Alamosa Redevelopment Agency's Early Learning Program for children from disadvantaged families. She knew many of the families well, often visiting them in their homes to assess their needs and support their children.

---

[1] An ICE detainer—or immigration hold—is one of the key tools ICE uses to apprehend individuals who come in contact with local and state law-enforcement agencies and put them into the federal deportation system.

While he was not always on the same page with his wife when it came to immigration issues, Frank had learned a lot from Sheri's work in the community and appreciated her insights. She had even convinced him a year earlier to team up with Oswaldo Luna, a local Indigenous Mayan from Guatemala, to offer free driving lessons for local Spanish speakers. Since then, Luna had occasionally served as a translator of the Q'anjob'al language for inmates in the jail.

Over dinner Frank commented, "I feel that as sheriff I've done a lot to build up trust with Alamosa's Hispanic community. Federal immigration enforcement enlisting local police officers and county sheriffs in its war against unauthorized immigration could destroy that trust. I'm all for a border wall, and I'm not even opposed to deporting undocumented immigrants who have committed crimes, but enlisting local law enforcement to question people about their immigration status and asking sheriffs to detain people beyond when they should be released could mean that Hispanic community members will stop coming to the police for anything. As a result, we'll lose their cooperation on cases. Merging local law enforcement with federal immigration enforcement will have a chilling effect on crime reporting in immigrant communities, which will lead to increased crime and less safe neighborhoods."

Sheri replied, "We are in difficult times. Many of the families I visit are worried that family members could be deported. In addition, the increasingly negative rhetoric about Central American and Mexican immigrants has led to increased harassment of the most disadvantaged residents of Alamosa. I keep hearing people say that immigrants are taking American jobs, but I don't see any white people lining up to harvest vegetables in the fields or process meat at the slaughterhouses. The wages are way too low, and the work is much too dangerous."

"We do need secure borders, but we don't need all this xenophobia," Frank responded, after sawing off a good chunk of his pork chop. "I like that we have a mixed-race parish at St. Mary's and that our priest is even from Africa. Alamosa is an ethnically diverse town, and we all need to work together to make it a good place for everyone to live."

Sheri replied, "I wish you'd come with me to the Social Justice Committee meetings at church. Just last week Father Samuel quoted Pope Francis that we need to protect and defend the fundamental rights and dignity of immigrants, and that our catechism makes it very clear that we need to support the intrinsic dignity of all human beings."

Frank countered, "I certainly don't condone racism, and I agree that we should support everyone's intrinsic dignity, but that doesn't mean we have to open our borders to all immigrants who want to come to the United States for a better life, does it?"

Thinking back to these conversations, Frank wondered what his next step should be in response to the ICE detention request. Javier had looked so scared behind the glass jail wall last night. Javier's father, Miguel, had come to the station for a brief time when Javier was first arrested, but he had no immediate resources to post bail and he needed to return to his job at the meat-processing plant. Looking at Deputy Eugenia Sanchez's report on Javier's arrest, it appeared that Javier had been arrested for failing to follow the rules of his school suspension by going back on school property and getting into a fight. It was likely, however, that Javier would be released on his own recognizance and with a promise to appear for his court hearing. Frank decided it would be useful to talk to Deputy Sanchez for more context on Javier's situation.

Eugenia recounted what the high school guidance counselor had told her: "Javier is in his senior year and has been getting into trouble lately. He lives with his dad and other relatives in a two-bedroom apartment. He hasn't seen his mom and sister since he and his dad left El Salvador eight years ago. His father had no longer been able to make a living at his small corner store in El Salvador due to extortion by the gangs. They were threatening to harm Miguel's family if he didn't pay them more. Javier's parents were also terrified that Javier would get recruited by gang members. Javier's mom was too scared to make the trip to the United States with his young sister, so Miguel and Javier undertook the long and dangerous journey north. They crossed the border illegally in Texas with the aid of a 'coyote' guide who charged them a lot of money to help them get into the United States."

Eugenia continued, "After all that, Javier's parents divorced three years ago and since then his mom has remarried. This year Javier's sister has been sharing with him stories of their stepdad's abuse of their mom. Now that his sister is older, Javier has been trying to get his mom to leave her abusive spouse and travel to the United States for asylum. Javier gets very little parental support at his home in Alamosa with everyone in his household working long hours in the fields or the meat-processing plant."

Frank responded, "Do you think that the stress of his family situation is the cause of his negative behavior in school?"

Eugenia paused for a second and then replied, "That's probably one of many stresses he is dealing with. The guidance counselor says he is a smart kid but that he is being pressured by his dad and uncle to work more hours with them at the meat-processing plant. The counselor thinks Javier is most likely helping to support his mom and sisters with the money he makes. The counselor also said that there is tension at the high school between some of the white kids and the Hispanic kids. Those who speak English with an accent routinely get bullied."

Frank said, "It sure would be good if a talented young person like Javier had more opportunities beyond the back-breaking low-wage work his family is doing. I know the immigrants who work at the plant only make around $20,000 a year and the seasonal farm hands make even less. I wonder what danger Javier would be in if he got deported back to El Salvador. It's too bad he doesn't have DACA status like some of the other immigrant kids in town."[2]

"It seems crazy to focus on deporting hard-working people who are doing some of the most tedious and unsafe work in our economy," Eugenia said.

Frank had to agree. The Alamosa economy depended on all of the residents of the Hispanic community—both documented and undocumented. Frank knew that many sheriff's offices were cooperating and even partnering with ICE, while others located in sanctuary cities were not allowed to honor ICE detainers. He wondered how Alamosa's immigrant community would interpret any action on his part to detain undocumented immigrants in jail long enough for ICE to pick them up. Would such an action violate the Fourth Amendment of the Constitution? Some sheriffs had refused to comply with ICE detainers without a judicially approved hold or warrant. Frank clearly didn't have such a warrant for Javier. Frank needed to call the Denver ICE agent back the next day. He wished he hadn't been put in such a difficult situation. It wasn't clear what he should do or what the ramifications of his decision might be for others and for his own career.

---

[2] On June 15, 2012, then-Secretary of Homeland Security Janet Napolitano issued a memorandum entitled "Exercising Prosecutorial Discretion with Respect to Individuals Who Came to the United States as Children," creating a non-Congressionally authorized administrative program that permitted certain individuals who came to the United States as juveniles and meet several criteria—including lacking any current lawful immigration status—to request consideration of deferred action for a period of two years, subject to renewal, and eligibility for work authorization. This program became known as Deferred Action for Childhood Arrivals (DACA).

Commentary

Immigration is not a new phenomenon in the United States, nor is it currently a hot-button issue only in the United States. It is useful to view this case in relation to the larger global context of colonization, neocolonialism, and migration. In addition, an understanding of the history of US immigration and US involvement in Central America and Mexico is important when framing how Sheriff Styles might respond in this case.

IMMIGRATION IN THE UNITED STATES

There has always been a tension in the United States between economic concerns and expressions of nativism in relation to immigration. Economically, immigrants have helped to meet the labor needs in the United States, as is clearly the case in Alamosa, where immigrants work in the fields, in the meat-processing plant, and at other low-wage jobs. Nativism—stronger at some times than others—is a fear or scapegoating of particular immigrants who are seen as a threat, whether to national identity or to employment of citizens, as John voices to Sheriff Styles.

For years immigrants were allowed to enter the United States without a visa, but several times in our history nativism has led to immigration restrictions. In the 1840s, when labor needs were high due to the Gold Rush and economic development of agriculture, mining, and railroads in California, laborers were recruited from China. Racial discrimination was prevalent, however, and culminated in the Chinese Exclusion Act of 1882, which denied most Chinese in the country a path to citizenship and barred further immigration from China. Another episode of nativism, this time against Catholic immigrants from Ireland and Italy, was the impetus for the Immigration Acts of 1921 and 1924 that instituted a quota system limiting immigrants from certain countries.

When Chinese immigration was forestalled, Mexican workers began to fill the labor void, especially during World War I. In addition to the "pull factor" of the United States needing more workers, there were some "push factors" occurring in Mexico. Economic decisions made by President Porfirio Díaz from 1876 to 1910 created a large landless population, and the Mexican Revolution from 1910 to 1917 led many to flee for safety. The economic pull declined during the Great Depression; as a result, restrictions were implemented and deportations were increased. During World War II, labor was short again and the United States instituted the *bracero* agreement, offering visas to Mexicans for temporary contract work, especially in agriculture.

During the McCarthy era in the 1950s, nativism reared its head again and Operation Wetback was put into effect to apprehend anyone in the country illegally. Similarly, in 1986, concerns over growing Hispanic migration led to the Immigration Reform and Control Act, which fortified the Border Patrol, developed stiffer sanctions for employers hiring undocumented workers, and provided amnesty to those who could prove they had been in the United States since 1982. Following in this vein, the Illegal Immigration Reform Act and the Immigrant Responsibility Act of 1996 increased border surveillance, cut federal benefits to undocumented immigrants, and gave states leeway to reduce public services to immigrants.

After the attacks of September 11, 2001, the Department of Immigration and Naturalization (INS) was folded into the Department of Homeland Security, with INS activities and the US Border Patrol housed in the newly created Immigration and Customs Enforcement Agency (ICE). This move made control of terrorism and drug traffic central to immigration debates and continues to have a large influence on immigration policy and sentiment today. The views of Sheriff Styles on immigration reflect these structural changes.

ICE detainers have been used under presidents Bush, Obama, and Trump. In April 2018 US Attorney General Jeff Sessions announced that all prosecutors on the southwest border of the United States are "to have a zero-tolerance policy toward immigration." The goal was to prosecute all individuals who cross the border illegally. Enforcement of this policy led to twenty-three-hundred children being separated from their families. President Trump signed an executive order by mid-June to stop the separations of children from their families.

Sheriff Styles might defend a border wall and support stiffer immigration laws, but he seems hesitant to cooperate with ICE agents when it comes to handing over a high school boy who might simply be struggling under hardship. He also explains to John that the County Sheriffs of Colorado organization had advised sheriffs not to comply with ICE detainers because they are unconstitutional—they contradict the Fourth Amendment that prohibits holding people behind bars without a warrant signed by a judge. Sheriff Styles might also have cause to be wary because organizations like the National Immigration Forum have documented that detainers are misunderstood and misused by both ICE and state and local law-enforcement agencies, opening up room for lawsuits.

HISTORY OF UNITED STATES INVOLVEMENT
IN MEXICO AND CENTRAL AMERICA

Alamosa was part of Mexico before 1848, when the Treaty of Guada-lupe-Hidalgo was signed, ending the Mexican-American War and ceding a large chunk of land to the United States, including all of California, Nevada, and Utah, and parts of Arizona, New Mexico, Colorado, and Wyoming. Thus, Hispanic residents of Alamosa could have roots that go back generations. That being said, there has been regular migration from Mexico and Central America, in part due to US involvement and policies related to these countries.

In the late 1800s, the American corporation United Fruit Company was created to produce and transport tropical fruit (primarily bananas) to the United States. It controlled vast areas and transportation networks in Central America, and by the 1930s it owned 3.5 million acres in Central America and the Caribbean. In the early 1900s, President Theodore Roos-evelt instituted "gun boat diplomacy," which meant that US multinational corporations could expect the US military to protect their interests. Under his leadership, the United States played a large role in the development of the Panama Canal, a boon to US corporations. This military backing gave the United Fruit Company control over the governments of these small countries and immense power to set prices, taxes, and employee pay. Countries like Guatemala, Honduras, and Costa Rica became known as "banana republics." Land ownership in the hands of a few, and subsequent poverty and inequality, was the result of both US dominance and previous Spanish colonization.

Javier and his family are feeling the repercussions of years of political and economic instability in the region. In El Salvador the landed elite grew coffee, not bananas, with an oligarchy of fourteen families controlling most of the land and wealth. By 1979, chronic oppression led to a devastating thirteen-year civil war in El Salvador between the military-led government and guerrilla groups. According to the National Organization Committee in Solidarity with the People of El Salvador, death squads and massacres were in part financed by over $6 million of direct military assistance from the United States to El Salvador's government. While Peace Accords were signed in 1992, those responsible for war crimes were given amnesty and never held accountable.

Currently El Salvador has one of the highest murder rates of any country not at war. According to the World Bank, killings peaked at 104 per 100,000 residents in 2015. The violence is largely a result of two warring criminal gangs, MS-13 and Barrio 18. The MS-13 gang actually started in Los Angeles in the 1980s when people fled the civil war in El Salvador. Many gang members were deported back to the wartorn country in the 1990s, where there was little infrastructure and support for reintegration into the country. These young people turned to violence and extortion, with poor people as their targets. Javier's dad had been paying gang extortion fees in El Salvador to keep his corner store open, and he was only too aware that children as young as eight were being recruited into gangs.

In addition to civil unrest, Mexico and Central American countries face what some call economic neocolonialism in the form of structural adjustment programs (SAPs) that were instituted in the 1980s. From the 1950s onward, developing countries got low-interest loans from the World Bank for development projects based on the central premise of "modernization theory." The idea was that traditional societies could develop into modern states and reduce poverty through investment in industrialization. Poorer countries like those in Central America, however, did not have a trade advantage and found it hard to compete with the more developed and richer countries. When inflation rose in the late 1970s, the interest payments on variable-rate loans ballooned. By 1982, the Mexican government said it could no longer afford the interest rates and would have to default on its loans.

The International Monetary Fund, an international organization created to promote global economic growth and financial stability, knew that the global banking system would be in trouble if all developing countries defaulted on their loans, so they created "structural adjustment loans" to help countries continue to pay interest on their original loans. To receive structural adjustment loans, however, countries had to restructure their economies, which included privatizing state-owned enterprises, lowering wages, cutting public services and food subsidies, liberalizing trade and investment, and devaluing their currency. SAPs, while keeping countries from defaulting on their loans, have put them even more in debt, increased poverty and inequality, opened up pathways for multinational corporations to extract even more resources, and pushed many subsistence farmers off the land. While structural adjustment helped these countries pay off interest on their loans, poor families like Javier's suffered with lower wages, fewer public services, and loss of food subsidies. SAPs are a tool for increased economic globalization where capital and investment can cross borders at will but people cannot.

Free-trade agreements, another tool for economic globalization, have also had some particularly devastating effects on small farmers. In Mexico, for example, small subsistence farmers for centuries cultivated maize and sold part of their crop on the local market. The neoliberal economic philosophy undergirding economic globalization views small subsistence farmers as unprofitable. SAPs encourage and give subsidies to larger export-oriented agriculture, aiming to push small farmers into the cities. Free-trade agreements, like the North American Free Trade Agreement (NAFTA)[3] and the Central American Free Trade Agreement (CAFTA) have supported trade liberalization. In the case of Mexico, this meant eliminating tariffs on US corn entering the Mexican market. This benefited large agribusiness, while around two million small farmers were pushed off their land, according to the Food and Environment Reporting Network. Sustainable maize farmers simply could not compete with cheap US-subsidized corn. Now nearly half of Mexico's food is imported, including the corn that is a staple and religious symbol for the indigenous population. A country that was self-sufficient in corn is now dependent on imports. Some refer to these small Mexican farmers who crossed the US border as "refugees of NAFTA." While the increase in migration from Mexico and Central America since 1990 has multiple causes, economic globalization policies supported by the United States are a significant factor, pushing families like Javier's out of their home country in order to flee violence and extreme poverty.

HISPANIC IMMIGRATION

According to the Migration Policy Institute, the Central American immigrant population grew tenfold from 1980 to 2015, representing around 3.4 million in 2015 or 8 percent of all US immigrants. Eighty-five percent of those Central American immigrants are from the Northern Triangle formed by El Salvador, Guatemala, and Honduras. After four decades of rapid immigrant growth, Mexican migration stabilized around 2015, but Mexican immigrants account for over a quarter of the foreign-born population in the United States and constitute the largest immigrant origin group. Javier and his dad migrated from El Salvador because of violence. A 2017 report from Doctors Without Borders states that the Northern Triangle countries are experiencing "unprecedented levels of violence outside a war zone" and that "citizens are murdered with impunity; kidnappings and extortion are daily occurrences. Non-state actors perpetuate insecurity and forcibly recruit individuals into their ranks, and use sexual violence as a tool of intimidation and control." The El Salvadoran police can also be dangerous in their crusade to eliminate gangs.

To reach the United States, Javier and his father needed to traverse the length of Guatemala and then almost two thousand miles in Mexico. Many migrants speed up the trip by riding dangerously on top of a train called *la*

---

[3] In September 2018, the United States–Mexico–Canada Agreement (USMCA) was signed, replacing NAFTA. Overall, the changes to the old NAFTA are mostly cosmetic.

bestia (the beast); many migrants have lost limbs or even died under the wheels of these trains. Migrants are also vulnerable to theft, and women to rape and abuse. Doctors Without Borders found that almost 70 percent of these migrants become victims of violence during their transit. Javier's mom was aware of these dangers and chose to stay in El Salvador with Javier's sister. According to the *New York Times,* the cost to migrants is usually about $10,000–$12,000 per person, with $1,000 of the total smuggling price going to drug cartels for the right to pass. The last part of the journey, which involves crossing the southwest border of the United States after walking over miles of desert and traversing the Rio Grande River in inflatable inner tubes, requires a "coyote" guide. Many don't survive this trip, and many others who do are caught and deported. The current zero-tolerance policy that subjects anyone crossing the border without authorization to possible criminal prosecution means that fewer migrants are successfully entering the United States. Javier and his dad survived the ordeal but have probably been spending years paying back the loans they took to finance their trip.

Mexico has usually been considered a transit country for migrants from Central America, but recently many have made it their home. In 2014, however, Mexico implemented its Southern Border Plan to stem the tide of migrants from Central America. There is a containment zone in the State of Chiapas near the border of Guatemala, and according to *Newsweek,* Mexico has deported, with US support, over 500,000 Central Americans since the plan's inception, more than have been deported from the United States.

The United Nations 1951 Refugee Convention defines *refugee* as any person who, "owing to well-founded fear of being persecuted for reasons of race, religion, nationality, membership of a particular social group or political opinion, is outside the country of his nationality and is unable or, owing to such fear, is unwilling to avail himself of the protection of that country." In 2010, the United National High Commissioner for Refugees (UNHCR) broadened this internationally recognized refugee definition to include any "serious and indiscriminate threats to life, physical integrity or freedom resulting from generalized violence or events seriously disturbing the public order." Under the UNHCR definition, Javier and his family should be able to seek asylum as refugees. The reality, however, is that it is almost impossible for people fleeing violence in Central America to secure refugee status in Mexico or the United States. The United States views them as economic migrants rather than political refugees, and the current administration does not believe that fleeing gang or domestic violence should qualify someone for asylum. Thus, Javier's mom and sister will likely find it difficult to enter the United States legally.

The Trump Administration has described the border as out of control. It has described it as a war zone and even deployed National Guard troops to stop the "hordes" of migrants from crossing. According to the *Washington Post,* however, the reality is that there has been a fourfold increase in Border Patrol agents since the early 1990s. As a result, border towns have lower violent crime rates than the national average, and the slightly more than 300,000 people apprehended for coming into the country illegally in 2017 represent the lowest recorded number since 1971. Another reason the Trump Administration has given for building a border wall is to stem the opioid epidemic and to stop terrorists from entering the country. According to the *Washington Post,* the reality is that prescription opioids are sent through the mail, heroin trafficking has been primarily through official crossings, and the State Department reports that there is no indication that members of terrorist groups have traveled through Mexico to enter the United States.

The increased detentions of immigrants under the zero-tolerance policy have been a financial boon for the private, for-profit prison system, which, according to the Center for American Progress, provided 71 percent of all immigration detention beds in 2018. The two largest private-prison contractors in the United States, GEO Group and CoreCivic, are currently facing allegations that they have forced immigrant detainees to do unpaid labor in their prisons, and the US Commission on Civil Rights has documented that private prisons provide substandard care to those in their custody at a higher rate than public facilities.

DEBATES ON IMMIGRATION IN THE UNITED STATES

In the case, police officer John Kearny voices some of the arguments that are made in support of tougher immigration policies. One is that immigrants are taking jobs from American citizens. Another is that there are legal routes to come to the United States, and so no one should be entering illegally. Another that John did not voice is that immigrants in the country illegally are a drain on public services. A sentiment underlying many of the arguments for tougher immigration policies is the feeling that our American identity is changing. More bluntly, some people fear the "browning of America."

As Sheri points out to her husband, undocumented workers often take the backbreaking and low-paying jobs that native-born workers are not willing to do. Javier's dad, and the other people who live with him in Alamosa, are working in the meat-processing plant and in agriculture. According to the Department of Labor, almost half of the farmworkers in the United States are undocumented immigrants. With the current zero-tolerance border policy in effect, there is an agricultural-labor shortage. Scholars at the Brookings Institute note that immigration is connected to economic growth and innovation. They argue that a decline in immigration levels will be especially problematic as the US population gets older and fertility rates remain low.

There is disagreement among experts over whether the presence of undocumented immigrants in the workforce substantially lowers wages for native workers. The Brookings Institute argues that the decrease is negligible, while others think the downward effect on wages is considerable and that it is the lowest-skilled workers who are negatively affected—often former immigrants and people of color. It might also be useful to view workforce wages in the larger context of economic globalization because the policies that give large corporations more power also make workers more vulnerable. Undocumented workers like Javier's dad are susceptible to exploitation and have no bargaining power in the workplace. Their fear of deportation means that they often suffer bad working conditions, wage theft, and other abuses.

Proponents of stiffer immigration policy argue that those who come to the United States illegally have unfairly jumped ahead of those who are attempting legal entry. They believe that undocumented immigrants should go to the back of the line and respect the rule of law. Kearny thinks people who have entered illegally should be prosecuted and deported. At the extreme end are those who favor mass deportations, although others argue that such actions would result in dramatic surveillance and enforcement measures, most likely leading to racial profiling and overwhelming jail and court systems. Furthermore, mass deportations, many argue, would cripple the US economy. Sheriff Styles is caught in the middle of these conflicting views on how to deal with the undocumented population in the United States. On the one hand, he is supportive of deporting anyone who is a danger to the community. On the other hand, he knows that most undocumented immigrants are working hard and simply trying to provide for their families. How should he view Javier's case?

Some argue that undocumented immigrants from Central America and Mexico are a drain on the US economy because they are supported by our tax dollars for health care, education, law enforcement, and welfare. They claim undocumented workers cannot be turned away from emergency rooms for health care even if they don't have the means to pay; that the children of undocumented immigrants are a financial burden on the school system, especially when the schools meet their language needs; that among undocumented immigrants there are criminals who cost money when they end up in the prison system; and that undocumented immigrants disproportionately need welfare resources.

Others point out that undocumented immigrants are ineligible to receive many benefits, including Social Security, Medicare/Medicaid, food stamps through the Supplemental Nutrition Assistance Program (SNAP), disability insurance through Supplemental Security Income (SSI), children's health insurance (CHIP), and other forms of welfare. Some undocumented immigrants do send their children to public schools, get treated in emergency rooms, and receive aid from the Program for Women, Infants and Children (WIC), but most fear deportation, keep a low profile, and seek few public services. Undocumented immigrants pay more in taxes than they receive in services. A 2010 report by the American Immigration Council showed that undocumented immigrants pay almost $90 billion in taxes but only receive $5 billion in benefits. They pay a wide range of taxes, including sales tax, property tax if they own a home,[4] both state and federal income taxes, as well as Social Security and Medicare taxes, despite the fact that they are denied the ability to claim either of these benefits.[5] According to New American Economy, a coalition of business leaders and mayors that advocates comprehensive immigration reform, undocumented immigrants contributed $16 billion into Social Security funds and $3 billion to Medicare in 2016.

The United States is not only becoming older, it is also becoming more racially diverse. According to the US Census Bureau's annual population reports, in 1900 slightly over 10 percent of people in the United States identified with a race other than white; by the 1990s, 20 percent of the population was nonwhite; and by 2044, over 50 percent of Americans are expected to be a race other than white. For some, this reality of racial diversity challenges their conception of what it means to be an American, leading to nativism. John's comment about protecting American culture illustrates this perspective. Brown and black-skinned Hispanic immigrants are increasingly targets of this nativist sentiment today with calls for "English only" and references to Hispanic "gang animals." Others believe America has always been a nation of immigrants and they celebrate increasing racial and ethnic diversity. While Sheriff Styles seems to embrace the diversity of his town, he is also wary of increased Hispanic immigration. It is important to

---

[4] While many undocumented immigrants cannot afford to buy a home, there is no law against them doing so. They can pay with cash or through an ITIN mortgage. An ITIN is an Individual Tax Identification Number that was created as an alternative to a Social Security number so foreign nationals who own property can pay taxes on it.

[5] Some undocumented immigrants buy fake Social Security cards (often numbers of deceased people). When employers who don't look closely or don't care submit a W-2 form and a tax payment for such workers, the federal government keeps the payroll taxes, even if the Social Security number isn't linked to anyone on file.

analyze how conceptions of American identity can influence perspectives on immigration.

CARE FOR NEIGHBOR AND RESTITUTION

Sheriff Styles and his wife, Sheri, attend a Catholic church. One of their priests, Father Samuel, an immigrant himself, leads the Social Justice Committee. Father Samuel might have been quoting Pope Francis's message "Migrants and Refugees: Men and Women in Search of Peace." In this message Pope Francis seems to be responding to the current anti-immigrant sentiment in many nations: "Those who, for what may be political reasons, foment fear of migrants instead of building peace are sowing violence, racial discrimination and xenophobia, which are matters of great concern for all those concerned for the safety of every human being." The pope addresses some of the reasons for increased migration, such as war, poverty, and environmental destruction, and argues that migration will continue in the future. He very pointedly says that the rhetoric of national security and the high cost of welcoming immigrants demeans human dignity. He offers an alternative view of migrants as people ready to contribute and who bring "courage, skills, energy, and aspirations, as well as the treasures of their own cultures" to their new homes.

The pope calls Christians to engage in solidarity and sharing based on the view that all people belong to one family and thus have the same rights to sustenance and security. He evokes the image of a city with its gates always open to people of every nation, which is found both in Isaiah 60 and Revelation 21. Pope Francis draws on two of the well-known tenets of Catholic social teaching in this message: God's preferential option for the poor and the church's promotion of a common good. He argues that in pursuit of a common good, nations should adopt policies of welcome to asylum seekers, refugees, migrants, and victims of human trafficking. In particular, he says that immigration policies should welcome, protect, promote, and integrate these vulnerable groups of people.

This stance on immigration is commensurate with the pope's views on holiness outlined in his third apostolic exhortation *Gaudete et exsultate* in March 2018. For the pope, the ultimate judge of holiness is how Christians care for one another. Jesus states this view clearly in the Gospel of Matthew:

> For I was hungry and you gave me food, I was thirsty and you gave me something to drink, I was a stranger and you welcomed me, I was naked and you gave me clothing, I was sick and you took care of me, I was in prison and you visited me. . . . Truly I tell you, just as you

did it to one of the least of these who are members of my family, you
did it to me. (Mt 25:35–36, 40)

There is a biblical mandate not only to care for one's neighbor, but
explicitly to care for immigrants. Biblical scholars point out that there are
ninety-two appearances of the Hebrew word for immigrant, *ger,* in the
Bible. For example, in Leviticus 19:34, God says, "The alien [immigrant]
who resides with you shall be to you as the citizen among you; you shall
love the alien as yourself." Throughout scripture God's litmus test for justice revolves around the way society treats vulnerable groups of people—
especially immigrants, widows, and orphans.

Migration is central in the biblical story. Noah, Abraham, Moses, Joseph,
and Mary were all uprooted people of God seeking sanctuary and refuge.
Many migrants seek a "promised land," leaving their homes for any number of reasons. In scripture all sojourners are part of God's divine plan and
ought to be welcomed. Nevertheless, as is true today, there are some host
cultures in these stories that are compassionate and welcoming and others
that are not. What the stories tell us is that migration is a human condition
and that God is with all who are sojourning and/or homeless.

While hospitality and protection of the most vulnerable are clearly
important values to guide Christians, some Christian ethicists argue that
responses to immigration should be reframed to emphasize the values of
justice and restitution in support of structural change. For example, Christian ethicist Miguel De La Torre is critical of extolling the call to hospitality and welcoming the stranger at the expense of addressing structural
oppression and injustice. He argues that considering the colonization of
Mexico and Central America and the neocolonialist financial policies that
benefit the United States at the expense of our neighbors, Christians ought
to be calling for restitution instead. While hospitably welcoming undocumented immigrants is important, an emphasis on the virtue of hospitality,
he argues, can mask the structural injustices that caused people to flee their
home countries and does not challenge the power inequities between those
who are able to offer hospitality and those who are expected to be grateful. De La Torre writes in *The US Immigration Crisis,* "Maybe the ethical
question we should be asking is not 'why' are they coming, but how do
we begin to make reparations for all we have stolen to create the present
economic empire we call the United States?"[6]

Sheriff Styles might find insights from his Catholic religious heritage
helpful, but how is he to apply principles such as solidarity, sharing, care

---

[6] Miguel A. De La Torre, *The US Immigration Crisis: Toward an Ethics of Place*
(Eugene, OR: Cascade Books, 2016), 159.

for neighbor, and human dignity to the situation at hand? Does God's call to protect the vulnerable mean that nations need to open their borders to everyone? Don't nations have the right to promote the security and well-being of their own citizens first? What does a common good look like? And how do restitution and reparations fit into a common good? What are individuals like himself responsible for? Last of all, doesn't the Bible also tell Christians to follow laws and "submit to the governing authorities" (Rom 13:1)? Are Christians really called by God to protect undocumented immigrants who have not followed the law and entered the United States illegally? Sheriff Style's partner, John, doesn't think so.

While Sheriff Styles might ponder the ethical implications of US immigration laws and US economic and social policies in relation to other nations, his immediate dilemma is whether he should cooperate with ICE by letting them know when he plans to release Javier. If Alamosa were a sanctuary city, he would have the backing of city officials not to cooperate with ICE in this way. While sanctuary cities could lose federal funding by taking such stances, the Immigrant Legal Resource Center estimates that from 2017 to 2018, over four hundred counties strengthened their limitations on cooperating with immigration enforcement. Sheriff Styles does not have such support and must consider whether detaining Javier past his release date is ethical in relation to the religious principles that guide him, or even constitutional according to the Fourth Amendment.

ADDITIONAL RESOURCES

Bauman, Stephan, and Jenny Yang. "An Evangelical Perspective on Immigration," *Tikkun* 40, no. 5 (Summer 2013): 49–50.

Carroll R., M. Daniel. *Christians at the Border: Immigration, the Church, and the Bible.* 2nd edition. Ada, MI: Brazos Press, 2013.

Collier, Elizabeth W., and Charles R. Strain. *Global Migration: What's Happening, Why, and a Just Response.* Winona, MN: Anselm Academic, 2017.

De La Torre, Miguel. *Trails of Hope and Terror: Testimonies on Immigration.* Maryknoll, NY: Orbis Books, 2009.

————. *The US Immigration Crisis: Toward an Ethics of Place.* Eugene, OR: Cascade Books, 2016.

Myers, Ched. *Our God Is Undocumented: Biblical Faith and Immigrant Justice.* Maryknoll, NY: Orbis Books, 2012.

O'Donovan, Leo J., SJ. *Blessed Are the Refugees: Beatitudes of Immigrant Children.* Maryknoll, NY: Orbis Books, 2018.

Schaab, Gloria L. "Which of These Was Neighbour? Spiritual Dimensions of the US Immigration Question." *International Journal of Public Theology* 2, no. 2 (2008): 182–202.

Soerens, Matthew, Jenny Yang, and Leith Anderson. *Welcoming the Stranger: Justice, Compassion, and Truth in the Immigration Debate,* Revised edition. Downers Grove, IL: InterVarsity Press, 2018.

Related Videos

Crossing Mexico's Other Border. 23 minutes. Society. 2013.

Gangs of El Salvador. 66 minutes. Vice News Documentary. 2015.

Harvest of Empire. By Eduardo Lopez and Peter Getzels. 90 minutes. Onyx Films. 2012.

Immigrants for Sale. 33 minutes. Brave New Films. 2015.

Trails of Hope and Terror. By Miguel De La Torre. 53 minutes. 2017.

Related Websites

Interfaith Immigration Coalition
http://www.interfaithimmigration.org

PART IV

THE ENVIRONMENT

Case

Oil and the Caribou People

Ron Blanchard had eagerly accepted the invitation from Bill Sanders. As the head of legislative advocacy, Bill had invited Ron to represent their denomination at the clan gathering of the Gwich'in people, which had taken place earlier that summer in northeastern Alaska. Ron's academic special-ization was in ethics and public policy, and he taught at the University of Washington in Seattle. Even though Ron had grown up in the Northwest, he had never been above the Arctic Circle in mid-summer, and he had enjoyed the opportunity to learn more about Gwich'in culture.

Now that the trip was over, he had to produce a report for his denomina-tion's national office for legislative advocacy. Bill Sanders had asked Ron to develop recommendations about what stance the denomination should take about oil drilling in the Arctic National Wildlife Refuge (ANWR), which is on the North Slope of Alaska's Brooks Range and adjacent to land where the Gwich'in had roamed for centuries. Bill indicated that over one hundred organizations had already endorsed Gwich'in opposition to the drilling, including many religious organizations and indigenous groups. Due to recent legislation in Congress, the Gwich'in Steering Committee was interested in gathering even more support, which is why Bill had sent Ron to the clan gathering.

The Gwich'in are Athabascan people with an estimated population ranging from seven thousand to nine thousand. They live primarily in northeastern Alaska and northwestern Canada. Legend and archeological evidence support a long human presence on the lands now inhabited by the Gwich'in. Traditionally, the Gwich'in roamed the boreal forests of the region as hunter-gatherers in bands of six to eight families. They lived a harsh life in an unforgiving land with cool summers and long, frigid winters when starvation was an ever-present danger. Over the last century, however,

---

This case and commentary were prepared originally by Robert L. Stivers and have been updated by Laura A. Stivers and James B. Martin-Schramm. The names of persons and in-stitutions have been disguised, where appropriate, to protect the privacy of those involved.

this rigorous way of life radically changed as the Gwich'in regrouped into larger social units in small villages. The arrival of Episcopalian missionaries, the building of schools, and the acceptance of modern technology, in particular the rifle and snowmobile, hastened these changes.

The Gwich'in opposition to oil exploration and development stems from the threat they perceive it poses to their main source of subsistence, the Porcupine Caribou Herd, and to the culture and spirituality they have developed in relation to the herd. The Porcupine Caribou Herd, with approximately 218,000 animals, is one of the largest and healthiest herds of caribou in the world. It has been growing at a rate of 3–4 percent per year, while other caribou herds around the world are in significant decline.

The herd winters south of the Brooks Range on Gwich'in lands. In spring a great migration takes place. First the females and then the males trek through the passes of the range onto the North Slope, where calving occurs almost immediately, reaching its peak in early June. The Gwich'in refer to the coastal plain as *Iizhik Gwats'an Gwandaii Goodlit* ("the sacred place where life begins").

The herd migrates to the North Slope to take advantage of the rich tundra vegetation in the brief but fertile Arctic summer; to avoid its natural predators, who seldom venture onto the slope; and to gain respite from the hordes of mosquitoes in the winds off the Arctic Ocean. Beginning in late summer the herd makes its way once again south of the range and disperses across Gwich'in lands to endure the winter.

The herd has been the primary source of food for the Gwich'in's subsistence economy. The Gwich'in have harvested animals from the herd in substantial numbers and developed a culture closely bound to the herd and its migration patterns. The herd continues to do well in this habitat. The Gwich'in, in turn, have survived as a people, though not without considerable hardship.

To prepare himself for the trip, Ron had read scientific reports on the potential effects of petroleum development in ANWR and an anthropological study that described the ancient ways of the Gwich'in. It was interesting to compare the health of the Porcupine Caribou Herd with the welfare of the Central Arctic Herd—whose range includes areas affected by the drilling for oil in Prudhoe Bay since 1977. According to the US Fish and Wildlife Service, the Central Arctic Herd now consists of only twenty-two thousand animals and has experienced a 69 percent decline from its peak of seventy thousand animals in 2010. While the herd grew during three decades of oil drilling in the area, scientists are still concerned. The parts of ANWR slated for drilling, the so-called 1002 lands, are among the best feeding grounds for the Porcupine Caribou Herd. If this land is disrupted, will the caribou of the Porcupine Herd seek other, less nutritious feeding grounds more populated with predators? One thing the reports made clear was that reproductive success depends on summer weight increase and avoidance of predators. The scientists urged caution.

From the anthropological study Ron learned about the traditional no-madic way of life of the Gwich'in, their main food sources, and their rela-tion to the caribou. He understood intellectually their concern for the loss of both their primary food source and their traditional culture. He was not prepared, however, for the degree to which their traditional culture already seemed to be in jeopardy.

Throughout his stay during the clan gathering, Gwich'in tribal elders had been eager to recount the old days and their experiences. Barbara Frank, whose age was difficult to judge, but who looked to be in her sev-enties, told about the old days and of summer movements in small family groupings. The warm days added nuts, berries, and fruit to their steady diet of moose and small animals. In winter she remembered a harsh life in crude shelters and a diet of caribou and whatever other animals trapping produced. She expressed in deeply spiritual terms the close relationship of her people to the caribou. Although she spoke with nostalgia, she never once urged that the modern comforts of the village be abandoned for a return to the wilderness.

Another elder, John Christian, remembered the coming of the missionar-ies and the schools they established. He related how his parents and grand-parents were attracted to the village that grew up around the church and school. They were fascinated by the new technologies that added a margin to subsistence in the Arctic and by the amusements that brought variety and diversity. His family was subsequently baptized. They abandoned their given names for Christian names and assumed the superiority of the new and the inferiority of the old.

Alongside these private conversations were daily public gatherings with starting times that baffled Ron. It was confusing to have no schedule, no appointed time to begin. Things just happened. The sessions began when the spirit moved and ended when there were no more speakers. There was no set agenda. An elder kept order and transferred to each speaker the large decorative staff that conferred the right to address the assembly.

The general topic for the first public gathering was oil exploration in ANWR. Moses Peters, an important tribal elder, spoke in English and presented his assessment of the situation. He reviewed existing production procedures at Prudhoe Bay and the shipment of oil through the Trans-Alaska Pipeline. He claimed that operations at Prudhoe Bay had adversely affected the smaller Central Arctic Caribou Herd that summered in the vicinity. The herd, he asserted, was reluctant to cross the pipeline and did not graze in the vicinity of the wells.

Moses went on to say that the oil companies expect their next big find will be in ANWR. He feared that the one hundred miles of pipeline, four hundred miles of roads, the gravel pits, the production facilities, and the air strips would seriously disturb the migration routes of the Porcupine Herd at a crucial time in its annual cycle. "Caribou survival," he insisted, "depends on being born in the right place at the right time, and all of the caribou depend upon these summer months on the North Slope to rest and eat. It is this period of predator-free resting and feeding that prepares the caribou to reproduce and to survive the winter. I know the oil companies have improved their drilling techniques, but I am still worried."

Moses handed the staff to his daughter, Mary, who was brief and blunt: "Oil waste and the burn-off of natural gas will contaminate the tundra. The caribou will not be able to eat. If that happens, we won't eat either."

Mary returned the staff to her father, who concluded by saying that they needed to press urgently for the permanent protection of ANWR. "The recent [2017] decision by Congress to open up ANWR for oil production is a catastrophe. We have to find a way to stop it. The oil companies are eager to develop new supplies because the global demand for oil keeps rising and gas-hungry Americans consume more and more every year. We must get permanent protection now, by any means necessary! The Porcupine Caribou Herd is our main source of life, our very survival. We can't live without the caribou. All our traditional skills, our whole way of life, will be lost if there are no caribou."

Ron had been impressed by the sincerity of these appeals and the efforts of the Gwich'in to secure reliable scientific evidence and political support. Their views differed markedly, however, from those who supported oil production in ANWR. Ron had learned about these views in a conversation with Glen Stone, a friend who worked as an engineer at Northern Oil. They had discussed the issues prior to Ron's departure for Alaska. Glen had talked about his own involvement on the North Slope at Prudhoe Bay. He painted a rosy picture of the benefits of oil production to all Alaskans. "Oil money," he said, "builds schools, roads, and other public works projects. It keeps personal taxes low and enables the government to pay each resident a yearly dividend. The Native Americans benefit, too, perhaps most of all."

Glen went on: "Production at Prudhoe will not continue forever. We need ANWR to maximize our investment in the pipeline and to keep those benefits flowing to Alaskans. Northern Oil geologists say there are sixteen billion barrels of oil up there. We're consuming over seven billion barrels of petroleum every year in the United States. Why lock up such a valuable resource? As for ecological concerns of the environmentalists and Gwich'in, modern construction and containment techniques minimize negative environmental impacts. Believe me, we take great precautions. The Gwich'in have little to worry about."

Glen continued: "The electrification of transportation will probably happen but not on a large scale very soon. In the meantime, we will need all the fossil fuels we can get our hands on. Otherwise, the economy will come to a grinding halt and with it our whole way of life. We need to open ANWR up to development."

As he thought about it, Ron perceived something deeper at work. Oil exploration seemed to be symbolic of the invasion of modern technology and the threat it presented to traditional Gwich'in culture. It was an obvious enemy: alien, capitalist, consumer-oriented, and potentially destructive to the environment. What really seemed at issue was Gwich'in identity.

As he thought back to the clan gathering, the little that was said about oil exploration after the first day seemed to support this conclusion. Instead, the question of identity had dominated public sessions. Speaker after speaker decried the erosion of Gwich'in culture. Some in prophetic voice condemned the erosion outright. Others reflected their own personal struggle to preserve the best of the traditional culture while adopting chunks of modern life.

The speakers had focused their concern on language. Mary Peters reported through a translator that in some villages less than 20 percent of the children understand the Gwich'in language. She was troubled that the local schools taught English as the primary language and, worse, that some schools ignored native language altogether. For the most part she herself did not speak in English, believing that speech in her native tongue was a mark of integrity.

As he thought about it, Ron certainly agreed that language was crucial. But the matter seemed to run still deeper. He reflected on the one school in the village that had hosted the clan gathering. It was by far the largest, best-equipped, and most modern structure in the village. Built by the state of Alaska with money from oil royalties, its facilities were state of the art. Villagers could not avoid making comparisons between it and their own humble dwellings.

Even Ron, a total stranger, made the comparison, although he had not taken the time during the meeting to explore the implications. As he thought about it later, it seemed odd that Gwich'in from other villages and non-Gwich'in like himself had not been housed in the school but instead were put up in make-shift tents. He thought about his own backpacking tent and the mosquitoes that were so big villagers were said to build bird houses for them. How much easier it would have been to lay his pad on the floor of the school, away from the swarms of mosquitoes and in easy reach of flush toilets and showers.

Ron's reflections returned to the village itself and the things he had observed while hanging out and wandering around. Snowmobiles, while out of use for the summer, were everywhere in storage. Satellite dishes for television reception were common. The table in the laundromat was covered with glamour magazines. The teenagers roamed the village in groups without apparent direction, much like teenagers roam malls throughout North America. Joy riding and kicking up dust on big-tired, four-wheeled vehicles was a favorite pastime.

Perhaps the most obvious symbol of all this was the five-thousand-foot gravel runway that ran like a lance through the center of the village. As the place where visitors, fuel, mail, and supplies entered, it was the symbolic center of town.

Ron found himself thinking that oil exploration and production on the North Slope was an invasion by an alien culture and ideology. Yes, saving the caribou herd was important. Yes, teaching the kids the language was also important. But there were deeper questions. How can the caribou and Gwich'in culture survive the onslaught of modern technology and thought? How can a traditional people maintain its identity when much that is attractive to them comes from a more powerful and alien culture and seems to make life easier and more interesting? The problem for the Gwich'in was not just the oil on the North Slope. It was also the school, the runway, the motorized vehicles, the glamour magazines, and maybe even the churches.

The Gwich'in had devoted the last days of their gathering to stories of flight and return. A procession of witnesses, including Mary Peters, testified to the horrors of migration. Lost identity, alcoholism, drug addiction, a final bottoming out, and then a return to roots were common experiences. For each witness, Ron had wondered how many were lost in the bars of Fairbanks.

Ron had been impressed with the integrity of those who testified. They were no longer innocent about modern culture. They seemed to have returned much stronger for their trials and with a healthy respect for their traditions, the land, and the ambiguities of their situation. Perhaps these survivors and their children were the hope for a future that would be both easier and more satisfying. Maybe a new and stronger identity was being forged by this generation.

He had been moved to tears by Mary Peters's concluding remarks, communicated by an interpreter, in English:

> It is very clear to me that it is an important and special thing to be Gwich'in. Being Gwich'in means being able to understand and live with this world in a very special way. It means living with the land, with the animals, with the birds and the fish as though they were your

sisters and brothers. It means saying the land is an old friend and an old friend your father knew, your grandmother knew, indeed your people have always known. . . . We see our land as much, much more than the white man sees it. To our people, our land really is our life.

Ron's attention turned to the present and his report and recommendations to his denomination's national office for legislative advocacy. What should he say? Should he encourage his denomination to support the Gwich'in and their opposition to drilling for oil in ANWR? What if legislative advocacy is not enough? Should he encourage his denomination to oppose drilling in ANWR by any nonviolent means necessary? What might those measures entail? What about the members of his denomination? Should he urge them to make changes to their lifestyles and invest in new efficient vehicles?

Alternatively, should he accept Glen's optimistic assurances about minimizing environmental impacts and the positive financial benefits ANWR would bring to all Alaskans—including its indigenous peoples? Like it or not, oil is the lifeblood of the economy. If the oil companies don't drill for oil in ANWR, won't they just drill for oil somewhere else? If so, won't that also pose the threat of irreparable harm in those locales? Is it any better for the United States to import oil from Saudi Arabia or Nigeria, which are hardly exemplary democracies or good caretakers of the environment?

Commentary

Battles over oil drilling in ANWR have been raging since the 19.6–million-acre wildlife refuge for caribou, polar bears, and migrating birds was created in 1980. While most of ANWR was designated a wilderness area, section 1002 of the legislation set aside 1.5 million acres on the coastal plain for future oil exploration and development. Only one well has ever been drilled in the area. It was drilled by a consortium of oil companies in 1986 and the results have never been released to the public. While Glen Stone says there are 16 billion barrels of oil in the area, the US Geological Survey estimates the amount that is technically recoverable ranges from 4.3 to 11.8 billion barrels. If that proves to be true, ANWR would yield about as much oil as Prudhoe Bay has to date.

In 2017, the Republican-controlled Congress included a rider in a major tax reform bill that opened ANWR to oil exploration and production. The legislation authorized two lease sales over the next decade of around 400,000 acres each. The estimated $1.1 billion in revenues from the lease sales and oil royalties are to be split evenly between the federal government and the State of Alaska. Since the completion of the Trans-Alaska Oil Pipeline in 1977, petroleum revenues have provided over 85 percent of Alaska's budget. One way these revenues are distributed is through the Alaska Permanent Fund, which pays an annual dividend to each citizen of Alaska. In years when oil prices have been high, the dividend has exceeded $2,000 per person.

Many Inupiat Indians in the North Slope support drilling in the area, in large part because two companies owned primarily by Inupiats, the Arctic Slope Regional Corporation and the Kaktovik Inupiat Corporation, are considered "disadvantaged" under federal law and thus will receive preference in contracting. The Gwich'in, however, have been consistently opposed to drilling in ANWR and have recently renewed their efforts to bolster political support.

AN ETHIC OF INTEGRITY

To understand this case, a new appreciation of an old virtue, integrity, is helpful. The word integrity comes from the Latin *tango,* meaning "to touch." The past participle of *tango* is *tactus.* Add the preposition *in,* and the English word *intact* emerges. Further consideration yields other relevant related words such as *integration* and *integer*.

The Christian tradition speaks of the immanence of God, of the God who is revealed in Jesus Christ and continues to relate to the world through the Spirit. In an ethic of integrity, God is the power of integrity that creates and sustains in three distinct but related dimensions of existence: (1) personal integrity, (2) social integrity, and (3) nature's integrity. Jesus Christ is the embodiment of God's power of integrity and points to the experience of inner wholeness or integration that is God's primary work with humans.

Personal integrity, the first dimension, involves an inner harmony that is the foundation and source of inspiration for an outer harmony that seeks a consistency between act and intention. God's integrating power of love creates internal harmony in the self when the self is receptive. This internal harmony also creates the spirit and will to respond with love and justice. The relationship of God and the self that produces internal harmony is called faith. It empowers and frees the self to act in accordance with intentions.

Personal integrity is part of Mary Peters's reluctance to speak English in the public gatherings. She apparently sees speaking in her native tongue as an important element in the reinvigoration of Gwich'in culture and wants to match her words and deeds.

Ron Blanchard's personal integrity is also an issue in this case. Given his limitations as an observer, how is he to report his experience and make recommendations so that his intentions for the well-being of the Gwich'in, his own society, and the Porcupine Caribou Herd are realized?

Finally, personal integrity is a matter for everyone. In this case it involves knowledge of the issues, accurate understanding of the history of Native Americans, and sensitivity to finding one's way in a different culture.

Social integrity, the second dimension, is the harmony of act and intention in a community. Communities have integrity when peace and justice are foundational ethical concerns. While communities have fewer resources than individuals for receiving and acting on the power of God's integrity, peace and justice are deep wellsprings. To the Greeks, justice was the harmony of a well-ordered community where equals were treated equally. For the Hebrews, *shalom* and righteousness resulted from keeping the covenantal relation with God and following the guidelines of the law. They included a special concern for the poor. For both Greeks and Hebrews, peace and justice fed on each other and together nourished social integrity.

Christians melded Greek and Hebrew traditions, emphasizing basic equality in Christ and seeing in the person of Jesus the model and the power for both peace and justice. These understandings of peace and justice have developed further in Western traditions with the norms of equality and freedom. Persons should be treated equally and left free unless some ethically justifiable consideration justifies a departure from equality or freedom. Such departures, when adequately justified, are called equity.

While peace and justice are the spiritual and ethical foundation of social integrity, they presuppose the provision of sufficient consumption. The equal sharing of poverty can be as disintegrating as war and injustice. The definition of basic sufficiency is notoriously difficult, of course. Clear in the extremes of absence and excess but vague at the margins, the concept of sufficiency is useful for setting floors to poverty and discriminating about levels of consumption. As the commentary on the case "Rigor and Responsibility" makes clear, the norm of sufficiency establishes a floor below which a just society does not let its members fall. On the up side, it calls into question unsustainable consumption and efforts to justify environmentally destructive consumption. Sufficiency applies to plants and animals as well. They too need what is necessary to sustain their evolutionary trajectory.

Basic also to peace and justice are elements of a common culture. No society can long remain integrated without some minimum of shared understandings, symbols, values, and traditions. A culture can become so fragmented by invasion from without or conflict within as to lose its identity.

A consideration of social integrity is central to this case. From the side of the Gwich'in, the integrity of their culture appears to be in jeopardy. Their way of life depends on the land and their subsistence on the Porcupine Caribou Herd, which needs its special summer habitat in order to flourish. Their identity as a people depends on the maintenance of their language and respect for their traditions. Sensitivity to their situation calls for an understanding of the difficult changes they are facing, changes from the outside that may be too rapid for them to preserve that basic minimum of common culture.

From the side of the wider North American society, the Gwich'in and other native peoples deserve respect. In Christian perspective, this respect stems from the love of neighbor that stands at the center of the tradition and the norm of justice. There is also a need to address the dependency of industrial societies on the consumption of copious amounts of energy. Can such consumption be justified on grounds of economic sufficiency? Is it sustainable? Is it really integral to North American identity? These are questions North Americans should address before drilling begins in ANWR.

The third dimension is the integrity of nature. While human integrity and nature's integrity are separated in many people's minds, they are related because humans are a species in nature like any other species. All species must use nature as a resource to survive. The human species and other species are distinct because other species do not exercise intentionality, at least not in the same way or to the same degree. Therefore, it is incorrect to speak of a harmony of act and intention, justice, or sin in the rest of nature. These terms apply to humans. Still, the concept of integrity may be even more relevant to nature, considering the root meaning of the word.

The integrity of an ecosystem or species is its intactness, its capacity to evolve dynamically or sustain itself so that a variety of individuals and species may continue to interact or fit together. What comes first to mind is a pristine wilderness. This is too static a concept, however, and today a rare exception as humans have made themselves at home in an ever greater number of the earth's ecosystems. Rather than some abstract, pristine ideal, it is better to speak in terms of the norm of sustainability. This norm allows for human participation in and use of nature without endorsing activities that cause the disintegration of systems and species. Such activities should be named for what they are—sin.

Maintaining the integrity of ecosystems is not solely a prudential matter for humans. Nature in biblical understandings has more than use or utilitarian value. It also has intrinsic goodness, at least in the understandings of the writers of Genesis 1, where God sees nature as good independent of humans, and in Genesis 9, where God makes a covenant with all of creation. In Christian perspective, nature is much more than a resource, or backdrop, or something to be overcome. Nature is to be cared for (humans are to "till it and keep it," according to Genesis 2:15) as Jesus himself cared for others and sought their fullest realization. Humans are called to be good stewards in the image of God as that image is revealed in Jesus Christ, a concept discussed more fully in the "Sustaining Dover" commentary. God will eventually redeem the whole creation (Rom 8). Nature's integrity is represented in this case by the Porcupine Caribou Herd. Oil drilling in its summer range has the potential to degrade habitat critical to the herd. The integrity of the herd is threatened and with it the social integrity of the Gwich'in.

ENERGY AND AMERICAN INTEGRITY

The era of cheap and abundant fossil fuels (oil, gas, and coal) may be coming to an end. Conventional supplies of fossil fuels that have supported industrial societies are being depleted rapidly and are not renewable. For example, oil production at Prudhoe Bay peaked at 2 million barrels per day in 1989; today the area yields no more than 280,000 barrels per day. While hydraulic fracturing and horizontal drilling technologies have released copious amounts of unconventional oil and gas in the lower forty-eight states, these operations are quite costly and require higher commodity prices for drilling firms to make a profit. They are also plagued by a host of other social and environmental problems.

The primary limiting factor for fossil fuels, however, is not their finite supply but rather the effect their combustion has on the concentration of greenhouse gases in the atmosphere. Fossil fuels are decomposed organic matter that grew millions of years ago. When burned, fossil fuels produce a variety of gases that accumulate in the atmosphere and result in global warming. In the United States, carbon dioxide accounts for over 80 percent of greenhouse gas emissions, and the combustion of petroleum products is the primary cause. Transportation-related emissions are now the largest source of emissions in the United States. After declining for over a decade, US greenhouse gas emissions began to rise again in 2018.

Scientists all over the world are raising alarms about the escalating rate of global greenhouse gas emissions and the very real dangers of catastrophic climate change. The concentration of carbon dioxide in the atmosphere is higher today than at any time in the ten thousand years of human history and is higher than it has been for over 800,000 years. It has increased from 280 parts per million (ppm) at the outset of the Industrial Revolution to over 415 ppm today, and it could more than double by the end of this century.

These changes in the composition of the earth's atmosphere are producing a *rate* of warming that is unprecedented in human history. The planet has already warmed by over 1.4 degrees Fahrenheit since 1880 and will heat up another 8–10 degrees if present trends continue. Evidence of warming is now widely visible in retreating mountain glaciers, a thinner arctic ice pack, animal and plant shifts, rising ocean levels, and heat-damaged coral reefs. Scientists predict the inundation of low-lying areas, despoliation of freshwater supplies, more extreme weather events, hotter summers with more drought, significant reductions in agricultural production, and huge increases in heat-related illnesses and deaths.

It is an ironic, if not tragic situation. The very things (fossil fuels) that powered modern economies, improved the quality of lives, and increased human longevity for so many are now imperiling the future of human civilization and the vast majority of life on the earth. We desperately need to shift back to energy sources that are more renewable and sustainable.

The realm in which renewable sources of energy like wind and solar power reign in conjunction with energy conservation needs to be markedly different, however, from the present realm governed by economic growth, as measured by the Gross Domestic Product. Sustainability and sufficiency must guide energy decisions, not growth—at least not growth of fossil energy and resource-intensive production and consumption.

Between this realm and the one to come there will be a difficult period of transition that is already beginning and whose duration is difficult to predict because the rate of technological innovation cannot be known. The realm to come can be delayed if limits to growth are aggressively attacked with the so-called technological fix, that is, a commitment to find technological solutions to resource constraints.

Certainly new technology will have a role to play, but if the shape of human communities and the distribution of costs and benefits are disregarded in the rush for technological solutions, the new realm will hardly be worth inhabiting. Groups like the Gwich'in, if they can continue to exist in such a climate, will be peripheral. Social scale will be large and structurally complex, with hierarchical, centralized, and bureaucratic administration. Materialism accompanied by great disproportions of wealth will continue as the reigning philosophy. In short, social integrity will be under severe pressure from the demand to find "fixes" and to pay those who can do so.

Alternatively, a society geared to renewables and conservation will bring pressure on everyone to live sustainably and to be satisfied with basics. It will be a society where appropriate scale, simplicity, a greater degree of decentralization, and greater equality will prevail.

Energy choices are social and value choices. If a critical mass of North Americans decides on lives that consume large amounts of energy and natural resources, or alternatively, to live sustainably, it will simultaneously choose the economic and political structures to organize and sustain such decisions.

The issue of exploration for oil in ANWR is thus much larger than meets the eye when technological and economic calculations are the only factors. In its largest dimension the question is, What kind of society do present stewards of the earth want for themselves and their children? And beneath this lurks the basic question of social identity and character. Who are North Americans as a people? What should be the center of their common culture?

The amount and style of energy consumption currently enjoyed by North Americans are difficult, if not impossible, to justify. Energy sufficiency can certainly be endorsed and a case made for oil as necessary in any transition, but the unnecessary and wasteful consumption of the present not only violates the norm of sustainability but also the model of frugality and simplicity seen in the person of Jesus Christ. Yes, oil will be needed in the transition to a more sustainable society, but until North Americans reduce their high levels of consumption and consider their identity in a world of limited resources, all the oil in ANWR will make little difference.

GWICH'IN INTEGRITY

The view of the Gwich'in in this case is through the eyes of a non-native on a short stay who is unfamiliar with their culture and has no formal training as an observer. Any one of these limitations might skew his observations.

While caution is warranted, a few things are clear. First, the Gwich'in are deeply concerned about the Porcupine Caribou Herd for reasons of subsistence and social integrity. Their history is tied nutritionally and spiritually to the herd. Were the herd to lose its integrity, the Gwich'in would receive another rude shock to their identity.

Second, Gwich'in culture, like most native cultures in the Americas, is in jeopardy. Ron wonders whether there is enough common culture left to maintain social integrity. The Gwich'in worry about this too but also express words of hope and show signs of reinvigoration.

One way to approach the situation is to advocate closing ANWR to exploration and to pursue a policy of disengagement, leaving the Gwich'in to work out their own future. Such an approach has its attractions, given past injustices. The perceived need for oil, the many linkages among cultures in Alaska, and the intermingling of peoples on the land, however, make disengagement all but impossible.

Alternatively, policymakers could continue to pursue the two patronizing approaches that have governed US policy in the past. The first of these two approaches pictures Native Americans as backward savages in need of superior Western technology, social institutions, and culture. While still widely held, this picture must be dismissed outright and confession made for the expropriations, massacres, and deceptions it has promoted. The domination and elimination of Native Americans by people of European origins is one of the ugliest chapters in the annals of world history.

The other traditional approach is to idealize Native Americans as "noble savages." This idealization, while more sensitive than the first, leads to confusion about native care of the land, the moral superiority of native peoples, the ease and comfort of nomadic life in a harsh climate, and the place of native religions in modern technological society and in the environmental movement.

The Gwich'in have a different—not a superior or inferior—way of life. They are a shrewd and politically interested community of people who have learned how to negotiate from strength. They know of the potential monetary rewards of oil production in ANWR. They know that the Porcupine Caribou Herd is resilient and that the environmental consequences of oil production at Prudhoe Bay are not altogether clear. They know they have political support in the rest of North America, and they know how to use it. They know as sub-Arctic people that they have different political interests than the Inupiat on the North Slope. They know that northeastern Alaska is no Eden.

How then should North Americans view the Gwich'in? Most appropriate is a perspective that begins with respect and exhibits a concern for their social integrity. Included should be a frank recognition that a conflict continues between two cultures, the one closely linked to a subsistence way of life on land, the other more powerful, linked to modern technology and capitalistic economic organization.

Traditionally, the Gwich'in were hunter-gatherers who long ago migrated from Asia and settled in the sub-Arctic south of the Brooks Range in Alaska and the Yukon and Northwest Territories in Canada. They subsisted directly off the land, primarily on the Porcupine Caribou Herd, which they harvested in sustainable numbers. Life was difficult, but the people were resourceful. They relied on sharing, the extended family, and respect for the wisdom of others, especially elders.

Modern industrial society is obviously different, perhaps most obviously in how it relates to the land. Those in modern society are not as close to the land. They do not see it as sacred. They buy and sell it and encumber it as private property. They view it through the eyes of the economist as a factor of production and obtain its produce by selling their labor and purchasing the means of subsistence in markets far removed from the land.

The future of the Gwich'in's subsistence way of life is in jeopardy. Ron Blanchard's account, however, reveals considerable evidence of continuing social integrity. The Gwich'in have organized themselves to defend their interests. A spirit of resistance is expressed in the refusal by some to speak English and in opposition to oil production in ANWR. The Gwich'in recognize shortcomings in their school system and the importance of language to a cultural identity. Younger people are returning to the villages to raise their families. Many seem determined to overcome the ravages of alcoholism. Skeptics might view this evidence as staged by the Gwich'in to impress unsophisticated observers or as a failure to assimilate to a superior culture. In contrast, eyes of respect will interpret this evidence as a triumph of the human spirit.

Nor should the Gwich'in's subsistence way of life be dismissed. Granted, the Gwich'in have purchased tools to make that way of life easier and as a result must resort to wage labor. Granted also, they have supplemented their diets with food from the outside, thereby improving nutrition. These actions are not decisive, however. Their subsistence way of life will continue as long as they choose to live in rural Alaska, for the simple reason that a market economy will never produce a sufficient economic base to support them in this setting. Except for the oil, which is not on Gwich'in lands, there are not enough commercially valuable resources in rural Alaska.

Respect for the Gwich'in in their subsistence way of life is important in this case. From the outside it is a matter of justice and recognizing the legitimacy of Gwich'in concern about identity, the land, and the caribou. From the inside it is a matter of economic sufficiency and the maintenance of a common culture.

The Porcupine Caribou Herd is central to Gwich'in integrity. The caribou are the means of continued subsistence. Cultural identity is bound up with the land and the herd. Oil exploration is viewed as a threat to the herd and as another one of those barriers that wall the Gwich'in off from their identity. Respect in this case means listening to what these people are saying.

NATURE'S INTEGRITY

When anthropocentrism dominated discussions such as this, a commentary would have ended with the preceding section or with a short statement of the value of the Porcupine Caribou Herd as a resource for Gwich'in subsistence. Utilitarian considerations dominated analysis. The intrinsic value of landscapes, species, and ecosystems was left out or separated off into the realms of philosophy or theology. This is no longer the case. Analysis needs to be fully integrated and nature's systems viewed as having value of their own.

The issue for the integrity of nature in this case is the sustainability of the Porcupine Caribou Herd, whose survival depends on the preservation of summer habitat on the North Slope of the Brooks Range in ANWR. On the one hand, the need to preserve this habitat is symbolic of a more general problem: the worldwide degradation of land and ecosystems that causes the extinction of species and the reduction of biodiversity.

The causes of this wider degradation are complex, but certainly an increased human population that consumes more and uses more powerful technologies is principal among them. Oil exploration and development in ANWR on fragile Arctic tundra is simply another example of behavior that degrades the natural environment, Glen Stone and his safeguards notwithstanding. In some cases, and this may be one, any intrusion whatsoever can be destructive, and humans should probably stay out.

On the other hand, the issue is quite specific: the impact of oil exploration and development on the herd and other species that inhabit the Arctic ecosystem. Exploration itself may be innocent enough if all it means is looking around, overturning a few rocks, probing the ground here and there, and then leaving. Who could object? Producing oil is another matter.

The case itself offers important information about the Porcupine Caribou Herd, some of which bears repeating. According to the US Fish and Wildlife Service, the herd currently numbers about 218,000 animals and is growing.

Critical to the herd is its summer calving and feeding in areas believed to have the greatest potential for oil discovery. If the herd is displaced from its richest feeding grounds to others where the vegetation is less nutritious and predators are more numerous, the herd may suffer. Less nutrition means less weight gain. Weight gain is critical for the females and is directly related to calf survival and birth rates the following summer. Predators are found in greater numbers to the south in the foothills of the Brooks Range. Presumably the herd would move in that direction with displacement, since this is what occurs in years of heavy snowfall in the prime feeding areas. In good weather years displacement might have little effect, but scientists are concerned about other years, when displacement would add to already bad conditions and put the herd under stress.

The more than forty years of experience with the Central Arctic Herd at Prudhoe Bay is the only evidence that scientists have to predict effects on the Porcupine Caribou Herd in ANWR. The Central Arctic Herd currently numbers about twenty-two thousand animals. It grew rapidly in the 1970s and 1980s. After 1985, however, the ratio of calves per one hundred cows dropped, more so in areas in the herd's western range near oil production at Prudhoe Bay. The herd's population has declined significantly since 2010. Scientists are cautious about these data, however. There is no long-range information on numbers or calf/cow ratios. The estimates of herd size are based on aerial surveys. Natural fluctuations in ratios and size are to be expected, and without baseline data causes of short-range fluctuations are difficult to determine.

Scientists have arrived at several significant conclusions, however. The Central Arctic Herd avoids humans, roads, and production facilities at Prudhoe Bay, the females more than the males. In other words, production facilities displace the herd. Also, the herd as measured by calf density is in worse shape the closer its animals are to production facilities. This is the evidence that worries scientists and the Gwich'in, for displacement in ANWR would drive females to less favorable calving and feeding grounds.

PERSONAL INTEGRITY

Mary Peters's reluctance to speak English in public gatherings is probably difficult for most North Americans to understand. English is, after all, the main language of international communication, not to mention the language of common culture in the United States. If Mary's first priority is to get the Gwich'in's message out to observers such as Ron, it would behoove her to communicate directly instead of through an interpreter.

Mary is, however, speaking to her own community as well, and it is probably more important for her to establish her own integrity within the community before she speaks to outsiders. Whatever else, her reluctance to speak English should not be viewed by outsiders as a snub or as culturally backward. To expect Mary to give up what is central to her culture and her own identity is the epitome of cultural imperialism. Mary's act is in keeping with her intention to reinvigorate Gwich'in culture.

As for Ron Blanchard, he must decide how to word his report and what to recommend concerning oil exploration and production in ANWR. Personal integrity depends on receiving God's power of integrity. Ron's first act should be a prayer for openness and discernment.

Ron might next reconsider his intentions. The case makes clear that he is troubled by the threats to Gwich'in social integrity. The disintegration of the Porcupine Caribou Herd would threaten their subsistence way of life and arrest efforts to reinvigorate old traditions. Ron is no doubt aware of the tortured history of Native Americans in post-Columbian North and South America. Under the norm of justice with its concern for the poor and oppressed, he might well give the Gwich'in the benefit of the doubt about their motivations, their reading of the scientific evidence, and the political nature of their appeal. He should be careful not to cloud his judgment with patronizing illusions about Gwich'in nobility, however.

The case also reveals that Ron has convictions about excess energy consumption. He listens carefully to Glen Stone, who is convinced that energy sufficiency for North Americans is at stake, but does not appear to be swayed. Perhaps one of his recommendations should pertain to how members of his denomination use and conserve energy in general and petroleum products in particular. Much of the pressure on developing ANWR would be relieved if Americans demanded less oil.

The evidence on the threat of oil production to the integrity of the caribou herd should also be a consideration. If he is perceptive, Ron will pick up the caution of scientists who have studied the possible consequences. The lack of conclusive evidence should lead him to be cautious himself. No longer, he might conclude, can an ethic that considers only human integrity control outcomes. He should also remember that the Porcupine Caribou Herd has intrinsic value as part of God's good creation.

What Ron decides to do with his observations is finally his responsibility, as it is the responsibility of every visitor to other cultures. Ethical analysis can pave the way to good decisions, but good character and personal integrity are needed to translate analysis into good actions.

CONCLUSION

The case against exploration and production in ANWR is strong. It rests on three pillars: (1) respect for Gwich'in social integrity; (2) respect for nature's integrity; and (3) the failure of North Americans to curb their energy appetites. The case may not be as strong as it seems, however. ANWR is not on Gwich'in lands. The main link of the Gwich'in to ANWR is the Porcupine Caribou Herd. If it can be demonstrated beyond a reasonable doubt that oil production represents little or no threat to the herd, then Gwich'in integrity is not threatened and the first two pillars fall. Should North Americans curb their demand for energy and thereafter use the oil in ANWR to fuel the transition to sustainable energy consumption, then the third pillar crumbles.

For the moment, however, the three pillars stand. The effects on the herd are not clear, the herd is central to Gwich'in integrity, and North Americans have yet to make a determined effort to change their energy consumption habits.

ADDITIONAL RESOURCES

Bass, Rick. *Caribou Rising*. San Francisco: Sierra Club Books, 2004.

Congressional Research Service, *Arctic National Wildlife Refuge (ANWR): An Overview,* January 9, 2018, https://fas.org/sgp/crs/misc/RL33872 .pdf.

Dinero, Steven C. *Living on Thin Ice: The Gwich'in Natives of Alaska.* New York: Berghahn Books, 2016.

Dochuk, Darren. *Anointed with Oil: How Christianity and Crude Made Modern America.* New York: Basic Books, 2019.

Haycox, Stephen. *Battleground Alaska: Fighting Federal Power in America's Last Wilderness.* Lawrence: University Press of Kansas, 2016.

La Duke, Winona. *All Our Relations: Native Struggles for Land and Life.* Cambridge: South End Press, 1999.

———. *Recovering the Sacred: The Power of Naming and Claiming.* Chicago: Haymarket Books, 2016.

Madsen, Ken. *Under the Arctic Sun: Gwich'in, Caribou, and the Arctic National Wildlife Refuge.* Englewood, NJ: Earthtales Press, 2003.

Martin-Schramm, James B., Laura A. Stivers, and T. Spencer, *Earth Ethics: A Case Method Approach.* Maryknoll, NY: Orbis Books, 2015.

Moe-Lobeda, Cynthia D. *Resisting Structural Evil: Love as Ecological-Economic Vocation.* Minneapolis: Fortress Press, 2013.

Nash, Roderick Frazier, and Char Miller. *Wilderness and the American Mind.* 5th ed. New Haven, CT: Yale University Press, 2014.

O'Brien, Kevin J. *An Ethics of Biodiversity: Christianity, Ecology, and the Variety of Life.* Washington, DC: Georgetown University Press, 2010.

———. *The Violence of Climate Change: Lessons of Resistance from Nonviolent Activists.* Washington, DC: Georgetown University Press, 2017.

Porter, Joy. *Native American Environmentalism: Land, Spirit, and the Idea of Wilderness.* Lincoln: University of Nebraska Press, 2014.

Related Videos

Energy Crossroads: A Burning Need to Change Course. 55 minutes. Tiroir A Films. 2010.
Oil on Ice. 90 minutes. Bullfrog Films. 2004.

Related Websites

American Petroleum Institute
  http://www.api.org
Arctic Power, "Arctic National Wildlife Refuge"
  http://www.anwr.org/
Gwich'in Steering Committee
  http://ourarcticrefuge.org/
Gwich'in Tribal Council
  http://www.gwichin.nt.ca/
National Religious Partnership for the Environment, "Arctic National Wildlife Refuge"
  http://www.nrpe.org/arctic-refuge.html
National Resources Defense Council, "Protect the Arctic National Wildlife Refuge"
  https://www.nrdc.org/protect-arctic-national-wildlife-refuge.
US Fish and Wildlife Service, "Arctic National Wildlife Refuge"
  https://www.fws.gov/refuge/arctic/.

Case

Whose Water?

"How are you going to vote, Mike?" Sheila Bloom asked her husband as he prepared to leave home for the County Commission meeting.

"I'm not even sure that we are going to vote on the issue tonight," Mike replied. "Julie called and said there are so many people who have signed up to talk to the commissioners on the water issue that the commissioners might have to postpone our own discussion and vote at an extra meeting in two weeks."

As Mike put on his jacket and headed for the front door, Sheila impatiently said, "You know what I was asking—how do you think you are going to vote on it?"

"I still don't know, Sheila. I have to listen to all the different points of view first. That's why I was elected." At that, Mike went out and closed the door behind him.

"Humpff!" snorted Sheila in dissatisfaction. She was concerned for her brother Eli's interests and for those of many of her neighbors. Eli had been hired as assistant manager of the new bottled water plant that was to open in Butler six months from now. He was already deeply involved in overseeing aspects of the construction of the new plant, at which a number of her unemployed neighbors hoped to work. The plant would employ about one hundred people when it was up and operating.

But now all that was threatened by a mix of lawsuits that had been stirred up by a coalition of local and national environmental organizations.

Butler is a small city of five thousand in Pendleton County, a rural county of fifteen thousand people. Butler, like the county seat, Maysville, and virtually all of the county, gets its water from Cimery Lake, a dammed stretch of the Licking River. The year before the state water-testing service had notified the county's water-treatment plant that its water quality had

---

This case and commentary were originally prepared by Christine E. Gudorf and have been updated by Laura A. Stivers and James B. Martin-Schramm. The names of persons and institutions have been disguised, where appropriate, to protect the privacy of those involved.

failed to meet state standards for the previous six months. As a result, the county was being officially cited. The County Commission, which oversees the treatment plant, had six months to file a plan for bringing the water quality up to standards, after which it had eighteen months to demonstrate the effectiveness of that plan.

The reason for the notice of water-quality failure was obvious—the state itself had been cited by the federal Environmental Protection Agency (EPA) for insufficient state water-safety standards two years before, and when the state in response had set new higher standards, a number of municipalities and counties had failed to meet those new standards, including the Pendleton County plant. Most of those municipalities had neither the expensive equipment necessary to test for those pollutants nor the ability to treat them. In fact, one of the problems the state pointed to in Pendleton County's water was excessive levels of chlorine, which the treatment plant had been putting in the water hoping to knock out some of the things they were now supposed to test for but couldn't. An additional problem was, following winter runoff, the water in Cimery Lake required a level of filtration to remove manganese that the old plant could not do. The new standards would require a completely new state-of-the-art-treatment facility at a cost of over ten million dollars, a figure that was well beyond the county's reach. County and city officials had been stymied about how to comply with the state's demands—until they received the offer from the bottling company.

The bottling company offered to lend the county the funds without interest so the county could build the treatment facility at the current county site and operate it for the first three years at the current schedule of charges to users, and after that to keep rate increases under 4 percent per year. In return, the bottling company would build its own bottling plant on adjacent land bought from the county, and, after the county had paid back the loan in water for the bottling plant at current user rates, it would continue to buy water at the prevailing commercial rate. The only concession the bottling company asked was deferment of property taxes on the bottling plant for the first three years of the thirty-year contract. County and city officials had been more than relieved when this offer was made—in fact, they had been overjoyed. A free water-treatment plant without a raise in rates; a new industry to give jobs to locals; and, after three years, new property-tax revenues as well! What could be better?

So construction began. Then came the news about lawsuits by environmentalists. Sheila was not alone in thinking that any environmental problems down the road should take second place to current problems, like families without income. Eli's situation was especially worrisome. He had been out of work for twenty months when the new job offer came in. He and Betty had used all their savings in addition to his eighteen months of unemployment and her salary as a school-bus driver to feed the kids, to pay the mortgage, and to pay the premiums for health insurance. They were just about to default on the mortgage on their house when an even bigger disaster loomed. Betty had felt a lump in her breast, which a biopsy revealed was cancerous. Only weeks before this diagnosis the eighteen months of COBRA health insurance from Eli's job at the Sara Lee plant had ended. It had been a horrible time. Sheila and Mike had offered their own savings to help, but they did not have enough to pay the mortgage more than a few months, and not enough to make even a dent in cancer surgery and chemotherapy costs.

It was then that Eli got the interview with the bottling company and the job offer. Since his insurance had been lapsed less than sixty days, Betty's treatment was covered under the new insurance, and his new job allowed them to pay up on the mortgage and keep the house. Betty had had her surgery and started chemotherapy—things were looking much better for them, and better for many of their neighbors, some of whom had just been hired to construct the new treatment plant and some of whom were hired for construction at the bottling plant. Then the news about the lawsuits had hit the radio and papers.

Sheila helped the two youngest kids finish their homework, take their baths, and say their prayers. An hour later she was finally getting the oldest, Curt, to head to bed when she heard the garage door and looked up to see Mike come in.

"How did it go?" she asked.

"Come in the kitchen and get us both a cup of coffee while I hang up my coat," he replied.

Settled at the kitchen table, Mike began. "I have no idea what will happen, Sheila. I'm not even sure the commission is going to have much say in how this gets settled. It is really a mess. The crux of the issue is that the contract Butler and Maysville signed with the bottling company did not put any limit on the amount of water that the company could take from Cimery Lake. Some of the environmentalists have data that show that in other places, both in the United States and abroad, similar contracts with bottling companies have led to the companies taking so much water from the local reservoir that the municipalities had to buy water from other districts to have enough for their own people. That would be crushingly expensive. We would have to construct a pipeline to bring the water in from miles away. Additionally, in our case, since the dam constantly releases water from the lake to keep the Licking River flowing below the dam, a major draw down of the level of water in the lake could dry up the flow of the Licking into the Ohio River, depriving all those who depend on the Licking River for the water they need—not just the rafting and canoeing businesses, or the sport fishermen, but also the barge businesses docked on the Licking that work on the Ohio River.

"On the other hand, the bottling company seems to have a strong legal case. Since the Supreme Court says corporations must be treated as persons, they cannot be limited in their water use any more than any other customer. We have no regulations limiting water use for residents or for other businesses. In fact, Harry Bertram, who has been on the commission for forty years, thinks we signed a contract with the Sara Lee plant back in the 1970s that gave them unlimited water access at the residential rate for fifty years, which was the life of the contract. Bob Marshall, the town attorney, is checking on that. I think we are screwed either way it goes. We are going to be paying a fortune to lawyers to take it to court, and who knows how long it will take to settle."

"What is the interest of the environmentalists in this?" asked Sheila.

"Any significant drawdown in the level of the lake would endanger the flow of the Licking River below the dam, and that would have an impact on a number of species, a couple of which only exist here. I had never even heard of them, but one is a fish and two are some kind of local frogs," said Mike.

"What will this mean for Eli and Betty?" Sheila asked.

"Who knows?" Mike replied. "The company could stop construction, fire him, and wait out the results of a court fight. Or it can continue construction, open on time, and wait out the decision that way. I have no idea. Eli is not the only person concerned here—all the people with jobs in construction either at the treatment plant or the bottling plant are at risk."

Two weeks later, at a spaghetti supper at the high school to help raise money to send the band to a competition in Washington, the table Mike and Sheila sat at was deep in debate about the plant and the contract. One of their neighbors, Mary Posey, had just declared that everything would have been fine if the state had not adopted the new water standards. Another neighbor, the Methodist Sunday School teacher Ted Nelton, disagreed. "I don't think so, Mary. Our son, Tim, is an engineer for the Water and Sanitation Department in Charleston, West Virginia, and he has been telling us for years horror stories about the inadequacies of water treatment plants around the country, especially old rural ones in little towns like ours. Our treatment plant thought that adding chlorine alone made the water safe. But Tim explained that cities in the United States, even major cities, have had their water loaded with microorganisms that can cause serious disease in humans, such as giardia, because these old systems can't detect them. There are regular outbreaks of water-caused disease around the country. He said about a half a million were reported last year and that nearly seven thousand people died! Under the new standards there has to be testing for giardia and other microorganisms. Who knows how many people here have gotten sick or even died because of stuff in the water?"

Mary retorted, "But why do we never hear about this on the news? I have never seen a story on unsafe city water."

Ted's wife Grace leaned forward and said, "I asked Tim the same thing, Mary, and he said that the really big cases, when thousands of people in a big city get sick from giardia in the water, do make the news, but they are not that frequent. More often, smaller numbers of people get sick, many of them so mildly that they don't go to hospitals. The few who get most sick are often diagnosed without anyone knowing the source of the infection until long after the epidemic is over, and even then, the cases are not always connected. Often, these water-borne infections are simply the last straw for persons who are already seriously ill or immune compromised. When they die, their deaths are attributed to their chronic illness. But beyond that, most of these outbreaks are not publicized for fear of public panic. When they do publicize it—and we have all seen this—the water company just tells people to boil their drinking and cooking water for a few days."

David Cook, the local sheriff, spoke up. "Mike, do you really think that we have to worry about the bottling plant taking so much water it drains the lake? That is a huge lake! I don't understand it—there has to be some way to prevent the plant from increasing its draw on the plant to that extent. Doesn't the state—and the County Commission, too—have to approve the plans for the new treatment plant? Surely there is a limit to how much water the new plant can treat, and at that limit, the bottling plant couldn't take any more."

Mike replied, "Yeah, you would think so, but the way it was explained to us, if that point comes and the company is told it can't have more water, then neither could any other user. In addition, no new users could be added. That would mean no new homes could be built, no new businesses. It was made plain to the commission that this is a constitutional issue—the bottling company has the same right to water as you or I or any other property owner."

Sheila turned to Mike, "So tell them about some of the things the commission is looking into."

Mike said, "We have just begun to look at a number of possibilities, but we don't know if any are realistic. The state is giving us some help, but it is overextended because there are so many counties and municipalities in similar straits. They sent an engineering and accounting team here that did some research and determined that we are treating about 40 percent more water than people are using. When they reported that, we thought we were home free and had enough water after all. But what they were reporting was a *leakage rate* of 40 percent—the old plant sends out 40 percent more treated water than ever gets delivered to users. It turns out that we are only slightly higher than the average in our state, especially in the hilly eastern counties. The same shifts that cause mudslides and rockslides put pressure on old pipes, which leak at joints and sometimes even crack along their length. If we could capture that 40 percent lost to leakage, it would give us a margin for supplying the bottling plant without drawing down the lake level or lowering the downstream flow. But fixing the delivery system would be expensive, maybe more expensive than building the new plant. And some of that cost would be passed on to customers—we would all pay a surtax for pipe repair as well as being required to pay for fixing any leaks between the meters at our homes and the spot where we tap into the main water supply."

"I still don't understand why the environmentalists got into this issue," complained Sheila.

Grace looked surprised, "Well, they were the ones who knew of other ecological problems when bottling plants start draining high proportions of local water. They looked into it here when they read of the new contract with the bottling plant. If Cimery Lake disappears, so will the environment for many local animal and plant species. But the biggest loss would be for those downstream on the Licking River, which actually has two or three species of fish and frogs that have not been found anywhere else. That is the primary environmental interest in the issue, but those environmentalists were smart and publicized their research on the possible disappearance of those species downstream so that the businesses on that stretch of river would know that they had a bone in this dogfight, too. Lots of people who don't take the rights of fish and frogs seriously do know somebody with a business or a job that depends on the downstream Licking."

Just then Sheila's brother Eli walked over and sat down at the table. As he approached, conversation hushed. Eli looked around, "Guess I know what you all were talking about here. I know it's a mess. But the bottling plant is not the villain here. I don't say that just because I have a job there. The company wants a good relationship with the county, and that's why it was willing to build the new treatment plant on a no-interest loan, so that there would be a solid foundation of cooperation that would lead to renewing the contract again in thirty years. It has complied with the 1988 law that requires non-agricultural, non-thermoelectric users of more than ten thousand gallons a day to register with the state's Department of Environmental Protection, even though the company's initial plans call for using considerably less than that. All the workers, and more than half of the management at the company, will be local. Do you really think we would recklessly overuse the lake and dry up the river?"

When no one else answered, Mike lifted his head. "I'm not sure what any of us thinks really matters, Eli. Until the commission gets a formal answer from your company about how much water it will need for the next three to five years and what the maximum capacity of the new treatment plant will be, and we get some idea of how much we can draw from the lake in an average year without endangering local species, we won't know whether the county can go ahead with the present plans. If so, could we use zoning in the future to prevent an extension of the bottling plant that would overstrain the new water treatment plant? Or would addressing the leakage problem be enough?" At that, the group at the table began to turn in their trays and put on coats, ready to go home. After all, it was a school night.

The following Sunday the local public high school, Pendleton Senior High, played the local Catholic high school, St. Xavier, in boys' basketball—an event that always generated lots of excitement and was guaranteed to draw a crowd. Mike and Sheila sat next to Father Polk, the priest at the local Catholic parish. He had been Mike's coach when he played basketball at St. Xavier. During halftime their conversation turned to the water issue when Father Polk asked Mike what was happening on the County Commission. Mike said that it looked as though the contract with the bottling plant might be continued, but the issue of whether the county could institute a new rate structure that would have higher commercial rates than residential rates, and higher commercial rates for larger users—which could discourage huge expansions of the bottling plant—was still in the hands of wrangling lawyers. He concluded, "The one thing we are all sure of is that all of our rates are going to go up, and go up considerably."

Father Polk responded, "Mike, this is a county with a lot of very poor folks. Families have lost their jobs, then lost their homes—some of them are living two and three families in two-bedroom homes. The elderly who were already living very simply on Social Security are now trying to support their kids and grandkids on that same check. Water is the gift of God, intended to serve the needs of all. We all have an obligation to see that the poor continue to get water, no matter what the rates are. We have gone through this issue with the electric cooperative. It took us ten years to get its agreement that the poor who are on disability or the elderly who fall behind on their heating bills in the winter will not have their electric and heat cut off. We need to do something like that for water, too, and do it in the planning stages for the new plant."

Mike squirmed a little, then looked up at Father Polk and said, "I have been learning a lot about water and water systems and the role of water in the environment in the last few months. And I have to say that I think we need to be very careful in implementing the kind of program that you are talking about. I don't want the poor to have their heat *or* their water cut off. But a big reason that the price of water must go up is that we do not have a surplus of it, and clean drinking water is becoming more scarce all around the world, not just where new bottling plants are going up. If water is free, or extremely cheap, it is easy to waste it. When I was growing up, we thought nothing of forgetting to turn off the sprinkler at night. It watered the backyard all night long. After all the kids left home, my parents rented out the bottom floor of their home, but after the first two years of offering free heat to the renters, they put in a separate furnace and meter because the heating costs for the whole house more than doubled that first year with the renters—and stayed that high the second year. If it doesn't cost you, then you don't worry about turning down the heat when you go out or go to bed. If heat—or water—is free, people have much less incentive to conserve water."

"But how will the poor be able to pay higher rates?" asked Father Polk.

"We need to look at various ways to go," Mike replied. "You know Ben Habib, the recorder at the courthouse? He told the commission that in some Muslim countries, like Saudi Arabia and Iran, they have different rates for different kinds of use, based on the Qur'anic verses about care for the poor. Residential customers get a certain amount of water, enough for drinking in the average household, at a fraction of its normal cost. Then they get enough for the typical household to wash themselves and their clothing at a some-what higher but still subsidized level. Any water use after that is charged at the rate that is necessary to cover the cost of obtaining, treating, delivering, and reclaiming (recycling) the water in a closed-loop system. This full-cost rate—that is what we need to be moving toward if the county is not to deplete its water resources below the level needed by the next generation or two. We need a full-cost rate to establish a closed-loop system. You are pointing to the needs of the poor now—but I think we need to think about the needs of future generations too. My kids, and hopefully my grandkids, if I am blessed, will need to have water at affordable rates, too."

Father Polk bowed his head as the teams came back out on the floor and said, "We need to pray that God will take care of the future."

As Sheila and Mike herded their kids to the car after the game, Mike related to Sheila his conversation with Father Polk. "It's all very well to pray that God will take care of the future," he groused, "but those of us on the commission need to take care of the present *and* plan for the future. Lord knows we all pray about this, but we still have to make decisions that will affect thousands of people now and more in the future. Does he think we don't have obligations to future generations?"

Commentary

This case ends with Mike irritated that Father Polk suggested praying to God to take care of future generations, interpreting it as an abdication of human responsibility. It is perhaps natural for Mike to be annoyed, given the strain he and the other commissioners have been under. But, in fact, Father Polk had already shown his interest in addressing community problems rather than simply sitting back and waiting for God to take care of them. He had been involved in the campaign with the local utility to prevent the poor who were behind in their bills from having their heat and electricity cut off in winter. In addition, the concern he now voiced to Mike was the need to ensure that the new water rates would neither exclude the poor from access to water nor make it impossible for them to pay for other necessities. Praying for help to address the interests of future generations does not necessarily exclude planning for them now. He could just be recognizing that such planning is difficult because we can't always predict the conditions that will exist in the future. Prayer can sometimes be an aid to deciding how to act, not a replacement for action.

Both Mike and Father Polk voice important values. As Mike indicated, urban planners all over the world are clear that virtually everywhere it will be necessary to have closed-loop systems if potable water is to be available to meet human needs. A closed-loop system is one in which no water is lost; all treated water is recycled, retreated, used, and then recycled, retreated, and used again in a never-ending loop. Various cities and counties in the United States and around the world are already working on three of the most important aspects of progress toward closed-loop systems—solving systemic leakage problems, stopping the discharge of untreated sewage water into streams and oceans, and keeping down the volume of water that needs to be fully treated by separating sewage from stormwater. Sewage and stormwater runoff are combined in many places during heavy rains, and the combined volume requires the highest level of treatment in order to become potable. In fact, in many cities the capacity of the treatment plants is overwhelmed during storms so that the excess of combined raw sewage and stormwater is discharged into rivers and oceans. If the two waste streams can be separated, the stormwater runoff can be collected, minimally treated, then used for purposes that do not require the high standards of drinking water, such as irrigation in agriculture, cooling in power plants, and lawn watering. Many new suburban neighborhoods have done such separation and require that only "gray'"water from baths, sinks, washing machines, and dishwashers be used for watering lawns and washing cars. A number of tests have shown that there are no health dangers in using "gray" water to water crops eaten by humans.

But Father Polk brings up another value often understood as opposed to the environmental planning values that Mike advocates. Father Polk's concern is for the poor and their right to water as a basic human need. It is because water is such a basic human need that many issues around water are so contentious. Privatization of water supplies, like privatization of garbage pickup, prisons, and jails, and even some highways, has become increasingly common all over the world. In many places in the developing world there have been riots and political controversies because private companies that replaced municipal services have raised rates beyond the capacity of the poor to pay or have refused to extend water-system services to neighborhoods from which they could not make back their investment in a timely manner. Officials in these corporations understand that their primary responsibility is to their stockholders, unlike municipal services, which must answer to voters. The primary reason for the spread of privatization is that so many municipal governments, like Pendleton County in this case, are unable to raise the capital required to invest in replacing or expanding water treatment plants.

The county commissioners are not privatizing their plant, but their contract with the bottling company amounts to a partnership that could produce many of these same tensions. In fact, the whole issue of how much water the bottling plant would use in the future may pit the interests of stockholders, who may want to expand the plant in order to increase profits, with the interests of the residents, many of whom are poor or who have businesses or employment that depend upon the downstream Licking River. Environmental interests in preserving biological life in the area here cohere with the interests of many humans.

WATER AS A BASIC HUMAN NEED

What status should the human need for water be accorded? Some respond that because humans require both food and water simply to survive, water is a human right, an aspect of the right to life. The limitation on assertions that water, or any commodity, is a human right is that rights must be enforced, they must be provided by the larger community. Some people, in the form of institutions, must be obligated to provide those rights. In Pendleton County, this is the task of the county commissioners; in most societies, protecting human rights is the task of government—local, regional, or national. But governments have limited resources. Many governments around the world do not have the resources to provide potable water to all of their citizens. As in Pendleton County, government resources are dependent upon tax revenue; poor communities often do not generate enough tax income to meet all their obligations. In fact, privatization of basic services has often been the governmental response to such revenue shortfalls.

Religious responses to water as a basic human need support understanding water as a human right but also go beyond this. Christian treatment of the human need for water takes two forms; one is symbolic, and the other is an imperative. Water appears frequently as a symbol in the Christian and Hebrew scriptures and in rituals. Wells and pools figure prominently in Bible stories as the center of villages and towns. These wells were public; all citizens used the water to meet their needs for sating human thirst and that of animals, and for washing. Because everyone needed the water in the local well, wells were frequently meeting places. For example, Jesus meets the Samaritan woman at the well, and she draws water for him (Jn 4:11–26). In Genesis, Rebecca becomes the wife of the patriarch Isaac when the emissaries from his parents encounter her at the well near her home (Gen 24:11–27). In larger cities, such as Jerusalem, there were not only wells but pools from which residents could draw water for washing as well as drinking and cooking. Jesus heals a man among the many infirm he encountered at the pool of Bethesda in Jerusalem (Jn 5:2–9).

Water in the Christian tradition is a prominent symbol both of washing and of life itself. John the Baptist baptized thousands, including Jesus, in the waters of the Jordan River (Mk 1:9–11). For centuries the Christian ritual of baptism used complete immersion in water to signify the washing away of sin and the emergence of a "new" person, who was often given a new name as a further symbol of his or her new status. Just as babies emerge from the waters of the amniotic sac in birth, so emergence from water has signified new life in the Spirit through baptism.

The symbolic uses of and references to water in scripture reinforce for Christians the intimate relation between humans and water, and inculcate in Christians a sensitivity to water as a universal human need. There are also imperatives—commandments—in the tradition that bind all Christians, both collectively and individually, to respect the basic needs of everyone. The first commandment of this kind comes in the creation story in Genesis, when God appoints Adam and Eve the stewards of the earth and entrusts them with all the earth's resources (Gen 1:26–31). Through Adam and Eve all humans inherit this stewardship of the resources of the earth. But while God has gifted humans with water and all the other resources of the earth, this gift comes with obligations. Stewardship is not ownership. As stewards of God's creation, humans must manage creation for the benefit of all. This includes managing water to meet the needs of all. Thus, stewardship encompasses both Mike's concern for future generations and Father Polk's concern for the poor of the present day. (For more on stewardship, see the commentary in "Sustaining Dover.")

The second commandment that is directly relevant to Christian understandings of water usage is Jesus's command that his followers love their neighbor (Mt 22:39). This is not simply one commandment among many but the overarching commandment that sums up all the commandments of the Jewish Law under which he lived. When Jesus was asked by those attempting to discredit him which was the greatest of the commandments, he did not cite any one specific part of the Law but instead replied, as had previous great rabbis, that the greatest commandment is the sum of all the others: we must love God with our whole body, mind, and spirit, and love our neighbors as ourselves (Mt 22:34–40). Thus, if we recognize our own need for water and love our neighbor as ourselves, we must acknowledge an equal need in our neighbor.

Nor can we arbitrarily decide who our neighbor is. In the parable of the Good Samaritan (Lk 10:25–37) Jesus taught that the good neighbor was the outsider, one of the despised Samaritans, a group thought to be heretical by other Jews. The Samaritan was the good neighbor because he responded to the needs of the Jew who had been robbed and beaten and left to die in a ditch. Jesus instructed his disciples that the obligation to love our neighbor cannot discriminate between intimates and strangers, even enemies, but requires loving all. Therefore, one cannot love one's neighbors and allow them to go without water.

BALANCING RESPONSIBILITIES

There is a universal temptation to understand the command to love our neighbor as applying only to persons in close proximity, those with whom we personally interact, and thus to avoid applying the command in complex social situations. In this case Sheila is tempted by such an approach; she is impatient with Mike's determination to take all sides into consideration. She insists that priority should go to the needs of her brother and his family, and those of her near neighbors. She is not alone in such an approach, nor is this approach based necessarily in selfishness.

Many persons are intimidated by the complexity of economic and political decision-making and interpret Christian morality as involving only the personal avoidance of prohibited activity such as adultery, theft, or lying. They leave the complex decisions to experts and only become involved in wider political activity when their self-interest is threatened by policies of political and economic experts. But individual Christians in democracies, where citizens have responsibilities for making laws and policies, have an obligation to engage in the process of social decision-making based on their dual obligations to stewardship and love of neighbor.

Social policies involving water are extremely complex, and must differ from place to place depending on local circumstances. In this case the question of what Mike and the other commissioners should decide is not completely open. There are legal issues that constrain their decisions. It is possible that federal agencies could become involved and prevent any decision that would endanger the local species in the downstream river. The constitutional construction of corporations as persons before the law, having the same rights as citizens, has served important purposes historically in promoting economic prosperity. However, in this case and many others today, there are some very real dangers due to the size and wealth of many corporations. Mike seems to think that the only legal way to prevent the bottling company from expanding its water use to the detriment of the rest of the county is to use zoning to control the size of the plant.

It might be that constitutional interpretations of the status of corporations should be reviewed. It does not seem just that understanding a corporation as having the same rights guaranteed to individual citizens should allow a rich and powerful corporation to usurp local resources that belong to all. Certainly such an outcome seems contrary to all Christian social justice traditions, in which the integrity of divine creation, especially the dignity of humans, must take precedence over all human creations such as corporations.

In the past, water resources in the United States have only been understood as a problem in some limited areas of the nation, mostly in the West, where policies were established to allocate water for irrigation and to balance the rights of upstream and downstream river communities. These policies attempted to implement just water allocations to various human groups but did not take into account the environmental impact on other species or on preservation of water resources for the future. In the next decades policies must be established to deal with these issues and with new problems around water that are increasingly complex. These include many densely settled cities having depleted their underground water table, cities buying large amounts of water from other communities, and regions where underground water tables and surface waters have been polluted. In some coastal places the draw down on the water table from heavy settlement has resulted in saltwater seeping into the water table. While the Clean Water Act of 1972, amended in 1977 and 1987, has vastly improved the water quality of many US rivers and streams, comprehensive law regarding water systems and usage has yet to be developed—and is urgently needed.

Ironically, if Pendleton County did have a closed-loop water system, the issue of bottling plant usage would be moot, because except for the bottled water produced and sold by the bottling plant, all the water from the plant would be used over and over. In this case the county could legislate limits on, or higher rates for, all treated water that is not recycled. In the absence of such a system, Mike and the other commissioners must choose the most just option available, one that best protects everyone's interests.

ADDITIONAL RESOURCES

Alvez, Alejo. "Water as Private Property." *Latinamerica Press* 20 (October 31, 2007): 4.

Arnone, R. D., and J. P. Walling. "Waterborne Pathogens in Urban Watersheds." *Journal of Water and Health* 5, no. 1 (2007): 149–62.

Barlow, Maude, *Blue Covenant: The Global Water Crisis and the Coming Battle for the Right to Water.* New York: The New Press, 2009.

Chamberlain, Gary. *Troubled Waters: Religion, Ethics, and the Global Water Crisis.* Lanham, MD: Rowman and Littlefield Publishers, 2007.

Clark, Anna. *The Poisoned City: Flint's Water and the American Urban Tragedy.* New York: Metropolitan Books, 2018.

Eckstein, Gabriel. "Precious, Worthless, or Immeasurable: The Value and Ethic of Water." *Texas Tech Law Review* 38 (2005–6): 963–70.

Flórez-Estrada, Maria. "CAFTA Threatens to Turn Water into Merchandise." *Latinamerica Press* 20 (October 31, 2007): 6.

Gudorf, Christine E. "Water Privatization in Islam and Christianity." *Journal of the Society of Christian Ethics* 30, no. 2 (2010): 26–55.

Hall, David, and Emanuele Lobina. "Private and Public Interests in Water and Energy." *Natural Resources Forum* 28 (2004): 268–69.

Hanna-Attisha, Mona. *What the Eyes Don't See: A Story of Crisis, Resistance, and Hope in an American City.* New York: One World, 2018.

McKenzie, David, and Issha Ray. "Urban Water Supply in India: Status, Reform Options and Possible Lessons." *Water Policy* 11, no. 4 (2009): 442–60.

Myers, Ched. *Watershed Discipleship: Reinhabiting Bioregional Faith and Practice.* Eugene, OR: Cascade Books, 2016.

Pearce, Fred. *When the Rivers Run Dry.* Fully revised and updated edition. Boston: Beacon Press, 2018.

Robinson, Joanna L. *Contested Water: The Struggle against Water Privatization in the United States and Canada.* Cambridge, MA: The MIT Press, 2013.

Shiva, Vandana. *Water Wars: Privatization, Pollution, and Profit*. Reprint edition. Berkeley, CA: North Atlantic Books, 2016.

Stivers, Laura. "Water as Earth's Bloodstream or Commodity? Latina Ecofeminist Responses." In *Spirit and Nature: The Study of Christian Spirituality in a Time of Ecological Urgency,* ed. Timothy Hessel-Robinson and Ray Maria McNamara, 201–19. Eugene: Wipf and Stock Publishers, 2011.

Zenner, Christiana. *Just Water: Theology, Ethics, and Fresh Water Crises*. Revised edition. Maryknoll, NY: Orbis Books, 2018.

Related Videos

Blue Gold: World Water Wars. By Sam Bozzo. 90 minutes. Purpleturtle Films, 2009.

Flow: For the Love of Water. By Irena Salina. 33 minutes. 2008.

The Story of Bottled Water. 8 minutes. The Story of Stuff Project. https://storyofstuff.org. 2010.

Thirst. By Alan Snitow and Deborah Kaufman. 62 minutes. PBS, 2004.

Water on the Table. By Liz Marshall. 79 minutes. Bullfrog Films, 2011.

When the Water Tap Runs Dry. By Ron Meyer. 40 minutes. New York: Ambrose Video Publishing, 2009.

Related Websites

Food and Water Watch
   https://www.foodandwaterwatch.org/
Public Citizen
   https://www.citizen.org/
Global Policy Forum
   https://www.globalpolicy.org/home.html

PART V

BUSINESS

Case

Sustaining Dover

John Yeoman was relieved to be sitting in the folding chairs instead of his customary seat as a City Council member. He could get used to just being a regular citizen again. It had been a long seven years. In fact, division had been growing among the eight thousand citizens of Dover for more than a decade. When he was first elected to the City Council, the city was still licking its wounds financially after a failed effort to block a large developer from building Sunrise Plaza, a new retail center on the south edge of town. Concerned that the shopping center would harm the downtown business core, the city had denied the landowner's request to rezone the property. After a judge ruled in favor of the landowner, and all appeals were denied, the City of Dover was left with over $85,000 in legal fees. John's first duty as a City Council member had been to figure out where to cut thousands of dollars out of the city budget over the next few years in order to pay legal bills racked up by City Council members who had preceded him.

Now, at the end of John's second four-year term on the City Council, emotions were running high over the news that Walmart intended to build a 184,000–square-foot Supercenter on the eastern edge of Dover. Dwarfing all other stores in the community, including Walmart's 74,000–square-foot store in Sunrise Plaza, the Supercenter would be built on thirty-one acres of land, one-third of which had up to now been designated as a flood plain.

Sitting in chairs reserved for the general public, John had come to attend the last public hearing the Dover Planning and Zoning Commission would hold regarding Walmart's request to fill in the portion of their property in the flood plain and to reclassify the land from F-1 (Flood Plain) to C-4

This case and commentary were prepared and updated by James B. Martin-Schramm. While the case is based on actual events, names and places have been changed to protect the privacy of those involved. This case is a condensed and updated version of "Sustaining Dover: Urban Sprawl, Habitat Fragmentation, and Sustainable Communities," in James B. Martin-Schramm and Robert L. Stivers, *Christian Environmental Ethics: A Case Method Approach* (Maryknoll, NY: Orbis Books, 2003), 80–111.

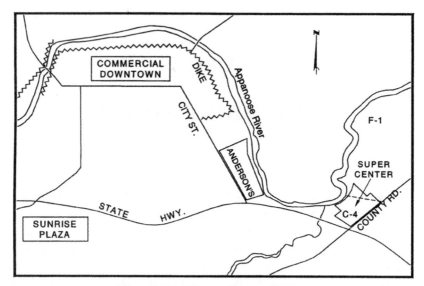

Figure 5-1. Map of Dover, Iowa

(Shopping Center Commercial District). Tonight, the Zoning Commission had to make a recommendation to John and the six other members of the City Council who would make the final, binding decision at an upcoming meeting.

Wincing at the thought of being back in the hot seat in a few weeks, John listened as the regional representative for Walmart, Max Walters, began his presentation. Dressed in casual business attire, Walters made three points in his presentation. The first was that the Iowa Department of Natural Resources (DNR) had just approved Walmart's plan to bring fill to the site in order to raise the land above the 100–year flood plain level. "I am sure you are as gratified as we are to receive this vote of confidence from the DNR," said Walters, holding the letter aloft. "Once the fill process has been completed, the land will no longer be in the flood plain; our land will be at the level of other commercial establishments in the area.

"Like all of you, Walmart is concerned about the water quality of the Appanoose River, which forms the western boundary of our property. As a result, we have worked with the DNR to design an eight-acre detention basin and riparian buffer zone. These two design features will filter petro-chemical and other wastes from our parking lot so that they do not enter the river. This will probably be the 'greenest' parking lot in the city! To our knowledge, all other parking lots in Dover and the city's forty miles of streets discharge their waste directly into the nearest storm sewer and thus ultimately into the river. In addition, the detention basin and riparian buffer zone will create a small area of wetlands that will create habitat for wildlife. Our plans for the site include a prairie-grass demonstration project, bat houses, and houses for songbirds. Ecologically, we want to do our part to be a good steward.

"Finally, whereas some developers have strenuously negotiated various tax breaks before investing in the community, Walmart will pay for all improvements to our site. We will bring city water and sewer lines to our property and add a turning lane to the county road that feeds the entrance to our store at no expense to the taxpayers of Dover. In addition, we have secured federal funds to provide walking and biking trails to the store. As always, Walmart will continue to be a good neighbor in the City of Dover."

Clapping heartily, Buck Sorensen, chair of the Planning and Zoning Commission, thanked Walters for his presentation and turned the podium over to Clara Laursen, coordinator of the Appanoose River Alliance—a loose coalition of environmentalists, bird watchers, anglers, hunters, and canoeists. Twenty years younger than Walters and a foot shorter, she addressed the audience dressed in khakis and a t-shirt emblazoned with the logo of the Alliance.

"Members of the Zoning Commission and fellow citizens of Dover, the Appanoose River Alliance opposes Walmart's request to fill in and rezone this portion of the flood plain for several reasons. The first and perhaps most important reason is that filling in flood plains destroys wildlife habitat. Habitat destruction is the single most important variable in the loss of biodiversity on our planet. For example, we have 390 bird species in Iowa and almost 40 percent of those that breed here are in decline. This is due, in part, to the loss of wetlands and flood plain areas. We would much prefer the wetlands nature provides to one constructed artificially and laced with toxic chemicals.

"Second, flood plains serve as natural sponges that soak up excess water in the spring after snow melts and in the summer after major storms or extended rain events. Without these flood plains, floodwaters are confined to the main channel of the river until they spill over the banks and cause considerable damage to dwellings and agricultural property—especially to communities farther downstream. Flood plains are nature's way of spreading out floodwaters so that they do the least damage and provide the most benefit through the dispersion of river nutrients and the provision of wildlife habitat.

"Third, the Alliance is not convinced that Walmart's detention basin and riparian buffer zone will protect the river from contamination by the road wastes collected on its eleven-acre parking lot while also controlling the volume of water from its four-acre roof. It is our understanding that the state DNR is only required by law to consider the effects of a 100–year flood upon the property in question. Left unstudied is the virtual certainty that the detention basin would fail in floodwaters that exceed the 100–year flood level. When we experience another flood of this or greater size, all of the concentrated petro-chemical wastes would suddenly be flushed into the river where they could seriously degrade the quality of the water for fish and other species.

"Finally, given the fact that the State of Iowa has designated the Appanoose as a 'protected water area,' the City of Dover has no right to spoil the natural and scenic quality of the river by allowing a big-box retailer like Walmart to construct a Supercenter right along its banks. Given these concerns, we strongly urge the Planning and Zoning Commission to reject Walmart's bid to fill in the flood plain and reclassify this portion of the land from F-1 to C-4. Any decision otherwise would constitute bad land stewardship."

As the room erupted in applause, Buck Sorensen thanked Clara somberly and then announced that there would be one more presentation before the floor would be opened for public comment. Coming to the microphone now was Tom Bittner, director of Dover Citizens for Sustainable Development, a coalition of local merchants, advocates for historical preservation, and farmers in the area committed to community-supported agriculture. A recent college graduate in political science, Bittner cared passionately about sustainable development but had little experience in local politics. Nevertheless, here he was, looking a bit uncomfortable in a shirt and tie, addressing a packed crowd.

"Ladies and gentlemen, Dover Citizens for Sustainable Development is in favor of economic growth when that development is conducted in a responsible manner and contributes to the sustainability of this community. We are not anti-growth, but the construction of a Walmart Supercenter in this flood plain would be both ecologically irresponsible and economically ruinous. This community worked long and hard after the Sunrise Plaza fiasco to develop Dover's comprehensive development plan. As those of you on the Zoning Commission know, that plan designates the downtown business area as a vital commercial district in Dover. In addition, the plan states that protecting the flood plain of the Appanoose River and its tributaries from 'incompatible development' will be given 'high priority.' Walmart's request to build a Supercenter on the banks of the river violates both of these major features of Dover's comprehensive plan. Sprawling development in the flood plain on the eastern edge of town will destroy our downtown, and it will forever end responsible farming in that portion of the flood plain. It is your responsibility, and the duty of the City Council, to enforce the comprehensive plan so that these two things do not happen.

"As you know, just the rumor that Walmart was going to build a Supercenter was enough to cause one of the three grocery stores in our town to close. Take a walk down Main Street. Count the number of empty store-fronts. Yes, the downtown area survived the initial battle when Walmart moved into Sunrise Plaza, but a Supercenter is too much. It will be the death knell for local merchants, and it will certainly clobber all of the other stores in Sunrise Plaza when Walmart moves to its new store. Just as important, it will be a devastating blow to the distinctive, historic character of our community. People come from far and wide to canoe in the Appanoose, to vacation in our campgrounds, and to enjoy the blessings of small-town life that all of us take for granted. The construction of a Walmart Supercenter along the banks of our lovely river is not progress; it is yet one more denial of our heritage and an irrevocable step into the boring homogeneity of American culture. We don't have to be like everybody else. We can control the nature of economic growth in our community. We can harness the power of that economic activity to preserve this community for our children and grandchildren as well as the countryside around us. Members of the Zoning Commission, I implore you: Don't sell our community down the river. Do the right thing: Say no to Walmart!"

Bittner's populist rhetoric struck a chord with many who leapt to their feet and applauded as he left the podium. Watching Bittner return to his seat like a slugger rounding third base, John found himself wondering if anyone in the room supported Walmart's bid to open a Supercenter in Dover. He didn't have to wait long.

Paul Petersen was the first to speak. "Forgive me, Mr. Bittner, but you were probably in middle school when Walmart first came to Dover. We had a lot of 'doom and gloom' rhetoric back then, too, but take a look around. Did downtown Dover dry up and blow away? Is Walmart the only game in town? Hardly. Many businesses downtown are thriving. Things are going so well that the city just spent $3 million on historic preservation and street improvements downtown. Dover has become a major retail hub in this corner of Iowa. We didn't enjoy that status before Walmart came to town."

Dale Murphy, a contractor in Dover, spoke next. He noted that Dover was built in a valley carved out by the Appanoose and that the eastern edge of town was the only outlet for growth in the region. Murphy went on to point out that the city's comprehensive plan acknowledged this reality because it designated this area as a corridor for future growth. "Close that end off, and the town will die. If you're not growing, you're dying," said Murphy.

Speaking next, Charlie Tieskotter commended Walmart for working so closely with the DNR and warned everyone that if the Zoning Commission or the City Council ignored the DNR permit and denied Walmart's legitimate request to fill in and rezone the land, the city could find itself back on the losing end of a court case.

Last, but not least, Gail Banks addressed the audience. Banks and her husband operate a modest dairy farm on the outskirts of Dover. Speaking forcefully, she said: "I'm tired of people turning their noses up at Walmart. Some of you only seem to be concerned about Dover's historical heritage. I've got news for you. My family has lived here for three generations. I'm proud of our heritage, but I'm more interested in the present and the future. Maybe some of you can afford to spend extra money on groceries and cleaning supplies, but we can't. We don't buy our clothes over the internet from Eddie Bauer, which, by the way, is what is really killing retail stores. We need the low prices that Walmart gives us, and we're not alone. Take a look at its packed parking lot. The reason Walmart wants to build a Supercenter here is because we're all shopping a lot at its current store. It is giving us more of what we want!"

Two weeks later John left his Goodyear dealership early, ate dinner with his pastor, and then took a long walk along the river on the eastern edge of town before the City Council meeting that evening. He knew that the vote would be close; in fact, it might come down to him breaking a tie. With a name like Yeoman, he was always the last one to vote.

He rehashed the arguments in his mind. On the one hand, Tieskotter was probably right. If they ignored the judgment of the Iowa DNR and rejected the recommendation of the Planning and Zoning Commission to rezone the land after it is filled, Walmart would almost certainly take them to court and a judge could rule again that the City Council's decision had been "arbitrary and capricious." On the other hand, if they approved the landfill and rezoning request, the newspaper had reported yesterday that a group of property owners intended to sue the city for increasing the danger of flooding on their land. John sighed. No matter what decision they made, it looked like the City Council was going to get sued.

He still didn't understand how the DNR could approve the filling in of a flood plain. Buck Sorensen had been helpful on that score, however, when he reminded him that the DNR's responsibility is to protect the lives and property of the people of Iowa. In this situation they had concluded that filling in this small portion of the flood plain did not produce a significantly increased risk of flooding. But the DNR's decision did not mean that Dover's hands were tied, because the state left final control of flood-plain areas and planning-related issues to local officials. It was up to the City Council to use the comprehensive plan to determine whether the Supercenter amounted to "incompatible development" in the flood plain. Legally, this was up to them. Given that the comprehensive plan makes protection of flood plains a high priority, the City Council would be on solid legal ground if they chose to deny Walmart's request. The reality, however, was that much of Dover was built in the flood plain and had regularly flooded until the 1940s, when the Army Corps of Engineers built the dikes that now protected the town.

But John still didn't like the idea of passing even more floodwaters along to communities downstream from Dover. Just because a dike protected Dover didn't mean the city shouldn't do something about the floodwaters it could still control. Just as important, he worried about the impact that commercial development would have on wildlife that relied on the habitat offered by the flood plain. Even though John knew that the Walmart land had once been home to a drive-in theater, it had been planted in either soybeans or corn for as long as he could remember. There was no doubt that the land provided habitat to some wildlife, especially near the river. And it *was* beautiful—even with Anderson's big gravel pit and road construction equipment parked on the western bank. How should he juggle his responsibilities to others downstream with his duties to the citizens of Dover? And what about the birds? Who represented their interests? Was this good stewardship of the land?

Having reached the site, John surveyed the 586–acre watershed and knew why it was so appealing to developers. Dale Murphy was right when he pointed out that this was the only area within current city limits that provided the kind of space necessary for large-scale commercial development. There certainly was no other thirty-acre undeveloped parcel available to Walmart elsewhere in Dover. As a businessman he understood the benefits of economic growth, but he also had a personal stake in the matter. It was likely that he would lose a good share of his tire and auto service business to Walmart. And even though he felt up to that competition, he found himself thinking about the impact the Supercenter would have on other business owners.

John also found himself thinking about the impact the Supercenter would have on the community of Dover and the county as a whole. He loved living here. Every year he could count on reading letters to the editor from visitors who praised the beauty of the town and the kindness of its citizens. It was true that Walmart's entry into Sunrise Plaza had led some local business owners to close their stores, but several years later the economy seemed strong, and it appeared to John that Dover was a stable and growing community. He wasn't so sure about the other towns in the county, however. The Supercenter's sixty thousand square feet in groceries would exceed the total amount of space in grocery stores in the county outside of Dover. Given the chance to couple savings with the convenience of one-stop shopping, John feared people who now patronized these rural grocery stores would probably take their business to the new Supercenter in Dover.

Finally, was Dover on the brink of losing its distinctiveness? Dover had certainly changed a great deal since John had arrived twenty-five years ago to enroll at the college in town, but the town still seemed healthy. Fast-food chains had moved in around the same time that Walmart arrived, but Sally's Kitchen was still a thriving downtown eatery for locals and college kids. Lawn-chair nights still pulled big crowds to listen to local entertainment on the steps of the County Courthouse in the summer. And the annual ethnic-heritage festival remained a huge draw for tourists. John found it ironic that one of the parties that had sold land to Walmart's land developer was Dover's museum. Recognized nationally for its unique collections honoring Dover's ethnic heritage, the museum board of directors had realized that the only way it could raise the funds to expand the museum was to sell land that had been given to the museum in a bequest. How do you preserve the identity of a people or a town? At what price?

Commentary

Ethical questions raised by this case are being debated all over the world as cities, suburbs, and towns grapple with the growth of big-box retailers in their communities. While the environmental aspects of the case are very important, there are also significant economic and social issues at stake. This case is not just about urban sprawl and its environmental consequences; it is also about jobs, the character of a major corporation, the heritage of a town, and the quality of life in Dover. Will Dover be a *sustainable* community if it allows Walmart to build a new Supercenter there?

In order to answer this question it is necessary to introduce the much-debated concept of *sustainable development,* a term used since the 1980s to describe development that, according to the United Nations, "meets the needs of the present without compromising the ability of future generations to meet their own needs."[1] Since then people around the world have been examining various ecological, economic, and social goals that need to be integrated in order for life to flourish on earth.

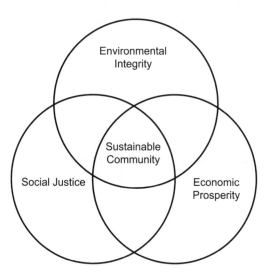

Figure 5-2. Sustainable Development Goals and Sustainable Community

---

[1] World Commission on Environment and Development, *Our Common Future* (New York: Oxford University Press, 1987), 8.

As an elected member of the Dover City Council, John Yeoman is wrestling with ethical questions related to each of the three key dimensions of sustainable development: environmental integrity, economic prosperity, and social justice. Environmentally, will the Supercenter development diminish habitat for birds and other wildlife? Will filling in this portion of the flood plain increase the likelihood of flooding in the future? Will wastewater runoff pose a water-quality problem for the Appanoose River? The economic questions are also difficult. Will the Supercenter help or harm the merchants in Dover? Is it more important for the Dover economy to grow or for there to be a larger percentage of locally-owned stores? On the social front, is it really the case that the character of the community is at stake? When do quaint towns lose their distinctiveness and tourist appeal?

As if these problems were not enough, Dover's comprehensive development plan requires John and the other members of the City Council to prioritize the three key dimensions of sustainable development. The comprehensive plan does a good job of identifying various social, economic, and ecological goals, but it is not clear how these goods should be reconciled when they conflict. The plan calls for protection of ecologically sensitive areas, but it also calls for economic growth that will benefit the citizens of Dover while preserving its downtown business core and the town's unique heritage. It is not evident how these goods should be ordered, and thus it is difficult for John to know what position he should take on Walmart's request to landfill and rezone a portion of the land for the site of the Supercenter.

THE IMPACT OF WALMART

Walmart is the largest retailer in the world. According to the company's website, Walmart employs 2.2 million people in 11,348 retail units under fifty-eight banners in twenty-seven countries. Walmart's total revenue of $514 billion in 2019 enabled Walmart to retain the number-one spot on *Fortune* magazine's list of the top five hundred corporations in the United States.

Much of this case revolves around the economic impact a Walmart Supercenter would have on a relatively small city in Iowa. Researchers at Iowa State University have studied the impact of Supercenters on communities in Iowa and Mississippi and have reported three important findings. First, once a Supercenter opens, total local sales usually increase because the huge stores encourage residents to shop in their own community rather than travel to larger communities nearby. In addition, Supercenters attract residents from outlying areas and thus affect the retail establishments in those areas. In many rural parts of the United States the size of the population is at best stagnant and often declining. As a result, retail competition is often a zero-sum affair, which means that increased sales in one community often result in reduced sales in others.

Second, merchants in towns that host a Supercenter do better if they do not compete head to head with Walmart on products. Examples are furniture stores, restaurants, various service businesses, upscale stores, and so forth. These firms tend to benefit from the spillover effect caused by new shoppers drawn to the community by the Supercenter.

Third, the opposite is true for those who compete directly with Walmart. Merchants selling the same merchandise as a Supercenter are in jeopardy. Local grocery stores and drugstores are usually the hardest hit, with sales declines of some independent stores reaching 25 percent or more a year. Other businesses that are hit hard by Supercenters are those that sell clothes, jewelry, sporting goods, tire and auto services, eyewear, and photo services.

The bottom line is that a new Supercenter makes the host community more of a regional trade center. Often other chain stores follow suit, which magnifies the economic impact. At the same time, there is no question that some businesses in the host city or county and surrounding areas will fail.

Other issues related to Walmart's business practices are not discussed in the case but bear some mention here. In 2019, Walmart admitted the company had used middlemen to bribe government officials to open new locations around the world. The settlement Walmart reached with the Department of Justice and the Securities and Exchange Commission was the culmination of one of the biggest investigations ever under the Foreign Corrupt Practices Act. Walmart paid a $282 million fine and spent over $900 million in legal fees on the case since the *New York Times* initially reported the story in 2012.

Walmart has also been battling class action lawsuits alleging sexual discrimination. In one of these cases the plaintiffs claimed that 72 percent of Walmart's hourly sales employees were women, but only 33 percent of the company's managers were women. Drawing on corporate data furnished to government regulators, the plaintiffs contended that 56 percent of managers at Walmart's largest competitors were women. Walmart resisted the lawsuit, claiming the complaints filed by these six employees were not sufficient to justify a class-action lawsuit that could affect 1.6 million workers. Ten years after the lawsuit was filed, the US Supreme Court voted unanimously that the case could not proceed as a class action in its current form. In 2019, however, another group of almost one hundred Walmart workers filed a new lawsuit in Florida alleging denial of equal pay for hourly and some salaried management positions.

On the labor front, unions are not very fond of Walmart. From its outset the company resisted efforts to unionize its workers. In 1970, Sam Walton hired a professional union buster to break up union organizing efforts in two small towns in Missouri. To this day unionizing efforts have borne little fruit. When eleven meat packers at the Walmart Supercenter in Jackson, Texas, voted to join the United Food and Commercial Workers Union, Walmart declared that it would only provide pre-packaged meats in all of its stores, thus eliminating the need for meat packers. When union organizers in a town in Quebec managed to unionize the workers at a Walmart store, the company closed the store, saying the increased labor costs would make the store unprofitable. And in 2018 Walmart publicly acknowledged in the settlement of a lawsuit that it violated federal labor laws when it threatened workers who supported strikes or efforts at union organizing at Walmart stores in California. Despite these incidents, Walmart insists it respects the right of its workers to unionize, and it is proud that few have thought it would be in their best interests to do so.

Walmart has made many efforts over the last decade to counter its critics and to burnish its reputation as an ethically responsible corporation. The company's website trumpets a host of initiatives by the company and its foundation. These include providing assistance for the victims of natural disasters around the world, subscribing to 36 one-megawatt community solar gardens in Minnesota, and providing a third grant to the International Justice Mission to combat human trafficking (modern slavery) in Thailand's fishing industry. In fiscal year 2019, Walmart and its foundation donated over $1.4 billion globally to various causes. In the United States over forty-seven thousand Walmart employees volunteered more than 776,000 hours for various community organizations.

Recent commitments Walmart has made in the area of sustainability have surprised many who have viewed the corporation's global reach, sprawling growth, and poor labor practices as a premier example of *unsustainable* business practices. More than a decade ago, however, Walmart set out to achieve three aspirations: achieve zero waste, be powered by 100 percent renewable energy, and deliver more sustainable products. The company's website provides updated information on Walmart's efforts to promote sustainability in its operations and in its global value chain of suppliers. The (self-reported) results are impressive. For example, in terms of operational sustainability, Walmart was the first global retailer to announce a science-based target to reduce its greenhouse gas emissions at the rate set in the Paris Agreement. It has received an A- rating by the Carbon Disclosure Project and has gotten over one thousand suppliers to sign on to Project Gigaton, which seeks to avoid one billion metric tons of greenhouse gas emissions from the company's global value chain. With regard to zero waste, the company aims to achieve that goal by 2025 in Canada, Japan, the United Kingdom, and the United States. Walmart is especially focused on reducing food waste and plastic waste both in its operations and in its supply chain. While some critics claim Walmart's broader sustainability measures are little more than "green-washing," it is hard not to be impressed by the scale and quality of its initiatives.

In addition, Walmart's unrivaled economic success could not have taken place without high rates of customer and employee satisfaction. As Gail Banks testifies, people around the world love to shop in Walmart stores. Walmart certainly appears to be doing some things very well. Why shouldn't John Yeoman support construction of the Supercenter? At this point it is time to do some ethical assessment of the moral issues posed by this case.

STEWARDSHIP AND SUSTAINABLE DEVELOPMENT

Over the centuries Christians have drawn on the stewardship tradition when they have been faced with balancing the various ecological, economic, and social goals associated with what is now called sustainable development. Several people in the case appeal to the concept of stewardship. Max Walters points to the detention basin, riparian buffer zone, and the accommodations for wildlife as evidence that Walmart wants to be a good steward ecologically. Clara Laursen takes the opposite view in her presentation. For her, the destruction of wildlife habitat, the increased dangers of flooding and water pollution, and the construction of a massive store on the banks of the scenic Appanoose all add up to a clear case of bad land stewardship. John Yeoman seems to sympathize with Clara's concerns. He finds it hard to see how filling in flood plains can constitute good stewardship of the land, though he acknowledges that dikes protect Dover from floods that used to plague the town.

It is clear, however, that John is wrestling with more than just the environmental matters related to this case. As a member of the City Council he is also concerned about the economic impact the Supercenter would have on other businesses as well as the social repercussions this project could have on the distinctive quality of Dover. Though he does not refer explicitly to the concept of stewardship when he considers these matters, it is clear that he feels an obligation as an elected public servant to make decisions that are in the best interests of the citizens of Dover, both now and in the future. John wants to be a good steward of Dover's resources.

This broader conception of stewardship is revealed through comments by some other characters in the case. Tom Bittner casts stewardship primarily in terms of preservation. He urges the Planning and Zoning Commission to preserve and protect the flood plain, local businesses, and the distinctive quality of Dover. Dale Murphy takes the opposite approach. For him, good stewardship is equivalent to economic development and growth in the area. Finally, Charlie Tieskotter's comments remind John that fiscal prudence is another important dimension of good stewardship. The city can ill afford another failed lawsuit. It would also not fare well if Walmart built the Supercenter in a different town instead.

Virtually nothing is said in the case about John's faith background, only that he has an early dinner with his pastor before the City Council meeting. The case does not say what they discussed, but it is possible that stewardship was one of the topics. If so, the pastor might have helped John trace the biblical foundations for the concept of stewardship in the Hebrew and Christian scriptures. With this background John would better understand how the concept of stewardship applies not only ecologically to the stewardship of land, but also to wise decisions involving everything God has made.

In the Hebrew scriptures interpretations of the two creation accounts in Genesis can render different concepts of stewardship. In Genesis 1:26–28 God creates human beings in God's image and blesses them, saying, "Be fruitful and multiply, and fill the earth and subdue it; and have dominion over the birds of the air and over every living thing that moves upon the earth." In Hebrew, the word that is translated "subdue" *(kabash)* means literally to put something under one's control, like a conqueror placing his foot on the throat of the vanquished. The term finds colloquial expression in the phrase, "They put the kibosh on that," which means that someone stamped out the possibility of a certain option. In this text the implication is that human beings have divine permission to control nature as they fill the earth and exercise dominion over it. This authorization to "subdue" the earth is tempered a bit, however, by two other key elements in Genesis 1. God's blessing to "be fruitful and multiply and fill the earth" is actually pronounced *first* to the birds of the air and the fish of the sea (Gen 1:20–22). Thus, even though God wants human beings to fill the earth, it would appear that this should not come at the expense of birds and fish. They have a right to flourish too. Also, the Hebrew word translated "dominion" *(radah)* refers to the type of rule that kings or queens exercise over their subjects. While this rule could be harsh or benevolent, it is clear from the rest of the Hebrew scriptures that God prefers rulers who care for the poor and vulnerable, maintain justice, and avoid idolatry.

Thus, the concept of stewardship that emerges from this interpretation of the first creation account in Genesis is one that views human transformation of nature as perfectly legitimate so long as it contributes to the flourishing of human beings and is not achieved through unjust means or by unduly imperiling the welfare of other living animals. The problem, however, is that too often stewardship as responsible dominion has been replaced with the notion that ownership sanctions rapacious domination. As modern notions of private property and increasingly powerful technologies have been joined with a permission to subdue the earth, the result has been enormous ecological and social harm. This logic of domination has sanctioned slavery, destroyed civilizations, and caused enormous ecological damage. In no way, shape, or form can this sort of behavior be construed as good stewardship. God's command to have dominion over the earth is not a license to exploit it ruthlessly.

Another conception of stewardship can be located in Genesis 2:4b–24. In this second creation account God forms the first human being *(Adam)* from the dust of the ground *(adama)*. Then God plants a garden in Eden and puts Adam in the garden with instructions to "till it and keep it." Next, concerned that Adam have a partner and not be alone, God forms out of the ground every animal of the field and every bird of the air and allows Adam to name these animals. When none of these animals proves to be a sufficient partner for Adam, God uses one of Adam's ribs to form Eve.

The conception of stewardship that can be drawn from this text is significantly different from the view in the first creation account. Whereas Genesis 1 emphasizes that human beings are created in the image of God, Genesis 2 emphasizes humanity's humble origins; God molds the first human from humus. In addition, humans share kinship with all other living creatures, because they too were formed from the ground. Later, in Genesis 3, Adam is reminded that he was created from dust, and that he will return to the dust when he dies. If the first creation account emphasizes humanity's independence and reign over all that God has made, the second emphasizes humanity's fundamental interdependence with the earth and kinship with other forms of life. Here the vocation of human beings is not to "subdue the earth" but rather to "till and keep" God's garden. In Hebrew, the word translated "till" *(abad)* also means "serve," or "benefit another." The Hebrew word translated "keep" *(shamar)* means "to watch or preserve" or "to guard and protect." These terms render a more static and less dynamic conception of stewardship. The emphasis is on serving and protecting what God has made. Humans are invited to care for the earth as God "blesses *(barak)* and keeps *(shamar)*" them (Num 6:24). Human beings are not set above other living things with permission to exercise dominion over them. Instead, God sets human beings apart to address the needs of other forms of life through acts of service.

The reality, of course, is that both texts are part of the book of Genesis, and thus both texts should inform contemporary conceptions of stewardship. It would appear that the ancient Hebrews realized that human beings would always be torn between the desire to preserve all that God has made and the need to use parts of God's creation in order to flourish. Stewardship is a complicated vocation.

Other texts in the Bible further illuminate the concept of stewardship. Good stewards are those who know their place and do the work of their masters (1 Chron 28:1), while bad stewards receive severe condemnation (Is 22:15). In terms of duties, stewards manage substantial economic assets and sometimes also wield political responsibility (Gen 43:16–19; Gen 44:1–4; Mt 20:1–16). For Jesus, the ideal steward is the one who stays on the job while the master is away and manages resources so well that all members of the household have "their allowance of food at the proper time" (Lk 12:35–48). Jesus even extols the example of a dishonest or shrewd steward in one of his parables (Lk 16:1–8). When a rich man confronted one of his stewards and charged him with squandering the master's money, the steward decided to cut deals with the master's debtors to ingratiate himself with them and also to recover at least some of the money that was owed to the master. When the steward presented these returns to the master, he commended the steward for his shrewdness. At this point Jesus laments that the children of light are less shrewd than others in society. On another occasion Jesus encourages his followers to be "wise as serpents and innocent as doves" (Mt 10:16). From these texts it is clear that stewardship requires trustworthiness, skill, experience, and cunning. It is not just a matter of preserving what God has made but also a matter of taking some risks and using God's resources wisely.

THE ETHIC OF ECOLOGICAL JUSTICE

This summary of the stewardship tradition provides a helpful background, but it does not resolve John Yeoman's dilemma. Somehow John needs to figure out what good stewardship entails in this particular situation. He has to prioritize and integrate the three key dimensions of sustainable development that function as interlocking but also competing spheres of moral concern. One resource John might use to reflect further on this case is the ethic of ecological justice, which has grown out of conversations in the World Council of Churches and has been utilized by member churches to develop official policy statements. The ethic of ecological justice, which is sometimes called eco-justice, is an attempt to unite in one broad scope of moral concern the ethical obligations Christians have both to present and future generations, and to all human and natural communities. Four norms rooted in scripture and Christian theology are central to this ethic: sustainability, sufficiency, participation, and solidarity.

The eco-justice norm of sustainability expresses a concern for future generations and the planet as a whole and emphasizes that an adequate and acceptable quality of life for present generations must not jeopardize the prospects for future generations. Sustainability precludes short-sighted emphases on economic growth that fundamentally harm ecological systems, but it also excludes long-term conservation efforts that ignore basic human needs and costs. Sustainability emphasizes the importance of healthy and interdependent communities of life as the basis for the welfare of present and future generations.

It is obvious that much economic activity in countries like the United States is not sustainable ecologically in the long run. Global warming, top-soil erosion, habitat destruction, and water degradation are all harming the ecological foundation upon which economic activity takes place. It is difficult, however, for most local politicians to consider seriously their duties to future generations because the voters that elected them are the ones that call on the phone and demand that their interests be represented *now*. This is why policy documents like Dover's comprehensive development plan are so important; they can give politicians some cover to make difficult decisions. But ultimately politicians have to muster the courage to use the plan to protect the future and not sacrifice it to the present. Since the protection of flood plains is a priority in Dover's plan, it is hard to see how filling in a flood plain reflects this priority. Given the high costs that are incurred each year as a result of flooding in the United States, it is clear that development in flood-plain areas is neither economically nor ecologically wise. Raising land to bring it out of the flood plain simply passes the burden of floodwaters further downstream, thus violating the norm of solidarity that calls for the equitable sharing of burdens and benefits. It is also reasonable to expect that wildlife will be affected by this development, though it is not clear to what extent. The case does not mention any specific species that would be endangered or threatened, but it is likely that loss of habitat would further contribute to the decline of birds in the area.

The norm of sustainability, however, can also be applied to the economic and social dimensions of this case. One of John's primary duties as an elected member of the City Council is to make decisions that enable Dover to flourish as a sustainable community. Economically it appears clear that Dover would be better off with a Walmart Supercenter than without one. If Walmart closed its store in Dover and built the Supercenter in a nearby town, Dover would lose a large number of jobs and a sizeable portion of its tax revenue due to decreased sales. At the same time, other long-range studies produced by Iowa State University indicate that total sales eventually decline in most towns whether they have a Walmart or not because larger cities in Iowa are gradually capturing an increasing share of total sales. This trend does not bode well for the future, but it is clear that having a Walmart store in the community helps to forestall this trend.

On the social side there are reasons to be concerned about the impact a Supercenter could have on Dover and the rest of the county. Some businesses undoubtedly would fail, especially grocery stores and others competing head-on with Walmart. Would the loss of these businesses erode the sense of community in Dover and diminish its vitality? It is true that Walmart's sales revenues are not recycled substantially in communities like Dover since they are transferred electronically to Arkansas, but it is reasonable to wonder how much money is currently recycled from the shaky local businesses that John fears will be tipped into bankruptcy by the arrival of the Supercenter. It is likely that the cash flow and financial assets of these businesses are already weak. At the same time John needs to consider what would happen to Dover if hundreds of Walmart jobs left the community. This would significantly harm the economy of Dover, and it would deal a blow to the town's self-image. While the preservationists would be delighted, others might well be discouraged about the long-term future of Dover.

There is no denying, however, that a Walmart Supercenter built on the banks of the scenic Appanoose River would be one of the first things people would see when they approached Dover from the east. The question is whether it will deal a decisive blow to the distinctive character of the community. Since dikes protect downtown Dover from floods, commercial enterprises will only encroach upon the aesthetic beauty of the Appanoose as development takes place beyond the dikes in the watershed on the eastern edge of town. In addition, since the Supercenter would be built on land on the fringes of the community, the homogeneity of its architecture would not detract from the historic character of Dover's downtown business district. At the same time, it is likely that the Supercenter will result in another round of business failures for merchants on Main Street. Thus, tourists may arrive only to tour a downtown with quaint buildings but a growing number of empty stores. Optimists will see this as an opportunity for new ideas and investment, but pessimists will look at the decimated downtown areas in other Iowa towns and be discouraged. No matter how one looks at it, however, change is going to occur in Dover. The issue is what kind of change will take place and whether it will help Dover to be a sustainable community or not.

The other eco-justice norms address additional ethical considerations in the case and deserve brief mention. The norm of sufficiency emphasizes that all forms of life are entitled to those things that satisfy their basic needs, but it also repudiates wasteful and harmful consumption and encourages the virtues of moderation and frugality. It is clear from Gail Banks's remarks that she is looking forward to low prices on more items at the Walmart Supercenter. There is no doubt that these savings will be a significant boon to people with limited means in Dover and in the rural parts of the county. But will the Supercenter actually increase the selection of goods available in the community? The failure of competing local stores could reduce the range of goods available. Will low prices also encourage higher rates of consumption among wealthier people? Undoubtedly they will, but virtues are always tested by vices. Mass discounters will always appeal to greed and envy, but this is not a new phenomenon, and avarice is an ancient character flaw that is not unique to any particular economic class.

Another factor to consider under the norm of sufficiency is that construction of the Supercenter in the flood plain will destroy some habitat that currently helps to provide basic needs to various animals. While the development does not apparently pose a dire threat to any particular species, it will perpetuate a pattern of habitat degradation and fragmentation that is a key factor in the loss of biodiversity—death by a thousand cuts.

The participation norm emphasizes that the interests of all forms of life are important and must be heard and respected in decisions that affect their lives. The norm is concerned with empowerment and seeks to remove all obstacles to participation constructed by various social, economic, and political forces and institutions. The norm places importance on open debate and dialogue and seeks to hear the voices or perspectives of all concerned. The participation norm is relevant to certain dimensions of this case. For example, like small merchants, small towns find it nearly impossible to match the power of the world's largest retail corporation. This lack of power can be seen in the fact that, apart from denying the landfill and rezoning request, there appears to be little the City Council can do to prevent Walmart from building the Supercenter. The city's comprehensive development plan does prohibit "incompatible development" in the flood plain, but the Iowa DNR's permit to fill in the flood plain appears to make the issue moot because the land would no longer be in the flood plain. Thus, if the City Council votes to prevent the construction of the Supercenter because it constitutes illegal and "incompatible development" in a flood plain, it is likely that Walmart will sue and present to a court the DNR permit that allowed it to fill in the land. In that event a judge in the local district court will make the final decision. The point, however, is that the deck appears to be stacked in favor of economic growth and large corporations. While communities have the power to regulate where growth takes place, this power is limited; the more jaded might say that it is largely illusory. These power dynamics are not an insignificant aspect of this case, and for some they may constitute the primary moral problem.

Finally, John grapples with the solidarity norm when he considers the impact the Supercenter will have on various merchants, especially grocers. This norm highlights the communal nature of life in contrast to individualism and encourages individuals and groups to join in common cause with those who are victims of discrimination, abuse, and oppression. Underscoring the reciprocal relationship of individual welfare and the common good, solidarity calls for the powerful to share the plight of the powerless, for the rich to listen to the poor, and for humanity to recognize its fundamental interdependence with the rest of nature. There is no question in this case that consumers assume they will benefit from lower prices, increased selection, and one-stop shopping, but the costs will be borne by some merchants who will not be able to compete, by workers in other nations paid meager wages, and by various species that used to rely on the habitat provided by the land that has now been developed. Thus, one could argue that the burdens and benefits of the Supercenter will not be shared equitably.

This is not a new problem. It is inherent in the capitalist economic system. Competition leads to survival or failure in business, but the customer always benefits from increased competition so long as monopolies do not form. Given Walmart's market saturation strategy (on average, each American lives within ten miles of a Walmart store), this is a real concern, but not one that the Dover City Council can resolve by itself. In the end, fervent societal beliefs in the pursuit of self-interest and the value of competition make it very difficult for individuals or communities to act in solidarity with those who might be adversely affected by the construction of a Supercenter. John was elected to champion the interests of his constituents, not those of residents elsewhere. It is very difficult to take a step back to see the broader picture, and politicians who do so are normally not reelected.

Nevertheless, the case indicates that as many as three of the seven City Council members may be leaning against approving Walmart's request to landfill and rezone the land. Should John join them and thus form a majority? Could he justify his stance by appealing to the stewardship tradition and the eco-justice norms? Or will those same moral norms lead him to conclude that the land should be filled and rezoned so that the Supercenter can be built? How should John vote?

ADDITIONAL RESOURCES

Dauvergne, Paul, and Jane Lister. *Eco-Business: A Big-Brand Takeover of Sustainability*. Cambridge, MA: MIT Press, 2013.

Evangelical Lutheran Church in America. *Caring for Creation: Vision, Hope, and Justice.* ELCA Social Statement. Chicago: ELCA, Division for Church in Society, 1993.

————. *Sufficient, Sustainable Livelihood for All: A Social Statement on Economic Life.* Chicago: ELCA, Division for Church in Society, 1999.

Fishman, Charles. *The Walmart Effect: How the World's Most Powerful Company Really Works—and How It's Transforming the American Economy.* New York: Penguin Press, 2006.

Halebsky, Stephen. *Small Towns and Big Business: Challenging Walmart Superstores.* Lanham, MD: Lexington Books, 2009.

Hall, Douglas John. *Imaging God: Dominion as Stewardship.* Grand Rapids, MI: Eerdmans, 1986.

————. *The Steward: A Biblical Symbol Come of Age.* Grand Rapids, MI: Eerdmans, 1990.

Hiebert, Theodore. *The Yahwist's Landscape: Nature and Religion in Early Israel.* New York: Oxford University Press, 1996.

Howard, Vicki. *From Main Street to Mall: The Rise and Fall of the American Department Store.* Philadelphia: University of Pennsylvania Press, 2015.

Humes, Edward. *Force of Nature: The Unlikely Story of Walmart's Green Revolution.* New York: HarperBusiness, 2011.

Martin-Schramm, James B., and Robert L. Stivers. *Christian Environmental Ethics: A Case Method Approach.* Maryknoll, NY: Orbis Books, 2003.

Massengill, Rebekah Peeples. *Wal-Mart Wars: Moral Populism in the Twenty-First Century.* New York: New York University Press, 2013.

Moreton, Bethany. *To Serve God and Walmart: The Making of Christian Free Enterprise.* Cambridge, MA: Harvard University Press, 2009.

Reich, Adam, and Peter Bearman. *Working for Respect: Community and Conflict at Walmart.* New York: Columbia University Press, 2018.

Rome, Adam Ward. *The Bulldozer in the Countryside: Suburban Sprawl and the Rise of American Environmentalism.* New York: Cambridge University Press, 2001.

Talen, William. *The Earth Wants YOU.* San Francisco: City Lights Publishers, 2016.

Young, Alistair. *Environment, Economy, and Christian Ethics: Alternative Views on Christians and Markets.* Minneapolis: Fortress Press, 2015.

Related Videos

The New Age of Walmart. 56 minutes. CNBC Original. 2010.

Rocktown: From the Small Farm to the Big Box. 90 minutes. CreateSpace. 2009.

Store Wars: When Walmart Comes to Town. 56 minutes. Teddy Bear Films. 2002.
Walmart: The High Cost of Low Price. 95 minutes. Brave New Films. 2005.

Related Websites

Making Change at Walmart
   http://changewalmart.org/
Walmart Corporation
   https://corporate.walmart.com/
Walmart Foundation
   https://walmart.org/.

Case

Executive Pay:
Reward or Excess?

Sally Young leaned back in the black leather chair that graced the expansive, polished table of the Cotto Inc. board room. The task before Cotto's board compensation committee was review of the compensation package for Cotto's chief executive officer (CEO), Robert Mossman. Deliberations had convened at nine o'clock, and it was now approaching noon. Young, in her role as committee chair, had anticipated a short discussion of the CEO's compensation package leading to quick agreement by the three-member compensation committee to forward a recommendation to Cotto's board for final approval. So far, that wasn't happening.

Cotto Inc. started manufacturing office furniture in 1953 in Bancroft, Illinois. The company quickly became a respected employer and earned a good reputation for its high-quality products. The growth of Cotto contributed to the growth of Bancroft. By the early 1960s Cotto was the largest local employer. The company expanded in the 1970s through acquisition of complementary product lines. Cotto's stock started trading on the New York Stock Exchange (NYSE) in 1975. The funds generated from selling the stock were used to purchase four other US companies that manufactured mail-processing equipment and copiers as well as two regional office-supply retail companies. By 1999, Cotto had an international market, reported $40 billion in annual sales, and was the second-largest company in the business equipment industry. Throughout the incredible expansion and growth, Bancroft continued to be the corporate headquarters location, and the original Bancroft manufacturing plant was in full operation.

This case was originally prepared by Ramona Nelson and the commentary by Laura A. Stivers. Both have been revised and updated by Laura A. Stivers and James B. Martin-Schramm. The names of persons and institutions have been disguised, where appropriate, to protect the privacy of those involved.

Since 2000, however, Cotto had endured multiple business challenges. Customers decreased their buying following the 9/11 terrorist attack. The recession in 2008 again decreased sales because business customers quit buying equipment as they reduced office space or encouraged their employees to work from home. Finally, Cotto experienced less customer demand for traditional office supplies as businesses went paperless. As a result, annual sales had not grown at all but rather had fallen by 10 percent.

Faced with the decline of the company and the retirement of the CEO, the board of directors established three performance goals for Cotto's management team: to improve Cotto's operating income; to reduce company spending on expenses not directly related to product costs; and to improve the reputation of Cotto stock in the public investor community.

To attract a new CEO with a strong record of success, Sally's compensation committee had engaged a compensation consultant to design a compensation package that would reward the CEO if these performance goals were achieved. The package incorporated a base salary, short-term performance-based bonus pay, and restricted awards of Cotto stock. Both the base salary and short-term performance-based bonus are to be paid in cash. The restricted stock shares are awarded in the current year, but the CEO does not receive full ownership of the stock until four years after the shares are awarded. If the CEO leaves Cotto before the end of the four years, all of the restricted stock is returned to the company. It is expected that the CEO will act in the best interest of all shareholders during the period of holding the restricted stock to improve the value of the company, which is measured by a higher market price for Cotto stock. If this happens, both the CEO and the Cotto shareholders reap the benefit.

The objectives of the company's CEO compensation program are to align the financial interests of the CEO with those of its shareholders, in both the short and long term; to provide incentives for achieving and exceeding the company's short-term and long-term goals; and to attract, motivate, and retain a highly competent executive by providing total compensation that is competitive with compensation paid at other well-managed companies in Cotto's industry.

Robert Mossman was hired as CEO under the terms of the new compensation program. At that time the market price of Cotto's stock was at $19 a share, which was a five-year low. The Cotto board had high hopes for Mossman. It was impressed with his executive experience; he had led two other major corporations to improved profitability and increased share market price. It was evident to the board that Mossman was motivated to make tough decisions to meet the board's expectations.

Incentivized by his compensation plan to achieve results quickly, Mossman immediately instructed his executive team to increase the effectiveness and efficiency of the Cotto business model. Over the course of the next three years, twenty-five thousand employees were laid off, another twenty thousand were moved to lower-paid positions, and all remaining hourly employees experienced a two-year pay freeze. In addition, fifteen underperforming office-supply retail stores, located throughout the country, were closed. Finally, six months before this compensation meeting, Cotto announced that the Bancroft manufacturing plant would be shut down the following year, with plans to move the production to Mexico. While this would create over two thousand jobs in Toluca, Mexico, it would come at the loss of a similar number of jobs in Bancroft, Illinois.

At the same time, however, Mossman announced plans to implement a new employee performance incentive pay plan to improve productivity. The profit-sharing bonus plan provides a 4 percent annual bonus to the base pay of all employees if Cotto's operating income increases by 5 percent. If the operating income increase is less than 5 percent, the non-executive employees will not receive a bonus.

The executive performance incentives produced positive economic results for Cotto and its shareholders. The following table summarizes key information for the three years Robert Mossman has served as CEO:

Cotto, Inc. *($ amounts in billions)*	Year 1	Year 2	Year 3
Revenues	$36.1	$38.5	$45.7
Operating income	$1.3	$2.4	$5.2
Operating expenses	$11.3	$9.6	$8.1
Number of employees	150,000	148,000	125,000
NYSE share price	$19	$21	$32
CEO Compensation Package *($ amounts in millions)*			
Base salary	$1.0	$1.2	$1.5
Performance bonus	$1.8	$2.5	$3.0
Restricted stock shares awarded	500,000	650,000	1,500,000

Figure 5-3. Three-year Economic Information

Given these results, Sally Young had expected that the compensation committee would reaffirm the executive compensation plan and vote to recommend that the board of directors renew it for the next three years. The discussion took a turn, however, when director John Jones voiced concern that Mossman's cash bonus was slated to increase 20 percent, from $2.5 million to $3 million. Three hours after they had begun the meeting, the board's compensation committee appeared to be no closer to resolution.

Young, Jones, and Ralph Smith, the third member of the board's compensation committee, found themselves locked in debate over rewarding Mossman according to the contractual terms of his pre-approved compensation package with clearly articulated performance incentives or reducing the bonus to make the CEO's pay consistent with the rank-and-file employees who were caught in the layoffs, pay reductions, or pay freeze. The three board members had reached a stalemate—each representing a different view on what action should be recommended to the Cotto board.

"The CEO's first obligation is to increase shareholder value," said Sally Young. "He's clearly achieved that, and he has exceeded the performance goals the board has established. Prior to Robert's hire, Cotto was clinging to an outdated business model against competitors who were better at managing their costs. The board hired him knowing cost-cutting measures would require personnel reductions. Robert has demonstrated strong leadership. The stock market's reaction is positive, as evidenced by the exceptional increase in Cotto's share price. We need to be true to our previous compensation agreement with Robert. We offered incentives for performance, and he has delivered."

John Jones squirmed in his chair before collecting his words to respond. "I've always thought a corporate board and management team should make increased shareholder value the first priority, but this situation is causing me to reflect on the fairness of paying a bonus to the CEO when the rank-and-file employees are forgoing pay increases, adjusting to reduced pay, or even worse, filing for unemployment because they are out of a job. Cotto has always had a good reputation in the communities where we operate. This year our employees are feeling the pressure of less pay, and the community of Bancroft will suffer the loss of a major employer when the plant is closed. How can we claim Cotto is a responsible corporate citizen if so many people are negatively affected by this year's business decisions? If we reduce Robert's bonus, it will convey a message that everyone associated with Cotto is doing with less as we all hope for long-term recovery. I trust that Robert will understand why we think his compensation should be decreased. If he doesn't, perhaps his personal values are in conflict with the leadership Cotto needs from its CEO."

A third perspective was advanced by Ralph Smith. "It's too early to change our direction with Robert. A talented leader needs time to identify a strategy, implement it, and then measure the results. If we reduce Robert's bonus this year, we are conveying the message that we don't value his leadership. The tough decisions he has made have improved the company's performance. Can we risk him leaving the company before the business improvements and increased profits are sustainable? The pay freeze is a temporary action until the new employee performance incentive plan is implemented next year. A guy with his talent has many opportunities, and we need to commit to him for the long term. The reduction of the work force and facilities will prove in the long term either to be brilliant or a knee-jerk reaction with only temporary cost reductions. Let's be patient and see how he can continue to reinvent Cotto with the remaining employees and a more focused business plan. To react now and alter the incentive for the performance he demonstrated will tarnish the trust he has in the board. That will harm Cotto and all of the company's stakeholders in the long term."

The three board members sat in silence. John Jones slowly turned to Sally and started to speak. "Sally, I had hoped the three of us would find a reasonable way to adjust Robert's compensation and demonstrate to the employees that we are sensitive to the negative effects they have suffered. I'm sure you remember Larry Able and Marcy Holmes from your high school class. They contacted me recently with concern about the abrupt change in Cotto's loyalty to its employees. Cotto has been their only employer since they finished high school. They are great examples of what the company has meant to Bancroft. Both Larry and Marcy have advanced to production management jobs. They called me to express their disappointment in the layoff decisions and their dismay about the pending plant closure. Even though they went to school with you, they did not want to pressure you to change Robert's compensation, but they felt they had to speak up. They hoped I could express their concern to you and Ralph. Finally, they asked us to consider the message the CEO's compensation package conveys to the employees and the community."

Shifting uncomfortably in her chair, Sally's memory flashed back to her high school days. Since graduating as valedictorian, thirty-two years ago, Sally had moved beyond her hometown roots, taking advantage of a full scholarship to Harvard. The prominent undergraduate degree presented Sally with many opportunities, and she joined the New York City office of Mercer Benham, a large international consulting firm. Through the years her talent was recognized and she advanced to her current position of senior vice president. Numerous invitations to join corporate boards had crossed her desk. Sally had been selective in accepting the invitations. When the

Cotto board extended her the invitation to join six years ago, she accepted immediately. Even though Cotto was suffering decreased profits and was confronted by many business challenges, Sally accepted the position, viewing it as a chance to give back to her hometown. She remembered Larry and Marcy; both were quality individuals who did not have the chance to earn a college degree. In fact, the three of them had grown up going to the same church. Larry's mom taught the fifth-grade Sunday School class. Sally had lost contact when her parents moved to Florida, twenty-five years ago.

When Sally agreed to join the Cotto board, she did not anticipate the internal conflict she was now facing. She started today's meeting thinking her expertise in executive compensation and her sense of commitment to the CEO's compensation agreement would guide her actions. Now she was confronted with her personal values. Thinking of Larry, Marcy, and the many other long-time employees tugged at Sally's sense of fairness and equity. It was less clear to her now what constituted a just and reasonable compensation package for Cotto's CEO.

Commentary

Sally came to her position as a board member of Cotto with a pro-business perspective, not realizing that her roots in the town of Bancroft and her Christian background might challenge some of her beliefs. While supportive of the need for corporations to cut employee compensation and downsize jobs to become more economically efficient and competitive, Sally is confronted this time by the actual people affected by these actions. If not for her connections to former classmates, she probably would not have thought twice about her beliefs that the main obligation of a CEO is to increase shareholder value or that contractual agreements that reward strong leadership and performance should be honored.

Once ensconced in an elite circle of executive leadership, it is hard to step outside one's position and ask ethically sensitive questions about what constitutes fair pay in a free-market economy and how pay should be structured to offer incentive for good performance while also ensuring equitable relations within society. Even more important is to ask what role corporations have in promoting healthy communities. Having grown up in the small town of Bancroft, Sally is aware of the importance of a major employer like Cotto for community well-being. And from her church roots there she has likely experienced the bonds of compassion and care within a close-knit community. Yet her Harvard degree and her New York jobs as international consultant and senior vice president have taken her a distance from her small-town upbringing and worldview.

FAIR PAY

While twenty-five thousand people have been laid off from Cotto and twenty thousand more have been reassigned to lower-paid positions, CEO Robert Mossman's pay, benefits, and perks have grown exponentially. Even when the US economy was still not out of the 2008–10 recession and millions were trying to hang on to homes and jobs, CEOs of major corporations were making as much as they were before the recession. CEO compensation has continued to rise since then. According to a report from the research firm Equilar, the median total compensation for top executives in the top one hundred largest public corporations was $15.7 million in 2017. At the top of the list was Hock Tan, chief executive of Broadcom, who made $103.2 million in 2017.

According to the Economic Policy Institute, in the 1960s CEOs were paid about thirty times the average wage of US workers, while today they receive 271 times the average pay. Many economists justify this wage differential by claiming it is simply what the market sets and is not about any sort of value judgment. In other words, if demand is high and supply of workers is low, pay will be higher and vice versa. In relation to CEO pay, the argument holds that there is high demand for the extraordinary leadership skills and talents that only particular top executives have exhibited, and therefore these executives are highly compensated. Executive pay consultants argue that just as there are few superstars like LeBron James in athletics, so too are there few gifted leaders in business. There are all sorts of other factors in addition to the market that determine pay, however.

The largest factor that determines CEO pay in relation to other jobs is how public policy is structured, especially tax policy. For example, in 1960 income over $400,000 (equal to about $3.4 million 2018 dollars) was taxed at 91 percent. In comparison, today's top tax rate is only 37 percent. And salary is only one piece of executive compensation. Mossman's compensation package includes a base salary, a performance bonus, and restricted stock awards. The latter are significant. If Cotto shares trade at its current level of $32 a share, his first 500,000 restricted stock shares will be worth $16 million at the end of his fourth year at the helm.

Mossman's executive compensation may also include health insurance, life insurance, a retirement plan, chauffeured limousine service, use of executive jets, club memberships, paid expenses, a housing allowance, and interest-free loans for the purchase of housing. In the 1990s, stock options rose from a quarter to a half of executive compensation. US corporations favored using stock options as compensation because stock-option accounting and tax rules allowed them to report stock-option expenses on their financial books at one value but use a different value when claiming an expense on their tax returns, resulting in substantial tax savings. When legislation was proposed that would have made firms report the costs of stock options like other compensation (thus limiting the growth of stock options), it was soundly defeated in the US Senate.

In other countries corporations use stock options, but payouts are linked to performance. Mossman does not receive full ownership of his stock options until after four years. The board expects that a higher market price per share will be an incentive for him to improve the value of the company, but they do not link his ownership of stock options to actual performance apart from share price values. The fact that the average CEO in the United States makes so much more than executives in comparable countries illustrates the effects of public policy. According to Statista, a leading provider of market and consumer data, Switzerland has the second-highest CEO pay levels, and yet executives are paid three-fifths of what American executives earn. In many European countries the role of CEO and board chair are separate, resulting in more-independent boards. Studies have shown that CEO compensation is higher when board members have been appointed by the CEO. Several European countries are able to curb CEO compensation through "Say on Pay" legislation where shareholders vote on executive pay.

Another justification for high CEO compensation, especially in the form of stock awards, is that such incentives will ensure good corporate performance (and thus increase shareholder wealth) by putting the CEO's interests in line with the shareholders' interests. It is not clear who is serving whom, however. Often boards are more beholden to CEOs than the reverse because the CEO influences the nomination of board members (often personal friends) and their pay and perks for their service as board members. There is usually a separation between the ownership of a corporation and the management of it. Most boards do not have the time or expertise to manage companies, and therefore shareholder votes only rarely alter corporate decisions. Furthermore, most shareholders are not individual investors but groups of investors (mutual funds) and insurance companies. Stock awards are often less about aligning CEOs' interests to those of board members and more about disguising the total amount of compensation CEOs receive. They are also a way to avoid the vagaries of the market by such maneuvers as "backdating" particular stock awards or deferring compensation to avoid taxes and interest.

Mossman did increase Cotto's shareholders' wealth substantially, but there is ample evidence that executive compensation is not necessarily linked to the profitability of companies. In fact, there are numerous stories of CEOs being rewarded for failure. According to *CNN Business*, the CEO of Sears, Eddie Lambert, received a 24 percent raise in 2017 even though annual sales plunged by the same percentage. Similarly, *CNBC* reports that the CEO of Viacom, Philippe Daumann, received a 22 percent raise even though shareholders lost 42 percent during the company's 2015 fiscal year.

So what is a fair wage or level of pay? There are various ways to define justice, each of which results in differing understandings of fair distribution of resources and opportunities. A classic Western definition of distributive justice, explicated by Aristotle, defines justice in terms of equality. This means similar cases should be treated similarly and dissimilar cases differently. But by what criteria do we consider cases similar? For example, are executive leaders and rank-and-file workers to be paid equally based on their common humanity, or are they to be compensated differently based on their roles, talents, responsibilities, or productivity? Most people believe incentives are important; that is, the CEO should be offered more pay as an incentive for increased responsibility, leadership, and expertise. Are current pay distributions based on the value of what people produce? Should they be based on performance? If so, then justice is being defined more on the basis of merit than equality. In this case, justice requires people getting what they deserve. Mossman has achieved the high expectations set by the board, but do his results warrant the extravagant pay he was promised?

While a biblical view does not discount justice according to equality or merit, it has a communal orientation and therefore places greater emphasis on fair burden and need. More often than not, biblical authors conceive of justice in terms of equity rather than equality or merit. That is, burdens should be distributed on the basis of one's ability to bear the burden, and benefits should be distributed on the basis of need. If cutbacks, including layoffs, are necessary to improve the efficiency and financial health of a company, who should shoulder the burden? If the point of wage cuts is to save money to benefit the whole, wouldn't it make sense to cut the largest salary? A handful of CEOs, in solidarity with workers, have refused raises, and some have even taken pay cuts, but such action has usually been voluntary, not mandated by their board. According to Christian norms of concern for the poor and a common good, there is something morally wrong with legal contracts that disproportionately reward a few but do not support equitable community relations.

Apart from legal responsibilities to honor the contract it made with Mossman, the Cotto board also has a moral obligation to keep its promise to compensate Mossman for a job well done. He not only achieved the performance goals the board established, but he exceeded them. It is only just that he be remunerated according to the stipulations of his contract for work done. Furthermore, the common good requires that contracts be honored. Companies will be unable to retain good leadership if they routinely renege on promised contracts, and societal stability and cohesion will disintegrate if there is no way to enforce contracts.

Modern contracts have roots in religious covenants that are central to Judaism and Christianity. While there is a reciprocal nature to much of biblical law that emphasizes divine blessing for human faithfulness, what is unique about God's covenant with humanity is that it ultimately is unconditional and not reciprocal. Despite human sin and humanity's persistent failure to keep up its end of the bargain, God remains faithful, loving, and merciful. The prophet Isaiah compares God's faithfulness to the care and compassion a mother has for her nursing child (Is 49:15–16). Human contracts are not the same as God's covenant because there is not always a personal relationship between the parties—and humans, unlike God, are fallible. Nevertheless, the covenant tradition can guide Christian thinking about keeping promises both out of duty and with respect to promoting the common good. As a covenant people, Christians have a duty to take seriously the importance of trustworthiness. At the same time, Christian morality requires pursuit of the common good. For example, *all* workers, not just CEOs, should be paid what they have been promised by their employer.

Often people view the morality of CEO pay on an individual rather than a societal level. Some decry the lack of virtue or sinfulness of CEOs who accept such excessive reward for work. The Bible has plenty to say about the idolatry of putting one's self and one's own desires in the place of God and of placing trust in material wealth over God (Ex 20:1–26; Ezek 16:48–50; Lk 15). We are not told much, however, about Robert Mossman's personality or desires, except that he is good at executing what he was tasked by the board to do. Many believe that those who work hard and rise to the top should be rewarded well. Mossman, like many CEOs, might believe that his compensation is the result of his own individual efforts, forgetting that he cannot run Cotto without the work performed by 125,000 other employees. His understanding of freedom might be a libertarian one—that wealth and income belong to the individual, not to the community. Paul taught, however, that God's love, sustenance, and salvation are a gift of grace, not merited by works (Eph 2:8–9). Before God, we are all equal, and furthermore, we are all part of the larger body of Christ (Rom 12:3–8).

From scripture comes the theological claim that all our wealth in this world is created and gifted by God to be used to establish justice, not for some to live in luxury while others struggle in poverty. The profits of a company like Cotto are a result of many factors, which include the efforts of the CEO, investors, managers, workers, and even the government through corporate subsidies and beneficial changes in tax laws. In the biblical view that workers like Larry Able and Marcy Holmes hold, it is a violation of both freedom and equality that a few line their pockets while others suffer pay cuts. The Hebrew scriptures teach us that we are not autonomous beings but are called to be stewards of that with which God has entrusted us. All of creation is God's property, to be subordinate to the purposes of the Creator. The biblical prophets were continually calling the people of Israel to account for their covenantal responsibility of making justice (Is 3:14–15; Jer 5:28; Amos 2:6–7). While God's grace is freely given, humans are nevertheless called by God to care for creation. In the Christian scriptures James warns the rich of future misery for their lack of stewardship: "You have laid up treasure for the last days. Behold the wages of the laborers who mowed your fields, which you kept back by fraud, cry out; and the cries of the harvesters have reached the ears of the Lord of hosts. You have fattened your hearts in a day of slaughter" (Jas 5:3–5).

Workers like Larry and Marcy might believe that Mossman was being idolatrous by accepting such extravagant compensation when he was laying off workers and decreasing the pay of those who were left. While they might see the need for both layoffs and pay cuts to keep Cotto competitive, a focus on distributive justice would hold that the sacrifice be shared more equitably.

A few CEOs are amazingly virtuous people, giving back to their communities a substantial percentage of their gains. An individualistic culture like ours deems it the prerogative of individuals to make as much as they can and to contribute to charitable causes if they see fit. On an individual level CEOs might be reminded of Jesus's injunction to the rich man to sell all that he owned and give the money to the poor (Lk 18:18–23), yet most people would find such a command to be an impractical and idealistic understanding of discipleship. The problem with focusing on an individual level is that it does not challenge cultural understandings about work and pay and the structures and policies that have institutionalized such widely differential compensation. We might ask whether Jesus's injunction is primarily about the rich man's salvation or about redistribution of wealth within society.

EQUITABLE SOCIETY

Interpreting Jesus's message to the rich man as a call for redistribution of wealth would put him in the long line of Hebrew prophets who argued for economic justice. God is a God of justice throughout the Hebrew scriptures. "For the Lord your God is God of gods and Lord of lords, the great, the mighty, and the terrible God, who is not partial and takes no bribe. He executes justice for the fatherless and the widow, and loves the sojourner, giving him food and clothing" (Dt 10:17–18). God repeatedly calls the people of Israel to act justly and reminds them that they were treated unjustly as slaves in Egypt: "You shall also love the stranger, for you were strangers in the land of Egypt" (Dt 10:19). The Mosaic economic laws were centered on limiting property rights so that all families had access to basic material goods. For example, farmers were instructed not to harvest all their crops so that people without adequate sustenance could glean the remaining grain (Lev 19:9–10). Furthermore, land could not be sold in perpetuity. If a family had to sell its land due to poverty, the land was to be returned in the year of Jubilee, a celebration that occurred every fifty years (Lev 25:8–17). While there is no evidence the redistribution of land ever occurred, Jubilee justice nevertheless functioned as an ideal for the people of Israel to strive toward.

This a far cry from where things stand in the United States today. According to a recent analysis by the Peoples Policy Project, the top 1 percent of Americans have gained $21 trillion in wealth since 1989, while the bottom 50 percent have lost $900 billion because they have more debts than assets. While our individualistic and capitalist culture tends to glorify the ability of executives and others to become massively rich, accumulation of wealth for those at the top is linked to the poverty of those on the bottom. This truth was fairly obvious in the agrarian societies of biblical times, when those who owned the most land had the lion's share of power. Mainstream economists claim, however, that capitalism is not a zero-sum game, one in which the economic pie is static and some lose out when others eat too much. Instead, they argue, capitalism increases the size of the pie, and while some might get bigger pieces, everyone gains. For example, industries like Cotto create jobs and corporate profits are reinvested into other productive endeavors that spawn new jobs. Board member Ralph Smith acknowledges the sacrifices Cotto workers experience in the company's short-term transition to better performance, but he believes that the reduction of the work force and facilities will in the long run put Cotto in a more competitive position, ultimately benefiting workers.

Non-mainstream economists and others critical of capitalism argue that while it creates wealth, not all benefit. The labor of many is exploited through poverty-level wages inadequate to sustain a family. Others are simply marginalized through unemployment, but even their status serves to keep wages down, creating more profit for the investors and owners. Workers like Larry and Marcy who are left at Cotto end up accepting lower pay simply to keep their jobs, knowing that there is a reserve of unemployed people ready to step in. Critics argue that the welfare of workers is subordinated to the quest for capitalist profits. Shareholders pay executives handsomely to increase the profits they receive, even if it requires the exploitation of workers and the degradation of nature. The unemployed and the degraded are made invisible through this relentless drive for profits.

Biblical justice is not simply about compensation for work done; it is also about right relations. A God of justice and liberation wants communities based on mutuality and respect. Such community building is difficult when executives make almost three hundred times what average workers make. Further, according to the Economic Policy Institute, 10 percent of the US population owns 75 percent of the wealth, and 1 percent owns 40 percent. This is a degree of economic stratification that approaches biblical proportions. Such a large gap between the rich and poor inhibits mutuality and exemplifies injustice.

Jesus criticized relationships of unequal power and patronage. Religious purity laws provided the ideological basis for who had status and power in his time. The Pharisees and Sadducees, the Jewish religious elite, justified their power and wealth by claiming to be more pure than others. They made a show of keeping the same purity code as the priests, such as a kosher diet, circumcision, and observance of Temple ritual and the Sabbath. Jesus, however, was concerned with the heart of the Jewish Law over the letter of the Law, teaching that the Law was created to promote the common good, not to justify new forms of oppression. In Jesus's time, women, Gentiles, and those who lacked bodily wholeness, such as lepers, blind people, or eunuchs, were deemed impure and considered outcasts. Yet Jesus continually challenged such status distinctions by creating inclusive community and purposely welcoming the "impure" (Mt 8:1–4; Mt 9:10–13). Crossing status boundaries as he did provoked hostility and resistance from those who used their positions of power to control and oppress people.

Paul was grappling with how the early church was to be organized. Would it adopt the cultural status distinctions of the Greco-Roman world, or would it embody the new form of community of mutuality and respect modeled by Jesus? He argued that both Gentiles and Jews should be included as participants in God's community and that membership should be by faith not works (Gal 3:23–29). That is, God's community, or in Paul's words, the *koinonia* community, includes all who believe in God, not simply those who appear religiously pure by human conventions. *Koinonos* in Greek refers to partner and companion. The *koinonia* community, in Paul's view, is one in which fellowship in God's grace abounds; it is a fellowship where sharing and generosity are prevalent and care and compassion for all are evident (Acts 4:32–37). True happiness and wealth are found in the relationships of love and hospitality, not in what members own.

While no community is perfect, and Larry and Marcy realize that Cotto needs to stay competitive to remain a viable business in a global economy, they are worried that the layoff decisions and pending plant closure will irreparably rupture their community. Furthermore, they expressed concern over the message conveyed when the executive leader of a company with long and deep ties to the community accepts exorbitant compensation in the face of such cuts. Such action is contrary to the fellowship, care, and sharing embodied in God's community. Implicit in the view Larry and Marcy hold is the value of solidarity—that if workers need to make sacrifices for the good of the whole, the budget cuts should be enacted in a fair way that respects all members. If we are all created in God's image and are part of Christ's body, then our institutions and institutional policies should respect the dignity of each and every member. This raises an important question: Should the norms of solidarity and inclusion be confined only to intentional koinonia communities or can they be applied to corporate board rooms and guide public policy?

What the people of Bancroft are experiencing is happening in multiple local communities. Many businesses are transferring production or services overseas in search of cheaper labor and production costs, leaving communities with a lack of employment opportunities. And for those businesses that remain, the threat of job loss is enough to lower wages and stifle workers' efforts to organize for better working conditions or pay. Those who retain their jobs are often overworked, and those who lose their jobs become demoralized. In both cases meaningful participation in community is lessened. On a national level the disparity between the rich and poor, and even between the rich and the middle class, threatens democratic participation, especially in a system where "money talks."

CORPORATE RESPONSIBILITY

Connected to the issues of just compensation and equitable communities is the question of corporate responsibility. Should corporations have responsibility only for their bottom line and return investments along with profits to shareholders, or should we expect more of them? Should Cotto be loyal to the workers and the community that have supported the company for years? Board member John Jones notes that Cotto has always had a good reputation in the communities where it operates and that he is concerned it will lose this reputation if it does not treat all employees fairly in its attempt to become more efficient.

The corporate charter, developed in the sixteenth century, was a grant from the governing king or queen that limited an investor's liability in the event of corporate loss to the amount of his or her investment. Such a privilege encouraged private investment in New World exploration and productive initiatives. In early America corporate charters were adopted to serve the public good but were only granted for a fixed number of years and were carefully monitored by citizens and government alike.

By the late 1800s, however, corporations had gained sufficient control over legislative bodies to influence the passage of laws that basically limited their liability and extended their charters in perpetuity. In 1886, the Supreme Court ruled that corporations had the rights of a natural person under the US Constitution, thereby entitling them to protections that individuals have under the Bill of Rights. These changes gave corporations even greater freedom and greatly decreased corporate accountability to the public. Today's corporations reach into every corner of the globe, and many are larger in size and power than most governments. International and domestic policy agendas are often more beholden to corporate interests than to labor or environmental interests.

A God of justice and liberation wants economic institutions and structures to promote the flourishing of God's amazing creation. Today's corporations are important for production of goods and services that support human welfare, and they are a crucial source of employment. That said, not all jobs promote human flourishing, nor is all corporate activity environmentally sustainable. Not only must people have access to the basic necessities to survive, but the opportunity to work and to participate in community life is important to individual self-esteem. Humans were created to be God's co-creators, to be faithful stewards in caring for God's creation. Thus, economic institutions should be designed so that people can participate as co-creators. Workers should be paid a just wage that allows families to afford the basic goods necessary for a sustainable and healthy lifestyle. Work places should encourage creative contributions, both so that workers can be fulfilled and so that organizations and businesses, and ultimately the economy, can benefit from the full array of gifts and skills workers possess. Economic institutions should also value the flourishing of human communities and the ecosystems that support them. To change the focus of corporate governance from short-term profit to sustainable community and environmental flourishing, however, would entail a radical transformation in corporate accountability to communities around the world.

Organizers in the late 1800s were able to institute some forms of accountability, such as child-labor laws, an eight-hour workday, minimum-wage standards, and modest safety regulations. However, transnational corporations like Cotto are increasingly transferring production to countries that do not have these same regulations. Workers in all countries are negatively affected by lack of corporate accountability. Solidarity among workers worldwide becomes important if any transformation is to be successful. While capital flows across borders freely, families suffer from displacement and communities become harder to sustain when employment opportunities are transient. Larry and Marcy are right to be concerned about the fate of their community if the Bancroft plant shuts down and moves production to Mexico, leaving an insufficient number of jobs for residents. Economic institutions should support the flourishing and freedom of all members of society and tread lightly on the ecosystems that they depend on.

How will Sally's connections to the Bancroft community influence her perspective on Mossman's remuneration for the work he has performed? Should the Bible's views regarding economic justice influence her views about corporate responsibility? Will she side with John Jones's perspective that reducing Mossman's bonus will show that Cotto is a responsible corporate citizen? Or should Sally side with Ralph Smith's claim that continued support in the form of a bonus for Mossman is crucial for the long-term success of the company? Will consideration of Cotto's legal and moral responsibilities to uphold contracts be most important to her? Or will she listen to the requests from her former classmates Larry and Marcy for distributive justice in light of the sacrifices Cotto workers have made? Finally, should Sally vote to renew the terms of Cotto's executive compensation plan for another three years or, given all of the concerns raised above, should the goals and structure of the plan be revised for good, ethical reasons? If so, what would that plan look like? Issues of fairness, equity, and corporate responsibility were not topics Sally thought she would have to grapple with when she accepted the invitation to be on the Cotto board. Now she and her fellow board members must decide what is best for Cotto, its stakeholders, and its employees.

ADDITIONAL RESOURCES

Association of Teaching Theologians. *Market and Margins: Lutheran Perspectives.* Edited by Wanda Deifelt. Minneapolis: Lutheran University Press, 2014.

Barnes, Kenneth J. *Redeeming Capitalism.* Grand Rapids, MI: Eerdmans, 2018.

Brubaker, Pamela. *Globalization at What Price? Economic Change and Daily Life.* Cleveland: Pilgrim Press, 2001.

Childs, James M. *Greed: Economics and Ethics in Conflict.* Minneapolis: Fortress Press, 2000.

Estey, Ken. *A New Protestant Labor Ethic at Work.* Cleveland: Pilgrim Press, 2002.

Evans, Joseph, and J. Alfred Smith. *Reconciliation and Reparation: Preaching Economic Justice.* King of Prussia, PA: Judson Press, 2018.

Finn, Daniel, ed. *The True Wealth of Nations: Catholic Social Thought and Economic Life.* New York: Oxford University Press, 2010.

Hicks, Douglas A. *Inequality and Christian Ethics.* Cambridge: Cambridge University Press, 2000.

Horsley, Richard A. *Covenant Economics: A Biblical Vision of Justice for All.* Louisville: Westminster John Knox Press, 2009.

Jones, Robert P., and Ted A. Smith, eds. *Spirit and Capital in an Age of Inequality.* Abingdon-on-Thames: Routledge, 2018.

Jung, L. Shannon. *Building the Good Life for All: Transforming Income Inequality in Our Communities.* Louisville: Westminster John Knox Press, 2017.

Lindsley, Arthur, and Anne Rathbone Bradley, eds. *Counting the Cost: Christian Perspectives on Capitalism.* Abilene, TX: Abilene Christian University Press, 2017.

Long, Stephen D., Nancy Ruth Fox, and Tripp York. *Calculated Futures: Theology, Ethics, and Economics.* Waco, TX: Baylor University Press, 2007.

National Conference of Catholic Bishops. *Economic Justice for All: Pastoral Letter on Catholic Social Teaching and the US Economy.* Washington, DC: USCCB, 1986.

Snarr, Melissa C. *All You That Labor: Religion and Ethics in the Living Wage Movement.* New York: New York University Press, 2011.

Tanner, Kathryn. *Christianity and the New Spirit of Capitalism.* New Haven, CT: Yale University Press, 2019.

Wallis, Jim. *Rediscovering Values on Wall Street, Main Street, and Your Street: A Moral Compass for the New Economy.* Brentwood. TN: Howard Books, 2010.

Related Videos

Inside AFLAC: CEO Dan Amos. 12 minutes. Princeton, NJ: Films for the Humanities and Sciences, 2008.

Smith Business School. *Setting CEO Pay: Executive Compensation.* 6 minutes. YouTube. 2009.

Creative Commons. *Wealth Inequality in America.* 3 minutes. YouTube. 2012.

PART VI

HEALTH

Case

Cut It Out!

Sofia Castro was wrung out emotionally. It had been a long, hard day. She had spent most of it trying to console her daughter, Carla, who was mourning the death of her best friend, Megan. They were home now after attending Megan's funeral and graveside service at the Lutheran church where Carla and Megan had both gone to Sunday School. They had grown up together on the same street in Durham, North Carolina, and had recently forged a deeper bond as starters on their high school soccer team. One week ago, in the middle of a game they were winning easily, Megan collapsed suddenly and died. An autopsy revealed that Megan had suffered from familial hypertrophic cardiomyopathy—a genetic disorder that results in the thickening of the heart muscle. While one in five hundred people have the condition, most are unaware of it or have only mild symptoms. Some, however, suffer sudden death. Sadly, Megan was one of them. Empathizing with their suffering, the pastor had preached that God was with those who suffer. Sofia took some comfort from his sermon but ultimately found it insufficient.

As a geneticist in a laboratory in the famed Research Triangle area of North Carolina, Sofia was all too familiar with hypertrophic cardiomyopathy. She knew that mutations in at least four genes were linked to the disorder and that a lot of research was under way around the world to correct it through gene therapy. These efforts had gained substantial new momentum with the discovery of a new approach in gene editing called CRISPR-Cas9. The technique was adapted from a naturally occurring genome-editing system in bacteria. In contrast to earlier forms of gene editing, CRISPR (Clustered Regularly Interspaced Short Palindromic Repeats) enables researchers to disable, repair, or augment any gene in any species. The therapeutic potential associated with this new technique is huge for medicine, but it

This case and its commentary were prepared by James B. Martin-Schramm. The names of persons and institutions have been disguised, where appropriate, to protect the privacy of those involved.

also could have a significant impact in agriculture. Researchers like Sofia had been working with CRISPR a lot over the last three to five years, but most members of the public didn't know much about it.

That all changed in November 2018 when a Chinese researcher, He Jiankui, announced the birth of twin girls whose embryos he had edited with CRISPR. Jiankui and his team had deactivated a gene that the human immunodeficiency virus (HIV) uses to infiltrate human cells. His motivation was to make the girls immune to HIV, because Chinese society stigmatizes those who are HIV-positive. It would have been one thing if he had merely edited the twins' somatic cells, but Jiankui edited the germline in both girls, which means his interventions will affect future generations if they reproduce.

Jiankui's actions were met with dismay and repudiation within the Chinese academy of scientists and around the world. The opposition was manifold. Some criticized Jiankui's actions as reckless, unnecessary, and amateurish. Others condemned the fact that he had violated one of the norms in his field, which limits such research to nonviable embryos. Most of the attention in the press, however, focused on the fear that parents would now work with geneticists to craft "designer babies." More than one columnist noted that the dystopian future imagined in the 1997 movie *Gattaca* now seemed not simply a subject for science fiction but a very real and present danger.

Sofia wasn't so sure. While she knew lots of parents would prefer to have children who are tall, smart, happy, and slim, the reality is that none of these attributes are associated with just one gene. In fact, researchers have identified hundreds of genes related to height and more than five hundred genes linked to intelligence. While a much smaller number of genes have been linked to happiness and obesity, the reality is that environmental factors play a huge role in human health and well-being. Sofia was worried that public concern about "designer babies" might wind up limiting the rapid pace of research into the use of CRISPR for all sorts of therapeutic gains. Labs around the world were researching the potential to treat or cure single-gene disorders like cystic fibrosis, hemophilia, and sickle cell disease. According to the *Journal of Gene Medicine,* twenty-six hundred gene therapy clinical trials had been completed through 2017.

Sofia's lab was focused on Huntington's disease—a progressive brain disorder caused by a single defective gene. Symptoms normally occur when people are in the prime of their life (ages 30–50) and result in significant deterioration of physical and mental abilities. The Huntington's Disease Society of America says it is like having ALS, Parkinson's, and Alzheimer's—all at the same time. Sofia's interest in the disease was personal. She had watched her father die from it and learned with relief as an eighteen-year-old that she had dodged the 50 percent chance of inheriting the faulty gene from her father. She was proud that her lab had demonstrated last year that they could use CRISPR technology to permanently deactivate the defective gene in mouse models and in cells from people with Huntington's disease. They had recently applied for additional research funding from the National Institutes of Health (NIH), and to the Food and Drug Administration (FDA) for permission to conduct a Phase 1 human clinical trial.

Two days after the funeral Sofia was back at work, and Carla was back at school. Sofia's lab was in a building that contained several biomedical research facilities. As a result, coffee breaks and lunch hours often led to great conversations with colleagues. Arriving a bit late for lunch, Sofia found a table that had one of the few available seats. She had met Ed Vance and Beata Klein before, but she didn't know them very well. Regardless, it didn't take them long to see that Sofia was a bit distracted and looked wan and sad. When Beata asked if she was all right, Sofia told them about Megan's sudden death from hypertrophic cardiomyopathy and how Carla remained virtually inconsolable.

After a pause, Ed Vance took the conversation in a whole new direction. He said, "I think Jiankui was on the right track. With CRISPR we have the ability to edit the human genome in ways that, over time, will significantly reduce and perhaps eliminate some devastating genetic disorders. Those of us in the health-care field have a moral obligation to reduce and end suffering if we can. There don't need to be more Megans."

After a moment, Sofia replied, "I agree that we should use CRISPR to develop somatic gene therapies for those suffering from these diseases now or who may manifest them in the future, but germline intervention is illegal."

"Actually, that's not quite right," said Ed. "It's true that the NIH won't currently approve experiments that involve germline genetic modification, and it is true that Congress has banned the use of federal funds for research that creates embryos or destroys embryos, but there is no federal law that prohibits genetic modification of human embryos. You just can't use federal money to do it."

"It may be legal, but it certainly isn't ethical," said Beata. "CRISPR has vastly improved our ability to edit genomes, but it isn't exact. There are still plenty of unintended effects. We aren't as proficient with the technology as we think we are."

"That's true," said Ed. "I'm not saying we're ready yet, but I think we will be soon. Remember what the NAS (National Academy of Sciences) said a couple years ago: 'Genome editing for purposes other than treatment or prevention of disease and disability should not proceed *at this time,*' but NAS said it can foresee a time when clinical trials 'might be permitted, but only following much more research' on risks and benefits, and 'only for compelling reasons and under strict oversight.'" Ed had clearly memorized these excerpts from the NAS report.[1]

"That would be a grave mistake," said Beata. "I think the international community should ban embryo gene editing as a means of human reproduction just as we've been able to achieve such a ban on human cloning. Unlike somatic gene therapy, germline modification of a human being is irreversible. In addition, it is unpredictable. We have no way to know with certainty what the epigenetic, personal, and social effects of our engineering of the human genome will be. The same gene that causes sickle cell helped humans combat malaria in the past. Who knows what sort of genetic problems we may be creating for our species in the future with germline interventions today? We are not as smart as we think we are. We can't foresee all of the consequences of our actions."

Ed replied, "Beata, we've had this argument before. You Germans are in love with the precautionary principle. It has its value, but applied relentlessly we will never be able to make scientific advances because we can't possibly foresee every possible consequence. We have to trust that future generations will grow in their scientific understanding and technological ability to fix any problems we create. Different challenges fall to different generations. Our generation is the first to be able to fix some of these devastating genetic disorders, and thus we have a moral obligation to do so."

Beata was visibly upset. "Yes, I am a German. You know damn well what my country did to people with disabilities when the Nazis were in power. Germline intervention opens the door again to delusions of engineering a master race. Even if that doesn't happen, the stigmatization of persons with disabilities will only get worse because now, presumably, something could have been done by their parents to fix or forestall their child's disability."

Now it was Ed's turn to be upset. "That isn't fair, Beata. You know my intentions are good. I just want to help people like Megan so that they don't suffer like so many have in the past. Every year, 6 percent of all children are born with a serious birth defect of genetic or partially genetic origin. Compassion drives me, not arrogance or hatred. We can help people with gene therapy. Sofia is demonstrating that in her lab. We are rapidly getting to the point where we can fix these problems for the long term. Therapy deferred is therapy denied."

---

[1] See National Academies of Sciences, Engineering, and Medicine, "Summary," *Human Genome Editing: Science, Ethics, and Governance* (Washington, DC: The National Academies Press, 2017), 7–9.

"Yes, but there is a huge difference between somatic gene therapy and germline engineering," said Beata. "Apply your compassion to this generation, Ed. Admit that we don't really know how our actions will affect future generations if we edit human germlines. Think about the way this technology will only widen the gap between the rich and the poor."

"Beata, the concerns you raise are not new but old. It has always been an advantage to be rich rather than poor. Higher measures of wealth and income tend to buy greater amounts of health and well-being—at least, up to a point. I agree that germline editing could widen the gap between the rich and the poor but the issue isn't the technology—it is our failure to pursue social justice. I know I need to spend less time in my lab and more time engaging in politics but these things are not mutually exclusive."

"Ed, the road to hell is paved with good intentions. The use of CRISPR to eliminate genetic disorders will rapidly lead to widespread efforts at genetic enhancement."

"Beata, there is no clear line between therapy and enhancement; it is blurry. Given the challenges our species faces in this age of rapid climate change and loss of biodiversity, we may need to evolve faster than we have in the past. We need to embrace our role as co-creators and not run away from it!"

At this point Sofia swept her lunch container and fork into her little meal bag and got up to leave. Ed and Beata were a bit mortified. They realized they had been debating the ethics of germline intervention and had not really invited Sofia into the conversation. Truthfully, Sofia was a bit relieved not to have offered an opinion. She wasn't sure what she thought, but she knew she did need to start thinking hard about these matters because the science and technology were moving quickly.

When she got back to the office, the mail had arrived. On the top of the pile was a letter from the NIH. She had been invited to become a member of the Novel and Exceptional Technology and Research Advisory Committee (NExTRAC), which would decide whether and when to approve germline interventions for therapeutic purposes. Sofia knew RAC's voice would be key as the US scientific community continued to grapple with the ethics of germline gene therapy. That meant her voice would be important. It was time to think more carefully about the stance she would take.

Commentary

The relentless pace of scientific discovery and technological change during the twentieth century is accelerating during the twenty-first century. This is especially true in the field of genetics. The discovery of CRISPR and the associated Cas9 gene-editing system has proven to be a game changer. CRISPR-Cas9 can be used for highly specific purposes such as inserting sequences into target genes, deleting genes, or turning genes off. To date, it is the most versatile genomic engineering tool in the history of molecular biology. At the time this book went to press, researchers at Stanford University and in other labs around the world were researching how to use CRISPR-Cas9 to disrupt the Covid-19 virus. While many worry about the new dangers this technology brings, there is no way to put the genie back in the bottle; it is simply too inexpensive. The ODIN, a company in Oakland, California, is just one of several that already sells gene-editing kits on the internet.

How should Christians engage the subject of gene therapy and germline intervention? Is it really that new and controversial? After all, human beings have been breeding animals for desired traits and grafting branches onto fruit trees for thousands of years. More recently we have developed hybrid and genetically engineered crops that are resistant to pesticides and herbicides as well as to drought and other threats to food production. Some families already use pre-implantation genetic diagnosis (PGD) to screen embryos produced through in vitro fertilization for genetic diseases before implantation in the womb.

What is new, however, is that we now have the capacity to direct the evolution of our own species while also having the capacity to alter the genomes of other species. With CRISPR-Cas9 we can turn off genes that produce horrific suffering through diseases like Huntington's, and we can select genes for a variety of desired traits. We can do this through gene therapy for present generations, which only edits patients' somatic cells and thus only affects persons during their lifetime. But we can also edit an individual's germline cells, which means the changes will affect all tissues in the recipient's body and will be inherited by future generations. Shifting from a focus on genetic intervention in human populations, we also now have the capacity to accelerate the traits of a population or even an entire species by engineering *gene drives,* that is, a system of biasing inheritance to increase the likelihood of passing on a modified gene more quickly than would typically occur through natural selection. According to a 2018 article in *Scientific American:*

The technology has the potential to stop insects from transmitting malaria and other terrible infections, enhance crop yields by altering pests that attack plants, render corals resistant to environmental stress, and keep invasive plants and animals from destroying ecosystems. Yet investigators are deeply aware that altering or even eliminating a species could have profound ecological consequences.[2]

Just as the human capacity to split the atom had a significant impact on the twentieth century, our new and growing capacity to edit genetic material will have a transformative impact on the twenty-first century.

Renowned Harvard biologist E. O. Wilson summarizes the situation well in his Pulitzer Prize–winning book, *The Meaning of Human Existence*:

> The advances of science and technology will bring us to the greatest moral dilemma since God stayed the hand of Abraham: how much to retrofit the human genotype. Shall it be a lot, a little bit, or none at all? The choice will be forced on us because our species has begun to cross what is the most important yet still least examined threshold in the techno-scientific era. We are about to abandon natural selection, the process that created us, in order to direct our own evolution by volitional selection— the process of redesigning our biology and human nature as we wish them to be. No longer will the prevalence of some genes (more precisely alleles, variations in codes of the same gene) over others be the result of environmental forces, most of which are beyond human control or even understanding. The genes and their prescribed traits can be what we choose.[3]

The stakes are huge. Bill McKibben, the founder of the environmental organization 350.org and the winner of the Gandhi Prize and the "alternative Nobel" (the Right Livelihood Prize), expresses profound concern about the dangers that climate change, artificial intelligence, and genetic engineering pose to humanity:

> The source of my disquiet can be summed up in a single word, a word that will be repeated regularly in this book: *leverage*. We're simply so big, and moving so fast, that every decision carries enormous risk. . . .

---

[2] Cynthia H. Collins, "Gene Drive: A Genetic Tool That Can Alter—and Potentially Eliminate—Entire Species Has Taken a Great Leap Forward," *Scientific American* (September 14, 2018).

[3] E. O. Wilson, *The Meaning of Human Existence* (New York: Liveright Publishing, 2014), 14–15.

As we shall see, humans have now emerged as a destructive geologic force. . . . And humans have simultaneously emerged as a massive *creative* force, in ways that threaten the human game not through destruction but through substitution.[4]

Finally, the world's most famous theoretical physicist and cosmologist, Stephen Hawking, admits in a set reflections published posthumously that his greatest fear is that a "new species" of genetically engineered "super-humans" would eliminate the rest of humanity.[5]

What does the future hold? Can Christians use CRISPR for laudatory therapeutic ends, or will our efforts at genetic engineering inevitably lead us down a slippery slope that accentuates anthropocentrism, deepens prejudices against those with disabilities, creates a whole new class of su-perhumans, widens the gap between the rich and the poor, and endangers ecological well-being? This commentary explores these questions and others by exploring theological and ethical resources in a social statement about issues in genetics produced by the Evangelical Lutheran Church in America (ELCA). It also explores three different stances toward these is-sues that are represented, to some extent, by the three scientists in the case.

GENETICS, FAITH, AND RESPONSIBILITY

While some Christian denominations have developed position statements about specific topics like embryonic stem cell research and pre-implantation genetic diagnosis, very few have developed wide-ranging statements on the many issues posed by modern genetic science. The ELCA is an exception. Like Wilson and McKibben, its statement *Social Statement on Genetics, Faith, and Responsibility*[6] emphasizes that "human beings increasingly bear the moral burden for the shape of nature and the very existence of future generations. The cumulative force of such unparalleled power and choice promise great benefit but also present qualitatively new levels of danger and ambiguity" (1).

The social statement emphasizes that there is no inherent conflict be-tween scientific findings and theological understandings of God as creator,

---

[4] Bill McKibben, *Falter: Has the Human Game Begun to Play Itself Out?* (New York: Henry Holt and Co., 2019), 14–15.

[5] Sarah Marsh, "Essays Reveal Stephen Hawking Predicted Race of Superhumans," *Guardian,* October 4, 2018.

[6] Evangelical Lutheran Church in America (ELCA), *A Social Statement on Genetics, Faith, and Responsibility* (Chicago: Evangelical Lutheran Church in America, 2011). Page numbers for quotations from this document appear in parentheses in this section.

redeemer, and sanctifier. To the contrary, science and technology are viewed as gifts from God that Christians need to use wisely and compassionately as they "respect and promote the community of life" (1). The social statement summarizes the ethical challenges associated with genetics this way:

> The ELCA's concern for benefit or harm, however, is not focused per se on any particular scientific or technological development. The concern, rather, focuses on the just and wise use of genetic knowledge and technology. For instance, the ELCA does not reject the use of genetic technology such as genetically modified organisms, prenatal diagnosis or pharmacogenetics. Like other gifts of technology, there are reasons for both encouraging their use and for cautioning against certain means of applying them. This church believes the use of any technology should be subject to moral assessment. (8)

For the ELCA, moral assessment begins with scripture and theological tradition. At the heart of the social statement is a conception of God as a creator who not only "originates, preserves, and will bring to completion the whole creation" (9) but also shares this work with human beings "to provide oversight as stewards" (10) to care for God's creation. The vocation of each Christian is "to continue what God is already doing for the earth—a calling to respect and promote the creation's flourishing" (10). This is what it means to be created "in the image of God" (Gen. 1:26–28). Just as Christ placed the interests of others over his own, so too should Christians "as innovative stewards . . . be guided by the goal to respect and promote the earth's abundance for the sake of the community of life" (10). Ed Vance appeals to this sense of stewardship when he tells Beata Klein that geneticists need to embrace their role as co-creators.

The ELCA acknowledges that human sinfulness can warp this vocation and it emphasizes that decisions about genetics take place in a world where powerful economic and political forces have a great deal at stake. In addition, the statement lifts up traditional concerns about the impact of human pride and hubris now magnified by unprecedented scientific and technological powers. It points out that Genesis 3 "depicts human beings as attempting to usurp the place of God" (11) by eating the fruit of the tree of the knowledge of good and evil. Here sin is manifested as excessive pride and leads to the misuse of human power. What is interesting, however, is that the ELCA considers sin in an additional way:

> Along with sin as excessive pride, Scripture also teaches that sin can be manifested as negligence or complacency, a lack of trust in God that despairs in human failures and limitations and neglects

responsibility for love and action (Mt 25:14–30). This manifestation of sin can translate into resignation and fatalism. Resignation can occur because genetic science, technology and commerce seem overwhelmingly complex and forbidding. It can follow and feed upon discouragement when individuals and systems are focused on self-interest and where commitment to care of the earth is tepid. Far too many become complacent or neglect their responsibility for the positive and constructive use of human powers. Far too many assume the role of a powerless bystander who believes little or nothing can be done to change the course of events. (12)

This view about sin and moral agency is an important contribution in the ELCA social statement.

Moving from theology to ethics, the ELCA summarizes its stance towards issues in genetics with a maxim: "Respect and promote the community of life with justice and wisdom" (14). Space here permits only brief excerpts from the social statement about these key concepts:

The Community of Life

The pursuit of genetic knowledge and its applications will rightfully give priority to serving the needs of existing individuals and the human community, with particular attention to the needs of the most vulnerable. These efforts, however, must not compromise the integrity of future human generations and should consider the integrity of the rest of the biosphere—animals, plants, soils and the ecosystem as a whole, including the water and air on which it depends. (16)

Respect

The fact that creatures across the multitude of forms exhibit both purposiveness and interdependence establishes the grounds for respect. . . . The placement of the directive to respect before the directive to promote indicates a priority for claims of integrity and dignity for members of the web of life. (17)

Promote

Human beings cannot create as God does, but they are to be imaginative, inventive and responsible caretakers (Ps 115:16). . . . The priority of respect over that of promotion means that not every possible enhancement or innovation should be pursued. Promotion must not violate the fundamental directive of respect. Efforts toward enhancement or innovation must be evaluated also through the norms of justice and wisdom. This church rejects striving after some imagined perfection or idealized state of human life. (19–20)

Justice

Previous ELCA social statements have identified four guiding principles that spell out the meaning of justice relevant to the study of genetics and its use: sufficiency, sustainability, solidarity, and participation. (21)

- *Sufficiency:* This church encourages governments, universities, nongovernmental organizations and private companies to seek ways to contribute to meeting basic needs and to broaden access for all who might benefit from genetic applications. (22)
- *Sustainability:* This church, however, believes overly restrictive regulation must not be a default response to novel genetic technology. Regulation must be justified by specified concerns for the potential harm of a genetic application and its delivery or by the necessity to regulate toward equal access and use. (22)
- *Solidarity:* The ELCA calls upon those in government and commerce to give emphasis to seeking the means to direct equitably the benefits of genetic knowledge and application. It urges attention to achieving access for all members of the human family regardless of which segments of society a person can be identified with. (25)
- *Participation*: This church encourages its members and all people of good will to be aware of, seek sound knowledge of, and actively participate in debates concerning public policies related to the application of genetic knowledge. (26)

Wisdom

In a century of growing genetic knowledge and practical power, the golden rule demands wise use of that knowledge and power. Wise use requires expert knowledge as well as humility and caution in the face of conflicting demands and uncertainty. (26)

The ELCA social statement on genetics concludes on a note of confidence yet accountability:

Human beings, as innovative stewards, have a distinctive freedom and power that are to be used for the sake of that community, but these powers are not unlimited, and we are accountable for their use. Human beings must use these gifts without knowing all possible contingencies or being able to guarantee outcomes. This church recognizes that good and sin, possibility and finitude, hope and anguish are always mixed together in earthly life. (35)

THREE STANCES ON "PLAYING GOD"

Ted Peters is one Christian theologian who is ready and willing to embrace the ELCA's emphasis on confidence and accountability. He served on the team of lay and ordained persons who developed the ELCA's social statement on genetics. In a 2017 article Peters explores three stances bioethicists can take regarding issues in genetics—including germline intervention, which is the aspect Sofia Castro is thinking the most about in the case.[7] At one end of the spectrum is Prometheus, the Greek Titan who defies the gods by stealing fire and giving it to humanity. At the other end of the spectrum are the anti-Prometheans, who think human beings should not usurp the authority of the gods and will be punished if they do so. Peters outlines a third, middle option, which is where he locates himself.

Who are the modern Prometheans? Peters lifts up Simon Young, who embraces genetic engineering and writes, "Let us cast aside cowardice and seize the torch of Prometheus with both hands."[8] Bill McKibben lifts up another example—Julian Savulescu, who teaches ethics at the University of Oxford and is the author of *Unfit for the Future*. In a TED Talk on this topic, Savulescu remarks:

> Science offers us the opportunity . . . to directly overcome those [moral] limitations [by producing embryos with improved] intelligence, impulse control, self-control—some level of empathy or ability to understand other people's emotions, some willingness to make self-sacrificial decisions for other people.[9]

In the case, Ed Vance seems to share some commonality with Young and Savulescu insofar as Vance embraces the idea that modern threats to human existence may require an acceleration of the normal rate of evolution

---

[7] Ted Peters, "Should CRISPR Scientists Play God?" *Religions* 8, no. 4 (2017).

[8] Simon Young, *Designer Evolution: A Transhumanist Manifesto* (Amherst, MA: Prometheus Books, 2006), 40.

[9] Julian Savulescu, "As a Species, We Have a Moral Obligation to Enhance Ourselves," TED guest author, February 19, 2014.

as well as the use of modern genetics to relieve suffering by eliminating single-gene disorders.

Who are the modern opponents of this Promethean attitude toward genetic modification? Peters points to Leon Kass, who in his role as the chair of the US President's Council on Bioethics, writes, "Not everyone likes the idea of remaking Eden or of man playing God."[10] Peters also lifts up James P. Eckman, president emeritus and professor in Bible and history at Grace University in Omaha, Nebraska. Eckman writes:

> Simply because society can pursue a particular medical, reproductive or genetic procedure does not mandate that it must! Especially in the area of genetics, "can" does not mandate "ought." The potential for power and control and its obvious abuse mandates an examination of this imperative. Perhaps with some of these procedures, such as gene editing, it would be wise to not do them at all.[11]

In the case, Beata Klein may fit in this camp—at least with regard to germline intervention. Like Vance and Castro, she sees the clear therapeutic benefits of somatic-cell gene therapy, but she also sees very clear dangers associated with germline intervention. This is a line she fervently believes should never be crossed. While we may be able to eradicate the threat malaria poses to human health through gene drives in certain mosquito species, who knows what ecological damage such unprecedented human intervention could cause? Beata is especially concerned about the impact genetic engineering could have on public perceptions of persons with disabilities and those too poor to afford the technology.

Peters locates himself between these two extremes. He uses a "stop light" analogy. While the Prometheans only see green, and the anti-Prometheans only see red, Peters sees yellow, looks both ways, and then proceeds with caution. He writes: "Keep driving ahead while perpetually assessing the risk; watch out for pot holes and avoid swerving into a ditch. This applies to germline intervention as well as somatic genome editing therapy."[12]

In a world where modern medicine routinely bars the doors to death and often produces miraculous results, the moral question for Peters is not whether humans should play God, but rather what kinds of human interventions are legitimate and which ones are not. Therapeutic editing of somatic

---

[10] The President's Council on Bioethics. *Beyond Therapy: Biotechnology and the Pursuit of Happiness* (Washington, DC: President's Council on Bioethics, October 2003), chap. 1.

[11] Jim Eckman, "The Ethics of Gene Editing." *Issues in Perspective*, May 16, 2015.

[12] Peters, "Should CRISPR Scientists Play God?" 2.

cells to cure genetic diseases is legitimate so long as success and safety can reasonably be assured. Germline intervention is another matter, however. Sofia Castro would undoubtedly be interested in the following comments by Peters on this topic:

> Suppose we would snip out of the germline the gene for Huntington's disease located on the short arm of chromosome 4. Huntington's is a neurodegenerative disorder leading to mental decline, dementia, uncontrollable body movements, anxiety, depression, and aggression. . . . What we don't know is the long-term effect of such large-scale changes in the genome. Genes work with other genes and other DNA in delicate systems like Swiss watches, mutually influencing one another. To eliminate one set of gears in an old-fashioned Swiss watch would cause it to self-destruct. Might this analogy apply to the human genome? We don't know yet. Without this knowledge, clinical geneticists cannot measure the risk.[13]

Appealing to the precautionary principle, Peters argues that more research is needed before germline editing can be justified. While Peters quotes the UNESCO version of the precautionary principle, he prefers the earlier (Wingspread) version that was formulated at the 1992 United Nations Conference on Environment and Development:

> When an activity raises threats of harm to human health or the environment, precautionary measures should be taken even if some cause and effect relationships are not fully established scientifically. In this context, the proponent of the process or product, rather than the public, should bear the burden of proof.[14]

Like Ed Vance, however, Peters notes that the National Academy of Sciences says that it is "essential for this research to be approached with caution, and for it to proceed with broad public input."[15] Peters concludes:

> Methodologically, I recommend that we proceed with developing and applying CRISPR/Cas9 while invoking the Precautionary Principle. There is no warrant either theologically or ethically for putting up a red stop light to halt this particular technology. Theologically, I

---

[13] Ibid., 5.

[14] Urban Governance, Wingspread Statement on the Precautionary Principle (1998).

[15] National Academies of Sciences, Engineering, and Medicine, *Human Genome Editing*, 7.

observe this: human creativity belongs inherently to the imago Dei, because we are created by the God who does new things (Is 65:17).[16]

CONCLUSION

Where does this leave Sofia Castro as she ponders the ethics of gene therapy and germline intervention? How would Megan view these issues? How about her father? What about Sofia's great grandchildren? Are the perspectives of some more important than others?

Given all of the gene therapy trials that have been approved by the NIH and the Food and Drug Administration (FDA) to date, there is a rapidly growing consensus around the moral propriety of somatic-cell gene therapy for present generations. The big issues revolve around germline intervention and the impact on future generations. While turning off or removing defective genes won't immediately eliminate the devastating consequences of diseases associated with a single gene, such germline intervention will reduce the number of carriers in the future and it will have an immediate impact for some families today who don't want to pass these diseases on to the next generation. If possible, why not spare families like Megan's the enormous grief and sorrow associated with her sudden death from hypertrophic cardiomyopathy? Ed Vance makes a powerful point—therapy deferred is therapy denied.

But what about the long-term, indeed eternal consequences of such interventions? Couldn't the elimination of a gene harm the human species in the future when environmental conditions might turn a genetic liability into an asset? What might be the unintended but potentially very harmful consequences of such actions? Think about nuclear power. After witnessing the horrible effects of the atomic bombs dropped by the United States to end World War II, many were eager to embrace peaceful uses of atomic physics in the form of nuclear power plants. Absent from much public reflection was the long-term challenge associated with storing and then disposing of high-level nuclear waste that remains toxic for hundreds of thousands of years. Our interest in short-term results seems to cloud our reflection about long-term consequences. Our technological prowess may be eclipsing our ethical wisdom.

Beata Klein is very worried about the use of CRISPR-Cas9 for genetic modification and enhancement—especially efforts to engineer the germline to produce a "master race." Given the persistent scourge of racism and appeals by some to various forms of social Darwinism, this concern

---

[16] Peters, "Should CRISPR Scientists Play God?" 2.

is legitimate and warrants substantial ethical reflection. Unfortunately, the likelihood is high that parents will seek the services of various genetics labs that will help them select the traits they want in their future children. Making such changes at the somatic cell level is one thing, but germline intervention would be quite another.

Either way, how can this technology be regulated? In the United States, the NIH's Recombinant DNA Advisory Committee[17] and the FDA appear to be doing a good job regulating somatic-cell gene therapies. It is less clear how to prevent fertility clinics from offering "enhancement" services as the cost to edit genes continues to fall. Beata Klein is attracted to the idea of an indefinite global ban on germline intervention, which thus far has apparently been achieved with regard to human cloning. It is hard to know whether such an indefinite ban on germline intervention could be achieved, however, especially since the US National Academies of Sciences, Engineering, and Medicine only says "genome editing for purposes other than treatment or prevention of disease and disability should not proceed *at this time*."[18]

When should it proceed, if ever? What criteria would need to be met? Teleologically, can we anticipate all of the possible consequences? How should the real goods be weighed against the possible harms? Deontologically, how should the precautionary principle be applied? Is it in conflict with the golden rule, which the ELCA embraces? Areteologically, given the rapidly falling cost of CRISPR-Cas9 and its ease of application, will the ethics regarding its use ultimately boil down to the moral character of the scientists using it in research and the moral character of the individuals who seek to utilize the technological fruits of their research?

Finally, what does it mean to be created in the image of God? Does that mean human beings are co-creators with God, or are we merely stewards of the gifts God has created? Is there, in the words of Karl Barth, "an infinite qualitative difference between God and man," between the creature and the Creator?[19] What does it mean, as the ELCA says, to "respect and promote the community of life with justice and wisdom"?

---

[17] This has now been renamed the Novel and Exceptional Technology and Research Advisory Committee (NExTRAC).

[18] National Academies of Sciences, Engineering, and Medicine, *Human Genome Editing*, 9, emphasis added.

[19] Karl Barth, *The Epistle to the Romans,* trans. Edwyn C. Hoskins (New York: Oxford University Press, 1965), 355.

ADDITIONAL RESOURCES

Advanced Gene Editing: CRISPR-Cas9. Washington, DC: Congressional Research Service. CRS Report R44824. December 2018.

Evangelical Lutheran Church in America (ELCA). *A Social Statement on Genetics, Faith, and Responsibility*. Chicago: Evangelical Lutheran Church in America, 2011.

Green, Ronald M. "Do We Have a Moral Obligation to Genetically Enhance Our Children?" *Hastings Bioethics Forum*. October 31, 2017.

Kane, Eileen M. "Human Genome Editing: An Evolving Regulatory Climate" (August 17, 2017). *Jurimetrics* 57, no. 3; Penn State Law Research Paper No. 15–2017.

Kolata, Gina. *Mercies in Disguise: A Story of Hope, a Family's Genetic Destiny, and the Science That Rescued Them*. New York: St. Martin's Press, 2017.

Marsh, Sarah. "Essays Reveal Stephen Hawking Predicted Race of Superhumans," *Guardian,* October 4, 2018.

McKibben, Bill. *Falter: Has the Human Game Begun to Play Itself Out?* New York: Henry Holt and Company, 2019.

Mehlman, Maxwell J. *Transhumanist Dreams and Dystopian Nightmares: The Promise and Peril of Genetic Engineering*. Baltimore: Johns Hopkins University Press, 2012.

National Academies of Sciences, Engineering, and Medicine. *Human Genome Editing: Science, Ethics, and Governance*. Washington, DC: The National Academies Press, 2017.

Peters, Ted. *God—The World's Future: Systematic Theology for a New Era.* 3rd edition. Minneapolis: Fortress Press, 2015.

———. *Playing God? Genetic Determinism and Human Freedom.* 2nd edition. London: Routledge, 2002.

———. "Should CRISPR Scientists Play God?" *Religions* 8, no. 4 (2017).

———. *The Stem Cell Debate*. Minneapolis: Fortress Press, 2008.

Peters, Ted, Karen Lebacqz, and Gaymon Bennett. *Sacred Cells: Why Christians Should Support Stem Cell Research.* New York: Rowman and Littlefield, 2008.

Peterson, James. *Changing Human Nature: Ecology, Ethics, Genes, and God.* Grand Rapids, MI: Eerdmans, 2010.

Savulescu, Julian. *Unfit for the Future: The Need for Moral Enhancement.* Oxford: Oxford University Press, 2012.

United Nations Educational, Scientific, and Cultural Organization (UNESCO), World Commission on the Ethics of Scientific Knowledge and Technology. "The Precautionary Principle." 2005.

Urban Governance. "Wingspread Statement on the Precautionary Principle." 1998.

Wilson, E. O. *The Meaning of Human Existence.* New York: Liveright Publishing Corporation, 2014.

Young, Simon. *Designer Evolution: A Transhumanist Manifesto.* Amherst, MA: Prometheus Books, 2006.

Related Websites

National Human Genome Research Institute, "About Genomics." https://www.genome.gov/about-genomics

National Institutes of Health, "What Are the Ethical Issues Surrounding Gene Therapy?" https://ghr.nlm.nih.gov/primer/therapy/ethics

Case

Keeping the Doors Open

Dr. Beatrice Gonzalez, newly appointed CEO of Washington Memorial Hospital, was speaking at her first meeting of the Washington Memorial Public Trust, the board of trustees for the hospital. Washington Memorial is a huge public hospital with an immense downtown complex and two satellite hospitals in the north and south ends of a county in south Florida. The hospital is owned by the county but the Washington Memorial Public Trust is responsible for the administration of the hospital.

"We face an immediate crisis," she announced. "The new auditing firm has informed me that we have the funds to remain open only seven to eight weeks. For next year we face a projected deficit of $200 million. We need at least $50 million simply to keep the doors open until the new fiscal year begins, and by then we will also need to have a deficit-reduction plan in place. The basic problem is that for many years the accounting department has continued to treat unpaid accounts as payable, not writing them off as bad debt, even though it was clear that minimum-wage workers without insurance were never going to be able to pay hundreds of thousands of dollars for extended ICU or surgical care."

The members of the trust looked stunned. "Why are we hearing about this for the first time if this practice has gone on for years?" demanded Peter Migone, a six-year veteran of the trust.

Beatrice replied: "Until recently there was sufficient income from insurance and paying patients to cover costs. The cost of health care has gone up substantially in the last ten years, and while the unemployment rate has gone down since the recession, the urban unemployment rate is still very high and the middle class is shrinking. While more people today are covered by insurance with the Affordable Care Act (ACA), some insurance plans

---

This case was prepared by Christine E. Gudorf and the commentary by Laura A. Stivers; both have been updated by Laura A. Stivers and James B. Martin-Schramm. The names of persons and institutions have been disguised, where appropriate, to protect the privacy of those involved.

have a high deductible and don't cover all forms of care. Over half of our caseload are patients either on Medicaid or with no insurance whatsoever. Fewer low-income families are covered by Medicaid in Florida than those states who opted to expand Medicaid under the ACA, and Florida is notoriously stingy in setting Medicaid reimbursement rates."

"I always figured that with almost 90 percent of the population now covered by insurance that public hospitals like Washington Memorial would be better off," said Peter.

Beatrice explained, "We couldn't compete with many of the for-profit and nonprofit hospitals that had better bargaining power with insurance companies to get many of the newly insured patients. The city and state also assumed, like you, Peter, that we would be better off with the passage of the ACA and offered less support. Under the ACA, federal funding to states for health-care costs was also decreased. Yet there are still many uninsured people who come through our doors. Florida has one of the highest rates of uninsured residents, in part because the ACA specifically forbids nonresidents of the United States, whether here legally or not, from signing up for the insurance exchanges."

"Why didn't the former auditors tell us about the amount of debt the hospital has? We have audits every year!" Peter exclaimed in exasperation.

Beatrice calmly responded: "When I asked that question of the new auditors, what I heard was that it is not easy to determine which unpaid bills should be written off. The general method involves time—bills that do not involve insurance and are unpaid after a year are either sent to collection agencies, which give us back a proportion of what they collect, or the bills are written off. There is some discretion involved in deciding whether to write them off or send them to collectors. As the proportion of unpaid bills went up, the staff got behind in handing them to the collection agencies, and the collection agencies' rate of recovery went down. Some of the insurance companies also seem to have delayed payment even more than usual in order to protect their own bottom line, although they deny it. The combination of these things created our crisis. In addition, all the flu admissions last winter didn't help because many of those who were sick were also too poor to pay their bill."

Elizabeth Walker, a long-term trust member who served on multiple metropolitan boards, asked the question in everyone's mind: "Did Michael Bender [the former CEO] know about this before he retired last month?"

"How could he not have known?" asked Miriam St. Jacques, director of a local education foundation. "He had to know that the three-month and six-month collectibles were increasing since the crash. Surely he was tracking the effect of that on the overall fiscal health of the hospital."

At that, John Bertrucci laughed. "Of course he knew! The man was sixty-seven years old. He had done a good job for years. He did not have the energy to tackle this coming crisis, and so he bailed! Frankly, most of us would have done the same. It's not like he took off with millions. He just retired. We all knew he would in the next year or two. Let's not make him a scapegoat for not solving this problem before it came to us." Other board members who had served with Bender nodded agreement.

The newest member of the trust, Fred Trask, a local businessman, tried to summarize the situation: "So, if I understand it, we need to tighten up the accounting practices, find emergency funds to tide us over for a while, and reduce the budget. Right?"

Beatrice answered him. "For decades health-care costs have increased faster than inflation. Our particular situation is going to be greatly affected by our long-term partner, the medical school at the university, which just opened its own hospital right across the street from us. The medical school shows no signs of wanting to end our contract, but how can it both partner with us and compete against us? Our historic advantage in being able to attract insured and even rich self-payers to Washington Memorial instead of local private hospitals has been that our doctors are on the faculty at one of the top medical schools in the nation; they are the best specialists in their fields, the ones who do the latest treatments in transplants, heart surgery, and neonatal care. For that kind of care people have been willing to put up with a shortage of single rooms, old linoleum floors, and sharing corridors and waiting rooms with homeless people. But now these paying patients are hearing the university's ads about getting these very same top specialists in a hospital with only single rooms, all newly decorated, with cable TV and wireless internet. Why should they come here? The university hospital has only been open two months, so we don't know the economic impact it will have on us, but we have to expect it to be drastic. It is likely that we will at least lose a significant part of our elective surgery patients with insurance coverage."

Elizabeth then asked, "Beatrice, obviously we will need to meet frequently for a while, and we'll also have to work on committees. How do you want to set them up?"

"The first order of business has to be to look for the support necessary to stay open in the immediate future," stated Beatrice. "We will need one committee to apply for city, county, and state emergency funds. Peter, Miriam, and Fred, you have good political connections. Can you constitute the committee to seek public emergency funding?"

"It would be crazy to think that we will get anything from the city and county, who are facing their own budget deficits," replied Peter. "We can try, but the state looks like the best bet. It is equally strapped, but it has some rainy-day funds tucked away that we might tap into."

With Peter, Miriam, and Fred agreeing to their assignment, Beatrice turned to John, who had donated two wings to the hospital in the past. "John, you know all the local philanthropists. Can you and Elizabeth form a committee to solicit individual and foundation contributions to our emergency fund?"

John grimaced. "We can try, but I think we will be lucky to get $5 million, much less the $50 million or more that we need. Every charity and university in the state has been soliciting these same people over the last ten years to make up the cuts they took from state budgets. And you know," he said, smiling, "many of us only like to donate when we get our names on buildings or suites. Filling in gaps in the operating budget isn't so attractive." The members laughed, knowing that John's name was prominently portrayed around the cancer wing and the paralysis-research wing he had donated.

Beatrice named Steve Garcia—the hospital's chief operating officer—the lead officer in the new accounting firm, and herself to a committee that would come up with options for closing the deficit by the next meeting. They then discussed how to present the crisis at the press conference on the following day. Fred said what was on everyone's mind: "Our big problem is going to be with the unions. They will know from the beginning that fixing deficits means cutting jobs, cutting salaries, or cutting benefits, and likely all three. We are in the same fix as the city and county—we negotiated very generous salary and pension contracts that we now can't fund."

Miriam added: "Yes, it will be a hard negotiation. But we will get no place at all with them if we are not perfectly transparent about how bad the situation is. The books must be open to the unions, if they are to be convinced that sacrifice is necessary."

No one responded. Beatrice thanked them all, and the meeting was adjourned.

The announcement of the crisis at the press conference the next day caused a frenzy. The news was full of interviews with indignant county officials and with representatives of the unions demanding explanations. Union officials declared that the problems caused by incompetent management should not be put on the shoulders of their members. Beatrice's subcommittee met the following morning. The initial discussion concerned the news stories, the most disturbing of which were interviews with county officials who demanded that the trust be dissolved and hospital management revert back to the county. Sixteen years ago the trust had been set up as an independent management body in response to mismanagement and corruption on the part of the county in administering Washington Memorial.

Steve Garcia reassured Beatrice that this threat was purely political. "The county commissioners have enough problems on their plate right now with their own deficit and corruption scandals; they do not want to take on Washington Memorial's fiscal problems too. But they will try to focus on our problems in the news as a way to take public attention off their own problems."

The committee went to work, and within a few days it had two initial options to present to the trust members. Beatrice explained to the full body: "We can invoke the fiscal emergency clauses in all the employee contracts—for the residents, interns, staff doctors, nurses, and maintenance staff. We will have to defend this in court, but that shouldn't be difficult—to impose a 5 percent cut in all employee wages. That will invalidate present contracts, which we will have to renegotiate in the coming months, but even a 5 percent cut will not be nearly enough to close the gap, which the accountants say continues to widen. We are also suggesting that we close the emergency room at Washington South, which has the highest proportion of uninsured patients, and the majority of these in the medical and surgical wards are admitted from the ER. If we close the ER, these patients will be taken to ERs in other private hospitals in the area—to Baptist Hospital and to Mercy Hospital. This would help stem the losses from Washington South. We are still investigating the situation at Washington North to see if closing that ER would significantly help."

"I can just imagine the protests from Baptist and Mercy," declared John. "They will say, with some justification, that we are the public hospital, funded by a special tax to treat the indigent, and now we are sending the indigent to them. And what about the unions—how many employees would be laid off if we close the emergency room at Washington South?"

"Somewhere between 125 and 160, depending on how many beds it empties in the wards," answered Steve. "Not nearly enough."

Fred demanded to know: "Why isn't the hospital run more like a business? Units that don't take in enough to cover costs should be closed and not be a drain on the rest."

Other members shook their heads. Beatrice responded: "There are lots of reasons why we can't do that, Fred. We can't close down units that have ongoing contracts for research without significant penalties. And every hospital administrator in the nation will tell you that some units, like the ER and maternity wards, never pay for themselves. But if couples can't come to us to have their babies, why would they come here for their kids' ear tubes, tonsillectomies, or appendectomies? How could our cardiology clinic keep patients—or for that matter, physicians—if we didn't have an ER to admit them with heart attacks or strokes? Our range of specializations is our strength; it's what makes us a full-service hospital."

Beatrice asked for a vote on proceeding with the salary cut and a provisional vote on closing the Washington South ER, pending further investigation on the size of the deficit. The vote was almost unanimously in favor of both. But she warned, "The size of the deficit is growing as the accountants dig further. We will certainly have to do more. We might have to close South altogether."

The following week Beatrice and Steve met with Dave Berry, the lead accountant conducting the new audit, and learned that the projected annual deficit was closer to $300 million than to $200 million. As they sifted through the figures, Steve pointed out that the cuts would have to be drastic, perhaps catastrophic. A 5 percent pay cut and even closing Washington South would not be enough. That afternoon they held the first negotiations with the unions, beginning with the nurses' union. Leona Simpson of the nurses' union pointed out that a 5 percent cut would put the salaries of nurses with less than five years of experience below that of most of the hospitals in the area. Beth Lisandro, director of nurses, volunteered that she would have a difficult time attracting new nurses to fill vacancies if Washington Memorial salaries were not equal to those of surrounding hospitals. Steve responded drily, "I doubt this will be a big problem, Beth. With the kind of cuts we are likely to have to make in nursing staff, at least at the satellite hospitals, there will be sufficient laid-off nurses to fill vacancies for the foreseeable future."

Leona, disturbed, asked, "You think there will be layoffs in addition to imposing a 5 percent salary cut across the board?"

"Leona, at our meeting this morning, we looked at the possibility of closing both satellite hospitals altogether. It might be necessary," insisted Beatrice. "There are no acceptable solutions, Leona. Neither of those buildings is fully paid for, so we might be paying for buildings and equipment that we don't use at all for the next seven or eight years. But the cost of doing that is much lower than paying the salaries of the five thousand employees that work there."

Steve added: "It is unlikely that we could find a buyer for either of those buildings. No other local hospital has the money to buy them, even on generous terms. And to reconfigure them for offices would cost a fortune. But if we don't air condition them, even while we don't use them, one summer of South Florida humidity will create a mold problem that will make them good for nothing but demolition."

Leona maintained that she saw no way that the nurses' union would agree to a contract with 5 percent reductions in salary if Washington Memorial was also laying off close to a thousand nurses at the two satellites. That evening the news was full of speculation about how the crisis would be resolved.

As Beatrice and her husband, Bill, ate dinner that night, she rubbed her temples and complained: "I don't know how to find the best solution. The members of the trust are lost and are looking to me for solutions. Nothing I have ever done has prepared me for this kind of disaster. Whose interests should come first? The employees? The patients? The institution itself? The taxpayers? What is best for the institution is to close the two satellites, because that would preserve all of the specializations and allow us to retain the majority of our doctors. But that decision would put five thousand employees out of work. I just found out today that we transferred some of the supervisors at those satellites from the central complex against their will because we needed their expertise in the new hospitals, and now we would be abandoning them. Many patients would be inconvenienced by having to go farther for care, but emergency care would still only be ten to fifteen minutes farther away by ambulance. It's the employees who would take the hit."

Bill, a professor of philosophy at the local university, asked: "So why not cut salaries more, on a temporary basis, while you find cost savings throughout the system. Would a 10 percent cut do it?"

Beatrice smiled. "That would cover about 85 to 90 percent of what we need. But if I do that, Bill, I suspect that within a year 30–50 percent of my physician staff will leave to work at hospitals in other states. We will not be able to attract new interns and residents. I will lose many of the best employees in all the services, because we would be talking about a 10 percent cut for at least three or four years, with no guarantees of ever catching up to where we were. The damage to morale would be tremendous. I am afraid of the consequences of even a 5 percent cut. The deeper the cut, the more likely we are to retain only the lowest-paid employees, those with the least professional credentials, who have fewer opportunities in other places. But we can't run a hospital with cooks, cleaning staff, nurses' aides, and clerks."

"That's true, Bea, but so many low-income people in our community depend on Washington Memorial, the only public hospital in our city, to meet their needs. Will the private hospitals serve them?"

"I don't know. That's the hard part about all of this. Tomorrow the board expects me to make a proposal. One of the nurses stopped me in the hall this afternoon and told me I should think about what Jesus would do in my situation. I wish I knew."

Commentary

Public hospitals have been places where all people can get medical attention no matter their status or their means. These hospitals have historically served low-income communities, and currently two-thirds of the patients who use public hospitals are minorities. Yet increasingly public hospitals are closing their doors. According to the American Hospital Association, hospitals, both public and private, have been closing at a rate of thirty a year. Public hospitals are especially critical for addressing societal health disparities, but they are receiving less and less financial support. Low Medicaid and Medicare reimbursement rates,[1] less financial support from the government, increased competition with private for-profit hospitals, and a steady stream of uninsured patients despite the Affordable Care Act (ACA)[2] have threatened the financial viability of public hospitals. Basically, they are experiencing a heavy demand for services on their already limited and quickly diminishing resources.

The budget shortfall that Washington Memorial Hospital is facing is not an isolated case. Escalating hospital closures, in both urban and rural areas, are raising concern about whether low-income people will receive quality health care and, further, whether health care will be seen as a public good in our society or simply an individual privilege. Public hospitals have been closing at a steady rate across the nation. Some major cities with high minority population now have no public hospital. Public hospitals require state support, but with the federal government decreasing the amount of money it gives states to cover the costs of serving the uninsured, cities and states are struggling to cover the shortfall. These hospitals are often older, and as the safety-net hospitals that care for the uninsured in most counties

---

[1] Medicaid is a joint federal-and-state-funded program that covers some medical costs for people with limited income. Medicare is a single-payer national health insurance program funded by a payroll tax. It provides health insurance for Americans over the age of sixty-five who have worked and paid into the system. It also covers some young people with a disability. A single-payer health-care system is one that is financed by taxes and administered by a single public system (for example, the government). Apart from Medicaid and Medicare, the United States has a multipayer system made up of multiple commercial health insurance companies.

[2] The ACA, signed in 2010 and fully implemented by 2014, expanded the eligibility for and federal funding of Medicaid. The program faced problems from the beginning (not surprising in such a huge program), from technical difficulties in implementation to a repeal attempt in 2017.

and/or cities, they have seen heavy use. Thus, they are usually in need of extra funding for infrastructure repair and upkeep.

When a public hospital closes in one area, patients are shifted to other struggling public hospitals or to nonprofit care providers who might or might not take them in. For example, when the Martin Luther King Jr. Hospital in Los Angeles's predominantly Hispanic South Central neighborhood was closed, patient load increased at the four remaining county public hospitals with no increase in their budgets. The closure of three hospitals in Queens, New York, led to an average wait of seventeen hours in the emergency room at the Jamaica Hospital Medical Center. Overcrowding can mean life or death when doctors are overworked and hurried and when ambulances are at a standstill waiting for their stretchers to be returned from the emergency room. The longer distance to access a public hospital also decreases the effectiveness of care. While all hospitals must by law provide emergency care, private hospitals can transfer patients to other hospitals once they are stabilized. Furthermore, private hospitals can turn away non-emergency cases, whereas public hospitals have to serve everyone who comes to their doors.

BASIC HEALTH CARE AS A RIGHT

The United States is one of the few developed countries that does not treat provision of health care as a basic human right. It is a wonderful system for those who can pay for services, but health care, apart from emergency medical care, is considered a privilege in US society. The Henry J. Kaiser Family Foundation (KFF) notes in its online "Fact Sheet" that by extending Medicaid coverage to many low-income individuals and providing marketplace subsidies for individuals below 400 percent of the official poverty level, the ACA decreased the number of uninsured from 44 million in 2013 (a year before the ACA went into effect) to 28 million at the end of 2016. According to the KFF estimates, the number of uninsured people in the nonelderly population was 46.5 million in 2010; by 2016 the estimated number was 26.7 million.[3] Coverage gains were the largest in states that expanded Medicaid, but Florida and several other Southern states decided against such expansion. Recent efforts to alter the ACA will likely increase the number of uninsured people in the United States. Already from 2016 to 2017 there has been a 1.3 percent increase in the number of people

---

[3] Rachel Garfield et al., "The Uninsured and the ACA," Henry J. Kaiser Family Foundation, January 25, 2019; see also Jennifer Tolbert et al., "Key Facts about the Uninsured Population." These and following quotations are found on the KFF website.

uninsured, leaving over 10 percent of the population (31 million people) uninsured in 2017. A Gallup and Sharecare report noted possible causes for the increased number of uninsured people, most notably rising premiums on the ACA's insurance exchanges in many states, decreased marketing of the program, and a shortened enrollment period. In 2019 repeal of the individual mandate went into effect, and the Congressional Budget Office projects that as a result four million more people will be uninsured by 2019 and thirteen million more by 2027.

Limited access to basic health care is both a class and race issue. About half of the nation's uninsured are people of color, yet people of color constitute only 35 percent of the US population. Southern states that have the highest poverty rate also have the largest percentage of people uninsured. Lack of health care compromises human dignity and basic well-being in multiple ways: from elderly people not taking life-saving prescriptions because they cannot afford them, to children not being able to concentrate in school due to abscessed teeth, to families filing bankruptcy over hospital bills. In fact, the KFF notes that medical debt is the number one reason Americans file for bankruptcy. It is a vicious circle: poverty leads to poor health in our country, and poor health negatively affects people's ability to participate fully in school, work, and community endeavors.

HUMAN DIGNITY AND HEALTH CARE

Jesus healed people, especially the outcasts—the blind, lepers, and the disabled. Preserving the dignity of the human person, especially the dignity of those who are most vulnerable, is a theme found throughout scripture. The sacredness of every person is grounded in our having been created in the image and likeness of God. This sacredness does not mean that we are entitled to every medical intervention or technological advance in relation to our health, but it does mean that we ought to have a basic right to those aspects of medical care that allow us to participate in the economic, political, and cultural life of our society. We are not isolated individuals; our human dignity can be realized only within communities and in solidarity with one another. The grounding of solidarity necessary for the respect of human dignity is not present in a society where health care is a privilege for those who can afford it. While rights are only guaranteed if society protects them, the right to the basic material needs necessary to live a life of dignity is founded in God, not society. Both the norms of love and justice call us to create social institutions that support the dignity of all people.

God calls us to love our neighbor (Mt 22:39), but what does this concretely entail? Jesus ministered to all people—especially the poor. The poorest and most downtrodden sought him out and, unlike the treatment they got from the dominant society, Jesus always responded to them compassionately. He intentionally directed his ministry to the communities of farmers and fisherfolk, not to the wealthy communities (Mt 10:5–6). Jesus expected his disciples and all who believed in God to minister to the poor: "Come, you that are blessed by my Father; inherit the kingdom prepared for you from the foundation of the world; for I was hungry and you gave me food, I was thirsty and you gave me something to drink, I was a stranger and you welcomed me, I was naked and you gave me clothing, I was sick and you took care of me, I was in prison and you visited me" (Mt 25:34–46). When Jesus ministered to the sick, he did not determine whose medical needs were more important but instead responded to whatever ailed people.

Love on an individual level is not enough, however. Justice on an institutional level is also required. In the United States health care is a right for some, which comes in the form of Medicaid for the most poor and Medicare for people with some specific disabilities or who are over sixty-five years old. These government-sponsored health plans address the health-care needs of many who might be the most vulnerable, but there are still plenty of people whose only access to health care is the emergency room at a public hospital or free health-care clinics run by nonprofit organizations.

FUNDING US HEALTH CARE

That public hospitals like Washington Memorial need to apply for city, county, and state emergency funds or look to philanthropists to stay open is indicative of the low value we as a society have given to social, economic, and racial justice. Rather than having a system of universal health care we have offered a rickety safety net for the most vulnerable and deemed it acceptable for health care to be an arena in which corporations decide what services will be provided to whom based on profits. Would Jesus have sought to profit from the care he gave to people? How do we understand his teaching that when we feed the hungry, welcome the homeless, and visit the imprisoned we have ministered to God? (Mt 25:35–46). Are we to see this teaching as counsel for individuals, or do we apply it to our larger communities and nation?

When hospitals are managed by private, for-profit businesses, society runs the risk that health care will not be universal. Most for-profit health care centers and hospitals prefer to cater to patients who have insurance and/or can pay for services. These for-profit hospitals can claim to be more economically "efficient" because they do not have to serve those who cannot pay for their care. There are many stories of for-profit hospital staff turning away people without funds and sending them to the nearest public hospital, or even illegally "dumping" homeless and chronically ill persons on the street after providing emergency care.

"Efficiency" in for-profit hospitals is also achieved by cutting back on salaries and benefits for hospital employees or by having employees do more tasks. For example, in many for-profit hospitals today, nurses are expected to serve more patients per shift. According to a report issued by the New England Public Policy Center and the Massachusetts Health Policy Forum, lower nurse staffing levels have been linked with patients' increased risk of pneumonia, urinary tract infection, post-operative infection, sepsis, ulcers, gastrointestinal bleeding, cardiac arrest, longer hospital stays, and, in some cases, death. The costs of people without health care, fewer jobs, and overworked and underpaid workers are not borne by the for-profit hospitals but are externalized to the community in the name of efficiency. Efficiency and hospital effectiveness are important, but not at the expense of the common good and the well-being of individuals.

Many doctors challenge the claim that the distribution of health care through the free market, with corporations and insurance agencies making a profit, is actually more efficient. They point to the amount of bureau-cracy and extra paperwork demanded by insurance companies that have doubled and tripled the number of office staff that doctors require. Much bureaucratic inefficiency could be eliminated with a single-payer system. Efficiency in hospitals could be achieved by ending the attempt of every hospital to offer the latest and most up-to-date technology in order to attract high-paying customers, and instead strategically locating different hospi-tal services. According to the Connecticut Coalition for Universal Health Care, administrative costs and profit-taking account for 20 to 30 percent of revenues at for-profit hospitals, whereas Medicare only spends 3 percent on administration and has no profit margin.

Government-provided health care is not without inefficiency, however. Medicare and Medicaid lose an estimated $60 billion or more annually to fraud, which contributes a great deal to the high per capita cost of health care in the United States compared to other nations. Neither government-sponsored health-care systems nor private insurance systems have been able to implement cost-containment measures that would shift from costly fee-for-service models that reward physicians and hospitals for maximum testing and treatment to a model that rewards them for maintaining patient health at lower cost.

Proponents of the current fee-for-service system argue that a single-payer universal health-care system (government run, with no intermediary insurance companies) would mean a decrease in both the quantity and quality of care and would be too costly. However, the KFF calculates that the United States spends 50 percent more per capita on health care than other industrialized countries that have universal government-sponsored health care, yet it ranks lower than these countries on many health indicators, such as infant mortality, life expectancy, and rates of immunization. In addition, many people do not have access to basic health services. It is clear, historically, that the private sector will not make health care more accessible to those without financial means without being forced to do so.

The ACA aimed to end some of the abuses of the insurance industry and increase health-care coverage. It required everyone to have health insurance by 2014. Large and medium employers were required to provide health insurance to their employees. Others would be covered by expansion of Medicaid among the poor and a requirement that middle-class people who are self-employed or work for small firms purchase their own policies. This legislation also helped children get health coverage, ended lifetime and most annual limits on care, allowed young adults under twenty-six to stay on their parents' health insurance, and gave patients access to recommended preventive services without cost. It also tried to increase coverage even before 2014 by offering tax credits to small businesses that provide insurance for their employees and by offering a preexisting condition insurance plan (PCIP) for those who are denied coverage by private insurance companies. However, this legislation did nothing to address directly the exponentially increasing cost of health care or insurance coverage in the United States. Universal health insurance coverage is a step forward, but if deductibles and co-pays are too high, health care will continue to be, for many, an elusive privilege.[4] Furthermore, minimally employed people who cannot afford insurance but do not qualify for Medicaid have a hard time complying with the requirement that they buy insurance. Therefore, this legislation does not represent universal health care coverage.

HEALTH CARE AS A PUBLIC GOOD

In many ancient cultures hospitals and caring for the sick were associated with religious institutions. In Judaism and Christianity, caring for those who had no one to care for them has been viewed as an aspect of religious duty (Ex 22:22; Is 61:1; Mt 25:35; Lk 7:22; Jas 1:27). The first hospitals in the United States in the 1700s were connected to the church and were originally houses for the poor and elderly—hence, the denominational

---

[4] According to the KFF, deductibles increased from an average of $303 a year in 2006 to $1,200 a year in 2016. People spent less on co-pays, however, from an average of $225 in 2006 to $140 in 2016.

affiliations still attached to many hospitals. In the early to mid-1900s many of these charities eventually turned into money-making enterprises, and entrepreneurs replaced church workers. Recent studies reveal that 20 percent of hospitals are still controlled by religious organizations, and a Mergerwatch report found that currently one in six patients is treated at a Catholic hospital. Furthermore, many churches and small nonprofits still run community health clinics today.

Provision of basic health care is not only about respecting individual human dignity, but is also imperative for promoting flourishing communities. The most obvious community benefit of health care as a public good is the prevention of communicable diseases. Sexually transmitted diseases, deadly viruses, and even the flu can affect all community members if not prevented and/or treated. Economic productivity also suffers when there is a lack of adequate health care. Many people without basic health care might not even realize what it would feel like to be in good health. Ill health affects the ability of people to participate fully not only in work but in all facets of community life. It is no surprise, for example, that disability and bad health are found in a higher percentage of people who are homeless than in the general population. Health disparities, exacerbated by the closing of public hospitals, have a negative effect on our communities and on our ideal of being a democratic nation that values equal opportunity.

DISTRIBUTING THE COST BURDEN

The dominant thinking in the United States is that we are an association of private individuals, each out for his or her own in competition with others. While Americans historically uphold the value of equal opportunity, we do not consistently ensure that such a reality exists. Rather than seeing the tax system as a way to provide goods and services to all, many tend to see taxation as a burden. The result of this anti-tax sentiment is a much lower rate of taxation than in other developed nations—and a resulting lack of funding for public goods. According to the Tax Policy Center, in 2015 US taxes at all levels of government made up 26 percent of gross domestic product (GDP), compared with an average of 34 percent of GDP for the thirty member-countries of the Organization for Economic Co-operation and Development (OECD). Only South Korea, Chile, Ireland, and Mexico had lower tax percentages.

The communal orientation of the biblical worldview is an alternative to our nation's individualistic focus. The biblical people of Israel were told repeatedly that their well-being was a gift from God, not earned. They were brought out of slavery by a God of justice and liberation. While God did not expect repayment, God did expect the people to care for those in their communities who were least well off, to treat each person with dignity, and to set up systems that ensured the well-being of all. Similarly, Jesus advocated for systems of liberation and justice. He overturned the tables of the moneychangers in the Temple because they were unjustly defrauding the poor. If we want to see a society of equal opportunity, health care coverage for everyone is a moral necessity. The early Christian communities understood this truth: "All who believed were together and had all things in common; they would sell their possession and goods and distribute the proceeds to all, as any had need" (Acts 2:44–45).

In the case, board member Fred Trask asks why the hospital isn't run more like a business. That is, why not close the hospital programs and units that are money losers? Apart from denying basic services to people if emergency rooms or maternity wards are shut down, there is the larger question of whether health care should be run like a business. Should we provide only those services that are money makers? Basic preventative care and public health interventions to prevent and manage diseases, injuries, and other health conditions are not where profit lies, but do we really want to determine what services to provide based on whether they make a profit? The God of justice and liberation expects humans to use the resources of this world wisely. There are justifiable reasons for health care rationing in response to limited resources, but the inability of people to pay for services or the ability of a service to garner profit should not be relevant factors in determining who does or does not get particular forms of health care. God would not condone a system that prioritizes profit over communal flourishing. The merits of rationing particular forms of health care or prioritizing specific groups should be debated publicly. The closing of public hospitals is an invisible way of rationing care in which the poor and people of color are being sacrificed. The larger question for us to ponder is whether health care is to be a public good or a private privilege only for those able to pay?

WORKER JUSTICE

Beatrice, as CEO of Washington Memorial, has negotiated with the unions. She says that in the past Washington Memorial offered generous salaries and pension contracts that it currently cannot fund. The practical answer is to make workers bear a share of the burden associated with the financial straits of the hospital. Clearly, Beatrice has limited options. In most public hospital closures workers were asked to sacrifice pay and benefits until it became clear that even this was not sufficient to keep doors open. Studies report that only 10–12 percent of public-sector workers were unionized in the 1950s and 1960s, compared to one-third to one-half of all private-sector workers. By the mid-1980s there was a reversal, with over one-third of the public-sector work force unionized and only 14 percent of the private sector. While unions have led to many different kinds of worker protections, such as work-place safety, standard work weeks, overtime pay, and child-labor laws, unions have also given workers vital collective bargaining rights with employers. All of these benefits have given workers more security and promoted flourishing communities. Officials of many American states, cities, and counties suffering from budget deficits and decreasing payments from the federal government claim that they are unable to fulfill the union contracts they have negotiated in the past. Beatrice's efforts to negotiate with the unions need to be viewed in relationship to this larger picture.

While Beatrice might have few other places to turn, the erosion of worker pay, benefits, and union organizing rights should be limited and short term. It is not right to place the burden for the hospital crisis on the workers; higher paid doctors, administrators, and the taxpayers should all bear a share of the financial burden. Also important to note is that the increasing privatization of public institutions has dealt a heavy blow to unionization because a larger percentage of public-sector jobs are unionized. Women and minorities are more negatively affected by these changes because they are more heavily represented in public-sector jobs. While unions were not a feature of biblical times, there are biblical stories that point to structuring work to meet the needs of people rather than only to garner profit for the employer. For example, in the parable of the Laborers in the Vineyard (Mt 20:1–16), the landowner pays all a wage sufficient to live on, regardless of the number of hours worked. Of course, business owners must be competitive to stay afloat in our economy as it is structured, but such competitiveness should not be at the expense of worker sustenance and security.

The consistent message of the Exodus narrative and the prophetic poetry is that the rich are to act in solidarity with the poor, not only through charity but also through just systems of governance and equitable distribution of resources. Moses taught: "You shall not withhold the wages of the poor and needy laborers, whether other Israelites or aliens [illegal immigrants] who reside in your land in one of your towns. You shall pay them their wages daily before sunset, because they are poor and their livelihood depends on them; otherwise they might cry to the Lord against you, and you would incur guilt" (Dt 24:14–15). Justice distributes power so that people can take care of themselves and participate in community life. Good jobs and just work places are integral to democratic society.

While unions are clearly important for securing worker justice, not all union policies and demands over the last decades have been wise or sustainable. Many public employees were granted generous benefits during boom times that are hard to sustain today. For example, some public-employee unions have full retirement after twenty to twenty-five years on the job, and so there have been cases of people retiring in their forties, getting a second public job, and then retiring at age sixty-five with two pensions funded from public coffers. While not common for most public employees, some hospital workers have benefited from such unsustainable retirement packages in the past. Public institutions like Washington Memorial might have legitimate reasons for limiting benefits that privilege workers unfairly and lead to inequitable distribution of resources. We should be careful not to forget, however, that union jobs offer a living wage and benefits, especially health insurance, that many jobs do not provide. These good-paying jobs not only help individuals but also support our economy and ensure that fewer people need to use governmental safety nets.

CONCLUSION

Beatrice has several short-term options for saving Washington Memorial Hospital. She will definitely have to tighten up accounting practices and find emergency funds to tide the hospital over for a while, but she will most likely need to take more drastic steps as well, such as cutting salaries, closing satellite hospitals, or both. Addressing the moral issue of health care as a right and as a public good will take longer-term solutions beyond those that CEOs of failing public hospitals can enact. Making provision of health care economically efficient will require exploration of cost-containment systems, and making health care universally accessible will entail reconsideration of funding systems, including single-payer schemes. If we are to achieve universal access to health care, the tax burden on the rich and on corporations will undoubtedly need to increase. Jesus's command to love our neighbor and the communal orientation of the biblical worldview call us to create systems that ensure the well-being of all, not only those who can afford health coverage. By making health care universally accessible, we would be acting in solidarity to support the dignity of each human person and we would be promoting healthier communities.

ADDITIONAL SOURCES

Berry, Leonard, and Kent Seltman. *Management Lessons from Mayo Clinic: One of the World's Most Admired Service Institutions*. New York: McGraw-Hill, 2008.

Branigan, Michael C., and Judith A. Boss. *Healthcare Ethics in a Diverse Society.* New York: McGraw-Hill, 2001.

Cahill, Lisa Sowle. *Theological Bioethics: Participation, Justice, Change.* Washington, DC: Georgetown University Press, 2005.

Craig, David, M. *Health Care as a Social Good: Religious Values and American Democracy.* Washington, DC: Georgetown University Press, 2014.

Dillard, Coshandra. "Critical Conditions: Caught in the Healthcare Crunch, Rural Hospitals Are Falling Behind—and Sometimes Closing." *Crisis* 123, no. 1 (Winter 2016): 32–35.

Graban, Marc. *Lean Hospitals: Improving Quality, Patient Safety and Employee Satisfaction.* New York: Taylor and Francis, 2009.

Kelly, David F. *Critical Care Ethics: Treatment Decisions in American Hospitals.* Eugene, OR: Wipf and Stock, 2002.

Lindrooth, Richard C., Marcelo C. Perraillon, Rose Y. Hardy, and Gregory J. Tung. "Understanding the Relationship between Medicaid Expansions and Hospital Closures." *Health Affairs* 37, no. 1 (January 2018): 111–20.

Valbrun, Marjorie. "Hospital Closings Jeopardize Care in Ethnic Communities." *America's Wire,* January 20, 2011.

Related Website

US Department of Health and Human Services
http://www.healthcare.gov/law/introduction/index.html.

PART VII

SEXUALITY/GENDER

Case

Drinking and Hooking Up?

Grace had been at Belmore University for six weeks. Her courses were interesting, and although she and her roommates were all very different, they got along well. It was exciting to have a group of friends again after the isolation of being homeschooled her last two years of high school due to an intestinal illness and surgery. She loved that she had been placed with four other girls in a suite with a central living space. Around the common room were three bedrooms with herself and Mae in one, Elanah and Kelly in another, and Beth in a single.

What was somewhat new for Grace was the party and hookup culture in college. Since she had been ill in high school she hadn't been fully immersed in the social scene. She started to feel better by the end of her senior year in high school and did attend prom and a post-prom all-night party at the Hilton. Still not well enough to drink, she remembers being the only sober person at the party. She also remembers with some distaste the way her girlfriends the next morning talked badly about the girls at the party who slept around, basically "slut shaming" them. She was bothered that only the girls, not the boys, were shamed.

Grace and her mom had long conversations about what to expect in college—how she was going to a college with fraternities and sororities, and probably a big party culture. Grace's mom, having married in her thirties, was pragmatic about sex before marriage and was open to Grace getting some form of birth control before leaving for college. She knew, however, that the contemporary hookup culture is different from when she was in college, and she wasn't sure whether it was particularly liberating

This case and commentary were prepared by Laura A. Stivers. The names of persons and institutions have been disguised, where appropriate, to protect the privacy of those involved. The case is inspired by a case described in Jennifer Beste's book *College Hookup Culture and Christian Ethics*.

for young women—or even men, for that matter. She worried especially about the incidents of sexual violence associated with the overuse of alcohol and drugs.

Grace had been raised in a mainline Protestant church and had been active in the youth group, participating in activities such as camping trips and Habitat for Humanity builds. Her youth pastor, however, did not help them to reflect theologically on the issues of sexuality, partying, or violence. She wasn't sure she wanted to attend a church while in college.

Still not fully sure about what her stomach could handle, Grace had only tried a couple of beers at the few parties she went to in her first six weeks. Her roommates were on a spectrum in relation to partying. Grace was glad that she shared a room with Mae, who didn't party at all; that way Grace didn't have to deal with late-hour drunkenness. Mae grew up in a conservative evangelical Christian household and had already joined a conservative Christian student club where she was meeting friends who held similar beliefs about partying and premarital sex.

Beth, Kelly, and Elanah all liked to go to parties, but they differed in their perspectives on hooking up. Just before coming to college Beth had broken up with her high-school boyfriend, whom she had dated and had sex with for a couple years. Now she was ready to meet someone new. She wanted a serious relationship and didn't want to sleep around with just anyone, but once she hit the party scene, it was clear to Grace that Beth was a flirt with loosened inhibitions. Kelly, on the other hand, had no reservations about hooking up. She felt liberated that she could have sex with no strings attached. She liked to party and had no interest in a serious relationship at this point in her life. Elanah liked to party and wasn't opposed to sex before marriage, but she wasn't a big fan of the hookup culture because she felt that any sexual relationship should be mutual, that is, one in which partners treat each other with dignity and respect. Grace admired Elanah's feminist perspective, but she worried that it might mean no relationships in college because the boys seemed so immature with no interest in committed relationships. Elanah felt the promiscuous party and hookup culture was a male-model of sexuality that treats the bodies of others, especially women, as objects for personal gratification. Like Grace's mom, Elanah also argued that this culture is intricately tied to sexual violence.

Saturday was the big homecoming football game with lots of fraternity parties scheduled afterward. While it was almost impossible for first-year males to get a frat party invite, cute first-year girls usually had unlimited access. Kelly had made friends with some frat boys in her chemistry course, and she asked Beth, Elanah, and Grace if they wanted to join her. She knew Mae wouldn't be interested. Grace had heard that her high-school friend John, a sophomore, had just joined this fraternity. Grace wondered if he had embraced the party hookup scene wholesale, since he hadn't been a big partier in high school.

While getting ready for the party, Kelly nudged Grace and asked, "Are you going to drink more than two beers and *actually* let your hair down? It'll be easier to talk to all the cute boys that way! Your friend John is pretty hot!"

Beth added, "Does anyone have that vodka from last weekend? I'm ready to p-a-a-r-t-a-y! But Grace, it's fine with me if you don't drink too much because then you can make sure I get home safely."

Grace wasn't sure how to respond to either of them. Couldn't she connect with boys without being drunk? And did she really want to be responsible for her friend's safety? Elanah chimed in, "I can't believe I've even agreed to go to a frat party with you all. It will probably just be a bunch of sexist immature guys, but it is homecoming and I wouldn't want all my besties having fun without me!"

The stands were awash in a wave of blue and gold. Clearly some had already had a few drinks at the pregame parties. The girls showed up a little late to the game, after primping to look good. Kelly and Beth had had a couple of pregame shots in their dorm suite. Sporting their Belmore attire, the girls cheered along with everyone else, supporting their team's narrow and exciting victory. After the game they went back to the room to don their party clothes—risque halter tops and short shorts, since the weather was still unseasonably warm for the end of September.

When they arrived at the big brick house with tall pillars on Greek Row, one of the drunken fraternity brothers yelled, "Hey, some fine-ass ladies are coming in! Sign them up for the upside-down shots!"

Elanah rolled her eyes.

"Hey, honey, can I get your number?" he asked, winking seductively at the girls.

"Yeah, it's 1-800-just-don't," Elanah joked with him.

Kelly headed to the back of the cavernous living room where a group of college kids were doing shots.

Beth called out to her, "Wait up!"

Elanah informed Grace, "I'm getting a beer from the keg in the back. Want one?"

At the keg Grace saw her high-school friend John. He poured her a beer and raised his cup to hers and said, "Cheers! Here's to your college party career!"

"Cheers to our football win," she said tilting her red Solo cup to touch his. She still was not sure she was up to drinking much more than two beers.

As the night wore on, the house got more and more crowded and louder. Grace had stopped drinking after a couple of beers and had taken a seat on one of the worn and tattered couches to observe. She quietly watched a game of beer pong, while boys hit on all the scantily clad cute girls, and couples made out in various corners of the house. She also watched a group of sorority girls twerking on the dance floor, one girl even doing a lap dance for a drunken basketball player. She scanned the party looking for Elanah but didn't see her. She had apparently left earlier. She did notice Beth in the crowd; she appeared to be quite drunk. Boys were flirting with Beth, getting extremely close to her face, and wrapping their arms around her. One drunken frat boy even put his hand down Beth's pants. She didn't move his hand away or try to get out of the situation. Grace didn't think Beth would have behaved this way if she were sober.

By 2 a.m., Kelly and Grace decided it was time to go back to the dorm, taking Beth with them. Troy, one of the drunken frat boys, clearly had something else in mind. When the three girls left through the front door, Troy kept pulling at Beth's hand, trying to drag her back into the party with him, saying, "Come on, baby. Let's hang in my room for a little bit."

In a slurred voice Beth declined, "No, not tonight. I need to go home."

On the way back to campus Beth admitted to Kelly and Grace, "Troy's cute but I don't really know him that well."

Then her phone buzzed with a text from Troy, "Please come back. You're really fine, and I just want to chill with you."

She stopped to text back, "Not tonight."

When they got back to their room Beth stumbled in, headed to her single, and fell asleep immediately.

Twenty minutes later Grace heard the main door to the suite crack open. Wondering who it was, she got out of bed to look and saw Troy. Someone must have let him into the dorm, and Beth, who came into the suite last, must not have locked the door. Troy mistakenly proceeded to open up the door to Kelly's and Elanah's room. He quietly closed the door and headed toward Beth's room. Grace listened as she heard the distinct noise of Beth's door open and slowly close. Grace wasn't sure whether she should do anything. She decided that Beth was a grown woman and could take care of herself.

All of the girls slept in the next morning. When Grace got up at 11:30 a.m. Troy was no longer there. Grace found Mae in the living room, "It's about time you all woke up. Let's go to brunch at Mel's. I'm starving."

So they all headed over to Mel's Café, Kelly and Beth looking like they might not be up to eating much. Grace noticed that Beth seemed desolate and detached, like she was dealing with more than a typical hangover.

Once they got their food, they went to the upstairs loft of the cafe and sat in a corner. Before even taking a bite of her food, Grace immediately prodded Beth, "Is something the matter? You don't look good. I saw Troy come in last night. Is everything all right?"

Beth let out a deep sigh, and Grace could tell she was holding back tears, "He came in and woke me up. He kept telling me how pretty I am and how he likes me and wants to be with me, even though we don't even know each other that well. I kept telling him that I was really drunk and that I just wanted to sleep, but before I knew it we just started kissing." Then, in a quiet voice with tears streaming down her face, she told her roommates, "Then we had sex. He didn't even ask if that's what I wanted. I just didn't know how to stop it." She was sobbing now and had to pause to catch her breath. "I just wanted to have fun at the party and flirt with boys. I really don't think that I would have had sex with Troy if I were sober last night."

Grace put her hand on Beth's shoulder consoling her, "Oh my god, Beth. I'm sorry. I should have stopped Troy and told him to get the hell out. He should have never followed you to your dorm room. There's no way you can really give consent to sex when you're drunk. Troy is a predatory creep!"

Not wanting Grace to feel guilty, Beth responded, "It wasn't your responsibility to protect me. I shouldn't have drunk so much last night, and I shouldn't have led him on. I should've just said no!" Between her queasy stomach and dazed state, Beth didn't think she could eat lunch. Although not wanting to leave her friends, she said, "I'm going to go back to the room to sleep. I really don't feel good."

Worried about Beth, Grace replied, "Do you want me to walk back with you?"

"No, I'll be fine. You should eat lunch," said Beth.

After Beth left, the girls starting talking about what happened.

Elanah was pissed. She said, "While it was Beth's decision to drink too much, she shouldn't have had to stop Troy from following her to her room and forcing sex on her! I agree with Grace that consent requires full cognitive ability, which Beth clearly didn't have last night. I'm so sorry this happened to her."

Mae chimed in, "These parties on campus scare me. There is so much drinking and casual sex. I want sex to be special. That's why I want to wait until I get married. My pastor from home talks about the Christian virtue of chastity. He tells all of us that we should be sexually pure when we get married. I understand you guys don't have the same religious beliefs as I do, but hooking up when you are drunk doesn't seem very healthy to me."

Elanah responded, "I agree that drunkenness and hooking up are not a good combo. Sexual assault is way too common on college campuses. I'm also Christian, but I've been raised to believe that sexuality is something positive and that people should have their own sexual freedom. I've also been taught and believe that individuals should respect the autonomy and dignity of each other when they are sexually involved. I want to travel and go to grad school after college. I don't want to get married anytime soon, but I'm definitely *not* going to be a virgin throughout my twenties!"

Kelly had been listening quietly to their conversation. "Well, you guys all know I'm not a virgin. I lost my virginity when I was sixteen to my high-school boyfriend. I've enjoyed having different sexual partners, and I think I'm probably like pansexual or maybe even bi. I don't know if I ever want to get married; it's really just an archaic and patriarchal institution. I mean, in Europe lots of couples are living together and just skipping the whole marriage thing. Sexual assault even happens within marriages. However, I think drinking, or even a little weed or ecstasy, can loosen inhibitions and make flirting and hooking up more fun."

Grace stayed quiet and just took in all that was being said. She wasn't sure where she stood in relation to the perspectives being shared. She thought sexual assault was a problem on college campuses, and clearly alcohol and drug use were related to assault. She didn't drink much due to health reasons, but she also wanted to be part of campus social life. Was it so wrong to get drunk every now and then? While raised Christian, she wasn't particularly religious. She wanted to have a boyfriend at some point, and eventually marry. She didn't see involvement with campus ministry as a way to meet guys, so wouldn't she have to go to some parties to do so? Was hooking up one of the only ways to find a boyfriend?

After lunch Grace left her friends to go study in the library. On the way over, she ran into her high-school friend John. She didn't feel that she could tell him what happened with Troy and Beth, but she wondered what his stance was on fraternity parties and hooking up. She timidly asked, "Do you guys party every weekend at the house?"

"Yeah, pretty much, but some of us who need to study or need a break come to the library or other places on campus and stay on the down-low," he replied.

"Yeah, I bet some of you need a break; that was a *wild* party. Do all the frat boys try to hook up with different girls each weekend? I mean, do any of you even have monogamy on the brain?" Grace asked, trying not to sound accusatory.

"I don't know that all of the guys are sleeping around *all* the time. I like hooking up with girls, but if I found someone that I would want to be serious with, I'd consider a monogamous relationship." He laughed, lightening the mood.

"Are any of your frat brothers concerned about the issue of consent and sexual assault, especially considering all the press related to the #MeToo movement?" Grace inquired.

"We like to party and have fun, but I think fraternities have gotten a bad rap with all of the incidents in the news lately. Of course I think consent is important, and I would *never* force myself on a girl. The girls I've hooked up with were all willing participants, and they were having just as much fun as I was," he added. "What's the harm in that?"

Grace responded, "Not all the guys in your frat are as trustworthy as you, John. I know some of your frat brothers have pressured girls to have sex when they are drunk and unable to fully consent." John nodded but stayed silent.

Grace trusted her friend John, but she had a lot to think about after the incident with her roommate Beth. She considered what responsibility she and others, both men and women, have for doing something about sexual assault on campus and in society. And how was she going to participate in the social scene at Belmore, where drinking and hooking up were so prevalent? Would she try drinking a bit more to fit in? How did she feel about hooking up with different guys? Or would she prefer to wait until she could find a boyfriend? And if she was even able to find a boyfriend, what were her views on sex in a committed relationship? Would her Christian upbringing influence her beliefs and actions, and if so, how? She reached the library and parted ways with John.

Commentary

While not all students are involved in the party and hookup culture on college campuses, it might appear to Grace that she needs to participate if she wants to fit in and have friends. Long before they arrive on a college campus, students have been inundated with media images of wild college parties with excessive drinking, eroticization of hyper masculinity and femininity, and displays of sexual exploits and promiscuous behavior. While the combination of drinking, drugs, and sex is hardly new, it was not the norm even in the 1960s that students *should* be involved in all three to have any semblance of a social life. That has changed. Peggy Orenstein, author of *Girls and Sex,* says that 72 percent of college students hook up at least once by their senior year, with the average number of hookups being seven.[1] Hooking up is defined as sexual activity without commitment or emotional investment. She notes that intercourse is involved in only a third of these hookups, however, and that young people usually overestimate how many of their peers have had sex as well as the number of their partners.

Our culture places great emphasis on success and individual achievement. Young people are told throughout high school that to get into college, they will need excellent grades and test scores, multiple AP courses, sports accolades, and more. They get the message that winners stand out from the crowd, have control of their lives, and are invulnerable. Technology and social media also give young people the expectation of instant gratification. Alcohol and drug use as well as casual sex in hookups can offer quick fixes from the stress of trying to achieve social status and "success"; they can also make participants feel less vulnerable and subject to the complexity, and often messiness, of deeper committed relationships. Youth learn to focus on ambition over romance, and freedom over interdependence, with the understanding that successful identity is built independent of relationships.

Similar to many other universities, Greek life is at the center of the party and hookup culture at Belmore University. Alcohol and excessive drinking are the social lubricants that lessen anxiety and loosen inhibitions. The fraternities provide the alcohol and try to have as many good-looking

---

[1] Peggy Orenstein, *Girls and Sex: Navigating the Complicated New Landscape* (New York: HarperCollins, 2016), 105.

256

girls attend their parties as possible. Many of the boys seek to prove their masculinity by the number of sexual conquests they have. Some girls, like Kelly, find casual sex liberating, but many do not. According to the National Marriage Project at the University of Virginia, both men and women are marrying at a later age than previous generations—twenty-seven for women and twenty-nine for men. Thus, unlike Mae, many have abandoned the idea of waiting for sex until marriage. While more men than women are satisfied with the hookup status quo, many students—both boys and girls—experience the negative physical and psychological consequences of hookups and wish for something different.[2]

POWER, GENDER, AND SEXUALITY

Troy's predatory behavior and Beth's acquiescence to it replicate popular culture's dominant story of gender norms. For men, the norms are to be heterosexual, to compete with other men, and to prove one's masculinity through sexual conquest without emotional connection. Women are given the message that to be desirable, they must be thin and should act passive, weak, and submissive—at least at parties. They learn that they will gain approval if they appear as a sex object. Before going to the party, Beth and her roommates made sure to change into short shorts and halter tops so they would be sexy. They were immediately called "fine-ass ladies" by the frat boys when they arrived at the frat house.

When drunkenness took over, the frat boys made their aggressive moves, and many of the girls acted out sexually by grinding and twerking on the dance floor, doing lap dances, and letting the boys touch their bodies. Grace thought to herself that Beth and probably many of the other girls wouldn't behave this way if they were sober. Excessive drinking not only serves to loosen inhibitions but can also keep insecurities and anxiety at bay; students can feel accepted and accomplished if they fit the social norms and are able to hook up with someone. Drunkenness can also give students an excuse from accountability for their sexual behavior, which is problematic when aggressive behavior turns into assault.

While sexuality is biological, our views of what is sexually arousing are culturally influenced and socially constructed. In particular, our culture eroticizes domination in sex. That is, men and women are socialized to view male domination as sexually arousing. Even the language we use to describe sex entails domination—screw, fuck, bang, nail. Women in this socially

---

[2] Reported in Jennifer Beste, *College Hookup Culture and Christian Ethics: The Lives and Longings of Emerging Adults* (Oxford: Oxford University Press, 2018).

constructed understanding of sex are to be submissive and powerless, and sexual arousal in heterosexual relations is connected to men overpowering women. Research shows that the domination/submission dynamic is central to sexual arousal for many men. While women report sexual fantasies connected to domination/submission, in their actual sexual experiences with men they report anger and feelings of powerlessness when they are sexually dominated; they are much more likely to prefer sex that is equal, mutual, and emotionally connected.

But what about the girls who say they are empowered by the hookup culture of sexuality? Kelly, for example, isn't interested in a serious relationship while in college and likes to have sex with no strings attached. For some women, casual sex might be fine, but for many it is not mutual and liberating. Orenstein, in her research, found that for the majority of girls who were beginning sexual experimentation, their focus was on pleasing their partner, rather than on their own pleasure; they were accustomed to coercion and discomfort, and they were afraid to say no for fear of appearing uptight. For many, gender equality gains in the public sphere do not apply to the private realm, with many girls and women still basing sexual satisfaction on their partner's physical pleasure. Orenstein also notes that only certain female bodies are sources of pride—those who are thin fit the sexually "hot" media image. Grace and her roommates, in their halter tops and short shorts, might feel empowered when they gain male approval and female envy, but who is left out, and how liberating is basing self-worth on an ideal image that few can realistically hope to retain over time?

SEXUAL ASSAULT
AND SEXUALLY TRANSMITTED DISEASES

Pornography is the quintessential eroticization of domination, where male violence and aggression and female subjugation and degradation are the norm. Orenstein notes that most boys have viewed pornography before they get to college, and many believe it portrays a realistic view of sexual relationships and seek to emulate it. Pornography can give boys an unrealistic understanding of sexuality, leading to inappropriate expectations of girls and women (for example, that they have a certain look, that they orgasm easily, that they are open to all forms of sexuality, and that love and feelings are inconsequential). Men as well can be harmed by the expectations set by pornographic sex (for example, that they must be hyper masculine and "well hung"). Pornography's most dangerous effect, however, is the blurring of boundaries between normal sexual relations and sexual assault or rape.

Racism is also endemic to pornography. Women of color are always portrayed in service to men's desires and often shown as prostitutes or strippers. They are also stereotyped as overly sexual and promiscuous, and as provoking sexual aggression. Black, and often brown, men are portrayed as violent and savage, ready to molest women at any time. These dominant narratives serve to justify historic and current oppression of people of color. According to the Women of Color Network, almost 30 percent of African American women suffer intimate partner violence, a rate 35 percent higher than that of white females. Almost 25 percent of Hispanic females and 37.5 percent of Native American and Alaskan Indian women are victimized by violence. The stereotype of dangerous black and brown men has resulted in a disproportionate percentage of them being incarcerated.

According to the Association of American Universities a little over a quarter of all female undergraduate students and a little over 6 percent of male undergraduate students experience rape or sexual assault. The US Department of Justice defines sexual assault as unwanted sexual advances and touching, as well as rape, which they define as "the penetration, no matter how slight, of the vagina or anus with any body part or object, or oral penetration by a sex organ of another person, without the consent of the victim."[3]

Many incidents, like that experienced by Beth, meet the definition of sexual assault but are not viewed by the perpetrators, or even the victims, as such. This is in part due to our cultural messaging around domination and sex. Does Beth think she was assaulted, and if so, will she report it? While more students are coming forward to report sexual assault, up to 80 percent of all cases never get reported. When students do report, universities can perpetrate secondary victimization by denying or minimizing the assault, blaming the victim, and/or failing to hold perpetrator(s) accountable. Since 1990, universities have been required to report all crimes occurring near or on their campuses to the Department of Education, but in 2006, 77 percent of campuses had reported zero sexual assaults, prompting a 2015 investigation of over a hundred colleges for the mishandling of sexual assault cases.

The prevalence of secondary victimization, of not being believed and in fact being blamed for having put themselves in vulnerable positions by drinking or engaging in any sexual behavior, keeps many female undergraduates from reporting cases of sexual assault. Women are all too aware that rape cases rarely result in criminal charges (less than 10 percent).

Prevention for sexual assault often focuses on what precautions women can take instead of addressing the root cultural and institutional factors that

---

[3] "An Updated Definition of Rape," blog, US Department of Justice Archives (January 6, 2012).

promote hyper masculinity and rape culture. Beste argues that our eroti-cization of sexual inequality and domination increases the likelihood that students will accept four "rape myths": (1) women cause male sexual ag-gression by what they wear or how they act; (2) women want to be coerced into sex; (3) sexual assault is an act of male lust that can't be controlled; and (4) women can always say no and fight off an attacker.

When universities do hold perpetrators accountable, they tend to focus on a small number of repeat offenders without addressing the broader issue of sexual violence and consent for all students on campus. Simply punishing the few "bad apples" does not touch the excessive drinking and drug use, the prevalence of sexual assault, and the toxic masculinity that permeates many campus cultures.

The power and privilege that men are led to believe is their right can lead some men to think that they can control or even possess another person's body. Some young college men who have been accused of sexual assault do not take responsibility for their actions but instead blame alco-hol, party culture, and sexual promiscuity. In the extreme they even justify sexual assault or rape. The truth is that conditions for sexual violence are fostered long before the drinking begins, yet we rarely have conversa-tions about toxic masculinity and its negative effects on both women and men. What if young men like John and his fraternity brothers hosted educational workshops on male power and privilege and alternatives to toxic masculinity?

While some of the girls seem aware of the connection of drugs, alcohol, and hookup culture to sexual assault and violence, none of them talk about the risk of sexually transmitted diseases (STDs). There are at least twenty-five different STDs that are spread through vaginal, anal, and oral sex. Cen-ters for Disease Control and Prevention estimates show that young people age fifteen to twenty-four acquire half of all new STDs, even though they only represent a quarter of the sexually active population. Even more star-tling is that one in four sexually active females in this age range has an STD. Youth in this age range account for 70 percent of all gonorrhea infections, 63 percent of chlamydia infections, and 25 percent of new HIV infections.

The higher prevalence of STDs among young people is due to behavioral reasons as well as possible barriers to accessing quality STD prevention and management services. Poverty and lack of health-care coverage make prevention of STDs more difficult. The fact that Grace and her friends aren't talking about the risk of acquiring STDs with casual sex is indicative of the silence that surrounds STDs. And a culture that values women's passivity and subordination also deters young women from adequately protecting themselves, either by refusing unwanted sex or by insisting on the use of a condom, even during oral sex.

CHRISTIAN SEXUAL ETHICS

Christian response to hookup culture—where sex is viewed from an individualistic, some may say narcissistic perspective, as simply an exchange between people without deeper meaning—is varied. While most Christian perspectives on sexuality do not hold that "anything goes," there is a divide between more conservative and liberal sexual ethics. Conservative Christians, like Mae in the case, argue that hookup culture has too many negative consequences for young people (especially women) and emphasize abstinence before marriage. They believe in the sacredness of heterosexual marriage and call young people to commit to purity and chastity before getting married. For conservative Christians, there are clear, biblically based moral rules in relation to sexuality. More progressive, often feminist Christians, like Elanah in the case, also tend to be critical of hookup culture but do not generally advocate against premarital sex; neither do they valorize heterosexual marriage in the same way conservatives do. They are open to differing sexual orientations and are more likely to draw on the biblical moral norms of love and justice to assess sexual behaviors in light of what promotes right relationality and human flourishing.

Since the meaning of sexuality is culturally conditioned and constructed, Christian sexual ethics has been dynamic and continually changing. Christianity was influenced by both Greek and Roman philosophical ideas as well as Jewish theology. The Greeks and Romans had a distrust of sexual desire and thought sexual pleasure was inferior to other human pleasures. They also gave more value to the mind or soul over the body. While they did not view sex as evil, they felt it was always dangerous and in need of control. The Stoics emphasized human reason and its ability to regulate emotion and irrational sexual desire.

In Judaism, sexual desire was considered a gift from God but in need of control, thus the historical emphasis on monogamous and lifelong heterosexual marriage. While the Christian tradition generally saw sexuality as a part of God's creation and therefore good, great emphasis was put on the Fall and human inability to control sexual passion. Many early Christian writers portrayed women, identified with the body and emotion, as temptresses who needed to be controlled by male reason. In patriarchal biblical times and for years after, this control equated to women being the property of men and having no sexual autonomy. For the majority of the Christian tradition, procreation was the primary purpose of sexual activity, and heterosexual marriage was the only socially acceptable venue for sex.

While our contemporary culture has clearly not jettisoned patriarchy, women are no longer considered property, and most Christian sexual ethics do not view procreation as the only purpose of sex. Most contemporary

Christian ethicists uplift sexual pleasure, intimacy, love, and human fulfillment as fundamental moral norms related to sexuality. Many Christians
view humans as embodied sexual beings with sexual desires, attractions,
emotions, and feelings, who are created by God as interdependent beings
made for relationship. Embodied human sexuality is much broader than
genital intercourse, and sex can be genital or non-genital, with or without
desire and/or pleasure.

The advent of birth control in the 1960s paved the way for the separation of sex from procreation, and since then sex has increasingly been
separated from marriage. Conservative Christians lament these changes
and responded in the 1990s with an abstinence movement based on the
Christian virtues of chastity and purity. Mae's local evangelical pastor has
likely taught her that marriage is a sacred institution between a man and
a woman, and has encouraged Mae and his other young parishioners to
abstain from sexual intercourse before marriage.

Evangelicals in the abstinence movement have sponsored Purity Balls
and "Silver Ring Thing" events where young people take a vow of chastity
before marriage. Mae might have attended a Purity Ball with her father, who
also would have made a vow at such an event to protect his daughter. The
Silver Ring Thing organization's vision is for young people to "embrace
a lifestyle of Christ-centered sexual abstinence until marriage." Inside the
ring is a passage from scripture: "God wants you to be holy, so you should
keep clear of all sexual sin. Then each of you will control your body and
live in holiness and honor" (1 Thes 4:3–4). While boys and girls are both
encouraged to choose abstinence, the emphasis on sexual sinfulness and
purity is more often aimed toward girls, in line with our Christian tradition
of viewing women as temptresses and our cultural tradition of purity and
modesty being gendered female.

While conservatives celebrate the sacredness of sex within heterosexual marriage, they make many arguments against sex outside marriage. Youth are taught that partners are using each other's bodies in
premarital sex, that such relationships lack an emotional connection, and
that they can have devastating consequences for self-esteem, let alone
the possibility of pregnancy out of wedlock or contraction of STDs. A
corresponding message is that their marriage relationships will be more
sacred and emotionally satisfying if they and their partners come to the
marriage as virgins. In a prominent purity campaign by the Southern
Baptist Church—True Love Waits—young people are encouraged to
reject our culture's message that we are self-serving individuals who can
shape our own identities and instead to adopt the countercultural message
that we are made for lives of holiness and that the way of Christ involves
holiness, love, humility, and self-sacrifice.

The Catholic Church has also had a conservative position on sexuality with its prohibition of premarital sex, birth control, homosexuality, and divorce. Pope John Paul II, in his series of lectures entitled *Theology of the Body*, writes that "sex is meant to be unitive, procreative, and sacramental." Union is between one man and one woman under God, based on Genesis 1:27: "God created man in his own image; in the image of God he created him; male and female he created them"; and Genesis 2:24: "Therefore, a man leaves his father and his mother and cleaves to his wife, and they become one flesh."

Elanah, and perhaps Grace's mom, seem to espouse a more liberal Christian sexual ethic. Neither is opposed to premarital sex, but they are critical of hookup culture, especially as it relates to female health and well-being. Elanah critiques what she sees as a "male model of sexuality" in hookup culture, where women are treated as sexual objects for males' personal pleasure. Both Grace's mom and Elanah connect our culture's emphasis on aggressive masculinity and passive femininity to sexual violence. In fact, media images socialize us to equate sexual activity with dominance and even sexual violence. Thus, a feminist Christian sexual ethic will emphasize both love and justice as important biblical moral norms. Liberals tend not to look to the Bible for a particular sexual ethic because they believe that the patriarchal culture and worldview of biblical times does not provide adequate moral guidance for a healthy contemporary sexual ethic. They are more likely to look to scripture for guiding moral norms, such as Jesus's call to love both God and neighbor, or the consistent message throughout scripture to promote justice.

Margaret Farley advocates for the concept of "just love" to guide sexual activity.[4] She argues for three norms in just love: (1) it affirms the concrete reality of the beloved; (2) it is subject to choice and offers itself to freedom; and (3) it promotes just and true desire (not desire grounded in love of ourselves or acquisition of some sort). The foundation for just love is the intrinsic worth of humans who are created and loved by God. Just love requires respect of persons as ends, not simply means. Farley argues that freedom and relationality are central features of human persons, and therefore our sexual relations ought to support autonomy and nurturing relationships. She believes that our freedom is found in right relationship; that is, relationships that nourish both love and justice.

Farley also outlines basic norms for just sex: (1) do no unjust harm; (2) free consent; (3) mutuality; (4) equality; (5) commitment; (6) fruitfulness; and (7) social justice. Sexuality is intimate and a place of vulnerability

---

[4] Margaret Farley, *Just Love: A Framework for Christian Sexual Ethics* (New York: Continuum, 2006).

for most people. While sex can foster deep bonds between partners, sex can also harm. It has the potential for instrumentalization and objectification, not to mention violence and/or exploitation. Grace is grappling with whether drunk hookups can ever be just or whether they are inherently about objectification, especially for women. For free consent to be present, wouldn't both partners need to avoid intoxication? Grace and her roommates didn't think Beth, in her drunken state, had freely consented to have sex with Troy. Beth and Troy also didn't know each other well enough to communicate comfortably and honestly about their sexual desires and boundaries.

Equality is a necessary condition for free consent and mutuality. Elanah embraces Farley's norms for just sex. She believes that the party and hookup culture is based on inequality between genders, with the dominant narrative portraying men as the aggressors in power and women as subservient. Heterosexual men have the most power to shape the rules of college party and sex culture, despite the fact that not all men benefit or would even choose hookup culture as the dominant norm. Female bodies are portrayed and treated as sex objects, with men as the pursuers. The eroticization of domination is premised on heterosexual male power and female submission. While our culture socializes both men and women to find domination and submission sexually erotic, the #MeToo movement, led primarily by women, is insisting that equality, free consent, and mutuality are necessary to counter sexual abuse. Are young men getting this message, and if not, how might they take responsibility for just sex?

For conservative Christians, commitment through heterosexual marriage is necessary for sex to be just. Progressive Christians define commitment more broadly and encourage it without claiming it is a requirement of just sex. They affirm committed non-heterosexual sexual relations as well as those outside of marriage. Farley argues that while brief encounters can open participants to relationship, they cannot have the depth of relationality of being known, loving and being loved. Kelly seems to disagree with this norm. She feels that casual sex in this stage of her life, with no strings attached, is liberating for her. Can Grace feel the same way?

While most conservative Christians no longer believe that all sex must be connected to procreation, they still emphasize the procreative value of sexuality. Progressive Christians are more likely to emphasize multiple meanings of sex, including pleasure, intimacy, and reproduction. "Fruitfulness," for Farley, does not allude simply to reproduction but to a love that is open to a wider community and not closed in on itself, that is, a love that moves beyond itself to nourish others.

The social-justice aspect of just sex is based in the fundamental Christian norm of respect for all people, which includes sexual autonomy and just relations. Attention to social justice entails assessment of the sexism, heterosexism, and racism of college party and hookup culture. Do all members of college communities—gay, straight, bisexual, differently gendered, black, white, or brown—have freedom for sexual expression and relations where they are not harmed and are treated as ends in of themselves, not simply as means in an oppressive system? The dominant norms within college party and hookup culture come from our broader culture. Will the students on campus have courses and mentors that help them to assess critically these dominant norms in relation to social justice? Our socially constructed understandings of sexuality do not just affect individuals but have larger social implications for who flourishes or is harmed in our society. Grace, her roommates, and the men in the case might only be considering what sexual ethics make sense for them individually, without thought to what promotes a healthy and flourishing campus community for all.

CONCLUSION

Like many students starting college, Grace must decide how she wants to relate to the college party scene and hookup culture, and as a female she needs to always be aware of the prevalence of sexual assault on college campuses. Put bluntly, Grace will have to negotiate the culture of casual sex and decide whether she wants to participate in it or not. Grace, her roommate, and the boys from the frat house all experience socially constructed norms and expectations that are different for men and women. How should Grace respond to these gender norms and the ways they influence behavior? How should she assess and view what happened to her roommate Beth? Should she do anything in response to what happened? In light of Grace's Christian upbringing, how should she personally view excessive alcohol or drug consumption and casual sex? How should she consider the larger social implications of the party and hookup culture on college campuses?

ADDITIONAL RESOURCES

Beste, Jennifer. *College Hookup Culture and Christian Ethics: The Lives and Longings of Emerging Adults*. Oxford: Oxford University Press, 2018.

Farley, Margaret A. *Just Love: A Framework for Christian Sexual Ethics*. New York: Continuum, 2006.

Freitas, Donna. *Sex and the Soul: Juggling Sexuality, Spirituality, Romance, and Religion on America's College Campuses*. New York: Oxford University Press, 2015.

Grenz, Stanley J. *Sexual Ethics: An Evangelical Perspective.* Louisville: Westminster John Knox, 1997.

Iozzio, Mary Jo, and Patricia Beattie Jung. *Sex and Gender: Christian Ethical Reflections.* Washington, DC: Georgetown University Press, 2017.

Moslener, Sara. *Virgin Nation: Sexual Purity and American Adolescence.* New York: Oxford University Press, 2015.

O'Malley, Timothy P. *Off the Hook: God, Love, Dating, and Marriage in a Hookup World.* Notre Dame, IN: Ave Maria Press, 2018.

Orenstein, Peggy. *Girls and Sex: Navigating the Complicated New Landscape.* New York: HarperCollins, 2016.

Ott, Kate. *Sex + Faith: Talking with Your Child from Birth to Adolescence.* Louisville: Westminster John Knox Press, 2013.

Rosenstein, Abigail. *Purity's Appeal: Sexual Culture and the Abstinence Movement.* Honors thesis in anthropology, Wesleyan University, April 2009.

West, Traci C. *Wounds of the Spirit: Black Women, Violence, and Resistance Ethics.* New York: New York University Press, 1999.

Related Videos

Liberated: The New Sexual Revolution. 86 minutes. Magic Lantern Pictures. 2017.

Related Websites

Center for Changing Our Campus Culture
http://changingourcampus.org/
Culture of Respect
http://cultureofrespect.org/
Faith Trust Institute
http://www.faithtrustinstitute.org/
Know Your Title IX
https://www.knowyourix.org/
Student Activists for Ending Rape (SAFER)
http://www.safercampus.org/

Case

Created in the Image of God

Eileen was a bit nervous as she drove toward Wesley United Methodist Church. She had approached the pastor, Jim Harris, last Sunday to see if he would be willing to meet with her. This last year, relations between Eileen and her husband, George, had become tense as they struggled over how best to parent their transgender daughter. Marlene, whom they had named Mark at birth, changed her name at the age of ten after several years of working with a counselor. Almost twelve, Marlene was asking that her parents allow her to take puberty suppressants to stop her from developing adult male characteristics.

Eileen trusted her pastor, but she didn't know how he would react to her dilemma of whether to allow Marlene to begin medically transitioning to a girl. She was also coming to the meeting feeling very worn out and fragile because her husband had increasingly been working more hours and taking long bike rides after work to avoid dealing with his conflicted feelings about raising a transgender daughter. Eileen was feeling that over the past several years she had been left to figure out what was best.

George had been thrilled when Mark was born a year after Silas, and he anticipated teaching his boys to hunt and fish. Shortly after they were born, he had said to Eileen, "They are your boys now, but someday they'll be my boys." George grew up in rural North Carolina in a small town of about twelve hundred people. His father had worked at a textile mill while his mother raised the kids, took care of their home, and sold Avon beauty products on the side. George grew up with traditional values—devotion to family and respect for country—that were reinforced at the nondenominational evangelical church they attended. No one in his family had gone

This case and commentary were prepared by Laura A. Stivers. The names of persons and institutions have been disguised, where appropriate, to protect the privacy of those involved. The case is inspired by and based in part on the story in *Becoming Nicole: The Transformation of an American Family* by Amy Ellis Nutt.

to college, so after high school George enlisted in the military, which was a practical and honorable choice in his community. While he didn't gain any useful vocational skills in the military, it gave him the opportunity to attend college afterward through the GI Bill. He even went on and got a master's degree in safety management, which had led to his current job as a safety-management inspector at a chemical plant.

Like George, Eileen grew up Christian and deeply valued family. Eileen, however, had been more open to educating herself about transgender identity when Marlene, as early as age three, insisted that she was a girl in a boy's body and asked when she got to be a girl. A few years later Marlene asked when she could get rid of her penis. George had been uneasy when Eileen had bought "girls' toys" for Marlene and let her wear "girls' clothes" at home, but he didn't intervene. George had tried over the years to get Marlene to act more "like a boy" by taking her hunting and playing baseball with her.

Eileen arrived at the church not exactly sure what to expect but knowing that she needed support and guidance as she figured out her next steps in parenting Marlene. Pastor Jim welcomed Eileen and asked if she wanted some coffee or tea. Sitting tensely on the sofa in the pastor's office, Eileen began to tell him her family's story. Pastor Jim was aware that Marlene had changed her name and her pronouns to *she* and *her,* but he didn't know any other details. Many of the parishioners had not been surprised and seemed genuinely accepting of the change since Marlene had grown up in the church and was loved. A couple of people, however, had expressed to Pastor Jim their discomfort with having a transgender person in the church.

Eileen began the conversation. "As you know, Pastor Jim, Marlene has always considered herself to be a girl. From an early age she wanted to play with dolls and was always the female characters when she and Silas were role playing. In fact, she was obsessed with Ariel in *The Little Mermaid.* She must have watched that DVD hundreds of times. Last year she asked everyone to call her Marlene instead of Mark. While most of the kids in her elementary school have been just fine with this, I know things are likely to be different when she goes to middle school next year. I'm worried about other kids bullying her. I've already been having discussions with Leticia, the school counselor, about how to prepare for middle school. We've talked about how to negotiate which bathroom Marlene should use and what to do about changing in the locker room before and after PE. At her current school the bathrooms are unisex and single stall, but that's not the case at the middle school. All of this is also a strain on Silas, who as an older brother feels that he should be there to protect Marlene."

Pastor Jim gently replied, "It sounds as though you are under a lot of stress."

"I was fine with Marlene changing her name and starting to wear more feminine clothes to school because over the years it just became clearer to me that Marlene is going to be who she is no matter what I think or do. George has had a harder time accepting these changes. What I am not so sure about are the next steps toward transitioning. The last few years we have been meeting with Dr. Ed Kwok, who works with transgender patients, and last year Marlene did her first psychological evaluation to confirm whether she has gender dysphoria. Since Marlene is a minor, it is our decision as her parents whether we allow her to take the next steps toward transition."

"And what are those next steps?" asked Pastor Jim.

"Dr. Kwok said that if Marlene passed the psychological tests, she could begin the 12-16-18 program. That is, she would take puberty suppressants around age twelve to slow down puberty. At age sixteen she would take female hormones so that she will develop breasts. At age eighteen she can decide whether she wants to have gender-affirming surgery. Marlene wants to start the puberty suppressants right now, but Dr. Kwok said that starting them too early could stunt her growth."

Eileen continued, "Marlene has been attending a summer camp for transgender kids since she was eight. This experience has made her more self-confident and more vocal about her needs. Just this week she said to me, 'Mom, Silas and my friends have viewed me as a girl for years. I need to be myself, and the other kids in school will just have to deal with who I am. I am a girl and want to play on the girls' sports teams and do all the things other girls are doing.'"

"If Marlene truly feels that she is a girl, what are your reservations?" asked Pastor Jim.

"I've done a lot of research, and although most studies show that it is rare for kids who truly have gender dysphoria to regret transitioning to another gender, these next steps seem so irreversible. I've also read about how children's brains don't fully develop until age twenty-five. Is Marlene fully capable of making a rational decision of such magnitude at her age? I realize that by the time she is eighteen years old, we won't have any say in her medical decisions, but if she has gender-affirming surgery she might not be able to have children, even though I've heard it is now an option for some transgender patients. I'm also worried about people not accepting her or even attacking her for being a transgender woman."

"You're right that these actions are life changing, but have you considered the implications if you don't allow Marlene to transition?" said Pastor Jim.

"Yes, over the past few years she has constantly been picking fights with Silas. Once when I asked her why she hit her brother, she said, 'Because he gets to be who he is and I don't.' I can only imagine how her anger could escalate. I don't want her to hurt anyone, and I also fear that her anger might even turn inward. The research bears this out, with a higher rate of depression and even suicide among youth who have not been allowed to transition."

"You said George has struggled with these changes. How is he reacting to the possibility of Marlene transitioning medically? Have you talked openly together about all the changes that are happening?"

With a slight sigh, Eileen replied, "I think George has been in denial, and it has been hard for us to talk about this, which makes me feel I'm carrying the burden of decision-making alone. He loves both of our children so much, and I think deep down he knows that Marlene needs to be who she needs to be, but her transgender identity challenges his core beliefs about gender, gender roles, and sexuality. He didn't stop Marlene from changing her name and identity, but he doesn't talk about it much. He absolutely refuses to look at any of the transgender research I've shared with him."

Pastor Jim reflected, "Are George's beliefs on gender roles and sexuality rooted in his religious upbringing? I think that for many people this is the case. In fact, the national Methodist Church (UMC) just voted against the 'One Church Plan' that would have allowed individual churches and regional conferences to decide whether to ordain and marry lesbian, gay, bisexual, transgender, and queer (LGBTQ) members. A majority opted instead for the 'Traditional Plan' that prohibits same-sex unions and ordination of LGBTQ pastors. Some church leaders are suggesting that churches opposed to the Traditional Plan should leave the UMC, while a group called Reconciling Ministries Network is advocating that dissenting churches remain and resist."

Eileen hesitated for a minute. "I wish he would talk to you about this. While we don't generally have theological conversations, George threw a Bible verse at me once when I let Marlene wear girls' clothes. It was something about it being an abomination to the Lord if a woman wears a man's clothes or vice versa, maybe from Deuteronomy. George grew up in a family and church that believed in traditional gender roles and definitely would have seen anything related to LGBTQ rights as sinful. While I have always been comfortable with the idea that masculinity and femininity are complementary roles that bring different strengths to marriage and parenting, raising a transgender child is prompting me to question my views on some things. The bottom line for me is supporting Marlene to be happy and healthy."

Pastor Jim replied, "While our congregation is currently following the national church's prohibition on same-sex marriage and ordination of LGBTQ clergy, I don't think using a single text from the Bible to prove a point without understanding the context of the quotation is particularly useful. I don't really know much about transgender issues, but I feel that it is my role as Marlene's pastor to support her mental, physical, and spiritual development and health. I have to admit, however, that balancing the needs of all parishioners isn't easy."

"Yes, I was pretty nervous coming to talk to you. I've been worried that we might get kicked out of the church. I know Marlene makes some people in the congregation uncomfortable, but my church family is important to me, so I'm glad that you are committed to supporting Marlene and our family." Eileen wondered, but didn't ask Pastor Jim, why pleasing all of the parishioners was necessary. Shouldn't he be more of an ally and move his church members toward acceptance of all people?

Pastor Jim responded, "I certainly cannot tell you what decision you should make in relation to the next steps about Marlene's transition, but I do encourage you to continue to reach out to George to be actively involved in the decision-making. It's important for both of you to listen to Marlene's perspective, even if you know that she is still maturing and will need guidance."

Eileen really wished that Pastor Jim would speak to George directly and encourage him to be an ally for Marlene, but she simply said, "Thanks, Pastor Jim. No matter what we decide, we'll have hurdles to overcome. Many people in our society are simply not ready to accept people whom they see as 'different.' I just hope that our family and Marlene are up to the challenge."

Commentary

In the United States we have historically assigned a sex to babies at birth, either male or female, and then, once a sex is assigned certain gender expectations follow. In fact, for most people, the terms *sex* and *gender* have been interchangeable. However, in recent decades new theoretical formulations of gender have argued that gender is more complex than a traditional binary framework and is related to three different dimensions: our bodies, our identity, and our gender expression. We experience our own bodies, but society "genders" our bodies by expecting conformity to specific gender norms related to being male or female. Our identity is our internal understanding of who we are—male, female, a blend of both, or neither. Gender expression is related to how we present our gender and how society both interacts with and shapes our gender.

Society tries to enforce conformity to particular gender norms, but we can interact with these gender norms in multiple ways. There are actually a range of possibilities for these dimensions despite the fact that our society generally views sex and gender as binary. While Marlene's identity doesn't really challenge the traditional gender binary, her experience challenges the conception that sex and gender are identical.

People who don't fit societal norms often face many challenges. According to the Williams Institute, there are at least 700,000 transgender people in the United States (0.3 percent of the population), but this is a conservative estimate due to the limited number of studies attempting measurement of the transgender population and due to the great diversity of the transgender community. People identify in various ways—as a man, a woman, genderqueer, nonbinary, and/or agender (no gender). Some transgender folks take hormones and have surgery, while others don't. And some identify as transgender, while others don't; they simply live in their chosen identity.

DEFINITIONS

To discuss this case, it is necessary to have some common definitions of terms and concepts. The first term is *gender expansive*, which refers to anybody who does not conform to a culture's binary gender options. *Transgender* refers to people whose gender identity doesn't match the sex they were assigned at birth; it includes transgender girls, transgender boys, and those who consider themselves nonbinary. It can also include people who cross dress. People whose gender identity and gender assigned at birth align are called *cisgender. Genderqueer* and *nonbinary* refer to people who do not identify as either a man or a woman; they might see themselves as a combination of genders, between genders, or even beyond gender. *Transsexual* refers to people who transition from one sex to another, either through the use of hormones and/or surgical procedures. While some people feel the term is dated and even offensive, others choose to identify as transsexual over transgender and vice versa.

Marlene, who was assigned male sex at birth but identifies as a girl, is considered a transgender girl. The difference between gender-expansive and transgender children is not always clear at first. While social experiences can shape a child's gender identity, medical experts generally agree that nature, not simply nurture and culture, also plays a role in a person's internal gender identity. Competent clinicians can generally differentiate between transgender and gender-expansive children. Marlene's therapist confirmed that she is transgender.

Children like Marlene, who from a young age are clear that their gender does not match the sex they were assigned at birth, are said to experience *gender dysphoria.* Children diagnosed with gender dysphoria have more severe distress over the mismatch between their sex and gender; the distress lasts for a long time and even worsens at puberty, because they *know* what they consider to be their real gender identity.

Often gender and sexual orientation are conflated, but each is a distinct part of our identity. Gender is personal and related to the way we see ourselves, while sexual orientation is interpersonal and related to whom we are physically or emotionally attracted. Our society tends to assume that if someone's gender expression doesn't match societal norms, that person is homosexual, but how people express their gender identity is separate from their sexual orientation.

BINARY SYSTEM VERSUS GENDER SPECTRUM

A binary system of thought sees sex and gender identity as either a man or a woman, with related gender expression delineated by societal understandings of masculinity and femininity. Yet throughout history and in many cultures there have been more than two genders, and in all societies there are people whose sex assigned at birth does not correspond to a binary model. For example, the organization Gender Spectrum notes that more complex understandings of gender are found in many different societies.

The Bugis Society in Indonesia has five genders that correspond to a cisgender male, cisgender female, transgender male, transgender female, and an androgynous or intersex person. In India the *hijra* are eunuchs or transgender people who have a specific role in their communities. Two-spirit people in some Native American communities fulfill a third-gender ceremonial role in their cultures. At least eight countries legally recognize a third gender.

The Intersex Society of North America estimates that in one out of fifteen hundred births atypical genitalia is noticeable. *Intersex* refers to a variety of conditions in which a person is born with reproductive or sexual anatomy that isn't typically female or male. The society also notes that there are a number of people who have subtler forms of sex-anatomy variation that show up later in life. For years, infants in the United States were subjected to *gender-normalizing surgery;* in 2013 the United Nations condemned these surgeries as unnecessary and often damaging to infants.

Despite biological evidence contradicting a binary model of sex and gender, most people struggle to move beyond gender binaries (as illustrated by George's discomfort with his daughter's gender identity). Even children whose parents are open to diverse representations of biological sex, gender identity, gender expression, and sexual orientation are confronted by binary societal norms. Before entering school, parents must identify on forms whether their children are male or female. Once at school, children are exposed to all sorts of gender expectations ranging from what types of imaginative play or extracurricular activities are appropriate to what they wear and what academic interests or careers they are encouraged to pursue.

While Marlene longs to adopt so-called feminine attire and activities, she nevertheless challenges the sex/gender binary by not identifying with her assigned sex. Other children might be fine with their sex as assigned at birth, yet not express their gender in the ways our culture expects. Some might even eschew traditional gender roles altogether. Of course, children who defy or transgress societal expectations of gender expression are often labeled and bullied; this is especially true for boys who are perceived as feminine.

While transgender identity is not related to sexual orientation, many people conflate the two, and sexual orientation is also subjected to a binary model of either gay or straight. The conflation of gender identity and sexual orientation can be confusing for children like Marlene, who are trying to make sense of their own identities. Binary understandings of gender, biology, and sexual orientation actually exclude the diverse identities of many people.

To make room for people who do not fit the binary options of man or woman, feminine or masculine, or straight or gay, scholars have proposed a spectrum-based model for sex, gender, and sexuality (see Figure 7–1).

Sex	Male	Typical male physiology
	Female	Typical female physiology
	Intersex	Physical sex markers not clearly male or female
Gender Identity	Male	Identifies as male
	Female	Identifies as female
	Nonbinary	Identifies other than male or female
	Transgender	Gender and sex assigned at birth differ
	Agender	Does not identify with any gender
Gender Expression	Genderqueer	Combination of, between, or beyond gender
	Masculine	Qualities traditionally associated with men
	Feminine	Qualities traditionally associated with women
	Butch	Masculine expression
	Femme	Feminine expression
	Androgynous	Mixture of masculinity and femininity
Sexual Orientation	Heterosexual	Toward persons of other binary gender and/or sex
	Homosexual	Toward persons of same gender and/or sex
	Bisexual	Toward persons of same and other gender and/or sex
	Pansexual	Towards persons of any gender and/or sex
	Queer	Any orientation other than straight/ umbrella term for marginalized sexualities and genders

Source: University of South Dakota

Figure 7–1. A Spectrum Model of Sex, Gender, and Sexuality

Since a spectrum model is fully inclusive, it also works well for people who fit more typical societal norms around sex, gender, and sexuality.

GENDER TRANSITION AND CHILDREN

In a 2008 study, social scientist Natacha Kennedy found that people become aware they are transgender at an average age of eight, and more than 80 percent are aware they are transgender before leaving primary school.[1] Marlene was clear about her gender identity even before she was eight years old. A consistent response from the transgender participants in the study was that at a young age they understood that they were different in a socially unacceptable way and thus, they felt the need to conceal their true feelings and identity.

George and Eileen have responded very differently to Marlene's self-identification that she is a girl. Eileen has done the work of educating herself about transgender children, gender dysphoria, and the stages of transition, but she is still worried about how to honor Marlene's autonomy while also being careful not to make any decisions that either of them might regret. After all, Marlene is still a child and her parents have the legal and moral responsibility for her well-being.[2] Marlene would like for the transition process to go more quickly, but Eileen questions whether Marlene is mature enough to envision all the consequences associated with transition.

In reality, Marlene has already started a gender transition by changing her name, wearing girls' clothing, and asking her family and friends to use female pronouns when referring to her. These steps are considered social transition. Since Marlene is a minor, her parents will have a say in what steps toward medical transition she is allowed to take next. Eileen wants to affirm Marlene's identity, but she is also worried about some of the possible implications of having Marlene take puberty blockers at age twelve and then gender-affirming hormone therapy at age sixteen (see Figure 7–2).

On the one hand, Dr. Kwok has probably assured Eileen that the effects of puberty blockers are reversible and that they can offer some time for Marlene to mature and further consider her gender identity. Dr. Kwok has also made sure that Marlene has had extended psychological evaluations, and Eileen connected Marlene to counseling support and gave her ways to

---

[1] Natacha Kennedy, "Transgendered Children in Schools: A Critical Review of 'Homophobic Bullying: Safe to Learn—Embedding Anti-Bullying Work in Schools,'" *Forum* 50, no. 3 (2008): 383–96.

[2] When parental consent is required by state law, medical decision-making is generally like other legal decisions made on behalf of a minor and depends on the custody arrangement of the family.

	Examples	Ages	Reversibility
Social transition	Adopting gender-affirming hairstyles, clothing, name, gender pronouns, restrooms and other facilities	Any	Reversible
Puberty blockers	Gonadotropin-releasing hormone analogs such as leuprolide and histrelin	Early Adolescents	Reversible
Gender-affirming hormone therapy	• Testosterone (for those assigned female at birth) • Estrogen plus androgen inhibitor (for those assigned male at birth)	Older Adolescents (as appropriate) Adults	Partially Reversible
Gender-affirming surgeries	• "Top" surgery (to create a male-typical chest shape or enhance breasts) • "Bottom" surgery (surgery on genitals or reproductive organs) • Facial feminization surgeries	Older Adolescents (as appropriate) Adults	Not Reversible
Legal transition	• Changing gender and name recorded on birth certificate, school records and other documents	Any	Reversible

Source: Human Rights Campaign

Figure 7–2. Stages and Options for Gender Transition

connect with other transgender children at a summer camp. On the other hand, Eileen might have found articles in her research from detractors of gender transition who argue that puberty blockers can cause long-term health effects and that not enough research has been done on the possible effects since the first puberty blockers were used on kids in 2007. Some people also claim that blocking puberty could cause children to persist in gender dysphoria rather than allowing them to mature and possibly come to terms with their birth gender. These claims, however, have not been supported by scholarly research studies.

While Eileen is legally and morally responsible for her child, she is struggling with the ethical implications of her role as a parent in decision-making about gender transition. Some people ask whether parents, or even medical professionals, should be allowed to make decisions in relation to transgender identity and transition when such decisions can alter substantially a child's life and psychological health. They argue that children with gender dysphoria are the ones experiencing a mismatch between their sex and gender, and therefore they have better insight than anyone about any transition decisions and what is necessary for them to feel comfortable in their own body.

Others argue that children with gender dysphoria should be allowed to go through puberty because their views might change. They hold that the mental and physical changes in puberty might change the way children feel about their body and their subsequent gender identity. Furthermore, as Eileen points out to Pastor Jim, children's brains have not fully developed. Should they make decisions of such magnitude without the guidance of parents and medical personnel? The fear is that children might make a rash decision without an adequate perspective of the long-term effects of their choice.

While clinicians generally have a gender-affirming approach to children who are gender expansive or transgender, there is a small group of health-care professionals who try to "correct" gender-expansive behaviors and advocate against gender transition. Some people take this approach out of fear that gender-expansive children are more likely to become homosexual. However, many professional organizations, including the American Academy of Pediatrics and the American Psychological Association, have rejected any efforts to change the gender expression or sexual orientation of children or adults. They argue that such efforts cause lasting damage to people and do nothing to prevent children from becoming transgender adults. Most experts agree that gender-diverse children will be healthier and more successful if they receive support for their chosen identity both at home and at school.

TRANSGENDER OPPRESSION

Eileen is right to worry about how society will treat her transgender daughter. Transgender advocates argue that the problem is not that people feel trapped in the wrong body, but rather that societal hate, lack of inclusion, and discrimination against transgender people are common. These advocates believe it is wrong to coerce any group of people to become who they are not and prevent them from expressing their identity freely without fear of reprisal. There is a great deal of evidence that societal oppression of transgender people and the resulting internalized transphobia many of them experience have an extremely negative effect on their well-being. Marlene's outbursts and anger are illustrative of the strains of pretending that her sex assigned at birth matches her gender identity.

Keeping one's gender identity a secret can be traumatic and can also isolate youth from their peers. Transgender youth whose self-identity is not supported are more likely to perform poorly in school and even drop out; have an increased risk of self-harm, substance abuse, or suicide; and can suffer from mental health issues into adulthood. Transgender youth who are not supported by their families are also at a higher risk of running away and becoming homeless. According to the National Center for Transgender Equality, 20 percent of transgender people have experienced homelessness at some point in their lives.

A study of transgender youth by the Gay, Lesbian and Straight Education Network shows that 90 percent of the youth surveyed experienced verbal harassment at school, half experienced physical harassment, a quarter experienced physical assault, and two-thirds do not feel safe at school. Most incidents were not reported to school officials, and school personnel rarely intervene when they witness gender-based bullying. Repeated bullying and victimization can lead to internalized transphobia and negatively affect adolescent psychosocial development.

Transgender adults also face discrimination, stigma, and systemic inequality. Currently, there is no comprehensive federal nondiscrimination law based on gender identity, although former president Obama added gender identity to the categories protected against discrimination through Executive Order 13672 in 2014. According to the Human Rights Campaign's State Equality Index, twenty-one states currently have laws in place that prohibit employment and housing discrimination based on gender identity. A 2015 report from the Movement Advancement Project and the Center for American Progress found that 15 percent of transgender people make less than ten thousand dollars annually, in contrast to 4 percent of cisgender people. For transgender people of color, poverty is even worse, with 34 percent of black transgender people reporting incomes at this level versus 9 percent of all African Americans, and 28 percent versus 5 percent for Hispanic transgender people. Lack of legal representation, due to poverty and/or bias, can also lead to unemployment.

Despite increased acceptance for lesbians and gay men, transgender people still face extreme stigma and are often seen as mentally ill, socially deviant, and even sexually predatory. This stigma leads to harassment as well as serious violence. Murders of transgender people, most of whom were transgender women and almost all of whom were people of color, have been increasing. The Human Rights Campaign calculates that 128 killings of transgender people have occurred between 2013 and 2018, with 80 percent of them people of color. Although transgender people face higher rates of physical and sexual assault, the National Coalition of Anti-Violence Programs found that nearly half are uncomfortable turning to police for help for fear of bias-based harassment from them.

There is insufficient data on health disparities among transgender people, but access to transgender-sensitive health care is a top priority for many transgender people. According to the National Transgender Discrimination Survey, almost 20 percent of respondents cited being refused medical care based on their transgender identity. Many avoid doctors or the health-care system for fear of discrimination. The Affordable Care Act (ACA) has been a very important law for transgender people because it prohibits sex discrimination, including anti-transgender discrimination, by a majority of insurance companies and health providers. Despite the passage of the ACA, almost one-third of transgender Americans still lacked health-care coverage in 2017, according to a survey by National Public Radio, The Robert Wood Johnson Foundation, and the Harvard T. H. Chan School of Public Health. Gender-affirming surgery is expensive, and therefore many transgender people do not get it, especially if they have no health-insurance coverage.

GENDER AND CHRISTIANITY

For many Christians the idea of a spectrum-based model for sex, gender, and sexuality is much too radical. For George, who grew up in a conservative evangelical church, gender duality is central. Organizations like Focus on the Family argue that in scripture, beginning from Genesis 1 when God created the universe, there are a series of "separations," including heaven and earth, light and dark, water and dry land. They believe that duality extends to humans, the pinnacle of God's creation, who were created separately from animals and were formed into two complementary sexes—male and female—both of which uniquely bear God's image or the *imago Dei*. Males and females are both called to reflect the image of God in their own unique and diverse ways. Even more important is the joining in marriage of male and female so they may be "fruitful and multiply and fill the earth" (Gen 1:28), thus spreading God's image throughout the world. George grew up with this worldview and for most of his life it probably never crossed his mind that it might be oppressive to some people. Marlene's identity challenges his ingrained perspectives, and he is having a hard time reconciling the two.

Love for his daughter might change George's views over time, as has happened for Eileen. For some, however, the opening up of gender categories that is occurring in society is to be resisted, as they feel it challenges the fundamental order that God (usually viewed as a male god) has established. The conservative Christian response to the existence of people who are intersex is to reinforce their understanding of a dualistically created order by marking difference as deviation from an established norm that reflects humanity's fallen nature. Nevertheless, they would argue, Christians should have love and compassion for all, because all people, no matter the disorders they are afflicted with, are created in God's image.

Conservative Christians might also cite particular Bible passages to argue against transgender identity. Eileen notes that George brought up a passage from Deuteronomy (22:5) that prohibits cross dressing. Similarly, in Deuteronomy 23:1, men are prohibited from participation in worship if they have lost their penis or testicles. Proponents of transgender identity argue that these admonitions were part of distinguishing Israel from its neighbors. In Deuteronomy and Leviticus there are many prohibitions against mixing things, many of which people would find out of date today (for example, Deuteronomy 22:11 prohibits wearing clothes made of wool and linen mixed together). Because transgender identity is a modern concept, biblical writers did not address it directly. Biblical texts do refer to eunuchs, that is, men who had been castrated and were no longer male or female and therefore were excluded from aspects of ritual life.

Proponents of transgender identity, however, point out a passage in Isaiah:

> Do not let the eunuch say,
>   "I am just a dry tree."
> For thus says the LORD:
> To the eunuchs who keep my sabbaths,
>   who choose the things that please me
>   and hold fast my covenant,

> I will give, in my house and within my walls,
>> a monument and a name
>> better than sons and daughters;
> I will give them an everlasting name
>> that shall not be cut off. (Is 56:3b–5)

They argue that this inclusion of all who keep the covenant with God counteracts the previous laws in Deuteronomy that excluded eunuchs from community and ritual life. They place emphasis on faithfulness and justice, not inclusion based on physical characteristics. Jesus himself seemed aware that there were more than two genders:

> For there are eunuchs who have been so from birth, and there are eunuchs who have been made eunuchs by others, and there are eunuchs who have made themselves eunuchs for the sake of the kingdom of heaven. Let anyone accept this who can. (Mt 19:11–12)

Jesus's reference to eunuchs from birth might refer to people with intersex conditions. Jesus does not judge or exclude but accepts that there are different ways of being human. Paul's vision for the early Christian community was that all Christians, no matter their race, status, sex, or other differences, are made in the image of God and one in solidarity in the Christian body: "There is no longer Jew or Greek, there is no longer slave or free, there is no longer male and female; for all of you are one in Christ Jesus" (Gal 3:28).

Organizations like the Center for LGBTQ and Gender Studies argue that the message of the Bible tends toward full inclusion of people, not exclusion based on physical differences. While scripture does not address transgender identity directly, they say that a story in Acts illustrates Jesus's message of love and inclusion. In the story a eunuch, who is different by race, nationality, gender, location, and religion from the members of the community he is traveling in, encounters Philip, sent by an angel of God. Philip shares the story of Jesus, and the eunuch asks if he can be baptized. Philip sees no reason that the eunuch can't fully participate in the community of faith, and immediately baptizes him (Acts 8:25–39). Jesus always teaches that his followers are to love their neighbors as they love themselves. For Jesus, all people are created in the *imago Dei*. Jesus models in all of his connections to others that to be created in the image of God does not mean Christians have particular bodily characteristics but that they are created to be in full and loving relationship with one another. People who are supportive of transgender identity would never see those who are intersex as having a disorder and therefore unable to fulfill God's plan;

instead, they would see all of the diversity in God's creation as something to be celebrated, not pitied or fixed.

Religious and theological interpretations can have major implications for people. Will Marlene's parents be able to celebrate her transgender identity and not see it as a disorder? Will their church community fully accept and include Marlene as a transgender girl? Should Pastor Jim play a leadership role in making that happen? Marlene's self-esteem and understanding of self-worth will be influenced by the way others do or do not accept her fully as a person of dignity created in the image of God. Not everyone in our society is religious, but dominant theological constructions can influence societal worldviews and perspectives.

Despite inclusive theological understandings of Jesus's message and God's will, many churches are still struggling to open their doors to full participation and inclusion of all. Marlene and her family attend a Methodist church. While many of the parishioners accept Marlene, the church itself is not formally connected to the Reconciling Ministries Network to resist the national Methodist Church's stance that prohibits same-sex unions and ordination of LGBTQ pastors. Will Marlene feel she can be a full participating member in a church that is not fully inclusive of her identity? Should Eileen make this her mission? Should Pastor Jim? The United Church of Christ, the Metropolitan Community Church, Unitarian Universalist, Presbyterian Church (USA), Disciples of Christ, Quakers, and Episcopal churches have all issued statements that transgender people have full inclusion in the church community and can be ordained as ministers. In many other denominations, like the Methodists, there are individual congregations that are "welcoming churches."

CONCLUSION

At eleven years of age Marlene seems clear about her gender identity and believes she is ready to transition medically to female. For her, being able to live fully in the gender she identifies with is more important than any oppression she might face as a transgender woman. Since she is not yet eighteen, however, her transition is not her decision alone. Eileen and George have had a steep learning curve in figuring out how to be supportive of their transgender daughter. They must now find a way to listen to Marlene and to communicate with one another in order to make the right decisions in relation to transition. They could let Marlene begin taking puberty blockers and later hormone therapy while she is a minor, or they could deny these treatments to her until she turns eighteen and can make her own health-care decisions.

Another issue is whether individuals and families have any ethical obligations in advocating for increased acceptance and policy changes within their church families and denominations. In the case of denominations that have changed their understanding of LGBTQ issues in recent decades, one of the major factors has always been the willingness of Christians to share their experiences and their stories as people of faith. Knowing the importance of personal witness and storytelling in challenging people to think about their theological understanding of sexuality and gender, do individuals have any ethical obligation to their community to share their story?

ADDITIONAL RESOURCES

Bader-Saye, Scott. "The Transgender Body's Grace." *Journal of the Society of Christian Ethics* 39, no. 1 (Spring/Summer 2019): 75–92.

Comstock, Gary David, and Susan E. Henking, eds. *Querying Religion: A Critical Anthology*. New York: Continuum, 1997.

Congregation for Catholic Education. *Male and Female He Created Them: Toward a Path of Dialogue on the Question of Gender Theory in Education*. Vatican City, June 2019.

Greytak, Emily A., Joseph G. Kosciw, and Elizabeth M. Diaz. *Harsh Realities: The Experiences of Transgender Youth in Our Nation's Schools*. The Gay, Lesbian and Straight Education Network, 2009.

Hartke, Austen. "Nonbinary Gender and the Beauty of Creation: God's Unclassified World." *Christian Century* 135, no. 9 (2018): 27–29.

Kennedy, Natacha, and Mark Hellen. "Transgender Children: More Than a Theoretical Challenge." *Graduate Journal of Social Science* 7, no. 2 (December 2010): 25–43.

Mollenkott, Virginia Ramey. *Omnigender: A Trans-Religious Approach*. Cleveland: Pilgrim Press, 2001.

Murchison, Gabe. *Supporting and Caring for Transgender Children*. Human Rights Campaign Foundation and American Academy of Pediatrics. September 2016.

Sheridan, Vanessa. *Crossing Over: Liberating the Transgendered Christian*. Cleveland: Pilgrim Press, 2001.

Stryker, Susan. *Transgender History: The Roots of Today's Revolution*. 2nd edition. Seal Press, 2017.

Tanis, Justin. *Trans-Gendered: Theology, Ministry, and Communities of Faith*. Cleveland: Pilgrim Press, 2003.

Yarhouse, Mark. "Understanding Gender Dysphoria." *Christianity Today* (July/August 2016), 44–50.

Related Videos

Judith Butler. *Your Behavior Creates Your Gender*. 3 minutes. YouTube. 2012.
Scott Turner Schofield. *Ending Gender*. 16 minutes. TED Talk. 2013.

Related Websites

Focus on the Family
   https://www.focusonthefamily.com
Gay, Lesbian, and Straight Education Network
   https://www.glsen.org/
Gender Spectrum
   www.genderspectrum.org
Genderbread Person v4.0
   www.genderbread.org
Human Rights Campaign
   www.hrc.org
National Center for Transgender Equality
   https://transequality.org/
The Center for Lesbian and Gay Studies in Religion and Ministry
   www.clgs.org

PART VIII

LIFE AND DEATH

Case

A Matter of
Life and Death

The antiseptic smell of clinics and hospitals had always made Sue Ann Thomas feel sick to her stomach. As she waited alone in the cold reception room, her mind flashed back to two weeks ago when she had told Danny she thought she was pregnant. He wasn't so much angry as he was confused and kind of dazed. They talked about what she could do.

Sue Ann was eighteen, a freshman at South Central Community College, and she was afraid to tell her parents that she was pregnant. Danny had also finished high school last year and had a job in a garage in South Chicago. She felt that Danny had been honest about how he felt. "You are really important to me, Sue Ann, but I don't think either of us is ready to get married right now. I guess we have to figure out what to do." They decided that by pooling their savings they could get together the six hundred dollars for an abortion.

Sue Ann remembered the name of Dr. Engles. Her mother had gone to him a couple of times. Making an appointment under another name, Sue Ann told him that she wanted an abortion. Dr. Engles talked to her after her examination when the pregnancy tests proved positive. He told her about what he thought was the best health clinic in Chicago for pregnancy termination. While Sue Ann was still there, he called the clinic for a counseling date and a surgery date the day after that, wrote out the papers for her to take in, and asked her to make an appointment with the nurse to see him three weeks after the abortion to make sure everything was all right. As Sue

---

This case was prepared by Alice Frazer Evans and the commentary by Christine E. Gudorf. Both have been revised and updated by James B. Martin-Schramm. The names of persons and institutions have been disguised, where appropriate, to protect the privacy of those involved.

Ann walked out of the office, she thought that the Wednesday counseling appointment—one week away—couldn't come soon enough.

The next week of waiting had been hell. Sue Ann was only seven weeks along, but she was sure she would begin to show. When Wednesday came, Sue Ann told her mother she was going over to a girlfriend's house for supper so she would be home late. When Danny came by early that morning in his old Ford to take her to class on his way to work, Sue Ann was sure her parents would never know what was going on.

But both her mother and her father had been bugging her for a couple of weeks now. She had been able to hide her nausea, but her mother said she didn't look well. Sue Ann knew they were worried about her. She also felt their pressure and their pride. She was the first member of the family who had ever attended college. Sue Ann thought that having a younger brother and sister who really looked up to her didn't help either. She knew her dad got pretty good wages working for a construction company, but her mom had started working part-time to help pay for her books and school fees.

Danny and Sue Ann didn't say much on their way into the city. Danny dropped her off at the community college and reassured her that he would pick her up at the clinic when he got off work about 5:30. After eating her packed lunch, Sue Ann took a city bus to the clinic for her afternoon appointment. She had seemed so confident, so sure of herself last week, and even this morning, but as she handed the papers to the receptionist and paid the clinic cashier, she was aware of how cold and clammy her hands felt. She jumped when the nurse called her into a small office to take her blood pressure and temperature.

Dr. Engles had told Sue Ann what would happen during those two days. Today was for a checkup and counseling. She was healthy and still in her first trimester, so the clinic doctor would likely do something called a "vacuum aspiration" tomorrow. This would take about fifteen minutes. Then she would have to wait at least an hour before she could leave.

Sue Ann was taken into a large room with four other women for a group counseling session with a social worker. Three appeared to be in their early to late twenties, and one looked to be in her mid-to-late thirties. She had known that at some time during the day before the abortion there would be a group counseling session. She remembered a couple of weeks ago telling her closest friend, Sharon, that she was pregnant. Sharon had blurted out that she could never have an abortion, that it was wrong and that she would feel too guilty. Sue Ann realized that Danny was the only other person she had told about her pregnancy. She was already afraid of having to talk with these women about it. Sue Ann chose a corner chair and stared out the window as she waited. It had begun to snow.

For the first time Sue Ann let herself think about Paul Reynolds. She hadn't dated anyone else during her last two years of high school. Paul was older. After high school, he had enlisted in the US Army. Over the first two years of his tour of duty they wrote to each other nearly every day. They planned to be married as soon as Sue Ann finished high school. But last summer the Army found that Paul had a heart defect. He came home on an extended leave, and he died in June. Sue Ann still couldn't really believe it. She had cried for weeks. Her friends and her mother said that she needed to move on and that she had to think about her own life. They all said that beginning college in September would be the best thing for her.

Sue Ann had known Danny since grade school and started dating him not long after her classes began in the fall. He was good company but nothing like Paul. She and Danny had a good time together; he made her laugh. When Danny said he loved her, Sue Ann thought that having sex with him would help her forget Paul, but it didn't. Paul had been a Roman Catholic. They had talked about sex a long time before they went to bed together. This was after they had decided to get married. Paul said that this meant having sex was okay with the church, but she wasn't sure he was right. She remembered reading that the Catholic Church was against premarital sex and also said abortion was murder. Sue Ann didn't want to think about what Paul would have said about her pregnancy. Getting an abortion had seemed the only thing to do.

The social worker came in and introduced herself. The women began to talk, to tell their ages, and to give their reasons for choosing to have an abortion. A girl in her twenties, who introduced herself as Mary, laughed uneasily and asked if anyone had ever backed out this far along. Connie Davies, the social worker, responded very seriously. "Yes, over the past six months of this particular program there have been a few women who chose at the last minute not to terminate their pregnancies. A couple of them said they had decided to give their babies up for adoption. That's one of the reasons I'm here to talk with you, to make sure you are clear about what you are doing."

Sue Ann dug her nails into her palms and began to feel the tears well up in her eyes. She had come this far. What could she do if she backed out? Sue Ann was the only one who had not spoken. Connie Davies turned to her and waited.

Commentary

Sue Ann Thomas, with her boyfriend Danny, faces an agonizing decision: whether to terminate with medical assistance an unwanted pregnancy in its early stages. With her decision Sue Ann enters the arena of fierce public debates over the definition of human life, the meaning of motherhood, the issue of who should control the abortion decision, and the role of sacrifice in Christian life. If all this were not enough, she must also work through how she will relate to her parents.

In facing this decision Sue Ann needs to consider the facts about abortion in her society; the resources of scripture and Christian tradition regarding abortion; definitions of human life; parenting roles; and the choices and roles open to her and other women in contemporary society.

FACTS ABOUT ABORTION IN THE UNITED STATES

Sue Ann's option to elect to have a legal abortion is provided in the United States under the landmark 1973 Supreme Court decision *Roe v. Wade*, which ruled that in the early stages of pregnancy prior to the viability of the fetus, the decision to have an abortion must be left to a woman and her doctor. Only after viability may the state prohibit abortion, and then not when the woman's life is in danger. This ruling threw out the laws of most states enacted in the second half of the nineteenth century prohibiting abortion unless a physician could claim compelling medical indications.

Abortion statistics lag behind records of live births. Nationwide abortion statistics for the United States are available privately from the Guttmacher Institute and publicly from the Centers for Disease Control (CDC). Guttmacher's statistics are published every three years and are based on direct surveys of all known abortion providers in the United States. The CDC statistics are published annually and are based on the number of abortions reported to state health departments—with the exception of California, Maryland, and New Hampshire, which do not publicly report abortion totals.

According to the most recent report by the Guttmacher Institute, approximately 862,320 legal abortions were performed in the United States in 2017, which is a 7 percent decline from 926,190 abortions in 2014. Despite this decline, nearly one in four women in the United States (23.7 percent) will have had an abortion by age forty-five.

Almost one-half of US pregnancies are unintended. Approximately 40 percent of unintended pregnancies are terminated by abortion. Thus, about one in five pregnancies ends in legal abortion, with 88 percent of these being in the first trimester. Another 15 percent end in spontaneous abortion (miscarriage).

Of women who get abortions, about 86 percent are unmarried, 59 percent are already mothers, and 12 percent are under twenty years of age. The CDC reports that, as of 2017, the birth rate for US teenagers reached a new record low (18.8 per 1,000).

According to the Guttmacher Institute, as of 2014, 75 percent of women who had an abortion were poor or low-income as defined by the federal poverty rate. For the first time in two decades, however, the abortion rate declined among women whose family income was less than 100 percent of the federal poverty level ($19,790 for a family of three in 2014). Nevertheless, the abortion rate among poor women remains the highest at 36.6 abortions per 1,000 women of reproductive age.

Abortions are relatively safe for the women involved, especially if they are done early in the pregnancy. According to the Guttmacher Institute the risk of death associated with abortion ranges from 0.3 for every 100,000 abortions at or before eight weeks to 6.7 per 100,000 at 18 weeks or later in the United States. In contrast, the CDC reports that the US rate of maternal mortality associated with live births is 23.6 per 100,000—the highest in the developed world.

An increasing number of abortions in the United States are nonsurgical. In 2000, the US Food and Drug Administration approved the use of mifepristone for abortions up to ten weeks gestation. This alternative may be an option for Sue Ann, since she thinks she is only seven weeks pregnant. The cost is comparable to vacuum aspiration. Such medication abortions have increased from 5 percent of all abortions in 2001 to 39 percent of all abortions in 2017. Over the same period of time the total number of abortions in the United States has declined significantly—in 2017 reaching the lowest number since the mid 1970s.

Women seek abortions for many reasons. According to the Guttmacher Institute the top three (over 75 percent each) are concern for or responsibility to other individuals; the inability to afford raising a child; and the belief that having a baby would interfere with work, school, or the ability to care for dependents. About half of the women seeking abortions report using contraception in the month they became pregnant, most commonly condoms or a hormonal method.

Many abortion patients have a religious affiliation. In 2014, 24 percent were Catholic, 17 percent were mainline Protestant, 13 percent were evangelical Protestant, and 8 percent identified with some other religion. Thirty-eight percent declared no religious affiliation.

In the United States, opinion polls indicate substantial acceptance of abortion in cases of rape, incest, danger to the mother's life and mental health, and a deformed fetus. Most polls indicate majority approval of the *Roe v. Wade* decision, although a few polls indicate a fairly even split. Disapproval of abortion is greatest when it is viewed as a form of family planning.

The American Psychological Association published a report in 2008 that examined the relationship between mental health and abortion. It concluded that adult women who have an unplanned pregnancy have no greater risk of mental health problems if they have a first-trimester abortion than if they give birth to the child. The report went on to note, however, that "it is clear that some women do experience sadness, grief, and feelings of loss following termination of a pregnancy, and some experience clinically significant disorders, including depression and anxiety."

SCRIPTURE AND TRADITION

As one surveys Christian traditions, scripture, and the contemporary views and roles of women, five central issues rise to the fore. These are the goodness of life, natural law, self-sacrifice, freedom, and the well-being of women. In the rest of this commentary these issues are discussed from various perspectives.

Historically, abortion has not been a major issue in Christian traditions. For centuries it was unsafe; children were considered an economic benefit; and underpopulation, not overpopulation, was the problem. The Bible itself has nothing directly to say about the morality of abortion. Although the Bible does not legislate about abortion, the Hebrew scriptures do indirectly provide some insight. Within the Mosaic Law, fetal life was held to have value. Anyone who caused the loss of fetal life was considered guilty and subject to sanctions. But the loss of fetal life was not of equal weight with the death of the already born. Responsibility for loss of fetal life was not considered murder but a lesser crime for which payment in coin was to be made in restitution. It is perhaps most accurate to say that the Mosaic Law regarded fetal life as potential human life and therefore of value. The Christian scriptures do not directly deal with abortion or the value of fetal life.

The Christian theological tradition has been rather consistently against abortion since the early church. Some describe this as continuity within the tradition, but others make two points that undermine the value of the tradition's consistency. It may be useful at this point briefly to discuss those two points, for that discussion will help bring the key issues in the debate into focus.

The first point is that although abortion has been denounced within the theological tradition of the church, until relatively recently the term was understood to describe the deliberate termination of pregnancy after the infusion of the soul (ensoulment), which was generally held to occur anywhere from six weeks to four months after conception. Thomas Aquinas, the Scholastic thinker whose philosophy and theology were made normative for the Catholic Church in 1878, adopted Aristotle's teaching on fetal animation and held that God infused the soul into the fetus at forty days after conception for males and eighty days after conception for females. In fact, popular folk practice for over a thousand years in Christian Europe, until after the Reformation, was to regard quickening (first fetal movement) as the definitive evidence of ensoulment, which was understood to be the cause of animation. Quickening usually occurs about the fifth month. Until that time midwives consulted by desperate women regularly practiced various methods of terminating pregnancy, most of them dangerous to the woman.

Tradition carries great weight in theological and moral thought, especially when it has been consistent. This is based on the recognition that the Holy Spirit not only enlightens the present generation but has also enlightened past Christian communities who passed this tradition on. But if all Christian communities condemned abortion but permitted termination of pregnancy for weeks to months after conception, does this really constitute a consistent tradition for banning all termination of pregnancy?

A second issue raised concerning the critical views of the Christian tradition on abortion is the fact that at least some of the tradition's opposition to abortion rested upon false understandings about the biology of conception and the natures of men and women. Many of these beliefs are no longer accepted by Christians. In the past there was widespread agreement in the theological tradition that the primary purpose of marriage was procreation; that the only purpose of sexuality was procreation; that women as a sex had been created by God solely for motherhood (although they could renounce sexuality through religious vows of celibacy); and that a woman's sole contribution to the process of procreation was acceptance in her body of the self-contained seed of her husband, which it was her role to shelter and nourish. Christian churches have modified or abandoned all these beliefs.

Today, Roman Catholics and almost all Protestant churches agree that procreation is but one purpose of marriage and that the covenant of love between the spouses is equally or more important. There is similar agreement that sexuality is not an evil or near evil tolerated for the sake of children, and that sexual pleasure is itself legitimate and valuable for its role in bonding spouses to each other in love. All Christian churches accept the findings of biological science regarding the equal genetic contribution of parents in conception. All Christian churches recognize the equality of women, at least in theory, although there are tremendous divisions among and within denominations over whether women's nature is ordained for motherhood or is open to other roles that women might choose.

Those who oppose abortion are quick to point out that the above issues are not sufficient to reverse a centuries-old tradition. The heart of the issue, they say, is the preservation of human life. This is why much of the discussion within and outside the churches is about when in the process of gestation fetal life becomes human and should be protected by the law and about how much to emphasize the life of the fetus in relation to the life of the mother and others affected by a birth.

Finally, regarding the tradition as a whole, there is the matter of conscience. All churches, including the Catholic Church, which takes a definite and rigorous stance against abortion, have longstanding teachings regarding the moral necessity of developing and following individual conscience. There are very complex relations among one's individual conscience, the teachings of one's church, and the values of the society in which one lives, but all churches agree that the conscience is a linchpin of the process of making important decisions.

This would mean that Sue Ann should not make her decision based on the fact that the majority believes that abortion can be moral, or that those who approve abortion tend to be more educated and middle class. Nor should she make her decision based solely on the teachings of a religious tradition or authority. She must consult all sources and judge for herself. Religious traditions can furnish arguments that Sue Ann may find ultimately convincing. Sociological data about the opposing sides in the abortion debate can illuminate the reasons individuals are more influenced by some reasons than others. But it is never legitimate to circumvent the formation of personal conscience and blindly accept the conclusions of others.

GROUNDINGS OF
CATHOLIC AND PROTESTANT POSITIONS

In the ethical treatment of abortion in Christianity today great division appears at a number of levels. As was touched upon above, a primary division occurs over the definition and value given to fetal life.

The Roman Catholic Church has defined all fetal life as full human life, while most Protestant churches are unwilling to define any specific point at which the fetus becomes fully human. Pope Pius IX in 1869 stipulated excommunication for abortion and fixed conception as the moment when the fetus, in technical terms at this stage a zygote, becomes a person, and, religiously speaking, ensoulment occurs. In so doing he closed the door on the hitherto prevailing views that distinguished between an animate and an inanimate fetus; fixed the moment of ensoulment at quickening; and by implication, permitted abortion before quickening. Protestants in the United States, influenced like Catholics by more than a century of opposition to abortion by physicians attempting to take over the birthing process from "unscientific" and "untrained" female midwives, generally followed suit with the pope. From the 1870s to the 1960s the matter was settled and debate virtually closed.

Today, the Catholic Church's strong opposition to the practice of abortion as well as to allowing women the legal option of abortion is based primarily on two moral principles. The first is that according to the natural-law tradition, God's will is embedded in the patterns of creation and can be apprehended by the human mind. According to the Catholic interpretation of this tradition, a rational investigation of sexuality reveals that its innate purpose is twofold: procreation and mutual love. Therefore, every sexual act must be open to the possibility of conception and should express love. Anything that interferes with either thwarts God's intent. This perspective has been the backbone of Roman Catholic proscription of both abortion and artificial contraception for over a century. It is for this reason that abortion is understood as a sexual sin as well as a form of murder. In October 2018, CNN reported that Pope Francis compared abortion to hiring a "hitman to solve a problem."[1]

The second moral principle used by the Catholic Church in its rejection of abortion is one that absolutely forbids the direct taking of innocent life. This is not a prohibition against all taking of life. Not all life is innocent. It is not forbidden for the state to take the life of the guilty in capital punishment, or for soldiers to kill other soldiers who are presumed to be trying to kill them, or for anyone to kill in defense of self or others under attack. Further, under this principle it is possible that one would not be held responsible even for killing an innocent, if that killing were indirect. For example, indirect abortions can be permitted under this principle. If a pregnant woman has a cancerous uterus, a hysterectomy to remove the cancerous uterus is permitted if the delay until delivery poses a threat to her life. The purpose of the hysterectomy is to remove the diseased body part that threatens the woman's life. The loss of the life of the fetus is indirect

---

[1] Hada Messia and Laura Smith-Spark, "Pope Compares Having an Abortion to Hiring a Hitman," CNN (October 10, 2018).

and not intended, for the hysterectomy would have been performed had she been pregnant or not.

Most Protestants are not convinced by these Catholic arguments because they do not share Catholic biological interpretations of natural law or Catholic assumptions about full human life existing from conception. While virtually all Protestants accept the ban on direct taking of innocent life, many deny that fetal life is fully human and therefore protected by the ban. Nor have Protestants relied on natural law as a moral grounding. Historically, Protestant churches have understood the Fall to have corrupted human reason to such an extent that humans are without any natural capacity to comprehend God's will. They are instead dependent on God's grace for understanding.

Today natural law is receiving more Protestant attention than in the past largely because of its role in civil morality, but the biologically based model of natural law used by the Catholic Church is rejected in favor of models that draw upon other human capacities as well. For example, one might find that numerous actions and goals—preservation of human life by avoiding overpopulation or the use of abortion when family income is minimal or a mother's health is in danger—rest on equally compelling interpretations of natural law, based on the belief that God gives human beings the desire to preserve the species with dignity.

A further problem with natural law is the finiteness of human rationality. God's will can be intentionally or unintentionally misread and is always discovered through the eyes of a specific culture. What in one culture or historical period seems natural or clear does not in others. There is no way to decide what is natural for all short of imposing authority.

CONTEMPORARY ATTITUDES
TOWARD WOMEN AND MOTHERHOOD

Other religious arguments that favor or condemn abortion depend heavily upon the two issues discussed above: whether the fetus is a fully human life, and whether God's will can be determined through investigation of biological processes. How these two issues are interpreted not only shapes much of the basis for the way abortion is viewed but also affects our view of motherhood and the role of women in our society. As stated above, in Christianity much debate around the issue of abortion focuses upon nuances and inconsistencies in the Christian tradition's position on the nature of fetal life. Those positions and debates have been spelled out in the previous sections because they form part of the backdrop of and resources for Sue Ann's and Danny's decision. Without losing sight of those issues, this section will shift the focus to the varying conceptions of women and motherhood that are powerful aspects of Sue Ann's context as she strives to reach a decision about her pregnancy. A cornerstone in the debate about motherhood and women's roles is the norm of well-being, with its attendant norms of self-sacrifice and self-development, freedom, and justice and equality. The emphasis in this section is upon the perspective that stresses freedom, justice, self-development, and equality for women. The reason for emphasizing this perspective is that it has been a catalyst for the current debates about abortion.

Well-being

At the heart of the clash over abortion and what constitutes the well-being of women are two quite different views of motherhood and the role of women in society. Sue Ann is caught between these views, and her struggle runs much deeper than the decision of whether or not to abort. It involves how she understands herself as a woman and mother. There is, of course, a great variety of views on women's roles and what constitutes their well-being. Without doing too much injustice to these views and for the sake of clarity and discussion, these many views will be arranged under two opposing headings, the *traditional view* and what we will label a *late modern view*.

The traditional view stresses that a woman's well-being is fulfilled through her service to her children and husband. Such service is what truly frees. This traditional view is held by many of the most ardent opponents of legalized abortion. In part rooted in the natural-law position discussed above, this view holds that there are intrinsic differences between men and women, differences that lead to dissimilar roles. Men work in paid jobs and provide for women, whose primary role is childbearing and childrearing. Male leadership, exercised in a benevolent way, is considered normal and right. Freedom for women to work outside the home or to control the birth of children may even be a threat because it appears to upset the natural pattern and downgrade traditional roles. Thus, at one end of the spectrum of what constitutes women's well-being is the position that stresses self-sacrifice and honorable service to children and husband.

Opposed to the above position is a view that women's well-being is fostered through equality with men and through the freedom to make choices about a host of issues—from careers to motherhood to the structure of relationships between men and women. Those who advocate this position hold that the context of women's lives today is radically different from the context in which the traditional view of women's roles developed. They point out that, for instance, dramatic changes are now occurring in the relation between men and women, changes partially indicated by the great increase of women in the work force. In 1970, 43 percent of all women age sixteen or over were in the work force. By 2016 the Bureau of Labor Statistics reported that women represented 56.8 percent of the US work force. This is not a mere change in numbers. This shift reflects a new concept of women as free and equal partners in society, capable of doing what men do and having the right to pursue nontraditional roles.

This new understanding of women, dominant among those who advocate women having a choice about abortion, sees men and women as substantially equal. Traditional roles are seen as reflecting not the order of nature but the ideology of a male-dominated society. The combination of male domination and oppressive ideology inhibits the full development and well-being of women. Being a mother is important, and many will elect it, but it is not the only role for women. According to this view, women must have choices about service and sacrifice, two central Christian affirmations we would do well to explore in greater depth before moving on to the critical issues of choice and equality.

Self-sacrifice

Within the Christian tradition there are various views of self-sacrifice, all largely stemming from interpretations of the words and actions of Jesus. One powerful image that is frequently raised here is that of Jesus on the cross and the implied mandate to sacrifice self for others. In very broad terms, many who stress this interpretation of Jesus urge a woman such as Sue Ann to choose against having an abortion and opt to sacrifice for the fetus she carries. But here the discussion returns to the questions raised above: Is the fetus fully human? Does it constitute one of the "others" for whom Sue Ann is called to sacrifice?

There are also questions about the understanding of self-sacrifice. Counter to the more traditional position is one that stresses a different interpretation of Jesus's sacrifice on the cross. In this interpretation Jesus did not go to the cross for the sake of self-sacrifice but to bring others a full and new life in the realm he announced. Self-sacrifice was a means, not an end; the end is entrance into the realm of God. Thus, what is normative is bringing others to this realm. Still, self-sacrifice, or, in less extreme terms, service to others, is often a good means to this end, so much so that in certain circumstances it is legitimately normative. The legitimacy of self-sacrifice depends on whether there is a self to sacrifice or to give in service freely. The self in its fullest realization is a gift given by God through Jesus Christ and received in mutual love and community. Under conditions of oppression or under the influence of repressive ideologies, the self in its fullest realization is often not possible and is replaced by false consciousness. In a sense, there is no self to give. It cannot therefore be commanded or exhorted from individuals. This is crucial. Calling for self-sacrifice from someone under such conditions, for example, a slave or an abused and passive woman, is not a call to new life but to further slavery and oppression because it does not produce but impedes the mutual love and community to which the realm of God calls us.

These crosscurrents over self-sacrifice are, or at least should be, affecting Sue Ann and the decision she faces. Sue Ann must carefully evaluate her personal situation. She must try to understand what kind of relationship she and the child would have and whether it ultimately could be one that supports the mutual growth of each. She must, in short, try to come to conclusions about the relative values of fetal life, her life and personal choices and development, and the life within the communities of which she is a part.

Freedom of Choice and Equality for Women

As has been discussed, the decision Sue Ann faces is in large measure left to her conscience. Hers is the freedom to exercise conscience, although the responsible use of conscience means consulting the wisdom available from the larger community, including her religious tradition, if any, and her society. Sue Ann must decide whether the use of her freedom to abort in this situation is a legitimate exercise of her power to control her own body or a misuse of her power to control her body by denying life to the fetus she carries.

Freedom is part of the biblically based understanding of justice that has evolved in Western thought. In the United States the legal system provides for individual freedom unless democratically determined laws are broken. The norm of freedom places the burden of proof on those who would restrict the control that Sue Ann and other women have over their bodies. Opponents of legalized abortion are convinced they have satisfied this burden. They argue that just as society rightly denies freedom to a murderer, so it should deny a woman the right to abort a fetus, which in their view has full rights as a person. Proponents of legalized abortion counter by denying full legal status to fetal life in the early stages of pregnancy and point to the injustice of the state or any other body compelling Sue Ann to bear a child. They argue that women should have the freedom to control conception in order to control their bodies and their lives. At issue is whether the power to control conception includes the right to abort a fetus, and whether this power to control fertility is essential to women's well-being.

Obviously, this notion of the right to control one's own body is a key element in the position that sees abortion as an option. Those who hold this position argue that in order for women to take control of their lives and to construct a meaningful life plan, they must have the capacity to break the link between sex and procreation. Otherwise their bodies, or whoever controls their bodies, will control them, and pregnancy will interrupt all possible plans except mothering. Statistically effective contraceptives and safe, affordable abortions make breaking the link possible for the first time in history. For many who support choice, the right to choose is more than just a symbol of the newfound freedom and equality of women. For those who hold this view, the freedom to choose is fundamental to all other justice claims of women. They argue that without the right to choose contraception to prevent pregnancy, or abortion to terminate an undesired pregnancy, women will be discriminated against. Employers, for example, may be reluctant to train women for or employ them in significant positions because those employers will anticipate that women will be in and out of the work force. There can be no equality in the work place when women and men function under the assumption that a woman's occupation will be subordinated to each and every pregnancy.

In essence, then, those who stand for women's choice argue that, for women, the capacity to choose is the capacity to gain equality, new identities, and new avenues for vocation. The very well-being of women is at stake, and society has a moral obligation to further this well-being. Part of the well-being of women includes openness to the growth possibilities inherent in childrearing and homemaking. If women are to be free to choose how to pursue their lives, then obviously they must be free to choose childrearing and homemaking as focal points of their lives. It does no one good to draw the options as a choice between passive, dull housewives and active, responsible career women. There are many paths between these stereotypes.

SEX BEFORE MARRIAGE

Sue Ann and Danny by mutual consent engaged in sexual relations outside of marriage. Sue Ann also had sexual relations with Paul Reynolds. These relationships raise the ethical issue of premarital sex.

Christian reflection on the ethics of premarital sex is in a state of flux and has become part of the cultural wars that now rage over the family and sexual relations in general. At one end of the spectrum are those who say the norm is clear and leads to only two moral outcomes: chastity outside of marriage and fidelity within marriage. This traditional view is still the official one in most churches, although adherence is hardly universal. Sexual relations outside of marriage are commonplace today, as they have been in other historical periods.

At the other end of the spectrum is the view that sex outside of marriage is appropriate for consenting adults. While not endorsed by many churches, this view is widespread both among Christians and in secular quarters, as evidenced by the increasing number of couples living together and even raising families without marrying.

In between these two ends of the spectrum are a number of other perspectives. There is no consensus.

The more traditional perspective with its legal approach has certain attractions. Sexual relations are far more than physical intercourse that satisfies a strong instinct. They involve great emotion and go to the core of a person's being. They involve the giving and the receiving of the self that can lead to a deep sense of inner wholeness. They are one of God's greatest gifts, and it is not too much to say that humans may even experience God through them.

The same vehicle serves sin, however. Some do not love but seduce. They take advantage of a vulnerable other person in order to serve their own selfish purposes. Hurt and alienation follow, and this is one reason why Christian traditions have put up so many warning signs around sex. "Proceed with caution," they seem to say.

Even if seduction is not conscious, physical sex is easily mistaken for love. Momentary sexual attraction can give the illusion of deeper intimacy. Love is easily trivialized. Sexual relations should therefore be part of a deeply loving and committed relationship, and normally such relationships take time to mature.

Another critical reason for caution has to do with children. Marriage, or at least a two-parent family, is still the best context for raising children. Social scientists are in fundamental agreement that children of single-parent families, especially those in poverty, face heightened risk. They drop out of school at a much higher rate. They have higher unemployment rates and are more likely themselves to have a child before age twenty.

On the other side of the issue, many single parents do admirable jobs. Marriage is no guarantee of love or well-raised children. Marriage relationships are often unloving, some even involving spouse and child abuse. Loving relationships can be found outside of marriage. The prohibition on sex outside of marriage is part of a patriarchal tradition that has been oppressive to both men and women.

Today's more open sexual relations are also a breath of fresh air in the catacombs of prudery where sex is dirty and the inferior cousin of celibacy. They bring a measure of joy back to sex. For these and other reasons a rigid legalism is misplaced. But so is the contrasting perspective that offers no normative guidance, often trivializes sex, and is not nearly as "open" as it purports.

THE CHOICES

Sue Ann apparently has not reflected in any depth about her future role as a woman. She had planned to marry Paul Reynolds as soon as she finished high school. This suggests that she envisioned a more traditional role. After Paul's death and her graduation, however, she enrolled in a community college, the first in her family to do so. This suggests she may have other plans for her life that giving birth and mothering may change, especially if she becomes a single mother.

Her options are to give birth or to have an abortion. If she gives birth, she may keep the baby or allow someone else to adopt the infant. Adoption may be an attractive alternative, but she should be prepared for the bonding that develops between the mother and the unborn child that makes giving the baby away difficult. According to the US Adoption Network, about 135,000 children are adopted in the United States each year and 15 percent (20,250) are voluntarily relinquished babies. According to the National Center for Health Statistics, there were 3,791,712 live births in the United States in 2018. This means that 0.53 percent of all live births in 2018 resulted in children being relinquished for adoption as infants. This statistic is sobering. The reality is that virtually all mothers decide to keep their infant children after birth.

The Mosaic view that regarded fetal life as potentially human and therefore of value, the norm of the goodness of life, and considerations of legitimate self-sacrifice would lead Sue Ann in the direction of preserving the fetus. The norm of freedom makes her morally responsible for the decision.

If abortion may be read as too "pro-self," then in contrast the decision to go to term and reject abortion may seem to her too "pro-birth." The norm of self-giving and self-sacrifice may be perceived as an alien demand forcing her to negate herself endlessly for childbearing and childrearing, unless she chooses the path of adoption.

Danny's response might influence Sue Ann's decision. Danny seems to be dumbstruck by the pregnancy, and there is no indication what he intends to do. He is not pressing her to marry him at this time in their lives. Sue Ann does not say how she feels about marrying Danny but does not object to Danny's reading of the situation. Sue Ann is on the rebound from Paul Reynolds and probably had sex with Danny more in response to her grief than love for him. Danny says, "You are really important to me." This is a lukewarm statement of affection. He does, however, pay his share of the $600 for the abortion. This may be an indication he will provide further support, but the job he holds probably does not pay very well.

Should Sue Ann and Danny marry now that she is pregnant? Marriages under these circumstances are at risk. There was a day when both church and social norms would have put pressure on them to marry. These norms have weakened in recent years for a variety of reasons, including the high divorce rates of teens that marry without much love under pressure from family, church, and society. Perhaps the best advice is to proceed with caution.

Danny does have responsibilities to Sue Ann, however. If she decides to have the baby, he is responsible for providing support, as he is able. He should participate in the birth and the care of the child and act as a loving father. He should also care for Sue Ann by giving her emotional as well as financial support. Who knows, their love may grow into a mature, stable relationship where God is present. Or it may not.

Rather than facing alone an impossible choice between the potential life within her and her own needs, Sue Ann may be freed by considering her interdependence with other persons. She might ask how her decision would enhance not only her well-being, but also the well-being of her family and those in the wider community.

The place to start is probably with her own parents, whom she has not consulted. Her parents are concerned about her health, but Sue Ann is reluctant to tell them she is pregnant. Normally, young women in her situation are wise to seek their parents' help. Most parents are understanding, however disappointed they may be. Whether she is afraid of letting them down or being criticized by them, the case does not say. In some situations past abuse by parents may justify not telling them, but there is no indication of that here. Sue Ann's parents may also have different views about abortion than she does and could possibly put heavy pressure on her at a time when she is already under stress. Sue Ann certainly is not the first young woman to be reluctant to tell and seek help from her parents.

Whatever the decision, Sue Ann's choice between an agonized decision to abort and resentful surrender to having a child, even if only temporarily should she opt for adoption, must be faced. Perhaps both Danny and Sue Ann know the healing power of grace that comes through faith in Jesus Christ. The task will be to unite head and heart so that this power can do its work.

ADDITIONAL RESOURCES

Bellinger, Charles K. *Jesus v. Abortion: They Know Not What They Do*. Eugene, OR: Cascade Books, 2016.

Bolz-Weber, Nadia. *Shameless: A Sexual Reformation.* 1st ed. New York: Convergent, 2019.

Burack, Cynthia. *Tough Love: Sexuality, Compassion, and the Christian Right.* Albany: State University of New York Press, 2014.

Farley, Margaret. *Just Love: A Framework for Christian Sexual Ethics.* New York: Continuum, 2006.

Gushee, David P., and Glen Harold Stassen. *Kingdom Ethics: Following Jesus in Contemporary Context.* 2nd ed. Grand Rapids, MI: Eerdmans, 2016.

Harrison, Beverly Wildung. *Our Right to Choose: Toward a New Ethic of Abortion.* Boston: Beacon Press, 1983.

Hitchcock, James. *Abortion, Religious Freedom, and Catholic Politics.* Piscataway, NJ: Transaction, 2016.

Kaczor, Christopher. *The Ethics of Abortion: Women's Rights, Human Life, and the Question of Justice.* New York: Routledge Press, 2010.

Lewis, Andrew R. *The Rights Turn in Conservative Christian Politics: How Abortion Transformed the Culture Wars.* Cambridge: Cambridge University Press, 2017.

Maguire, Daniel C. *Sacred Choices: The Right to Contraception and Abortion in Ten World Religions.* Minneapolis: Fortress Press, 2009.

Miller, Patricia. *Good Catholics: The Battle over Abortion in the Catholic Church.* Berkeley and Los Angeles: University of California Press, 2014.

Moore, Russell. *Adopted for Life:The Priority of Adoption for Christian Families and Churches.* Updated and expanded edition. Wheaton, IL: Crossway, 2015.

O'Brien, George Dennis. *The Church and Abortion: A Catholic Dissent.* Lanham, MD: Rowman and Littlefield, 2010.

Parker, Willie. *Life's Work: A Moral Argument for Choice.* New York: Atria, 2017.

Peters, Rebecca Todd. *Trust Women: A Progressive Christian Argument for Reproductive Justice.* Boston: Beacon Press, 2018.

Schlesinger, Kira. *Pro-Choice and Christian: Reconciling Faith, Politics, and Justice.* 1st ed. Louisville: Westminster John Knox Press, 2017.

Steffen, Lloyd H., and Dennis R. Cooley. *The Ethics of Death: Religious and Philosophical Perspectives in Dialogue.* Minneapolis: Fortress Press, 2014.

Tooley, Michael, Celia Wolf-Devine, Philip E. Devine, and Alison M. Jaggar. *Abortion: Three Perspectives.* New York: Oxford University Press, 2009.

Related Videos

Legal History of Abortion in the US. 73 minutes. C-Span. 2018.
Abortion: Stories Women Tell. 92 minutes. HBO. 2017.
The Abortion Divide. 55 minutes. PBS Frontline. 2019.

Related Websites

Adoption Council, "US Adoption Statistics."
    https://adoptionnetwork.com/adoption-statistics
American Psychological Association, "Mental Health and Abortion."
    https://www.apa.org/pi/women/programs/abortion/mental-health.pdf
Centers for Disease Control
    https://www.cdc.gov/reproductivehealth/data_stats/abortion.htm
Guttmacher Institute
    https://www.guttmacher.org/united-states/abortion
National Adoption Council
    https://www.adoptioncouncil.org/

Case

Death, Duty, and Dignity

Professor Theresa Christiansen gazed out her office window after reading the letter for a second time. A large ecumenical organization had invited her to give the keynote address at a conference that would be held in the state capital in six months. The conference theme, "Death, Duty, and Dignity," had been prompted by a new proposal in the state legislature to pass a bill identical to Oregon's Death with Dignity Act. As in Oregon, the proposed legislation would make it legal for a person in the last stages of a terminal illness to hasten his or her death with the assistance of a physician.

Theresa assumed she had been invited to give the keynote address because she had been an outspoken critic of the Oregon law when it was first debated in 1994. Drawing on her training as a historian of the Reformation, Theresa had contrasted the *ars moriendi* (the art of dying) in the medieval and modern eras. She had opposed physician-assisted suicide because she felt it reflected an individualistic worldview grounded in appeals to rights and autonomy, which is foreign to a Christian worldview that emphasizes subservience to God and duties to others. Theresa had reminded her audiences in print and in person that religious leaders like Martin Luther had viewed their deaths as an opportunity and an obligation to witness to their faith—to use their deathbeds as teaching moments. In contrast to those who appealed to the rights of privacy and autonomy as the legal foundations for access to physician-assisted death, Theresa had emphasized that Luther viewed his death as a public affair in which he had a moral obligation to testify to his faith in the resurrection despite his suffering. To die well is one's final responsibility to others in the community. Dependence on God—not independence from others—is one of the hallmarks of a Christian

---

This case and commentary were prepared and updated by James B. Martin-Schramm. The names of persons and institutions have been disguised, where appropriate, to protect the privacy of those involved.

worldview. It is precisely because Christ's suffering was redemptive that our suffering should not be avoided.

Theresa was disappointed when Oregon's public referendum on the Death with Dignity Act passed in November 1994 by a slim majority, 51 percent in favor to 49 percent opposed. After the US Supreme Court ruled in June 1997 that there is no constitutional right to die and that this issue is best addressed by the states, she was a bit surprised when the citizens of her home state defeated a ballot measure to repeal the Death with Dignity Act by a 60 percent to 40 percent margin. By then Theresa had left Oregon to take up a new teaching position and had not been able to participate in the second round of debate. Theresa had not thought much more about the issue until last year, when her father called from the home Theresa had grown up in back in Portland, Oregon. Theresa remembered the call all too well. She had been totally unprepared for it.

Theresa's father, Ted Christiansen, had been a dentist for forty years when he retired at the age of sixty-five. Theresa's mother, Mary, had married Ted the year he graduated from dental school. Their two children, Theresa and Peter, followed in short order. They were a close and loving family. After the children went off to middle school, Mary went back to work as a teacher. She retired at the same time Ted retired from his dental practice. They had thoroughly enjoyed retirement. The couple had visited family in Scandinavia and had seen many spots in the world they had long wanted to visit but had been unable to do so while they had both been working. In Portland they were active in their church, and both belonged to different civic organizations like the Rotary Club and the League of Women Voters. Their three grandchildren absolutely adored Grandma and Grandpa. Ted and Mary had been blessed in many ways, and they had also been a blessing to others. One of these blessings had been the gift of good health for over a decade of their retirement.

A couple of years ago, however, her dad had not been feeling well. He had been having trouble with his vision and was increasingly nauseated and forgetful. The initial consult with his doctor led to an appointment with a brain specialist, an MRI, and finally a biopsy. Ted called his son and daughter after the specialist informed him that the result of the biopsy was brain cancer. More specifically, he had a grade IV glioblastoma multiforme (GBM), which is an extremely fast-growing and lethal form of brain cancer. The doctor had informed him that without any treatment the median survival time from diagnosis was three months. With surgery and perhaps radiation and chemotherapy, the median survival time was about eleven months. Theresa remembered hearing her mother sobbing in the background on the other phone.

After a week of prayer and reflection, Ted called Theresa and Peter to tell them he had decided to have the surgery to remove as much of the tumor as possible. The surgery took place about two weeks after that and went well. The brain surgeon set Ted up with regular doses of radiotherapy because studies showed that these treatments almost doubled the post-surgical survival time. Ted recovered fairly quickly from the surgery and was able to communicate and walk quite well. After about six months, however, his nausea and blurred vision increased significantly, and he began to experience increasingly severe headaches. Ted discussed the matter with his specialist, who sent him to a colleague for a second opinion. Both concurred that Ted had less than six months to live.

That night Ted and Mary shared this news with Theresa and Peter. About a month later they called both children and asked them to come home the following weekend so that they could tell them how they intended to handle the last stages of Ted's disease. Theresa had not anticipated what would follow. Seated around the kitchen table, Ted told his children that he had asked his lifelong friend and their family physician to assist him in hastening his death. With Mary holding his hand, Ted explained that he saw no point in dragging this on to the inevitable end. As the disease progressed he would experience more and more pain, and while his doctors assured him they could keep the pain to a minimum, they could not guarantee how long he would retain his memory and cognitive powers. Ted explained that he did not want to die unable to recognize his family and friends gathered around his deathbed.

Ted reached into a file folder and pulled out an article that Theresa had published during the height of the debate about the Death with Dignity Act in Oregon. He looked directly at Theresa and said that he could not be more proud of her and her work. He agreed that as a Christian he should testify to his faith at the end of his life. He explained, however, that he thought he could be a better witness while he retained the cognitive abilities he had left. With tears in his eyes he told Theresa and Peter he loved them with all his heart. He added that this decision was made easier by his confident faith in the resurrection. He concluded by saying he could never do this without the unqualified support of Mary, who nodded her sure assent through the tears streaming down her face. It was a moment Theresa would never forget, nor could she forget the actual day about two months later when Ted's life came to an end.

Ted chose to die on Reformation Sunday. Their pastor had agreed to come to their home, where Ted was now in hospice care, to lead a worship service for the family, friends, and members of their congregation that Ted had invited. Peter's wife, Faith, had refused to come, however, and had insisted that Peter not take their three children. While she loved her father-in-law, she thoroughly disagreed with his decision. As a Roman Catholic she firmly believed that suicide was a sin. She thought it would be sinful to participate in the service in any way because, in her mind, the service was sanctioning the sinful act that would follow. She said physician-assisted suicide was just the first step down a slippery slope that in the future could lead to a host of human rights abuses. She had urged Peter and Theresa to talk their father out of his decision, but they knew his mind was made up.

During the service Mary read Romans 14:7–8: "None of us lives to himself, and none of us dies to himself. If we live, we live to the Lord, and if we die, we die to the Lord; so then, whether we live or we die, we are the Lord's." Theresa's father followed with John 11:25–26, which he read haltingly: "'I am the resurrection and the life,' says the Lord; 'he who believes in me, though he dies, yet shall he live, and whoever lives and believes in me shall never die.'" The pastor gave a short homily giving thanks for Ted's ministry to others through his dental practice and in his service to the congregation and the wider community. The pastor also emphasized that each Christian has been baptized into the death and resurrection of Jesus Christ and thus can fully embrace life on earth as well as eternal life in heaven. During the prayers that followed, Ted's and Mary's friends surrounded him with love as they offered prayers of thanks and reassurance. Afterward the pastor celebrated the Eucharist. Mary dipped the small portion of the host in the cup and gave it to her husband, saying, "This is the body and blood of our Lord Jesus Christ given and shed for you." At the end of the service the pastor offered a closing prayer: "Lord Jesus, by your death you took away the sting of death. Grant to us, your servants, so to follow in faith where you have led the way, that we may at length fall asleep peacefully in you and wake in your likeness; to you, the author and giver of life, be all honor and glory, now and forever. Amen."

After the service ended Mary invited their friends to say their last goodbyes to Ted. About an hour later Peter, Theresa, and Mary gathered in Ted's bedroom with their pastor and their family physician. It was all Theresa could do to walk back into the bedroom. Mary asked Ted if he was ready. Brimming with emotion Ted quietly said, "Yes." He reached out and grasped the hands of Theresa and Peter and told them how much he loved them. Finally, he did the same with Mary. Still holding her hand, he used his other hand to lift the small cup that held the liquid opiates that had been prescribed for this purpose. Fully aware of his actions, context, and surroundings, Ted pointed to the Dag Hammarskjöld quotation on a print across from his bed: "For all that has been—Thanks. For all that will be—Yes." Shortly after Ted drank from the cup, he lost consciousness. About ten minutes later his friend and physician pronounced him dead.

Theresa sat in her office weeping quietly. It had not yet been a year since her father had died. Her emotions were still raw. She held the invitation in her hand. She felt she should accept the invitation, but what should she say about death, duty, and dignity? Her father had chosen to end his life while he still had the ability to testify to his faith with his loved ones around his deathbed. Had this profound experience led her to change her views about physician-assisted death and the *ars moriendi* in the twenty-first century? Are laws like Oregon's Death with Dignity Act compatible or incompatible with a Christian worldview?

Commentary

This case grapples with the topic of euthanasia, which, in Greek, refers to a "good death." For many, it is impossible to separate a good death from what constitutes a good life. While modern medicine has worked wonders and extended the length of human life, it has not always improved the quality of human life—especially in the last few years before death. In addition, while modern palliative care has made it possible to relieve virtually all physical pain for those who have access to these services, drugs do not necessarily relieve the emotional and psychological pain associated with losing control of one's physical and mental abilities as well as the loss of one's independence. Both of these factors have given rise to what has come to be called the death-with-dignity movement around the world.

Ethical discussions about this topic draw upon important distinctions between passive and active euthanasia as well as voluntary and involuntary forms of euthanasia. Passive euthanasia is typically described as not preventing death but rather allowing nature to take its course, whereas active euthanasia is typically described as taking a deliberate action to hasten and cause death. Voluntary euthanasia occurs when a person consciously decides no longer to fight death or takes steps to end his or her life. Involuntary euthanasia occurs when others decide either to let a person die or to hasten death without that person's explicit consent.

Voluntary, passive euthanasia is widely accepted legally and morally. All fifty US states permit individuals by themselves or through others named in a living will or advanced health-care directive to refuse or to withdraw futile medical treatments or interventions. Typical examples involve refusing surgery, ceasing medications, and turning off ventilators. Involuntary, passive euthanasia takes place when others authorize steps like these or otherwise allow someone to die—but without the patient's explicit consent. Similarly, involuntary, active euthanasia takes place when a loved one or physician takes steps to hasten a person's death without their consent. These "mercy killings" take various forms. Sometimes they involve a physician prescribing so much pain medication that it causes sedation and then shallow respiration to the point of death. On other occasions they involve parents, spouses, and friends euthanizing loved ones they can no longer bear to watch die a lingering and painful death. For obvious reasons, active and passive forms of involuntary euthanasia are not morally accepted. Normally they are legally pros-ecuted, although often without severe punishment.

This case involves voluntary, active euthanasia, in which a person takes deliberate steps, with or without the assistance of others, to hasten the end of his or her life and to ensure a certain death. For example, a patient could choose voluntarily to stop eating and drinking in order to hasten death. This requires enormous strength of will, however, to overcome the natural desire to eat and drink. A person could also try to commit suicide, but these attempts often fail because people either do not know how to kill themselves, lack access to sufficient means, or simply are physically incapable of doing so because they are bedridden and immobile. It is precisely for this reason that many terminally ill patients like Ted Christiansen have asked their physicians or loved ones to assist them in their death.

Active, voluntary euthanasia is legal in the Netherlands, Belgium, Luxembourg, Colombia, and Canada. While confined to competent persons suffering from a terminal illness, laws in these countries permit physicians to assist patients with their deaths, but they also permit physicians to administer the means if the patient is unable to do so but has requested to end his or her life in this manner. Assisted suicide is legal in some US states and in Switzerland, Germany, and the Netherlands. In Switzerland, assisted suicide is deemed a crime if the motive is selfish. In order to establish the motive, assisted suicides in Switzerland are typically videotaped and then reported to the police, who interview the family and others involved. If the police do not establish a selfish motive, the assisted suicide is not deemed a crime.

As the case explains, by two public referendums in the 1990s Oregon became the first US state legally to permit physician-assisted suicide. After various legal challenges that reached as high as the US Supreme Court, the state's Death with Dignity Act became law on January 1, 1998. A little more than a decade later, the state of Washington passed a ballot initiative in November 2008 establishing a similar law modeled on Oregon's initiative. To date, six other states have passed death with dignity legislation (California, Colorado, Hawaii, Maine, New Jersey, and Vermont), as has the District of Columbia. In addition, Montana's Supreme Court has ruled that physicians in Montana need not fear criminal prosecution if they write lethal prescriptions for mentally competent patients with terminal illnesses.

Given the location of Ted Christiansen's death—in the state of Oregon—this commentary first provides more information about the state's Death with Dignity Act before turning to discuss Christian views about the morality of euthanasia in general and physician-assisted euthanasia in particular.

OREGON'S DEATH WITH DIGNITY ACT

Enacted on October 27, 1997, Oregon's Death with Dignity Act (DWDA) allows terminally ill Oregonians to end their lives through the voluntary self-administration of lethal medications, expressly prescribed by a physician for that purpose. The following summary of key provisions was published in the journal *Bioethics*:

> Any resident of Oregon who is at least 18 years old, is capable of making and communicating health-care decisions, and has been diagnosed with a terminal illness with less than 6 months to live can request a prescription for lethal medication. The request must be made to a licensed Oregon physician.[1]

The following provisions are written into the Oregon law:

- The patient must make two oral requests to his or her physician, separated by at least 15 days.
- The patient must provide a written request to his or her physician, signed in the presence of two witnesses.
- The prescribing physician and a consulting physician must confirm the diagnosis and prognosis.
- The prescribing physician and a consulting physician must determine whether the patient is capable.
- If either physician believes the patient's judgment is impaired by a psychiatric or psychological disorder, the patient must be referred for a psychological examination.
- The prescribing physician must inform the patient of feasible alternatives to assisted suicide, including comfort care, hospice care, and pain control.
- The prescribing physician must request, but may not require, the patient to notify his or her next-of-kin of the prescription request.

If all steps are followed and a lethal prescription is written, the prescribing physician must file a report with the Oregon Department of Human Services. Physicians are not required to participate in [physician-assisted suicide] PAS, nor are pharmacists or health-care systems.

---

[1]   J. M. Dieterle, "Physician-Assisted Suicide: A New Look at the Arguments," *Bioethics* 21, no. 3 (2007): 128.

From 1998 to 2018, 1,459 patients have died from ingesting medications prescribed under the Death with Dignity Act. These deaths constitute 0.218 percent of the 676,922 deaths in Oregon from 1998 through 2018.[2]

While the number of DWDA deaths represents a tiny fraction of deaths in the state of Oregon, the number of persons requesting and dying from lethal prescriptions has been growing over time. The following information is excerpted directly from the state's 2018 annual report:

- As of January 22, 2019, OHA had received reports of 168 people who had died during 2018 from ingesting the medications prescribed under DWDA, an increase compared to 158 during 2017.
- During 2018, 249 people received prescriptions for lethal doses of medications under the provisions of the Oregon DWDA, compared to 219 during 2017. Of the 246 patients for whom prescriptions were written during 2018, 157 died from ingesting the medication, and one patient ingested the medication but regained consciousness before dying from the underlying illness (therefore is not counted as a DWDA death).
- Of the 168 DWDA deaths during 2018, most patients (79.2%) were aged 65 years or older. The median age at death was 74 years. As in previous years, decedents were commonly white (97.0%) and well educated (47.3% had a least a baccalaureate degree).
- Patients' underlying illnesses were similar to those of previous years. Most patients had cancer (62.5%), followed by neurological disease (14.9%) and heart/circulatory disease (9.5%).
- Most patients (87.5%) died at home, and most (90.5%) were enrolled in hospice care. Excluding unknown cases, most (99.3%) had some form of health-care insurance. The proportions of patients who had private insurance (32.4%) and Medicare or Medicaid insurance (66.9%) in 2018 were similar to those reported during the past five years (35.8% and 63.3%, respectively).
- As in previous years, the three most frequently reported end-of-life concerns were loss of autonomy (91.7%),

---

[2] The websites listed at the end of this commentary provide access to the most recent annual reports and additional information about the Death with Dignity Act in Oregon and the one in Washington.

decreasing ability to participate in activities that made life enjoyable (90.5%), and loss of dignity (66.7%).
- In 2018, three of the 168 patients were referred for formal psychiatric or psychological evaluation.

These statistics and others reveal that Ted Christiansen's case is in many ways typical, though his death is still quite exceptional. His case is typical because males have constituted 52.3 percent of all DWDA deaths over the life of the program. In addition, he is among the vast majority who have been diagnosed with cancer and who have died while enrolled in hospice care. Ted's death is exceptional, however, insofar as DWDA-related deaths represent just over two-tenths of 1 percent of all deaths in the state of Oregon since 1998. Nevertheless, this tiny fraction of deaths has been part of a large debate within Christian communities about the morality of euthanasia and physician-assisted death.

CHRISTIAN VIEWS REGARDING PHYSICIAN-ASSISTED EUTHANASIA

Christian opposition to euthanasia and physician-assisted suicide has been relatively widespread across denominations. For various reasons the Roman Catholic Church has tended to be at the forefront of public opposition and thus receives substantial discussion in this commentary.

Deontological Arguments

At the heart of a deontological argument is the claim that moral agents have obligations to obey authorities that are extrinsic to themselves. These authorities can be sacred scriptures like the Bible, the teachings of religious leaders and councils, the laws or principles that govern a community, or the rules of a home and accountability to one's parents. Deontological perspectives offer greater assurances of moral consistency over time, but deontologists also find it hard to compromise because certain options are precluded by the authorities they are obligated to respect. What follows is a discussion of five deontological arguments related to physician-assisted euthanasia. This is not the term that is typically used in public debates, however. Opponents to this practice normally refer to it as physician-assisted *suicide,* whereas proponents prefer to call it physician-assisted *death*. These different terms are used below depending on whether the argument supports or opposes physician-assisted euthanasia.

1. Physician-assisted suicide transgresses God's commandment not to kill innocent life (Ex 20:13), it usurps God's sovereignty over our lives, and it violates our obligations to serve others and the common good.

Ted Christiansen's daughter-in-law, Faith, appears to agree with this argument because it is consistent with her Roman Catholic tradition. In 1980 the Vatican's Sacred Congregation for the Doctrine of the Faith issued a "Declaration on Euthanasia." The statement emphasizes that "no one can make an attempt on the life of an innocent person without opposing God's love for that person, without violating a fundamental right, and therefore without committing a crime of the utmost gravity." The statement also stresses that

> everyone has the duty to lead his or her life in accordance with God's plan. . . . Intentionally causing one's own death, or suicide, is therefore equally as wrong as murder; such an action on the part of a person is to be considered as a rejection of God's sovereignty and loving plan. . . . Suicide is also often a refusal of love for self, the denial of a natural instinct to live, a flight from the duties of justice and charity owed to one's neighbor, to various communities or to the whole of society.

Given this wide-ranging condemnation it is interesting to note that suicide is not uniformly condemned in the Bible, and where it is discussed, it is often associated with an act of sacrifice or a death with dignity. For example, in the Hebrew scriptures Saul and his armor-bearer fall on their swords rather than be captured by the Philistines and subjected to a humiliating death (1 Sam 31:1–7). In addition, Samson prays to God to renew his strength so that he can pull down the house of Dagon and thus bring death to himself but also to his enemies (Judg 16:23—17:2). In the Apocrypha, Eleazar stabs a war elephant from underneath knowing that it will crush him, but he thinks it will help his compatriots win their battle (1 Macc 6:43–47). Like Saul, Razis falls on his sword and tears out his entrails rather than be captured by the enemy (2 Macc 14:41–42). In the Gospel of John, Jesus emphasizes that "no one has greater love than this, to lay down one's life for one's friends" (Jn 15:13).

Texts like these reflect the fact that biblical authors did not view life as an ultimate good that must be preserved at all costs. As a result, they could sanction acts in which persons gave up their lives for the benefit of others. While suicide motivated by despair violates God's sovereignty over one's life, the Vatican's Sacred Congregation for the Doctrine of the Faith acknowledges that "one must clearly distinguish suicide from that sacrifice of one's life whereby for a higher cause, such as God's glory, the salvation of souls or the service of one's brethren, a person offers his or her own life or puts it in danger (cf. Jn 15:14)." In the case presented here it does not appear that Ted Christiansen's decision is motivated by despair. Instead, he testifies to his faith in the resurrection, he trusts in God's goodness, and he wants his death to be edifying both for his family and for others in his faith community.

2. Physician-assisted death is justified by the Golden Rule that implores us to treat others the way we would want to be treated.

Paul Badham makes this argument in *Is There a Christian Case for Assisted Dying?* Badham is professor emeritus of theology and religious studies at the University of Wales and an ordained Anglican priest. He believes Jesus summarized the essence of Christian theology and ethics when he was asked by the Pharisees to identity the greatest Jewish commandment. Jesus replied: "'You shall love the Lord your God with all your heart, and with all your soul, and with all your mind.' This is the greatest and first commandment. And a second is like it: 'You shall love your neighbor as yourself.' On these two commandments hang all the law and the prophets" (Mt 22:37–40). Badham draws two important points from this key biblical passage. First, Christians who love God with their heart, soul, and mind do not fear death but rather view it as "the gateway to eternal life." Second, denying our neighbors and loved ones their repeated requests to die lacks compassion and violates Jesus's injunction to "do to others as you would have them do to you" (Mt 7:12). Badham asks, "If we truly love our neighbor as ourselves how can we deny them the death we would wish for ourselves in such a situation?"[3] Badham implies that Jesus would support a humane, physician-assisted death because Jesus broke the law to heal on the Sabbath (Mk 2:27). That is, Jesus was willing to break the law and violate social custom in order to do what was humane for a person who was suffering.

There are two primary responses to this argument from conservative Christians. The first is that some human actions, like murder, are always objectively wrong regardless of the motivations or circumstances. After all, Jesus heals the man on the Sabbath; he does not kill him out of mercy. The second is that compassion is best expressed when it leads Christians to bear one another's sufferings rather than terminate them. Pope John Paul II summarizes both views in his 1995 papal encyclical, *Evangelium vitae*. He writes, "Suicide is always as morally objectionable as murder. The Church's

---

[3] Paul Badham, *Is There a Christian Case for Assisted Dying? Voluntary Euthanasia Reassessed* (London: SPCK, 2009), 122.

tradition has always rejected it as a gravely evil choice." Regarding assisted suicide he writes, "To concur with the intention of another person to commit suicide and to help in carrying it out through so-called 'assisted suicide' means to cooperate in, and at times to be the actual perpetrator of, an injustice which can never be excused, even if it is requested." Regarding compassion the pope states, "True 'compassion' leads to sharing another's pain; it does not kill the person whose suffering we cannot bear." Anticipating involuntary euthanasia, Pope John Paul II concludes: "The height of arbitrariness and injustice is reached when certain people, such as physicians or legislators, arrogate to themselves the power to decide who ought to live and who ought to die. Once again we find ourselves before the temptation of Eden: to become like God who 'knows good and evil' (cf. Gen 3:5). God alone has the power over life and death: 'It is I who bring both death and life' (Dt 32:39; cf. 2 Kgs 5:7; 1 Sam 2:6)."

While it is true that human beings have sought to become like God in their quest for the knowledge of good and evil, it is also true that modern medicine has been able to bar the doors to death for well beyond what has been viewed as a natural or normal lifespan. Badham and other proponents of physician-assisted death think it is odd to ignore the way modern medicine seems to arrogate or deny God's powers over life and death, while at the same time we find fault with those like Ted Christiansen who are ready to embrace their mortality and welcome death as the gateway to eternal life.

3. Physician-assisted suicide rejects the power of redemptive suffering and the apostle Paul's promise that "God is faithful, and he will not let you be tested beyond your strength" (1 Cor 10:13).

The Christian gospel message is often summed up in John 3:16, "For God so loved the world that he gave his only Son, so that everyone who believes in him may not perish but may have eternal life." Isaiah 53:3–5 emphasizes that the suffering servant was "wounded for our transgressions" and "bruised for our iniquities." Jesus connects the cross to suffering and discipleship in all three of the Synoptic Gospels (Mk 8:34; Mt 10:38; Mt 16:24; Lk 9:23). Christians refer to the anniversary of Jesus's crucifixion as *Good* Friday. Central to the Christian gospel is the belief that suffering can be redemptive.

It is precisely for this reason that the Vatican's Sacred Congregation for the Doctrine of the Faith says in its "Declaration on Euthanasia" that suffering is not pointless: "Suffering, especially suffering during the last moments of life, has a special place in God's saving plan; it is in fact a sharing in Christ's passion and a union with the redeeming sacrifice which He offered in obedience to the Father's will." Pope John Paul II qualifies this stance later in *Evangelium vitae* in a section devoted to palliative care and pain relief: "While praise may be due to the person who voluntarily accepts suffering by forgoing treatment with pain-killers in order to remain fully lucid and, if a believer, to share consciously in the Lord's Passion, such 'heroic' behavior cannot be considered the duty of everyone" (no. 65). Pope John Paul II did accept the vocation of suffering in his own life, however, choosing to live out his last days with minimal pain relief in the public eye.

While Pope John Paul II emphasized that the vocation of suffering is voluntary, some evangelical Christians firmly oppose this view because, from their perspective, the whole point of Christ's death on the cross is that it, by itself, achieves reconciliation with God apart from any actions on the part of humanity. Christ's sacrifice on the cross is sufficient for atonement; no additional human suffering is required. More liberal Christians are repulsed by the very notion that a good and gracious God could only achieve reconciliation by the torturous death of a crucifixion. Some Christian pacifists also encourage caution with regard to "taking up one's cross" because they believe the related suffering stems from persecution for following Jesus and living out the values of the kingdom of God in a hostile world. While Jesus certainly has compassion for those who suffer from painful diseases like stomach cancer, some pacifists would not describe this as one's "cross to bear." Finally, even though suffering related to illness is often borne bravely and can provide occasions for one to bear witness to his or her faith, there are also times when this form of suffering no longer seems to bear any redemptive or salutary purpose and can jeopardize faith.

4. Physician-assisted death is justified by the same rights to privacy, autonomy, and self-determination that enable a person to refuse or withdraw medical treatments.

Pain is not the only thing that produces suffering. While palliative care can treat physical symptoms of suffering, drugs are far less effective at alleviating the suffering people experience as they experience the loss of their freedom, cognitive faculties, and control over their bodily functions. The statistics from Oregon and Washington, which have permitted physician-assisted euthanasia to longest, bear this out. The reasons most frequently given by those who have chosen to utilize physician-assisted death are loss of autonomy, decreasing ability to participate in activities that made life enjoyable, and loss of dignity. While many fear that the legalization of physician-assisted death may lead to the euthanizing of vulnerable populations, the statistics in Oregon and Washington reveal that those who value responsibility, independence, and personal autonomy are most likely to want to exercise these capacities in relation to the manner and timing of their deaths. It is important to note that these are not merely secular values. Ted Christiansen, in the case, utilizes his autonomy and self-determination to bear witness to his Christian faith upon his deathbed, albeit in a very untraditional way.

Opponents to this view challenge it on both legal and ethical grounds. Legally, they point out that courts have based the right to withdraw or refuse medical treatment not on the right to autonomy but rather on the right to self-defense and protection from assault. In 1977 the US Supreme Court ruled in *Vacco v. Quill* that the negative legal right to refuse medical treatment on the basis of freedom from abuse does not translate into a positive legal right to freely choose physician-assisted suicide, though the court did leave this up to the states to decide. Ethically, the Roman Catholic Church establishes a moral foundation for refusing or withdrawing medical treatments by distinguishing between proportionate or ordinary care and disproportionate or extraordinary care. These key terms are defined in the most recent edition of *Ethical and Religious Directives for Catholic Health Care Services,* which is published by the US Conference of Catholic Bishops. Proportionate means "are those that in the judgment of the patient offer a reasonable hope of benefit and do not entail an excessive burden or impose excessive expense on the family or the community." Disproportionate means "are those that in the patient's judgment do not offer a reasonable hope of benefit or entail an excessive burden, or impose excessive expense on the family or the community." Catholic patients are obligated to pursue proportionate health-care services and to reject disproportionate and futile services.

The Roman Catholic tradition also draws upon the *principle of double effect* when faced with life and death decisions, including those associated with medical treatment in the last stages of a terminal illness. The reality is that many actions have more than one effect. For example, the use of morphine as a form of palliative care is intended to relieve pain, but at certain levels it can also cause shallow breathing and respiratory failure. Intentions matter. If a physician prescribes a level of morphine with the intention of hastening the death of his or her patient, then this would constitute euthanasia in the eyes of the Roman Catholic Church. If the intent of the physician is merely to relieve the patient's pain, but the morphine does hasten the patient's death, then the bad effect of hastening death, while foreseen, is not unethical because the primary intention and good effect were to relieve the patient's pain.

5. Physician-assisted suicide forces doctors to violate the Hippocratic Oath and can force church-affiliated health-care institutions and their employees to violate their codes of ethics.

This argument appears to be quite persuasive on its face but upon closer examination has less moral force. What follows are two important provisions in the Hippocratic Oath: "I will prescribe regimens for the good of my patients according to my ability and my judgment and never do harm to anyone. To please no one will I prescribe a deadly drug nor give advice which may cause death." The reality, however, is that the American Medical Association does not espouse the Hippocratic Oath in its current principles of medical ethics. In fact, very few medical schools in the United States and Europe use the Hippocratic Oath at graduation, and almost none require students to swear by it. Instead, the World Medical Association emphasizes the Geneva Declaration, which requires a physician more generally to "consecrate my life to the service of humanity" and to "maintain the utmost respect for human life." Thus, the vast majority of physicians would not face a moral dilemma due to the Hippocratic Oath if one of their patients asked them to assist them with their death. In addition, one of the key provisions in Oregon's and Washington's Death with Dignity Act is that physicians, health-care workers, and health-care facilities are legally exempted from any obligation to participate in the program if they believe it violates their conscience or ethical commitments.

Teleological Arguments

At the heart of a teleological argument is the desire of the moral agent to reach an end or goal *(telos)*. These goals can vary, but within the context of this case relevant goals might be to relieve suffering, promote human dignity, and proclaim the gospel. Certainly Ted Christiansen wants to maximize his opportunity to witness to his Christian faith at the point of his death. A teleologist weighs various alternatives and chooses the alternative that best achieves the desired end or goal. Consequences matter. One advantage of a teleological approach to ethics is that it can tolerate compromise in order to draw closer to the goal. While ideals are important, teleologists don't want the perfect to become the enemy of the good. The danger, however, is that the desire to achieve the end may lead one to justify virtually any means. This is typically what produces conflicts with deontologists; both groups can agree on the ends, but they often do not agree on the means.

What follows are four teleological concerns that have been raised in opposition to physician-assisted suicide. Arguments in favor of physician-assisted death are almost always framed around deontological appeals to a person's individual rights to autonomy, privacy, dignity, and self-determination or to a principle like the Golden Rule. These arguments have been discussed above. While it is possible to convert these rights or principles to values and then to seek the teleological maximization of autonomy, privacy, dignity, self-determination, and humanitarianism, this is not normally done, and thus no teleological arguments in favor of physician-assisted death are discussed below. Unlike deontological arguments, teleological arguments can be substantiated or refuted with empirical evidence. Insofar as the explicit arguments below are refuted on the basis of empirical evidence, implicit teleological arguments that support physician-assisted death do emerge.

1. Physician-assisted suicide will weaken the prohibition on killing and be the first step down a slippery slope that ultimately will end with involuntary euthanasia of persons with disabilities and others that society does not value.

Nigel Biggar, Regius Professor of Moral and Pastoral Theology at the University of Oxford, addresses this concern in his book *Aiming to Kill*. Biggar discusses the Nazi euthanasia campaign that systematically ended the lives of sixty thousand to eighty thousand physically or mentally ill people the Nazis thought did not deserve to live. He argues that this early euthanasia campaign cleared the path for the Holocaust, which took the lives of over six million people:

> Whatever proportion these [Nazi euthanasia] crimes finally assumed, it became evident to all who investigated them that they had started from small beginnings. At first there was a subtle shift in the emphasis in the basic attitude of physicians. It started with the acceptance of the attitude, basic in the euthanasia movement, that there is such a thing as a life not worthy to be lived. This attitude in its early stages concerned itself merely with the severely and chronically sick. Gradually the sphere of those included in this category was enlarged to encompass the socially unproductive, the ideologically unwanted, the racially unwanted and finally all non-Germans.[4]

Biggar emphasizes that "the infinitely small wedged-in lever" from which this entire trend of mind received its impetus was the attitude toward the "non-rehabilitable sick."[5]

Could this happen in the United States? Will physician-assisted death in states where it is legal lead inevitably to horrible human rights abuses akin to those perpetrated by the Nazis? Will these laws undo all of the good work the disability rights movement has done to present a view of people with disabilities as different, not less valuable? Anything is possible, and history does have a way of repeating itself, but it is worthwhile

---

[4] Nigel Biggar, *Aiming to Kill: The Ethics of Suicide and Euthanasia* (Cleveland: Pilgrim Press, 2004), 159.

[5] Ibid.

to remember at least two things. First, physician-assisted death has been approved by democratic majorities in seven US states plus the District of Columbia, where it is regulated strictly by several specific and limiting legal provisions. The Nazi euthanasia campaign was conducted only after the Nazis had seized power, and the Holocaust was perpetrated only after Adolf Hitler had secured complete totalitarian control. Second, none of the statistics from Oregon or Washington indicates that involuntary acts of euthanasia are on the rise. Since the legal option of physician-assisted death has been made available, the contrary appears to be the case. In addition, while the statistics from Oregon and Washington do not indicate whether DWDA patients have disabilities, it is clear that in both states approximately 98 percent of those dying do not perceive their illness as a disability that might lead them to value their lives less and end their lives prematurely.

2. Physician-assisted euthanasia will lead vulnerable groups like women, minorities, the poor, and the elderly to be encouraged or coerced to end their lives prematurely.

The statistics from Oregon and Washington do not support this claim. Since death with dignity has been a legal option in both states, more men than women have chosen to end their lives with the assistance of a physician. In Oregon, males have represented 52.3 percent of all DWDA patients from 1998 to 2018; in 2018, males represented 51.8 percent of the state's DWDA patients. In Washington, males represented 55 percent of all DWDA patients in 2009, the first year the state's law went into force. In 2018, however, men represented 44 percent of the DWDA deaths in Washington, whereas women represented 56 percent of DWDA deaths. If women were being encouraged or coerced to end their lives prematurely, one would expect to see female DWDA deaths significantly outnumber male DWDA deaths. That has not been the case. It would be helpful to know, however, whether women disproportionately decide to pursue physician-assisted death out of a concern that they are a burden on family, friends, and caregivers. While Oregon and Washington do track this end-of-life concern along with several others, neither state breaks down its data by gender. In both states, however, fear of being a burden to others ranks low (25–35 percent) in comparison to concerns like loss of autonomy, loss of dignity, and being less able to engage in activities that make life enjoyable (84–91 percent).

The claim that minorities, the poor, and the elderly will be encouraged or coerced to end their lives prematurely also is not substantiated by the data from Oregon and Washington. In Oregon, whites represented 96.4 percent of all DWDA patients from 1998 to 2018, and in 2018 whites represented 97 percent of those who ended their lives in this manner. In Washington, whites represented 98 percent of all DWDA deaths in 2009 and 96 percent in 2018. If health-insurance coverage and level of education are used as proxies for degrees of wealth and poverty, neither measure lends credence to the claim that the poor are being coerced to end their lives prematurely. Over the life of the Oregon program only 1.2 percent of all DWDA patients have lacked health insurance. In Washington, no DWDA patients lacked access to health insurance in 2009, though 10 percent either lacked insurance or had unknown coverage in 2018. In addition, only 7.2 percent have had less than a high-school education in Oregon, and only 5.8 percent have had less than a high-school education in Washington. Data regarding the elderly is less conclusive. In Oregon, the median age of DWDA from 1998 to 2018 is seventy-two years of age. It is important to note that 27.1 percent of all DWDA patients in Oregon have been under the age of sixty-five. The numbers are similar in Washington.

3. Physician-assisted suicide will reinforce the solitary nature of death and diminish improvements in palliative and terminal care.

According to a 2016 study published by the US Centers for Disease Control and Prevention, the percentage of people who die in hospitals declined from 50 percent in 2000 to 37 percent in 2014. Nevertheless, more than one-third of those dying experience a reality of death that is often highly institutionalized and very expensive. Given this information, it is interesting that 90.5 percent of all 2018 DWDA patients in Oregon, and 92 percent of all 2018 DWDA patients in Washington, died while enrolled in hospice care. The executive director of the Oregon Hospice Organization initially opposed the law but later acknowledged that fears were unfounded and that the program has resulted in an increase in hospice and palliative care in the state. In the case Ted Christiansen dies at home while in hospice care surrounded by his family and friends.

4. Physician-assisted suicide will increasingly lead the dying to feel they not only have a right to die but also a duty to die.

There is no question that the annual number of persons requesting a lethal prescription under Oregon's Death with Dignity Act has grown steadily each year since the program was initially made legal in 1998. Nevertheless, DWDA deaths still represent just over two-tenths of one percent of all deaths in Oregon. Oregonians are not flocking in droves to end their lives in this manner. Only 168 of the 35,953 deaths in 2018 were due to the Death with Dignity Act. While Oregonians do possess the right to an assisted death, it does not appear that many perceive this as a duty to die. The same is true in the state of Washington.

CONCLUSION

Theresa Christiansen is trying to decide what she will say if she accepts an invitation from a large ecumenical organization to speak at the Death, Duty, and Dignity conference. In many respects her previously articulated views about physician-assisted suicide were more areteological in nature and not as focused on the deontological and teleological arguments reviewed above. In Greek, *arête* refers to the excellence of one's moral character. An areteologist does not focus on whether a decision will maximize the good (like a teleologist) or reflect obedience to an authority (like a deontologist). Instead, an areteologist is concerned about whether an action or decision will reflect a good moral character or diminish it. Areteologists want to cultivate various virtues and minimize related vices.

In the case, Theresa focused on the moral and religious character of those who are dying and of the people who should be there to support those who are dying. Theresa had argued that Christians have an obligation to die well—witnessing to their faith upon their deathbeds. She offered these views, however, prior to experiencing her father's physician-assisted death and the religious service that preceded it. As a result, several questions have emerged. Has this experience changed her views? Can physician-assisted death be supported on Christian areteological grounds? Is it consistent with the classic theological virtues of faith, hope, and love, or does it undermine and erode these virtues? Should Christians affirm physician-assisted death on the basis of compassion, care, and love? How might Theresa appropriate or reject related deontological and teleological arguments as she works through her areteological position on the issue?

Finally, should Theresa draw a distinction between her moral views and what constitutes wise public policy? That is, could she remain opposed to physician-assisted suicide for various ethical and religious reasons while not opposing its legalization if it is carefully regulated? Given the gradual aging of populations in industrialized societies, and the value given to freedom and self-determination in nations like the United States, questions related to physician-assisted euthanasia are likely to increase in coming years.

ADDITIONAL RESOURCES

Badham, Paul. *Is There a Christian Case for Assisted Dying? Voluntary Euthanasia Reassessed.* London: SPCK, 2009.

Battin, Margaret Pabst. *Ending Life: Ethics and the Way We Die*. New York: Oxford University Press, 2005.

Biggar, Nigel. *Aiming to Kill: The Ethics of Suicide and Euthanasia*. Cleveland: Pilgrim Press, 2004.

Boer, Theo A. "Recurring Themes in the Debate about Euthanasia and Assisted Suicide." *Journal of Religious Ethics* 35, no. 3 (Summer 2007): 529–55.

Carr, Mark F., ed. *Physician-Assisted Suicide: Religious Perspectives on Death with Dignity*. The Jack W. Provonsha Lecture Series 2006. The Center for Christian Bioethics, Loma Linda University. Tucson: Wheatmark, 2009.

Dieterle, J. M. "Physician-Assisted Suicide: A New Look at the Arguments." *Bioethics* 21, no. 3 (2007): 127–39.

Dowbiggin, Ian R. *A Merciful End: The Euthanasia Movement in Modern America*. New York: Oxford University Press, 2003.

Engelhardt, H. Tristram Jr., and Ana Smith Iltis. "End-of-Life: The Traditional Christian View." *The Lancet* 366 (September 17, 2005): 1045–49.

Gorsuch, Neil M. *The Future of Assisted Suicide and Euthanasia*. Princeton, NJ: Princeton University Press, 2006.

John Paul II. *Evangelium vitae*. Vatican.va.

Kimsma, Gerrit K., and Stuart J. Youngner. *Physician-Assisted Death in Perspective: Assessing the Dutch Experience*. Cambridge: Cambridge University Press, 2012.

Küng, Hans, and Walter Jens. *Dying with Dignity: A Plea for Personal Responsibility*. New York: Continuum, 2005.

Neumann, Ann. *The Good Death: An Exploration of Dying in America*. Boston: Beacon Press, 2016.

Quill, Timothy E. "Physician-Assisted Death in the United States: Are the Existing 'Last Resorts' Enough?" *Hastings Center Report* 38, no. 5 (September–October 2008): 17–22.

Sacred Congregation for the Doctrine of the Faith. "Declaration on Euthanasia." Vatican.va.

Steffen, Lloyd H., and Dennis R. Cooley. *The Ethics of Death: Religious and Philosophical Perspectives in Dialogue*. Minneapolis: Fortress Press, 2014.

Warnock, Mary, and Elisabeth Macdonald. *Easeful Death: Is There a Case for Assisted Dying?* New York: Oxford University Press, 2008.

World Medical Association. Declaration of Geneva. WMA.net.

Young, Robert. *Medically Assisted Death*. New York: Cambridge University Press, 2007.

Related Websites

Death with Dignity
  https://www.deathwithdignity.org/
Oregon Department of Public Health, "Oregon's Death with Dignity Act."
  https://www.oregon.gov/
Washington State Department of Health, "Death with Dignity Data."
  https://www.doh.wa.gov/

Appendix

Teaching Ethics
by the Case Method

The authors' use of the case method to teach Christian ethics is conscious and deliberate. The method is problem-posing and dialogical, in contrast to traditional teaching approaches of the teacher/expert transferring information to the student/novice. Traditional methods, although well suited for some purposes, do not explicitly invite students to think for themselves, learn by discovery, and engage the teacher and other students.

The discipline of Christian ethics involves the transfer of information. Students need, among other things, to know facts, theories, and contexts of situations. They need to be acquainted with Christian theology and ethical traditions. They need to understand how to apply Christian insights to the analysis of situations.

The discipline, at least in the minds of the authors, involves more, however. It finds its basis in faith, which, in Paul Tillich's understanding, includes reason, emotion, and will. The relationship of faith is a centered act of the whole person, something to be experienced, not just thought about. Information is only one part of its dynamic. The case approach encourages students to become part of the situation, willingly to suspend belief, to act as if they were one of the characters, and to make decisions that engage mind, will, and emotion.

In addition, one aim of teaching ethics is to enhance the limited freedom each person possesses to make choices. By freedom the authors mean freedom *from*, that is, freedom from ignorance, prejudice, paralysis of decision, oppressive ideology, and ultimately, sin. Freedom *from* opens the door to freedom *in* and freedom *for*. Freedom *in* is the freedom that comes through God and others and frees the self to be *for* others.

The authors think that a problem-posing, dialogical method is well suited to help people of faith learn to enhance the limited freedom they possess to make choices. Cases in this volume are not intended to give answers. Rather, they pose problems and encourage students to go through a relational process and experience their own freedom to decide. Cases taught in a dialogical style encourage this relational process. Whether in classes or discussion groups, the case approach allows students and teachers to learn from one another. Everyone participates in a process of discovery. The use of cases over time frees students to discover how to go about making ethical decisions so they are not stymied at the start by lack of direction and at the end by indecision. They become accustomed to making choices, even tough ones.

Finally, cases are useful in character formation. Students discussing cases unavoidably find themselves evaluating the characters, comparing themselves, and, one hopes, adjusting their own characters in accordance with the discoveries they make. They develop their own "habits of the heart," to use Robert Bellah's phrase, by putting themselves in the shoes of others.

The case approach opens doors to freedom, but it also opens other doors. First, it introduces students to contemporary ethical issues. The authors contend that thorough knowledge of issues is one of the first steps in a liberating education. Parenthetically, teachers may have to provide background in advance of case discussions using more traditional methods, especially in complex cases.

Second, cases are a way of entry into Christian traditions. At some point both teachers and students need to ask how the Bible, theology, and the church inform issues. The cases on life and death, for example, raise questions about abortion, euthanasia, the nature of God, the purposes of human life, and the meaning of death. Similarly, the cases on violence lead to an investigation of the church's different historical stances regarding punishment, peacemaking, and coercive force. At the same time that students are addressing issues and making decisions, they are in a position to learn the content of Christian tradition and how to apply it.

Knowledge of traditions is liberating if it helps students detect selective and self-serving attempts to manipulate authority for the purpose of supporting conclusions arrived at on other grounds. Traditions provide alternative perspectives from which to understand and challenge cultural myopia. Traditions provide the wisdom of experience, lend authority, offer general guidance, set limits, and designate where the burden of proof lies—all helpful in finding ways through the maze of experience and conflicting opinion and on to appropriate moral choices.

Third, repeated use of case studies encourages students to economize in the way they approach ethical problems. That is to say, cases teach ethical method. The more cases are used and the more explicit methodological awareness is, the more indelible a pattern for making choices becomes. However little students retain of the content of a given issue or the theology that informs it, the authors are convinced they should leave a course in ethics knowing how to address ethical problems and how to avoid the confusion of too many options and conflicting guidelines.

The authors also believe that an essential component of any pattern of learning is drawing on the insights of others. Discovery of the limitations of individuals acting alone and of the liberation in learning to trust others in community is an important benefit of this dialogical approach. The case setting calls on participants to listen to one another, to challenge their own and others' perceptions, and to build on one another's insights and experiences.

Fourth and last, the case approach is an experience-based form of education. As one veteran case teacher put it: "Cases are experience at a fraction of the cost." The cases in this volume represent the experiences of others that students can make their own without going through all the turmoil. The cases encourage students to express and apply their own experience. Finally, the cases push students to practice resolving complex dilemmas such as parenting, personal responsibility, individual and community rights, and thus to add to their own experience.

CASES FOR GROUP DISCUSSION

As stated in the Introduction, there are numerous types of cases used in contemporary education. These range from a hypothetical problem to a one-page critical incident or verbatim report of an actual event, to a four-hundred-page case history describing a situation. The type of case employed in this volume is modeled after those used by the Harvard Law and Business Schools and the former Association for Case Teaching; that is, each case consists of selected information from an actual situation and raises specific issues or problems that require a response or decision on the part of one or more persons in the case. The problem should be substantive enough and so balanced in its approach that reasonable people would disagree about the most effective or appropriate response. As a pedagogical tool the case calls for a response not only from the case characters but also from those studying the case.

Although cases can be extremely useful for inducing reflection by an individual reader, they are specifically designed for group discussion. They might be used in classrooms, retreat settings, community gatherings, or with any group seeking to gain new perspectives.

As this is a distinctive educational approach, the authors believe it is important to offer suggestions for guiding a case discussion. To begin with, while it is possible to hand out copies of shorter cases—for example "Rigor and Responsibility"—and ask participants to read them immediately prior to discussion, the quality of discussion is heightened by careful advance reading. The case leader might suggest ahead of time that participants (1) read through the case at least twice; (2) identify the principal case characters; (3) develop a time line to indicate significant dates or events; (4) list the issues that surface; and (5) think through a number of creative alternatives to the dilemma posed.

The case leader functions primarily as organizer, catalyst, probe, and referee. Good case leaders know where they want to go with a case and what they want to teach. They highlight insights and assist in summarizing the learning from the discussion. As a facilitator, case leaders are responsible for clear goals and objectives for each discussion session and for guiding the quality and rhythm of the discussion. Many who have worked with cases suggest that the most crucial factor for a rewarding case experience is the leader's style. Openness, affirmation, and sensitivity to the group create the climate in which genuine dialogue can occur. Second in importance is that the case leader thoroughly master the case facts and develop a discussion plan or teaching note.

It is important to keep in mind that there is no single way to approach a case. The Introduction to this volume highlights the elements of making an ethical decision, and the commentaries offer authors' analyses of more specific issues. Case leaders might order the discussion of cases by proceeding from analysis to assessment to decision, suggesting that students not read the commentaries until after the initial case discussion. Alternatively, leaders might integrate the material in the commentaries and the discussion. Neither the Introduction nor the commentaries should constrain teachers or students from taking different entry points or addressing different topics or issues.

Whatever approach is taken should draw participants into dialogue, uncover what is needed to make an informed ethical decision, and push students to a critical consciousness and finally to a decision that will help them when they encounter similar situations in their own lives.

There are no right answers to the dilemmas presented in this volume. This means that the problems posed are open to a number of creative alternatives. This approach stands in contrast to a closed, problem-solving approach in which the right answer or solution can be found in the back of the book. In contrast, the case approach calls for participants to become active subjects in the learning process, to consider various responses, and to analyze the norms that inform their decisions.

Experienced case leaders report that recording the essence of participants' contributions on newsprint or on a board gives order and direction to the discussion. A skilled instructor is able to help participants show relationships among contributions. The leader should be willing to probe respondents for additional clarification of points.

Honest conflict of opinion is often a characteristic of case discussions and can be quite constructive. The case leader may need to assume the role of referee and urge participants to listen to one another and to interpret the reasoning behind their conclusions. It is often helpful to put debating participants in direct dialogue by asking, for example, "Laura, given your earlier position, how would you respond to Mark's view?" The leader's role as mediator is also significant, especially as a discussion nears conclusion. It is helpful to encourage group members to build on one another's suggestions. One constructive process for closing a case discussion is to ask participants to share their insights from the discussion.

Case leaders employ two additional techniques. Leaders might focus and intensify discussion by calling participants to vote on a more controversial issue. For example, in a discussion of the "Sustaining Dover" case, one might ask, "If you were a member of the Dover City Council, would you vote to approve Walmart's request to fill in the flood plain and rezone the property?" The dynamics of case teaching reveal that once persons have taken a stand, they frequently assume greater ownership of the decision and are eager to defend or interpret their choice. Voting provides an impetus for participants to offer the implicit reasons and assumptions that stand behind a given decision. It can also be a test of the group's response, especially if one or two outspoken participants have taken a strong stand on one particular side of an issue. If a vote is taken, it is important to give participants an opportunity to interpret the reasons behind their decision.

Another way to heighten existential involvement in a case is to ask participants to assume the roles of characters in the case for a brief, specified period of the discussion. When individuals are asked to assume roles before a group, they can either be asked ahead of time or invited on the spot from among those who have shown during the discussion that they identify with the characters and understand the issues. It is often most helpful for individuals in a role play to move into chairs visible to the entire group. Case leaders can guard the personal integrity of those who assume roles by giving them an opportunity to "de-role." This is easily done by asking them how they felt during the conversation and by asking them to return to their original seats. Then group members can be called on to share what they learned from the experience.

Notwithstanding the preceding suggestions for case teaching, the authors wish to acknowledge that a good case discussion is not ultimately dependent on a trained professional teacher or a learned group of participants. A gifted leader is one who listens well, encourages participants to do the same, and genuinely trusts the wisdom, insights, and personal experiences of the group. To benefit significantly from the cases a reader needs to be willing to wrestle honestly with the issues in the cases and to evaluate with an open mind the insights of the commentaries.

SAMPLE TEACHING NOTE

Most case teachers prepare in advance a teaching note with suggestions for the general direction of the discussion as well as clear, transitional questions to move from one topic to the next. The following note is intended as an illustration of how the first case in this volume, "Rigor and Responsibility," might be taught in a short session.

A. Read the case if not pre-assigned. (ten minutes)
B. Have the class sketch a biography of each character. (ten to fifteen minutes)
C. Identify the basic questions: How is a family to live in a poor and environmentally degraded world? Alternatively, should an affluent family follow the rigorous holy poverty of Jesus or another option, which might be called responsible consumption, stressing right use and good stewardship? (one to two minutes)
D. Identify alternative issues. (five minutes) This category could be eliminated if the basic question is the focus. Or one of the following issues could become the main issue:
    1. Stewarding an inheritance
    2. Living in an impoverished, malnourished, and environmentally degraded world
    3. Discovering the biblical and theological witness on justice, wealth, poverty, possessions, and consumption
    4. Overworking in modern society
    5. Making a family decision
    6. Dealing with guilt
    7. Acting as an individual in a world dominated by mass consumption
    8. Distributing income and wealth
    9. Raising children
E. Ask each student to identify with one of the following: (ten minutes)
    1. Nancy or Clea
    2. Nathan
    3. Al
    4. The children

F. Adjourn to four separate groups. (twenty minutes)
   1. Discuss what is and what should be the normative position of the character selected. Point to:
      a. Biblical and theological views of justice, wealth, poverty, and consumption
      b. The two normative positions identified in the title of the case
      c. The norms of justice and sustainable sufficiency

OR

   2. Discuss the family relationships and how they should be worked through to arrive at a decision. Point to:
      a. The involvement of the Trapp family in a number of issues, the extent of its giving, and the crisis of the family in the United States
      b. Cultural attitudes in the local community
      c. Poverty, malnutrition, and environmental degradation in the world community
      d. Traditional patriarchal family patterns

OR

   3. Discuss the method question. How is a Christian family to decide?
      a. Point to the alternatives of using deontological, teleological, or areteological approaches
      b. Apply each to the case and note the differences

OR

   4. Discuss the character question. What are the characteristics of a person who responds well to the main problem? Point to:
      a. Basic character orientation, loyalties, and worldviews
      b. Character-building aspects of this situation

G. Conduct a role play, selecting one person from each group. Add David as an option. (ten to fifteen minutes). Role players discuss what the Trapps should do and how it relates to the main issue and to the alternative issues selected in "D" above.

H. Debrief and generate discussion. (ten minutes)
   1. "De-role"
   2. Ask students to identify what they have learned
   3. Open a general class discussion of the main issue

If time allows, the case leader can provide background in lectures, readings, films, small study groups, and so on. The more background, the more open-ended the small group discussions can be.

CASES AND COURSE DESIGN

How might cases be used in a course in Christian ethics? For starters, the authors recommend using the case approach in conjunction with other teaching methods. Cases can be overworked, and the freshness they bring lost.

In terms of overall design the teacher might select one of the cases with high student interest and open with it the first day of class. Cases are good discussion starters, and early use can introduce students to the method, to the use of critical consciousness, and to the goal of liberating education.

Following this, several general sessions on ethics would be appropriate, including the elements of making an ethical decision discussed in the Introduction and how to use Christian sources to derive norms. Use of a case or two to illustrate specific aspects of the ethical discipline would also be appropriate.

The remainder of the course could be devoted to the specific issues in this volume. Using all of the cases in a single semester might be ill advised. Selectivity on the basis of student interest and teacher expertise would be more suitable.

The authors recommend that students write briefs, that is, a four- to five-page analysis of a case. This process accomplishes several things. First, it brings writing into a course. Second, particularly if graded, briefs heighten interest by increasing the stakes. Discussion is more intense because preparation is more thorough. Third, briefs offer less vocal students another avenue of expression. Fourth, briefs are a vehicle for method, since method is implicit in any act of organization. Methodological awareness is more pronounced if the teacher requires a certain approach, or better, if the teacher insists that the students be cognizant of the approach they are taking. Finally, briefs may serve as the first draft of a research paper.

If briefs are used, students must be selective in what they cover. Four to five pages are not sufficient to analyze fully any case in this volume. In organizing their briefs students might follow the order of analysis, assessment, and decision outlined in the Introduction. Somewhere in the brief the "problem" should be clearly stated. The larger part of the brief should be devoted to ethical assessment, that is, to the derivation of norms, to the relating of norms to situations using one or more method, and to the relationships involved in the case. Briefs may be expository and present the various sides in a case, or they may be persuasive and argue one side in depth. While the commentaries in this volume avoid arguing for a particular side of an issue, students should make a decision and justify it.

Lack of time makes selectivity a cardinal virtue in a workshop setting. The typical one-hour class session is long enough for a good discussion of a single case, especially if it has been read prior to the session. Needless to say, the teacher should have a very clear idea of what he or she wants to accomplish and try to keep the class on task. An alert teacher, picking up on points in the discussion, can even insert background material through mini-lectures or asking students to elaborate. Small groups and role plays are especially helpful in stimulating discussion and breaking complex cases into manageable units.

LIMITATIONS OF THE CASE APPROACH

The case approach is not without limitations. First, case material must go through the personal filter of a writer. The situation is seen through the eyes of a single character with all the limitations of perspective. Seldom is enough information provided to satisfy participants. Crucial signals can be misread or misunderstood.

A second drawback is that the success of this form of education and presentation of material is dependent on the critical thinking and participation of students. This can be quite disconcerting, even threatening, for those who are accustomed to a process in which they are handed a complete analysis from the lectern. For most learners tutored in an educational system that fosters uncritical acceptance of the teacher's wisdom and authority, passive reception of information is the comfortable norm. This is, however, also the pattern of uncritical acceptance of the world as it is and contributes to a loss of vision. Case leaders need to develop a mode of open rather than closed questions to induce critical thinking and genuine dialogue.

Third, case discussion can consume more time and emotional energy than the direct communication of information. Intelligence is imperfectly correlated with the propensity to speak. Some participants are bent on dominating the discussion rather than learning from others. Tangents can carry the discussion into dead ends. These limitations call for good referee skills from the case leader.

Fourth, the forest can be lost for the trees, the macro for the micro, and the social for the individual by focusing on the particulars of a given situation to the exclusion of the context. For example, to reduce the discussion of abortion to a personal moral decision in the case "A Matter of Life or Death?" is to lose sight of a critical social question about who should control the decision, the woman or the state. The cases, and in particular the commentaries, have been written to help avoid this problem, but it is well to keep it in mind. Teachers can easily do this by including these elements in their background material and case plans.

Finally, relative to other methods the case approach is limited in its capacity to convey large blocks of factual information. This drawback does not mean teachers need to revert automatically to lectures. There are alternatives to "depositing" information, and even the lecture style can be approached with a different spirit. Many case teachers, for example, use mini-lectures in case discussion to introduce relevant and updated material when it is needed.

The case approach is no panacea and must be seen as only one of many effective educational instruments. The authors have attempted to respond to the limitations of the approach. They have not removed them. They trust, however, that the cases in this volume and the approach itself can lead to constructive, liberating engagements with what they think are critical contemporary issues. Their trust is based on many years of experience with the approach. They are convinced that the approach is not only a valuable and liberating pedagogical instrument, but also a way to build community in the classroom.

Authors and Contributors

AUTHORS

James B. Martin-Schramm is professor of religion and director of the Center for Sustainable Communities at Luther College in Decorah, Iowa. He is an ordained member of the Evangelical Lutheran Church in America and holds a doctorate in Christian ethics from Union Theological Seminary in the City of New York. Most of his scholarship has focused on issues related to ethics and public policy. He is the author of *Climate Justice: Ethics, Energy, and Public Policy;* co-author of *Earth Ethics: A Case-Method Approach* and *Christian Environmental Ethics: A Case Method Approach;* and co-editor of *Eco-Reformation: Grace and Hope for a Planet in Peril.*

Laura A. Stivers is professor of ethics and dean of the School of Liberal Arts and Education at Dominican University of California. She holds a doctorate in Christian ethics and social theory from the Graduate Theological Union in Berkeley, California. Most of her scholarship has focused on economic and environmental ethics. She is the author of *Disruptive Christian Ethics: Alternative Christian Approaches;* co-author of *Earth Ethics: A Case-Method Approach;* and co-editor of *Justice in a Global Economy: Strategies for Home, Community, and World.*

CONTRIBUTORS

Kristen Erickson is a social-work major at Luther College and president of the student-led Social Work Association. She served as a research assistant for this edition and did invaluable work identifying material that needed updating as well as providing feedback on the new and revised cases.

Alice Frazer Evans is retired director of writing and research at Plowshares Institute, Simsbury, Connecticut; senior trainer for the Center for Empowering Reconciliation and Peace, Jakarta, Indonesia; and an adjunct faculty member at Hartford Seminary, Hartford, Connecticut. She is co-author of *Casebook for Christian Living; Pastoral Theology from a Global Context; Peace Skills for Community Mediators;* and *Transforming Urban Ministry.*

Christine E. Gudorf is professor emerita of religious studies at Florida International University, the state university in Miami. She holds a doctorate in Christian ethics from Union Theological Seminary in the City of New York. Most of her scholarship has focused on sexual and environmental ethics. She is the author of *Comparative Religious Ethics: Everyday Decisions for Our Everyday Lives* and *Body, Sex and Pleasure: Reconstructing Christian Sexual Ethics*; and co-author of *Boundaries: A Casebook in Environmental Ethics*.

Jean Larson is a retired pastor in the Evangelical Lutheran Church in America, clergy leadership coach, and volunteer for Moms Demand Action for Gun Sense in America. She lives in Missoula, Montana.

Ramona Nelson is professor emerita of accounting and management at Luther College in Decorah, Iowa. She is a certified public accountant, serves on a community bank board, and stays active with volunteer service and travel.

Robert L. Stivers is professor emeritus of Christian ethics, Pacific Lutheran University, Tacoma, Washington. He is an ordained minister in the Presbyterian Church (USA) and holds a doctorate in Christian ethics from Union Theological Seminary in the City of New York. Most of his scholarship has focused on environmental and economic ethics. He is the author of *The Sustainable Society and Hunger, Technology, and Limits to Growth;* co-author of *Christian Environmental Ethics: A Case Method Approach;* and co-editor of *The Public Vocation of Christian Ethics; Reformed Faith and Economics;* and *Resistance and Theological Ethics*.